4 July 1983

Best Wishes—

the ROOT

The Marines in Beirut
August 1982—February 1984

Eric Hammel

Harcourt Brace Jovanovich, Publishers
San Diego   New York   London

LIBRARY OF CONGRESS CATALOGING IN PUBLICATION DATA

Hammel, Eric M.
   The root : the marines in Beirut,
August 1982–February 1984.

   Bibliography: p.
   Includes index.
   1. Lebanon—History—1975-   .
2. United States. Marine Corps—History—20th century.
3. Beirut (Lebanon)—Bombing, 1983 (October 23)
4. Beirut International Airport. I. Title.
DS87.H335 1985   956.92′044   85-805

ISBN 0-15-179006-X

Designed by Michael Farmer
Printed in the United States of America
First edition
A B C D E

*For the Marines, Sailors, and Soldiers
Who Died in Beirut—
and for Their Families*

Contents

Maps and Illustrations

Acknowledgments

I owe my greatest debt of gratitude to LtGen Al Gray, who commanded 2d Marine Division during the Beirut deployments and while I was interviewing participants. Al Gray told me to "get the whole story," and then he passed "The Word" along to the officers and Marines who had been in Beirut that it was okay with him if they told me "everything" about which I asked. This narrative could not have been completed without Al Gray's blessing and active support.

Marines who helped me in official capacities include: Col Jim McManaway, Director of Public Affairs; Maj Fred Lash, who both contributed his recollections and provided material support as a member of the Public Affairs staff; BGen Ed Simmons, Director of the Marine Corps History and Museums Division, and Col John Miller, the division's deputy director; Maj Dale Baird and Capt Craig Fisher, of the Joint Public Affairs Office at Camp Lejeune, North Carolina; CWO-4 Ron Frazier, Joint Public Affairs Officer at Twentynine Palms, California; and LtCol

Dick Wenzell, commanding officer of Battalion Landing Team 1/8 at the time this book was being researched—and their staffs. Valuable unofficial assists were provided by BGen Hugh Kerr and Col Dick Camp.

I spoke or corresponded with just over 200 Marine and Navy veterans of the deployments, mainly members of Battalion Landing Team 1/8, MAU Service and Support Group 24, and Marine Medium Helicopter Squadron 162. No contribution made by any of the participants, whether or not I used it directly in this narrative, was anything less than vital in bringing this project to completion. To all of you, my heartfelt thanks. I hope I have adequately returned the trust by opening my mind and hearing what you had to say, for we met before the pain and wonder had quite worn away.

Glossary

Special Military Terms and Acronyms

AAV.	Amphibious Assault Vehicle (also *amtrac; hog*)
Actual.	Commander; not the person speaking for him
Admin.	Administrative
AK-47.	Soviet-made Kalashnikov Submachine Gun
ALO.	Air Liaison Officer (pronounced *ay-lo*)
Alpha.	Phonetic A; first or forward
ANGLICO.	Air-Naval Gunfire Liaison Company
APC.	Armored Personnel Carrier
Arty.	Artillery
BIA.	Beirut International Airport
Binos.	Binoculars
BGen.	Brigadier General
BLT.	Battalion Landing Team; Battalion Headquarters Building
Bravo.	Phonetic B; second or rear
Cammies.	Marine Camouflage Utility Uniform
CH-46.	Marine/Navy Medium Cargo Helicopter
CH-53.	Marine/Navy Medium Cargo Helicopter
Charlie.	Phonetic C
CINCEUR.	Commander-in-Chief, Europe (pronounced *sink-yur*)

CINCNAVEUR.	Commander-in-Chief, Navy, Europe
CO.	Commanding Officer
Coax.	Coaxial
Cobra.	AH-1 Gunship Helicopter
COC.	Combat Operations Center
Comm.	Communications
CP.	Combat Post; also Command Post when used after squad, platoon, etc.
CPO.	Chief Petty Officer
CWO.	Chief Warrant Officer
Delta.	Phonetic D
Deuce Gear.	Webbed Equipment (e.g., packs, flak jackets)
Doc.	Navy Medical Corpsman
Dragon.	Wire-Guided Antitank Missile
Echo.	Phonetic E
EOD	Explosive Ordnance Disposal
ETC.	Electronics Technician Chief
Exec.	Executive Officer
FAC.	Forward Air Controller (pronounced *fack*)
FASTAB.	U.S. Army Experimental Target Acquisition Battery
FMFLant.	Fleet Marine Force, Atlantic
Fox.	Phonetic F
FROG.	Free Rocket Over Ground (Soviet missile)
FSSG.	Force Service Support Group
G-3.	LAF 7.62mm Service Rifle
Golf.	Phonetic G
Grunt.	Infantryman
Gunner.	Warrant Officer
Gunny.	Gunnery Sergeant
GySgt.	Gunnery Sergeant
Head	Lavatory
H&S.	Headquarters and Service
HM3.	Hospital Mate 3d Class
HMC.	Hospital Mate Chief
HMM.	Marine Medium Helicopter Squadron
HN.	Hospital Corpsman
Hog.	Amphibian Tractor
Hotel.	Phonetic H
HST.	Helicopter Support Team

Huey.	UH-1 Utility Helicopter
Illume.	Illumination
Incoming.	Incoming fire
India.	Phonetic I
Intell.	Intelligence
IV.	Intravenous
JCS.	Joint Chiefs of Staff
JPAB.	Joint Public Affairs Bureau (pronounced *jay-pab*)
Juliet.	Phonetic J
Katyusha.	Soviet-built 122mm Rocket
Kilo.	Phonetic K
LAAW.	Light Antitank Assault Weapon (pronounced *law*)
LAF.	Lebanese Armed Forces
LCdr.	Lieutenant Commander
LCpl.	Lance Corporal
LCU.	Landing Craft, Utility
Lima.	Phonetic L
LNO.	Liaison Officer
LPH.	Landing Ship, Personnel, Helicopter
Lt(jg).	Lieutenant, Junior Grade
M-113.	U.S. Armored Personnel Carrier
M-16.	U.S. 5.56mm Service Rifle
M-198.	U.S. 155mm Medium Howitzer
M-203.	U.S. 40mm Rifle Grenade/Launcher
M-60	U.S. 7.62mm Medium Machine Gun
M-60A1.	U.S. Main Battle Tank
MAB.	Marine Amphibious Brigade (pronounced *mab*)
MAF.	Marine Amphibious Force (pronounced *maff*)
MAGTF.	Marine Air-Ground Task Force (pronounced *mag-taff*)
MARG.	Mediterranean Amphibious Ready Group (pronounced *marg*)
MAU.	Marine Amphibious Unit (pronounced *mau*)
MNF.	Multinational Force
Medevac.	Medical Evacuation
Mike.	Phonetic M
MRE.	Meal, Ready-to-Eat Ration Pack
MSgt.	Master Sergeant
MSSG.	MAU Service and Support Group
NCO.	Noncommissioned Officer

NCOIC.	NCO in Charge
Net.	Network
November.	Phonetic N
ODO.	Operations Duty Officer (pronounced *owe-doe*)
Ops.	Operations
Oscar.	Phonetic O
Panhard.	LAF Six-wheeled Armored Car
Papa.	Phonetic P
PLA.	Palestine Liberation Army
PLO.	Palestine Liberation Organization
PO.	Petty Officer
PT.	Physical Training
Quebec.	Phonetic Q
Recon.	Reconnaissance
Romeo.	Phonetic R
RPG.	Rocket-propelled Grenade or Launcher.
S-1.	Personnel and Administration Officer/Section
S-2.	Intelligence Officer/Section
S-3.	Operations Officer/Section
S-4.	Supply Officer/Section
SAM.	Surface-to-Air Missile (pronounced *sam*)
SEAL.	Navy Air-Amphibious Commando
SFC.	Sergeant 1st Class
Sierra.	Phonetic S
SNCO.	Staff Noncommissioned Officer
SOG.	Sergeant of the Guard
SP4.	Specialist 4th Class
SSgt.	Staff Sergeant
STA.	Surveillance and Target Acquisition
TAB.	Target Acquisition Battery
Tac.	Tactical
Tango.	Phonetic T
Top.	Master Sergeant
TOW.	Wire-Guided Antitank Missile (pronounced *toe*)
Uniform.	Phonetic U
Victor.	Phonetic V
Water Buffalo.	Large Water Tank Trailer
Whiskey.	Phonetic W
Willy-Peter.	White Phosphorus
WO.	Warrant Officer

X-Ray.	Phonetic X
XO.	Executive Officer
Yankee.	Phonetic Y
Zulu.	Phonetic Z
Zuni.	Air-Ground Missile

Introduction

The Root is about the U.S. Marines involved in Beirut between August 1982 and February 1984, with particular emphasis upon the August–October 1983 period. The viewpoint of this narrative is mainly that of the participants.

This is *not* a book about Beirut or Lebanon in the wake of the June 1982 Israeli invasion, nor is it about the Lebanese people, the Lebanese religious and political factions, Lebanon's problems with its Syrian and Israeli neighbors, nor even the goals and aspirations articulated by the Reagan administration with respect to its hastily conceived and cosmetic solutions for the ongoing Lebanese tragedy. All those factors are part of this book only insofar as they impact upon Marines who were in Beirut.

The title of this book—*The Root*—is what some of those Marines called the city.

The bombing is etched as indelibly in my mind as is the day John Kennedy was murdered.

I had returned home the evening of Saturday, October 22, 1983, from several days as a guest of my good friend, Col Dick Camp, then commanding officer of the 1st Recruit Training Battalion at the Marine Corps Recruit Depot in San Diego. I had been talking about history and its lessons with eager officers and, also, interviewing Dick and several of his contemporaries about an obscure Vietnam battle that is the subject of a long-term historical project. I was also a guest at the graduation of several hundred fresh Marine recruits who had been trained under Dick's guidance. I had been living and breathing Marines for days. I returned home exhausted by a bad flight and fell asleep with the radio on and dreamed all night of dead and dying Marines. I was knocked out of bed at dawn when I realized that my dream was reality. I spent the next three days glued to the television.

The notion that *I* should write a book on the bombing came first from my editor, Don Knox. I am embarrassed to admit that I probably never would have thought of doing this book without Don's bringing it up. As it was, I let about twenty minutes of lunchtime conversation pass before I even reacted to the thought!

When I began planning *The Root* in late 1983, I frankly knew little of the multifaceted Lebanese crisis beyond what I had read or viewed by chance in or on the national media. It appeared then that I would be focusing upon the tragic events of October 23, 1983, when the Battalion Landing Team Headquarters was blown up and several hundred sleeping Marines, sailors, and soldiers were killed or maimed.

It took several months to get the Marine Corps to go along with the project. I am not sure I know why I was provided with complete access to the participants of the ill-fated adventure in Lebanon. Perhaps my earlier books and my long association with the Marine Corps played a major role. What I do know is that the wheels were greased by hands and forces I have yet to directly encounter.

I was ultimately given carte blanche to interview willing participants, to ask any reasonable questions, and to receive candid responses restricted only by the needs of something called "operational security." That single stricture, whatever it might have meant, had little impact upon my learning what happened, and no effect I know of upon *The Root*.

I am proud—and honored—to be the only civilian author given complete access to the people, if not to the records.

The effects of my clearance were so pervasive that officers who were at first reticent to share their experiences were soon telling me everything I felt I needed to know (and quite a bit besides), and then telling enlisted Marines—in my presence—to provide full and complete cooperation, to "Tell Mr. Hammel *anything* he wants to know."

Given that oft-repeated introduction, it is very strange that the military services provided me with *no official papers* describing events in Beirut. The U.S. Navy would not even allow me to conduct an exchange with a chaplain who happened to be in Beirut at the time of the bombing, though such an exchange could hardly have led to more than the addition of some human interest material to this narrative.

I did not press the issue of obtaining documents. I had determined early in my effort that the crucial unit records compiled as events were unfolding had been destroyed in the Battalion Landing Team Headquarters on October 23, 1983, and that nearly all efforts to reconstruct them were not proceeding. Since that time, by order of senior military and civilian authorities, all the official records concerning Beirut have been locked away. Even the unpublished manuscript of the official Marine Corps monograph—written as a training aid—has been sealed from public view. As far as I know, even senior Marine officers have been denied access to it.

I am advised that at least thirty years will pass before the last secret White House, State Department, and Defense Department documents are unsealed.

All of the tapes and documents I have compiled are in the care of the Marine Corps Historical Division. All of these materials will remain under my control for some years, and they will be made available to serious students of events in Beirut.

I conducted my first interviews in Washington, D.C., and at Camp Lejeune, North Carolina, in March 1984.

The first interview of combat veterans I conducted in Washington was a fluke—fortuitous and unexpected—and, in its way, critical to my understanding of the whole affair. I was making a personal call on BGen Carl Mundy, who figures in a Vietnam project I have under way, when the general told me he had a young lieutenant working for him who had been in the unit that was bombed on October 23, 1983. I met briefly with 1stLt Jerry Walsh—to set up a meeting for later in the week—and he told me that a survivor of the bombing itself had reported in to General Mundy's offices that very hour. Thus I also met 1stLt Chuck Dallachie, who was just back from months of recuperative leave. In over five hours of often-emotional discussion held on a Friday and Saturday just five months after the bombing, I learned not only the details of the lieutenants' experiences, but I was also given a crucial outline and important details of the "family" relationships operative in a Marine rifle battalion in a hostile environment. The insights I gained about how the battalion worked were pivotal. Equally important, the two lieutenants volunteered names and addresses of fellow veterans who had been transferred to commands throughout the country. This was my first break away from strictly official channels of information-gathering; I had the cooperation of two insiders, which would be useful in winning the trust of other insiders.

As the research gained momentum, I told my contacts at the various Public Affairs offices what I wanted and with whom I wanted to speak, and they delivered. Nothing I know about was held back. Background and informational briefings by very senior Marines were almost too numerous. After years of writing about old wars, I was quickly brought face to face with today's Marine Corps and educated in its peculiar vernacular and advancing ethos; I was immersed in "Marine things."

The settings for the interviews at Camp Lejeune were not always conducive to candor, but the young men—nineteen-year-olds of every background and ethnic group, from all across our nation—were superb. Indeed, many of them demanded to be heard in greater detail than I believe they had ever before achieved. It was evident that many participants viewed the interview sessions as some sort of sanctioned healing sessions. The tapes we made together are full of trial-and-error emotional voidings, of tears that are not quite tears, of unstated visions that time might never erase.

I have spent several decades getting to know old warriors of my father's generation and of my own. I was faced in this case, and for the first time, with men who were predominantly half my age and, in all but ten or a dozen cases, at least a few years younger than myself.

I must speak here of my impressions of those men.

They come in all sizes and shapes and textures. Some are incredibly articulate, others are people I would take to be average in all ways. They share little in terms of mental or physical or social or even emotional attributes. Some are highly complex individuals who would excel in any setting. Others are simple souls who, when I stop to think about it, form the backbone and blood and sinew of our civilization. Some will be Marines for decades while others have already left the Marine Corps and would never willingly return. Do they represent a cross section of our nation's youth? I do not know. They all have subjected themselves to the ongoing test that is the Marine Corps. Some, I am sure, have fallen short of their self-images as men and as

Marines. But that is of little moment, for I found all of them to be caring people who share all things with other men they might shun in other, less intimate, less resolutely manly settings. The mutual dependency, the tangible mutual respect, the bantering affection, the commonality of shared danger and pain prevailed in every conversation of from two to fifty of them.

I spoke mainly with high-ranking unit commanders, and service and combat support personnel of all ranks, during that first junket. On the very last day of the trip, however, I spoke with small batches of combat infantrymen. From those interviews a new story emerged, one that caught me so unawares that I was miles away from Camp Lejeune that night before its full impact hit me.

A month later, in April 1984, at the Marine Corps desert training facility at Twentynine Palms, California, I met exclusively with that half of the 1st Battalion, 8th Marine Regiment, which had both weathered Beirut and had remained with the unit as it prepared for yet another cyclic junket to the Mediterranean.

By the time I visited with these combat veterans in April, I had learned the outlines, but only a few of the details, of an entirely unreported *American war* in Beirut during the sixty days leading up to the bombing. I had quite literally stumbled upon a story of intense ground combat that went virtually unreported in our usually aggressive national press. I was thus able to piece together a story that takes up more than one-half of this book. I had earlier learned, in a very broad sense, that the "sniping" incidents and "spillover" fire about which we had been reading in September and October 1983 were merely parts of an unremitting ground war between Marines and Lebanese Moslem—and other—factions. As you will see, my week with Marine riflemen in April dazzled me with details of that war.

One of the more amazing realizations regarding the Marine Corps and its attitude toward events in Beirut came during the course of three "briefs" I gave in mid-1984 at the Marine Corps Recruit Depot in San Diego and at 12th Marine Corps District Headquarters in San Francisco. None of the officers and staff NCOs who heard me speak had advance knowledge of any of the facts, though all were amply armed with astounding misconceptions arising out of the rumor mill and the national press. A comment I made about this paucity of institutional interest to the editor of a Marine Corps professional publication drew an incredulous response; he knew only what he had heard through official channels, and that amounted to nothing of significance. Since then, I have raised the issue with numerous officers who served in Beirut, and all have agreed that the immediate military lessons of Beirut—not to mention the core events themselves—have been largely ignored by the institution. Indeed, a number of officers who served in Beirut have yet to be asked any questions whatsoever by their colleagues at new duty stations. This attitude is mystifying. It took the intercession of the colonel hosting one of my briefs to prevent a captain from accusing me of fabricating the whole story.

As I write this a year to the day after the bombing, I am assured by a senior participant that this state of affairs remains unchanged.

Another thing: I have become convinced that the tragic event of October 23, 1983—the bombing—was an incident that had very little to do with and was wholly apart from the actual fact of our "presence" in Lebanon or, indeed, of the Lebanese civil war. Rather, I believe, the bombing was the direct outgrowth of our leaders' having made available a target of unprecedented magnitude in the center of a chaotic situation.

That our combat force was declawed and placed in a static position with no clear mandate or any clear means for eluding the wishes of a maniacal anti-American regime or regimes was a bonus. Those maniacs were in large part not Lebanese, and they would have been satisfied to take out any American symbol in the

Middle East. They were, I am sure, willing to go to far more trouble to achieve what our leaders allowed them to achieve with, really, very little effort and at laughably little expense.

But that last is speculation. What was real—and not reported —is the war our Marines fought in Lebanon in the weeks just before and just after the bombing we do know about.

A few additional points about *The Root:* To help you get to know these Marines better, the language is, as far as possible, the language of the participants, raunchy and foul-mouthed and filled with jargon. Additionally, as stated, the book tells only a little more than the participants knew to be fact. In some cases, the facts that are revealed are merely the perceptions of the Marines. As I say in more than a few places and in many ways throughout the narrative, perceptions by far outweigh objective reality. Finally, and most important, this is a book about people, and not necessarily about events.

Eric Hammel
Pacifica, California
October 23, 1984

the
ROOT

PART I

Invasion
and Rescue

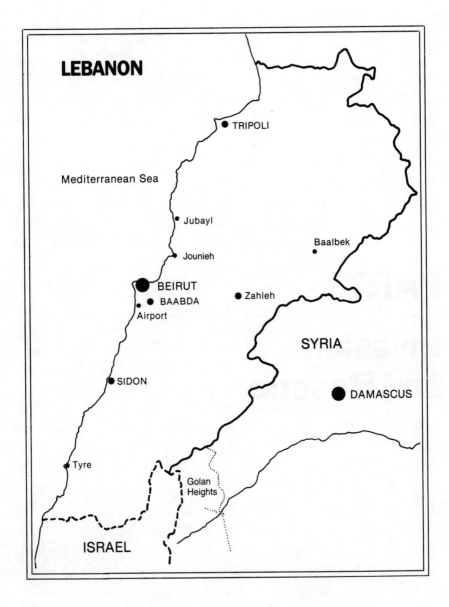

1

Immense Israeli armored and mechanized formations breached the fence that divides Israel from southern Lebanon at 1100 hours June 6, 1982 and fanned out to reduce Palestine Liberation Organization (PLO) positions and garrisons within range of Israeli villages.

The operation, dubbed "Peace in Galilee," was presented to the world as a limited clearing operation following six years of lawlessness in Lebanon, during which the PLO had, with total impunity, terrorized not only northern Israel but vast segments of the Lebanese civilian population. Military analysts worldwide speculated that the massively strong Israeli armored fist would, as it had twice in the past four years, punch through to a distance of only about forty kilometers to the Litani River.

In the two or three years before the invasion, the PLO had painstakingly built up a regular military force organized into battalion units of about 1,500 fighters. The battalions were brigaded with artillery and rocket units and companies of ancient Soviet-built T-34 tanks. Depots throughout southern Lebanon held vast caches of vehicles, weapons, and ammunition, including heavy artillery. There were, in fact, far more weapons than there were trained PLO fighters. Whatever use the PLO and their Syrian and Soviet benefactors had in mind for this massive arms buildup was made moot by the Israeli invasion.

For all practical purposes, the PLO had established a heavily armed state-within-a-state in southern Lebanon. It had assumed control over many of the essential civilian services and had ejected numerous Lebanese citizens from their homes and, indeed, from whole towns. The PLO ruled southern Lebanon by the gun and by holding hostage many prominent and ordinary Lebanese citizens. Any resistance, no matter how slight and whether by Christian or Moslem Lebanese, was dealt with in brutal fashion.

Also facing the advancing Israelis were major components of the Syrian army, which had been invited into Lebanon in 1976 in the hope that it could quell the mounting struggle between native Lebanese factions and the foreign PLO. The Syrian government, which considers Lebanon to be a part of Greater Syria and which has never had official diplomatic ties with the Lebanese government, had gleefully complied with the request, though the imposition of a Syrian solution upon the Lebanese civil war was to the detriment of Syria's unruly client, the PLO.

The Syrian army based upward of 70,000 soldiers in Lebanon, mainly in the Beqa'a Valley, but also in Beirut and other coastal sectors. The best-armed, -equipped, and -led force in Lebanon, the Syrians were consistently able to exert their will throughout the 1976–82 period. And all their will went into destabilizing Lebanon for the good of Greater Syria, of which, in their minds, Lebanon was and is an errant province.

A third foreign force occupying Lebanese soil was the Palestine Liberation Army (PLA), a sort of Arab foreign legion, bankrolled and commanded by Syrians and manned by fighters from throughout the Arab world. The PLA is so closely identified with Syria as to be considered an adjunct of the Syrian army.

The Israeli advance to the Litani was a work of art, marred only by the tragic inability of Israeli gunners to distinguish at times between PLO targets and the homes of Lebanese civilians. It is, as the world has seen, a standard PLO tactic to emplace their fighters in neighborhoods occupied by women and children. The Israelis are a nervous people under fire who tend to retaliate massively and without discrimination in the general direction of anything resembling resistance.

The Israelis advanced along three main axes, all aimed at destroying the PLO within a region from the Lebanese-Israeli border to the Litani. In addition to the destruction of the PLO in southern Lebanon, the Israelis openly challenged Syrian forces along and to the south of the strategic Beirut-Damascus highway. All the senior Israeli commanders were veterans of the desperate 1973 fighting on the Golan Heights; they knew the Syrians and had mastered them nine years earlier, when there were far more Syrians than Israelis in the fight. These blooded colonels and generals had little regard for Syrian fighting ability, a notion that easily permeated the ranks of the first-line Israel Defense Force (IDF) units they commanded in Lebanon.

The IDF mechanized spearheads sliced through their objectives, destroying PLO units where and when they stood and cutting off PLO units and individual fighters scattering for safety to the north and east.

There were hard fights, particularly in the streets of Tyre and around Beaufort Castle, an old Crusader aerie that had been refurbished as a PLO artillery fire-direction center.

The Syrians reflexively moved one of their best tank brigades directly into the path of the Israelis advancing through the southern Beqa'a, obviating the IDF plan to reach the Litani without a major confrontation with its very strong neighboring enemy. More important, PLO units that the Israelis particularly wanted to neutralize scuttled behind the Syrian armored screen.

The Israelis immediately passed messages, via Washington, to assure Syrian President Hafez al-Assad that they had no desire to fight a protracted war with Syria, that Peace in Galilee was a clearing operation designed to neutralize the PLO within artillery range of the Israeli-Lebanese border. The Israelis suggested that the Syrians might avoid direct conflict merely by quelling the destructive impulses of their PLO clients.

The Syrians ignored the Israeli proposal and brought their best armored and infantry units into the southern Beqa'a.

Israeli columns operating on the coast and in the center had consolidated their initial rapid gains by the morning of June 8. Then they combined to advance farther to the north while follow-up units, mainly infantry, engaged PLO forces hiding out among civilian neighborhoods in Tyre and Sidon.

Israeli forces in the center and on the right were fired on by Syrian units on June 8, and they returned fire. The sparring continued through the day while each side tested the other and built up its resources. Six Syrian and no Israeli jets were downed during the day.

The government of Israeli Prime Minister Menachem Begin decided during June 8 to forcibly push the Syrians from the path of the advancing IDF.

Perhaps the most significant event of the war came on June 9, when Israeli jets mounted suppressive strikes against the Syrian surface-to-air missile (SAM) sites throughout the Beqa'a. To the Israelis, this was a prudent move, aimed less at Syria than as a means for assuring continued aerial superiority against PLO targets behind Syrian lines. Nineteen SAM batteries were destroyed during the afternoon, an unprecedented achievement in that not one Israeli jet was lost. The Syrian air force launched 100 assorted first-line MiG and Sukhoi jet fighters to challenge the Israeli air force. Twenty-nine of the MiGs and Sukhois were downed, again without the loss of a single Israeli jet.

On the ground, on June 10, Israeli coastal columns advanced to Damour, just eighteen kilometers from Beirut's southern suburbs. The town, a former Christian community that had been utterly raped and occupied by the PLO in 1976, fell after bitter fighting. Israelis on the central axis engaged strong Syrian tank formations within three kilometers of the vital Beirut-Damascus highway. The Syrians fought here with everything they had in the hope of denying the Israelis access to the highway, the key to central as well as southern Lebanon. Syrian forces in the Beqa'a, including the army's premier tank division, were outgunned and outmaneuvered by the much larger Israeli eastern force. The Syrians lost 150 main battle tanks in the Beqa'a.

It was by now clear that the IDF was intent upon advancing at least as far as Beirut. Whether this had been its original intent or a matter of exploitation of initial gains is neither clear nor relevant. What is clear and relevant is that the PLO *and* the Syrian army in southern Lebanon were well along the trail to defeat at Israeli hands, in a war and in a place of Israel's choosing. Israeli Defense Minister Ariel Sharon had stated months earlier that he desired to link the IDF physically with Israel's Christian Phalange clients in north-central Lebanon. Suddenly, this was a very real proposition.

June 11 was marked by heavy Syrian counterattacks in the central Beqa'a Valley. These were all blunted.

As Israeli ground units sought to shape the battlefields from the coast to the Beqa'a to their own advantage, the Begin government announced its intention to impose a unilateral cease-fire at noon that day, June 11. The Syrian government immediately announced its intention to observe the cease-fire, though Israel made it clear that PLO units operating within range of Israeli guns would not be spared, even if they were behind Syrian lines or under Syrian protection.

The cease-fire found the Israelis in possession of a line from the coast just south of Beirut to Ein Dara, on the Beirut-Damascus highway, and then southeast across the Shouf massif and the Beqa'a, roughly paralleling the road, to within five kilometers of the Syrian border. The Israelis held complete mastery of the air over southern Lebanon.

The tacit accord broke down within two hours, when a Syrian brigade trapped in Beirut attempted to fight its way east to link up with other Syrian units. The move denied the Israelis access to an important road link between their own columns, so they moved to outflank the Syrian gains, which they did.

June 12 found Israeli mechanized columns consolidating gains and reaching for strategic objectives on the roads and in the hills around Beirut. One armored force, in fact, secured the official residence of the Lebanese president at Baabda.

U.S. Special Ambassador Philip Habib, hard at work from the outset of the Israeli move into Lebanon, secured agreements to a second cease-fire only after Israeli forces had completely surrounded Moslem West Beirut and linked up with Christian Phalange forces in East Beirut.

Israeli military leaders felt the Syrians had been left too close to the siege line the IDF was erecting around the Moslem sections of greater Beirut, so the second cease-fire, uneasy and often violated, was shattered on June 22, when Israeli forces moved against PLO and Syrian units near Aley and Bhamdoun, on the Beirut-Damascus highway. The limited action took the Israelis sixty hours to achieve and was their costliest single fight of the war. But the Syrians were pushed east from Bhamdoun, and the Israelis had a noose around the PLO leadership and fighters remaining in and around the capital.

A third cease-fire took effect late on June 24. To the amazement of all parties, this lasted, with the usual spates of killing, through July 14, when the Lebanese government officially asked all non-Lebanese military units to remove themselves from the country. This was the first time the Lebanese themselves sided with a policy put forth by the United States and wholeheartedly supported and accepted by Israel. That solution, however, could not have been further from Syrian and PLO designs. Absent a positive response, Israel announced that it would retain the option of proceeding by force into West Beirut.

2

The five ships of Mediterranean Amphibious Ready Group (MARG) 2-82 bearing the 32d U.S. Marine Amphibious Unit (MAU) arrived off Rota, Spain, before dawn on June 6, 1982, the day the Israelis crossed into Lebanon.

Rota is a regular stopping point for the 1,800-man U.S. Marine amphibious units that regularly "cruise the Med" as part of the permanently stationed U.S. 6th Fleet. The ten days scheduled at Rota would be used by the Marine infantry, service, support, and aviation units constituting 32d MAU to get ashore while the crews of the five transports had an opportunity to reprovision and undertake necessary maintenance. Thirty-second MAU's sister unit, 24th MAU, was due at Rota in a few days and would make a brief stopover on its way home to Morehead City, North Carolina, following its routine six-month cruise. In fact, 24th MAU had left Ashdod, Israel, the evening before, June 5. Once 24th MAU reached Rota, 32d MAU would be officially attached to 6th Fleet and would commence a busy schedule of amphibious exercises in Portugal, Italy, Turkey, and, possibly, Somalia. Interspersed among the amphibious drills would be liberties at Lisbon, Palma, Ashdod, Mombasa, and Cannes. It looked to be a good cruise.

The ten-day stopover in Rota lasted ten hours.

Whenever and wherever war or civil unrest erupts, the U.S. government properly sets into motion contingency plans aimed at securing at least the lives and, if possible, the property of American citizens based or living in the threatened area. Certainly, most of this attention on June 6, 1982, was directed at the potential danger to the American embassy in Beirut. Ronald Reagan owed his presidency to the American public's perceptions of Jimmy Carter's handling of the embassy takeover in Tehran. Thus, upon confirming news of the Israeli invasion of Lebanon, the appropriate military channels down through components of 6th Fleet informed the commander of 32d MAU that his unit might be involved in guarding American lives and property in the new hot spot.

The Word arrived on June 7, amid a blizzard of reports describing Israeli progress through southern Lebanon. The commander of MARG 2-82 was ordered to make directly to a point about 100 nautical miles off the coast of Lebanon and stand by to support possible operations ashore.

The as-yet-formless mission was precisely the reason the MAUs cruise the world's seas. The exercises run jointly with allies and friends of the United States, the liberties, the weeks and months of crushing ennui to which the sailors and Marines of the amphibious ready groups are subjected, are all aimed at securing American lives, property, and strategic interests wherever oceans touch land. No one aboard those five ships knew what to expect. Most secretly feared the possibilities, but the situation could potentially rescue them from boredom, testing combat skills acquired in many hours preparing for combat and forging that common bond all servicemen share—the possibility of using their skills in combat.

Surprisingly few of the 1,800 Marines in 32d MAU had ever seen action, though it had been only ten years since the last Marines were pulled out of Vietnam. Col Jim Mead, on the first of two scheduled deployments as 32d MAU commander, had flown twenty-eight fighter-bomber strikes and had logged many hours in observation aircraft in Vietnam in 1967 and 1968, earning a Silver Star and numerous other personal decorations. LtCol Bob Johnston, commanding officer of 2d Battalion, 8th Marine Regiment (BLT 2/8), the chief component of 32d MAU, had held a staff job in Vietnam in 1965, then had commanded a rifle company in northern I Corps in 1967. Of course, there were other field-grade officers and senior noncommissioned officers who had been to the wars, but perhaps as much as 90 percent of the MAU was virgin.

MARG 2-82 steamed in circles for two weeks as the war in Lebanon unfolded. About the only value derived from two weeks of cutting holes in the water was the opportunity afforded the MARG and MAU staffs to compile plans for the possible evacuation of from 300 to 5,000 American citizens and designated foreign nationals from Lebanese cities and towns. Nevertheless, the focus of the planning was on the American embassy in West Beirut. Several State Department staffers familiar with the embassy were flown out to brief the MAU staff on the layout of the city and the embassy itself. The United States was not going to get caught with its pants down this time. A carrier battle group was just over the horizon, ready to support the possible evacuations with close air support or airborne radar and other electronic surveillance capabilities. And a pair of destroyer escorts was on hand to provide direct naval gunfire support to any Marines who might be sent ashore.

Word arrived that several hundred eligible civilians would be

given safe conduct to the Christian Phalange stronghold at Jounieh, a small port about ten miles north of Beirut. The MAU was
to secure their safety in the town and escort them to landing
craft that would carry them to the transports.

Eight hundred Marines, the bulk of Lieutenant Colonel Johnston's BLT 2/8 and some service units, undertook last-minute
training and briefs. Officers and staff NCOs agreed that the level
of interest among the troops was considerably heightened. The
plan was by no means set in stone, so contingency orders of all
sorts were issued. It was assumed that the operation would be
conducted in what planners call a "permissive" environment—
that is, in a relatively peaceful area where civilians would continue to go about their daily routines. Still, worst-case situations
were factored into the operational orders.

The Christian town of Jounieh held many surprises for the
Marines of 32d MAU. Amid reports from around Beirut that
tens of thousands of artillery rounds were being traded daily by
Israelis, Christian Phalange fighters, Palestine Liberation Organization (PLO) fighters, Palestine Liberation Army fighters, and
Syrian regulars, Marines going ashore at Jounieh to help in the
evacuation of several hundred American and foreign civilians
could see no signs of war. The beaches at Jounieh were packed
with sunbathing Christian men, women, and children, and
water-skiers and wind-surfers had to be diverted from the paths
of landing craft sent into the port to carry the evacuees to the
ships of the MARG.

Were it not for the flash and thump of distant gunfire, the
news on the radio, and the specific comments of the evacuees
themselves, the sailors and Marines would have had no clue that
a war was raging a mere score of miles to the south.

In all, 581 members of more than two dozen nationalities
were evacuated by bus to Jounieh and by landing craft from the
port in an utterly routine operation, not much different from the

evacuation training exercises commonly undertaken by the MAUs and MARGs before they set sail from North Carolina.

While two transports ferried the evacuees to Cyprus, the flagship and the bulk of 32d MAU remained off Beirut.

Two days were used up for the Jounieh evacuation, then the MARG was reconstituted off the coast, where it remained through July before heading for Naples to pump bilges and get the troops ashore for some relief from the morale-destroying boredom.

The Marines and sailors were promised fifteen days of rotating leaves, but they received only four.

The Israelis were going in for the kill.

Special Ambassador Philip Habib had been at work for nearly two months trying to find a formula by which all the major antagonists could live and retain at least a facade of pride in the face of the microscopic attentions lavished upon them by the world press. Successive cease-fires had gone into effect and routinely failed.

It was all very wearing upon the Israelis, who could not continue taking even minimal losses without a clear resolution to the fighting. Already, the brave and highly decorated commander of Israel's premier armored brigade had resigned from the army to protest the use of Israeli soldiers in the painfully slow, street-by-street reduction of PLO positions in West Beirut. The casualty figures were rising and the net gains seemed to diminish. At length, Israeli Defense Minister Ariel Sharon ordered the use of massive air and artillery bombardments as a low-cost means for achieving the long-desired total destruction of the mainstrength of the despised PLO.

Whole neighborhoods of West Beirut became heaps of pulverized building stone and concrete. Uncounted hundreds of Palestinians and Lebanese died in the conflagration. Yet PLO chieftain Yasir Arafat announced his determination to hang on, and he continued to allow his heroic fighters to hide behind the skirts of Palestinian and Lebanese women as an appalled world watched the carnage nightly from its living rooms.

The PLO was offered a way out as early as July 6, when Ronald Reagan announced his willingness to provide American troops to escort PLO fighters from their positions to the Port of Beirut. Arafat responded with anger and petulance, but administration spokesmen announced that theirs was a standing offer, good at any time. President Reagan stated, "The United States has pledged to do all it can to bring peace and stability to the Middle East, and we must keep that pledge." Arafat responded with bombast: "Definitely, I won't accept."

The offer of help was reiterated time and again through the weeks of death and destruction that followed. Arafat put a brave face on his plight, and the Israelis fought on with uncharacteristic ambivalence, not quite mustering sufficient killing power to destroy the PLO and not quite easing the pressure.

At last, in the first week of August, there was a whimper from the besieged PLO headquarters in Beirut. The world viewing audience sucked in its breath and held it as Arafat made yet another convoluted pronouncement that seemed to say he was willing to be saved.

The PLO asked that any evacuation be handled by the United Nations, which has favored the organization for years. The Israelis refused to allow the United Nations to intervene in the conflict; nothing nice has been said about the UN in Israel since 1948. The United States, Italy, and France agreed to form a Multinational Force (MNF) to interpose itself between the warring factions and see to the safe evacuation of Arafat's fighters. All parties found this a suitable compromise, then got down to serious haggling over details while hundreds more people died in the streets of West Beirut. Arafat's primary concern was the fate of thousands of Palestinian civilians who would have to be left behind in the heavily populated Sabra and Shatilla refugee camps. He insisted upon receiving from the United States a written statement guaranteeing the safety of the civilians. Philip

15

Habib complied, adding his personal assurances that U.S. forces would remain ashore for up to thirty days, ample time to find a long-term solution.

The haggling was undertaken by a committee of interested parties convened at the American ambassador's residence at Yardze, a quiet suburb in the hills overlooking peaceful Christian East Beirut. The Americans on the committee were mainly State Department types led by Ambassadors Habib and Maurice Draper and included a military liaison team sent by the Commander-in-Chief of U.S. Forces in Europe.

Two senior Marine officers, one fluent in French, were joined by LtCol Bob Johnston, another French-speaker selected to represent 32d MAU, which had been designated the U.S. MNF contingent. The three Marine officers were to translate the wildly shifting discussions of the committee into a concrete plan that would see Marines of 32d MAU safely into and the PLO safely out of Beirut. Backing the recommendations of the liaison team were the MAU and MARG commanders, their staffs, and, farther back, the full weight of the U.S. Department of Defense. Despite all the support in the background, it would be things that Bob Johnston personally heard and saw that were of critical importance in planning and executing the unprecedented mission facing 32d MAU.

The committee meetings were chaired and dominated by Philip Habib. Political formulas and ramifications were endlessly debated, and contingency plans and briefs were presented at frequent junctures. It was clear almost from the outset that the American contingent could have little or no dealings with the Israelis, who were the dominant force in the area. It was essential, Habib averred, that the United States be seen as an honest and neutral broker, that nothing would come of the planning if there was the least perception that the United States favored one side over the other. Habib's interdict meant that 32d MAU would not be able to trade liaison officers with the IDF units in

Beirut. Thus there was no limit on potential misunderstandings. And, just possibly, fighting might erupt between Marines and battle-hardened Israeli veterans. Detailed planning for the evacuation was left to military officers.

Despite the extremity of his situation, Yasir Arafat continued to hold out for every conceivable advantage. For example, the Marines had the capability to build an artificial port for the evacuation, and they preferred doing so because there were ample beaches well away from built-up areas and all the problems attending a deployment among high-rise buildings. The PLO wanted to leave via the Bain Militaire, the officers' club used by the French during the years they had occupied Lebanon following World War I. In the end, all the parties agreed to run the evacuation through the Port of Beirut in the once-thriving commercial center of the once-thriving city. This decision bothered Colonel Mead not one bit; his troops would have their backs to the sea, from which they would come and to which they would return once the job was done.

The plan to which all parties had agreed by August 20 called for the collocation of MNF units with elements of the Lebanese Armed Forces (LAF), the official but by no means only army in Lebanon. Together, LAF and MNF units would interpose themselves between the Israelis and Phalange units dominating East Beirut and the PLO and Syrian army units trapped in West Beirut.

The French, who would be deploying 800 parachutists and foreign legionnaires, asked to be given control of the area around the French embassy and the former seat of their mandate government. The 400-man Italian contingent was to operate the main crossing point at the Galerie Semaan, on the so-called Green Line, the border between East and West Beirut. The U.S. contingent would secure the vital port area.

Thirty-second MAU vegetated aboard ship, tied down in Naples, through the two long weeks of negotiations at Yardze.

Since MARG 2-82 was on round-the-clock alert and would have to be off the coast of Lebanon within seventy-two hours of getting The Word, the troops had to live on board and the crews were unable to undertake any but the most rudimentary preventive maintenance. Morale balanced precariously between boredom and the underlying energy currents fed by rumor and imagination.

The MARG was ordered out of Naples on August 16 and the MAU was alerted to a possible landing to take place on August 20. Medical units were beefed up and military hospitals throughout Europe and the eastern United States prepared to receive casualties. Translator teams fluent in all the required languages were on the scene within thirty-six hours.

Bob Johnston was relieved at Yardze by the MAU executive officer on August 20 and flown to amphibious helicopter carrier *Guam,* the MARG flagship. Once aboard, the battalion commander changed from the civilian attire he had been wearing for two weeks into the camouflage utility clothing ("cammies") sported by every other member of 32d MAU. He slipped right into the planning routine and oversaw the intense last-minute briefings and training undertaken by the combat elements with which he would be going ashore as early as August 25. As had been the case before the Jounieh evacuation, Johnston's officers and staff NCOs had no problems holding the unwavering attention of all hands. Elsewhere aboard the thrumming helicopter carrier, the air and maintenance crews of the MAU's helicopter squadron worked brutally long hours to bring themselves and their aircraft up to peak operational effectiveness.

No offensive weapons, not even mortars, were to be taken ashore because, it was feared, the fragile agreement underlying the evacuation might dissolve if the PLO and Syrians felt there was real danger of a major confrontation. Both groups were doubtless and understandably paranoid about placing themselves in the hands of three nations that had at least formal relations with the Israeli enemy. Even the pair of Cobra helicopter gunships that accompanied the MAU would remain aboard ship—though ready to launch at a moment's notice. Destroyers and the carrier battle group would be on station below the horizon, out of sight but well within striking range.

The French went in first, testing the waters on August 21. They oversaw the evacuation of nearly 2,500 PLO fighters from the port over the next three days. MARG 2-82 arrived on station on August 24 and circled through the night while the units designated to land got set to go.

Everyone would move to the port via ramped landing craft. To facilitate the move, the transports moved to within 1,000 meters of the breakwater of the port at 0100 hours, August 25.

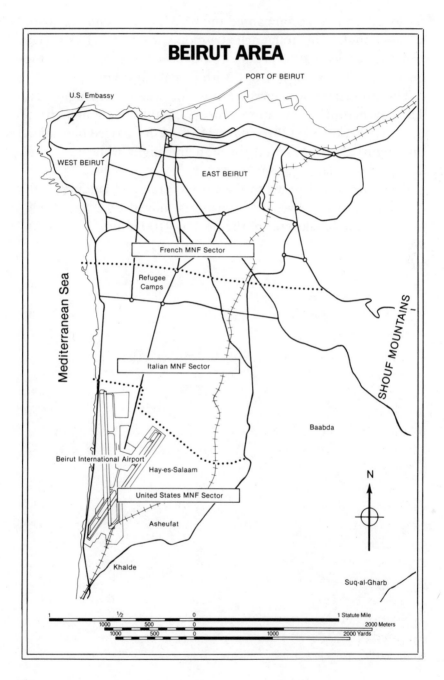

BEIRUT AREA

PORT OF BEIRUT

U.S. Embassy

WEST BEIRUT

EAST BEIRUT

French MNF Sector

Refugee
Camps

Mediterranean Sea

SHOUF MOUNTAINS

Italian MNF Sector

Baabda

Beirut International Airport

Hay-es-Salaam

N

United States MNF Sector

Asheufat

Khalde

Suq-al-Gharb

1   ½   0   1 Statute Mile
      1000   500   0   2000 Meters
      1000   500   0   1000   2000 Yards

3

Second Lieutenant Ken Lyles spent his twenty-fourth birthday, August 20, traveling to God-knew-what fate. A tall, blond, blue-eyed Georgian, Lyles was on his first deployment since becoming a Marine officer. As commander of the combat engineer platoon attached to LtCol Bob Johnston's Battalion Landing Team (BLT) 2/8, Lyles would accompany the command element ashore.

Lyles spent the long night aboard *Nashville* on deck with the lieutenants from Echo Company. It was clear and cool, really quite pleasant. There was not a whole lot of conversation among the officers, for all were deep in thought. The mission before them was utterly unprecedented in American military annals; there were no reassuring legends on which to fall back. Still, Ken Lyles was certain that everything would come off as planned.

Most of the troops gave little thought to history. They simply dropped their gear and caught whatever sleep the cool night and their own rampant imaginations allowed.

The Green Line, the border between Moslem West Beirut and Christian East Beirut, was startlingly defined that night; the Christian half of the city was brightly lit, normal-looking, while the Moslem half was completely dark but for the incessant bursts of tracer fired as "victory" salutes by Palestine Liberation Organization (PLO) units staging into the port.

Ken Lyles was on *Nashville*'s signal bridge in the predawn hour, watching the dark shore through a pair of stanchion-mounted "big-eyes" binoculars. He could not make out any activity on the beach until dawn broke just prior to the 0500 landing, at which moment Echo Company's first landing craft dropped its ramp. Flash units erupted along the shore as waiting news photographers greeted the tense, relieved Marines at the water's edge. Capt Ken McCabe, Echo Company commander, and Col Jim Mead were the first to step ashore through the milling mass of about a hundred newspeople. Mead was greeted by an entourage of VIPs personally led by Ambassador Habib.

The relief went off without a hitch, largely because Bob Johnston, members of his BLT staff, and all his company commanders had journeyed ashore the day before to receive a thorough briefing from the French Foreign Legion commander. The Marines began taking over legion positions as soon as they landed and, at 0730, the French commander was officially relieved of responsibility for the port. The tricolor was lowered and the Lebanese national colors raised, a pointed reminder that the United States was involved only insofar as it supported the government of Lebanon.

Second Lieutenant Ken Lyles's engineers landed at 0630 and fell to the task of clearing out a warehouse that had been designated the BLT command post. Resourceful engineers hot-wired several civilian forklifts they found in the area, and these were used to great advantage. The warehouse, which the engineers had cleared by early afternoon, was riddled with shrapnel holes, there was no electricity, and the water supply was unpotable. The buildings on the Green Line occupied by Echo Company were befouled with human and animal feces in varying stages of decomposition.

Lightly armed Marines established blocking positions and checkpoints as far out as the wire fence surrounding the port facility. One of the battalion's three rifle companies was held back for internal security and as a reaction force.

Sol Gorgius, the first evacuation vessel of the day—one of a small fleet of Greek-flag ferries hired for the evacuation—arrived at the port at 0915, and the American mission got under way.

At 1000, Jim Mead and Bob Johnston drove up to Checkpoint 54, the western entrance to the port. On the way, Colonel Mead was particularly impressed with the amount of destruction he observed in the port area and on city streets he could see from the road; the area in front of Checkpoint 54 looked "like pictures I have seen of Berlin at end of World War II."

Lebanese Armed Forces (LAF) trucks carted the first contingent of PLO fighters to Checkpoint 54 minutes after Mead and Johnston arrived. The crescendo of gunfire, which was always in the background, dramatically increased, and rocket-propelled grenades (RPGs) suddenly burst about 200 feet overhead. It seemed to Jim Mead that everyone was firing—people in the vehicles, people in the buildings nearby, people lining the road. They all appeared to be having a good time.

Marines and LAF soldiers manning the sandbagged checkpoint called the trucks forward, one at a time. The Marine Amphibious Unit (MAU) commander noted that, while most of the passengers were men, a few women and children were sprinkled through the departing column. A Lebanese official in civilian clothing checked each vehicle while LAF and Marine officers looked on. A Marine rifle squad stood in the street behind the checkpoint to control the traffic. Other armed Marines manned positions in and around nearby buildings.

The trucks and their occupants were briskly checked for weapons other than the light personal arms—AK-47s, rifles, and pistols—allowed under the evacuation agreement. Upon completion of the inspection, each truck moved forward with Marine foot guides and rounded a corner, out of sight of the checkpoint, where it was made to stop. Each group of four or five trucks that rounded the corner would be allowed to proceed toward the evacuation vessel. Bob Johnston led the first convoy of five trucks the 300 meters to dockside, and Jim Mead and a Marine lieutenant led the second.

The PLO fighters were off-loaded at the quay and processed through stations manned by LAF infantry. Each evacuee had only to give his name to be allowed to walk up the stern gate of the waiting *Sol Gorgius*. Weapons and ammunition were to be left beside the vehicle entrance, but no one standing on the dock could see if the rules were being followed. When one PLO fighter refused to give up his RPG, LAF officers simply blocked his access to the ship until he complied.

By late morning *Sol Gorgius* was fully loaded. It stood into the harbor and then disappeared over the horizon. Jim Mead celebrated by radioing his superiors, "The Marines have landed and the situation is well in hand."

A routine quickly evolved. A PLO lieutenant colonel was always on hand at Checkpoint 54 to negotiate in the event of trouble. So was an LAF brigadier, who always accompanied the LAF truck convoys that brought the PLO fighters to the gate. The senior Marine officer on the gate, usually Capt Ken McCabe, did all he could to facilitate the flow of traffic. Marines just wanted to get as many people through the port as quickly as possible.

One cause for serious concern was the attitude of the local Israeli commanders. Israeli gunboats were known to be patrolling just over the horizon. These appeared offshore at frequent intervals and some turned back departing Greek ferries, which caused great consternation among Marines because of the sheer volatility of so many armed groups in so small an area. An Israeli security detachment (including, as it turned out, a photo-surveil-lance team) established a post in a nearby building. Many PLO fighters wore their kaffiyehs across their mouths and noses to stymie the photographers. Finally, several Israeli tanks and ar-mored personnel carriers, about ten vehicles in all, made occa-sional sweeps at the periphery of the American area—a forceful reminder that the evacuation would proceed only as long as the Israelis wanted it to. Soon after landing, Bob Johnston took the advice of his French predecessor and surrounded the Israelis in the port area with his own troops—an American reminder.

Though Lieutenant Colonel Johnston always stood at the ramp of each ship just to see that no heavy weapons were brought aboard, Israeli observers were certain, on one occasion, that several RPGs had been smuggled on. Johnston responded through the American embassy that he had seen no RPGs, and he attempted to dissuade the Israelis from stopping the evacua-tion. To take the edge off the implied Israeli threat, the Marine battalion commander and the PLO lieutenant colonel with whom he worked made a ten-minute sweep through the PLO berthing compartments, then reported, truthfully, that they had found no RPGs.

One day, 2dLt Ken Lyles looked up in time to see what he took to be a dogfight between an Israeli and a Syrian jet. He definitely saw a pair of missile contrails and then spotted one plane head-ing north. Lyles heard that night that a Syrian jet had crashed into the mountains above East Beirut.

The greatest potential for danger, other than an outright fight in the port area, lay in the hundreds of thousands of spent rounds that rained constantly upon East Beirut—the detritus of the "victory" salutes fired at all hours by the departing fighters and, it appears, by all their kith and kin.

The pattern emerged at the start. Women standing near Checkpoint 54 would begin chanting while a few male bystand-ers pumped lead into the air. A speaker truck would crank up and further incite the gathering crowd with brave exhortations. The progress of the arriving convoy could be easily followed by the increasing volume of massed victory fire. At length, the LAF trucks, festooned with banners and photographs of PLO leaders and martyrs, would come into sight amid frenzied chanting and, if possible, even more victory fire.

Bob Johnston admired the PLO's effort to go out looking victorious. For example, it was plain to him that they considered the early evacuation of casualties to be a sign of defeat, so they waited a few days before sending the wounded to the port, and even then they made certain that the wounded did not leave with organized units.

Every PLO fighter who passed through Checkpoint 54 wore a brand-new camouflage battledress uniform, and each appeared to be carrying a brand-new rifle or AK-47. The PLO lieutenant colonel on regular watch at the gate once asked Bob Johnston, "Now what are you thinking? Regular or irregular? Aren't they more than a band of guerrillas?" Johnston would not admit it to the Palestinian, but he did find the PLO units well disciplined.

Less disciplined were the onlookers. Several live grenades were rolled out of the crowd toward the sandbagged checkpoint, no doubt to see how the Marines would react. No one was hurt, so there was no reaction, but Marines manning M-60 machine guns on nearby roofs could have wreaked awesome damage.

Few PLO fighters fired their weapons once they passed through Checkpoint 54. In the event, the Marines would not allow the trucks to proceed until all weapons had been silenced.

As the evacuation from the port settled into a routine, the evacuation committee turned to the repatriation of Syrian army and Syrian-sponsored Palestine Liberation Army (PLA) units to Syria. The overland evacuation was under Italian direction. The problems faced during this operation were formidable, but about 6,200 PLA and PLO fighters and Syrian soldiers were carried out of the besieged city aboard Syrian army and LAF trucks.

Colonel Mead was ordered on August 28 to prepare to escort Yasir Arafat safely through the port area on August 30. The PLO high command had begun moving through the port the day before, August 27, and there had as yet been no incident to mar their passage. Arafat's departure, however, was seen as something else again, perhaps the occasion for a direct challenge by the PLO leadership to what they still perceived as American support for Israel. On top of that, it was well known that certain Palestinian factions would assassinate Arafat if the opportunity arose.

Mead ordered an immediate beefing up of security measures throughout the port area. Arafat would not be Mead's problem until he arrived at Checkpoint 54, but he would be solely Mead's responsibility from then until his ship cleared the harbor.

The BLT swept the port area in the wee hours and stood on full alert until the Greek ferry *Atlantis* arrived at 1000, August 30. Arafat was scheduled to go on board at 1100.

By 1000 a huge crowd had gathered at Checkpoint 54. It was an emotional gathering, far too large to be controlled in the confined area near the gate. Women and children predominated, but there were armed guards, presumably Palestinians, hundreds of newspeople with bulky equipment that was to be *aimed* at Arafat, and many, many armed LAF soldiers with no-one-knew-what scores to settle with the PLO chieftain.

Arafat arrived in his Mercedes pretty much on schedule, ringed by his own armed honor guard. Jim Mead and Bob Johnston, who were on hand, would have liked to see the man simply pass through the checkpoint and hurry on his way, but they knew that was not to be.

As the cheering crowd pushed in to touch their chieftain, Arafat's honor guard deployed in the confined space in front of the sandbagged checkpoint and formally presented their leader with the colors of two PLO units that had accompanied him to

27

the port. Arafat then waved at the crowd and proceeded toward the gate in his Mercedes.

When the PLO chieftain and his honor guard attempted to pass the Marine guards in contravention of agreements there would be no martial displays by the PLO in the port area, the squad of Marines nearest the gate closed ranks and stood across the roadway. The PLO fighters threatened the American youngsters with their weapons, but the Marines stood their ground, then slowly pushed the PLO fighters back through the gate.

French Ambassador Marc Henri insisted upon making a play for Palestinian hearts and minds by showing up with a fifty-man honor guard arrayed in trucks and armored cars. Henri planned to personally lead the march to the quay to see Arafat off.

Bob Johnston had 1,000 Marines looking after the PLO leader so he was having none of this political grandstanding. Lieutenant Lyles was seated in a jeep beside the checkpoint, ready at a nod from Lieutenant Colonel Johnston to swing in behind Arafat and cover him all the way to the quay. When Johnston shouted for Lyles to bar the way, three Marine jeeps swung out onto the roadway, effectively blocking the path into the port area. Tensions were running high.

Ambassador Henri accosted Johnston and said, "This has been agreed with the American ambassador."

"Well, it hasn't been communicated to me," Johnston replied, at which point several French vehicles forced their way through the Marine checkpoint. Johnston clearly saw that it was time to compromise. His objective was to get Arafat safely away, so he let Henri and some of the French soldiers pass. Then the Marine battalion commander held the convoy up long enough to place the Italian and Greek ambassadors in the column, following which he led the entourage from his own jeep.

(When Johnston had time to think about it later, he realized that the LAF units that were supposed to have been manning the gate had somehow contrived to evaporate, leaving the Marines holding their bag.)

The quayside send-offs were well under way when, suddenly, there echoed through the confined and crowded area the crack of a single gunshot.

A deathly hush fell over the crowd at the quay. A French rifle had accidentally discharged. The air was stiff with tension, but nothing happened and Arafat sailed in due course.

The last of the PLO left the next day, September 1. The MAU remained in port until September 10, during which time it was visited by Secretary of Defense Caspar Weinberger and U.S. Senator Charles Percy, the first of uncountable VIPs who would, in the coming year, contrive to find Beirut an essential stopover.

On September 10 the MAU returned to its ships, which sailed for Naples.

•

PART II

Evolution of The Mission

4

The chasm that separates perception from reality in the Middle East yawned extra wide within days of the Palestine Liberation Organization (PLO) evacuation.

The first fracture appeared with the September 8 assassination of President-elect Bashir Gemayel, the charismatic Phalange military chieftain who had been elected by the Lebanese parliament following the Israeli invasion and who had become the first Arab leader to agree to an accord with Israel since Egypt's Anwar as-Sadat had ventured to Jerusalem. Bashir's younger and more pliable brother, Amin, was elected in his place by the Lebanese parliament, but Amin was an unknown factor whose very presence at least temporarily upset the very little apparent stability the nation enjoyed.

There was little the United States could do to redress the loss of Bashir Gemayel, for by then President Reagan had professed that his nation had no strategic interests in Lebanon and would thus refrain from leaving troops there, a policy that had resulted in the earlier-than-anticipated, earlier-than-agreed withdrawal of 32d Marine Amphibious Unit (MAU) and the liquidation of the Multinational Force (MNF).

Next, the Israelis reneged on the terms of an oral pledge that had allowed Ambassador Philip Habib to strike a bargain with Yasir Arafat's high command. The Israel Defense Force (IDF) invaded Moslem West Beirut. The Begin government gave as its reason the protection of Palestinians in the Sabra and Shatilla camps, a duty the Israelis believed to be the responsibility of the MNF for at least thirty days following the PLO departure from Beirut. Perhaps unwilling to offend world opinion, the Israelis restrained their natural desire to enter the camps themselves but permitted Christian allies to do so.

A stunned world awoke on September 18 to the news that between several hundred and several thousand Palestinians (the number would come close to 800) had been ruthlessly and brutally murdered by Christian militiamen who, on September 16, had entered the Sabra and Shatilla refugee camps under the guns of IDF units surrounding the former PLO stronghold. Israeli connivance in an apparently premeditated plot to implement these mass murders has not been established; but there is no doubt that some burden of guilt for the massacre—which is not to say responsibility—may have been felt by the Reagan administration and its former MNF partners, France and Italy.

The reconstitution of the MNF was instantly requested by President Amin Gemayel and agreed to by all parties within forty-eight hours of the discovery of the massacre.

For reasons deeply rooted in American perceptions, and the realities from which *they* derive, the Reagan administration sought to legitimize its newfound and unwanted role by speaking of its commitment to the reestablishment and strengthening of the legitimate Lebanese government in the wake of the destructive Lebanese civil war. This last was an argument that washed well with nearly all the factions that resided in Lebanon in the late summer of 1982. If nothing else, all had agreed for seven bloody years that Lebanon's plight was due to the PLO. Absent the Palestinians, most Lebanese agreed, the chimera that was a unified Lebanon could be captured once again, allowing members of all confessions to prosper and, above all, live in peace. Thus it became the avowed intention of the Gemayel government and the MNF participants that the MNF would remain in Beirut until the Lebanese Armed Forces (LAF) was in a position to undertake the security of the capital.

The Reagan administration's professions of simply offering temporary help to the Gemayel government dovetailed so nicely with the perceived needs of the Lebanese peoples that it was readily accepted without qualm by virtually all interested parties. Thus a crucial fantasy was woven into the fabric of the ongoing Lebanese struggle to mold one nation from five or six intermingled nations. The MNF would provide an aura of stability and legitimacy for the rebuilding process most Lebanese doubted could be fairly or enduringly achieved but which many of all faiths fervently hoped could be.

As soon as its commander received orders on September 20, Mediterranean Amphibious Ready Group (MARG) 2-82 suspended maintenance and leave programs. The five-ship convoy, with a carrier battle group as escort, left Naples on September 22 to deploy off Beirut until specific details could be ironed out. The MAU executive officer was flown to Beirut to coordinate the upcoming deployment, provide up-to-the-minute situation reports, and personally reconnoiter potential bivouacs.

It quickly developed at the "committee" meetings overseen by Philip Habib at Yardze that the MNF contingents—American, French, and Italian—would have to slice West Beirut into three portions. There was no question of any of the MNF contingents entering East Beirut, which was in the hands of the Phalange. The French requested and were given the role of actively patrolling the port and downtown areas of West Beirut. The Marines desired an open piece of ground with easy access to the sea, so they were assigned Beirut International Airport (BIA). In its way, this was an extremely important assignment, for an open, viable airport symbolized a functioning Lebanon. By default, the Italians were assigned the middle area, which happened to include the Sabra and Shatilla camps.

By pure coincidence, the Italian contingent commander, Col Franco Angione, happened to be reconnoitering his assigned sector when he drove into the middle of a scuffle between Phalange thugs and several Palestinians. Angione's jeep came to a screeching halt and the colonel jumped to the roadway, pistol in hand, and ordered the area cleared. The news of Angione's rescue of the Palestinians electrified the camps and assured the Italians a safe and pleasant stay in what might have been Beirut's most troublesome hot spot.

From the start the French kicked ass. It was a matter of style. They immediately put armed patrols on the streets of the central city and enforced an evenhanded but no-nonsense discipline upon the residents of their sector. They were never loved, nor even admired, but they were respected.

The Israelis receded into East Beirut on September 23 after turning their West Beirut checkpoints over to the LAF, which was then seen by most Lebanese as the "legitimate" arm of the Christian Phalange. Large Moslem residential areas remained under Israeli control both on the narrow coastal plain that is the city and on into the sprawl of towns climbing the Shouf escarpment.

The utter dominance of the Israelis over events and peoples in and around Beirut cannot be too strongly stressed. While the arrival and deployment of the reconstituted MNF established an *aura* of stability, it was the massive armed presence of the IDF that ensured whatever stability there was. As Marines noted from the outset, the Israelis "came to play." It would become a characteristic of the Israeli occupation that any resistance would be met with nothing short of draconian countermeasures.

The Israelis had a simple, brutal method for dealing with opposition: they blew away the source of the opposition, and everything around it.

These things were not so evident to the U.S. MNF contingent in the halcyon days of late September and early October 1982. Thirty-second MAU had other fish to fry and, more important, other, very different, precedents to establish.

5

Thirty-second Marine Amphibious Unit (MAU) was ordered on September 20 to land both through the Port of Beirut and by air directly into Beirut International Airport (BIA) to "establish a presence," a phrase no Marine commander had ever before seen on an operations order.

The imprecision of the "presence" phrase in Col Jim Mead's mission directive provided this able and ambitious officer with a crucial role in the command structure reaching down from the Oval Office. Indeed, Mead's responsibility for conducting U.S. foreign policy in Lebanon became, at the turn of a phrase, unique in modern American military *and* diplomatic annals.

It was evident at the outset to Mead and his staff that the primary threat facing the 1,200 combat and support Marines slated to go ashore would be isolated acts of terrorism and, initially, vast quantities of unexploded ordnance lying around the BIA. The MAU was organized to handle neither danger adequately, so Mead requested additional engineers, an explosive ordnance disposal detachment, an interrogator/translator team, additional intelligence specialists, and an air-naval gunfire liaison team. In addition, preventive medicine and public affairs detachments were requested. With these reinforcements, numbering about 100 officers and men, the MAU would be able to operate independently in an alien environment for an indeterminate period while remaining truly self-contained. Mead's request was "greased" by Fleet Marine Force, Atlantic, and all the additional personnel arrived, with their equipment, within thirty-six hours. But for a few additional specialist groups requested later, the MAU had taken the shape that would prevail for more than a year.

The political nature of the "presence" mission surfaced at the outset. While the amphibious Marines were perfectly able to land on beaches adjacent to the BIA, it was decided that a large detachment would reenter Lebanon via the Port of Beirut so it could be reviewed by President Amin Gemayel.

Even more important was the Israeli delay of their evacuation from the BIA until well after the deadline to which they had agreed in meetings with Ambassador Habib. The Israel Defense Force's (IDF's) political intent was obvious: if the Marines landed at the BIA while the IDF was still in possession, it would seem as though the Israelis were providing security for the Americans.

The Marines went ashore by landing craft and helicopter on September 29, 1982, a day later than planned, by which time the Israelis had been prevailed upon to move from the BIA. The delayed landing at the port resulted in a reshuffling of the presidential review, so a large Marine contingent had to be trucked back to the port, trucked past the presidential entourage, and trucked back to the BIA. The special considerations afforded President Gemayel had the desired effect; it was obvious to all that the Multinational Force (MNF) was indeed *his*.

There could be no rush occupying the BIA. The literally tens of thousands of unexploded ordnance devices littering the hotly contested airport kept all but specially trained Marine engineers firmly rooted to the hard-surfaced runways.

The task of clearing the dangerous explosives—125 different types from nineteen countries accumulated over eight years of heavy fighting—initially fell to 2dLt Ken Lyles's engineer platoon. Soon, three mine-clearance teams flown in that day from Camp Lejeune fanned out across the areas designated by LtCol Bob Johnston, the Battalion Landing Team (BLT) 2/8 commander, as most essential for billeting and security. Each team was equipped to find both metallic and nonmetallic mines and other explosive devices. So dense were potentially lethal devices that mine-detector operators were relieved every ten minutes to maintain peak efficiency.

Beginning at the beach over which the MAU would be supplied, the mine teams cleared and marked paths with agonizing precision throughout September 29. The hundreds of grunts who were not involved in necessary work simply sat on the hot runway surfaces, venturing only as far as the few heads (lavatories) and piss tubes that had been installed at the very outset.

The slow mine-clearing job continued into September 30, while a large infantry contingent busied itself at the MNF review. Communicators following in the traces of the mine-clearing teams installed communications wire, and sentries worked gingerly to install the first checkpoints.

Lieutenant Lyles was on his way back from surveying potential infantry installations around the Lebanese Science and Technical University, about a mile east of the BIA fence, when his dump truck was approached by a jeep heading north across the runways from Khalde, the town adjacent to the southern end of the runways. Lyles had a brief instant to glance into the back of the jeep, then uttered an involuntary "Holy shit!" His mind's eye had registered a crumpled human form awash in bright red blood.

The dump truck came to a slithering halt on the dusty road and the engineering platoon leader hit the ground running. Several of his young engineers and corpsmen were wiping blood from the face of Cpl David Reagan, an engineer who had been leading one of the mine-clearing teams.

Reagan was beyond help, though not quite dead. Lieutenant Lyles heard from eyewitnesses that he had been crouching over one of the tens of thousands of unexploded U.S.-manufactured cluster bomblets littering the BIA in the wake of the Israeli invasion. No one was quite certain what set off the otherwise inert device, but there had been a tiny explosion that drove numerous pellets into Reagan's abdomen, thorax, and head. At least one pellet had penetrated the twenty-five-year-old corporal's brain, undoubtedly desensitizing him to the mutilating wounds elsewhere in his body. He remained alive only as a result of cardiopulmonary resuscitation administered by a quick-thinking comrade, but he was truly beyond help and died a short time later at the temporary battalion aid station.

When LtCol Bob Johnston learned the details of Reagan's death, he took a more straightforward approach to the dangerous and agonizing task of clearing the airport. Most of the unexploded ordnance happened to be the same kind of bomblet that had killed Reagan; they were low-order antipersonnel devices that would have little or no effect on some of the heavy vehicles the Marines had brought ashore. Johnston pressed several of his amphibian assault vehicles (known variously as AAVs, amtracs, and hogs) into service along with Lieutenant Lyles, the amtrac platoon leader, and the Fox Company commander, whose sector was slated to be cleared first. Johnston and the amtrac officer boarded the lead vehicle, which was fully enclosed and lightly armored, and ordered its driver to sweep directly across an open stretch of ground in Fox Company's designated sector. The ground was soon covered by track marks, over which Fox Company Marines could safely traverse the area. While there was some danger of hitting an antivehicle mine, Johnston considered the risk acceptable in pursuit of minimizing the threat of antipersonnel bomblets to his troops. Fine-tuning the clearing operation was undertaken by newly arrived and highly skilled explosive ordnance disposal teams, but the Johnston method worked exactly as intended. The job of tactically deploying BLT 2/8 could now proceed apace.

The BIA was what is known in military jargon as a "permissive" environment, which is to say that it was open to civilians, that Marines would have to coexist with the hundreds or thousands of people who would have daily access to a functioning international airport. While this was a natural cause for concern to the security-minded Marines, it was the essence of the presence mission: the MNF was in Beirut precisely to ensure a sense of normalcy. The BIA was crucial to Lebanon's image as a nation capable of operating as a nation.

Neither Jim Mead nor Bob Johnston saw any reason to secure the BIA totally, to provide a doctrinal 360-degree defense. Indeed, the BLT and MAU headquarters were in secure buildings made available by the Lebanese government within the operational infrastructure of the airport. Buildings beside and around the BLT and MAU headquarters still functioned as, for example, the airport electrical engineering facility and the airport firefighting school. Parking lots and roads directly adjacent to the two Marine headquarters buildings and other facilities were completely open to civilian traffic of every variety.

The primary restriction on the tactical deployment Bob Johnston had proposed for his three rifle companies was the presence of IDF units in areas adjacent to the airport. A quick look at a map of the area incorporating the BIA convinced Mead and Johnston that they should establish Marine checkpoints along a meandering main thoroughfare known as the

Sidon Road, the link between Beirut and the southern city of Sidon. Johnston also felt that his battalion command post should be installed at the Lebanese University, east of the main runways and close to the Sidon Road. From here, BLT 2/8's rifle platoons could be easily directed should they be required to secure the presidential palace and the American ambassador's residence, in Yardze, and the Lebanese ministry of defense, in adjacent Baabda.

As it turned out, the Lebanese government had conceded to the IDF the use of the Sidon Road as its main supply route, linking Israeli units around Beirut to their checkpoints along the east-west Beirut-Damascus highway and in the Shouf mountains overlooking Beirut. Because of the State Department's strong opposition to any form of commingling—or even the perception of commingling—Marine units with the IDF, Lieutenant Colonel Johnston had to accept a much smaller area of responsibility than he had at first envisioned. This bothered Johnston, but was of some advantage in that the smaller area could be more effectively defended if the need arose. Thus the BLT deployed two rifle companies along the perimeter of the runways with checkpoints as far east as a railroad line running just to the west of the Sidon Road. The third rifle company was sent to an isolated position at the Lebanese University, where it was tied into the Italian contingent to the north. All Marine checkpoints were collocated with Lebanese Armed Forces (LAF) checkpoints, an important pretense in magnifying the image of this all-but-impotent army.

Bob Johnston was frankly surprised to be allowed to place a company as far east as the Lebanese University, and he welcomed the silence from higher headquarters because of the tactical advantages afforded him by having a strong infantry force on high ground. The company looked out over the Shiite Moslem quarter of Hay-es-Salaam, which was more or less a refugee area surrounding the main routes to and from the BIA. In addition, the battalion commander saw that any move by his

Marines or the LAF eastward from the BIA would be channeled across a bridge spanning a sluggish waterway deep enough to stop tanks. Friendly troops on the roofs of buildings at the university would be able to dominate these crossings against anyone seeking to contest them.

The environment might have been permissive, but Bob Johnston was determined to permit as little tactical advantage over his troops as the terrain and political strictures allowed.

Once it was clear to Johnston that he could not establish his command post at the Lebanese University, he agreed to do so in an administration building offered by the management of the BIA. This stoutly built four-story ferroconcrete structure was about the strongest building within Marine lines. It had served as a Syrian army headquarters prior to and during the Israeli invasion. As such, it had been hit by numerous heavy-caliber artillery rounds and had been struck on at least several occasions by Israeli fighter-bombers. Despite many pockmarks and uncountable broken windows, the structure itself had not been penetrated by any of the heavy ordnance that had been hurled at it. The best testimony to its integrity, Bob Johnston felt, was that the Israelis had used it in their turn as a major headquarters. It was centrally located, near the MAU headquarters and not far from the BIA control tower. Except for the tower, the building's large, flat roof provided by far the best observation platform anywhere within the airport complex. Within days, as many as 150 Marine headquarters staffers and communicators lived and worked in the building, which was secured by dismounted members of the tank and amtrac platoons. No one who was billeted in what immediately became known as "the BLT CP" had any qualms about being there.

Bob Johnston personally had only one direct contact with the Israelis, this on October 1, his third day ashore. He was approached by an Israeli captain who asked what the Marines would do if a terrorist got between the two forces—which were less than 200 meters apart in some places—and fired at one or the other. This was a serious question that raised long vistas of mayhem in the Marine battalion commander's mind. It was also the opening of an infrequent dialogue that would keep a succession of Marine senior officers in a quandary over how they should deal with an ally that higher authorities demanded they ignore.

In the end, Johnston settled for three company sectors, each somewhat isolated from the others. Within each sector, platoons and squads manned similarly isolated positions and checkpoints linked by a busy schedule of foot and motorized patrols.

Close combat air support, if needed, would be provided by a pair of missile-carrying AH-1T Cobra helicopter gunships stationed aboard the helicopter carrier offshore and, in dire emergencies, by Navy attack aircraft from 6th Fleet's carrier battle group. The balance of the MAU's helicopter squadron would also operate from the helicopter carrier both because the facilities could not easily be duplicated ashore and because the large CH-46 and CH-53 transport helicopters might prove to be tantalizing targets for terrorists if they were permanently based at the open BIA.

The six-gun 105mm howitzer battery that was attached to the MAU remained aboard ship as it was felt it would not fit in with the presence role ashore. The heaviest indirect-fire weapons on the beach were thus the eight 81mm mortars manned by BLT 2/8's mortar platoon, which could reach all Marine posts from its positions. Reinforcement in the event of ground attack was to be handled by the artillerymen, who were quietly brought ashore without their tubes and outfitted as a provisional fourth rifle company. The BLT's five M-60A1 main battle tanks were kept aboard ship, but the BLT did land its amtracs, which mounted .50-caliber heavy machine guns and provided excellent protection for troops and equipment.

Neither Jim Mead nor Bob Johnston was particularly concerned by the paucity of heavy weapons nor the widespread deployment of their infantry assets. Any potential opposing forces in the area were equipped with, at most, light artillery, mortars, and rockets and had few offensive weapons such as tanks, armored cars, or half-tracks. And, though it went essentially unstated, the overriding security consideration was that the immensely powerful IDF had its boot squarely on the neck of any potentially hostile faction with any sort of real offensive capabilities.

If anything, speculation ran heavily in the direction of an engineered confrontation with an Israeli ally, such as the Lebanese Christian militia commanded by Maj Saad Haddad. The fear was that Haddad might embarrass the United States by goading Marines into a firefight or some other form of confrontation.

It escaped no senior Marine's attention that an American force anchored to the BIA and other static positions could at any time serve as a convenient and useful target for any imaginable form of anti-American mischief.

One of the really striking features of the nearby Shiite Moslem town of Hay-es-Salaam was the absence of young males. As a group, the Shiites are the poorest of Lebanese Moslems, a large and burgeoning "religious minority" that has either not advanced or not been allowed to advance by the financially dominant but numerically insignificant Sunni Moslem sect, the secretive mountain-dwelling Druse sect, or the politically dominant and militarily ruthless Maronite Christian sect. When Bob Johnston asked an English-speaking resident of Hay-es-Salaam why there were no young men in town, he was told that they had fled the place during the fighting between the Israelis and the Palestine Liberation Organization (PLO) and were now afraid to return because access to the town could be gained only by passing through Phalange checkpoints. With the Sabra and Shatilla massacres very much in mind, Johnston was willing to suppress any doubts he might otherwise have had concerning this rather glib explanation.

It was something of a surprise—and deeply gratifying—when Marine patrols reported an outpouring of friendliness from Lebanese civilians—mainly Shiite Moslems—with whom they came in contact. There was some reticence at first when patrolling Marines were mistaken for Israelis, but the arrival of an abundant supply of American flags to be flown from Marine vehicles both relieved uneasiness on the part of the civilians and led to impromptu celebrations whenever Marines took a break or were stopped in traffic. A torrent of good feelings confronted these young Americans wherever they trod.

Courtesy calls were something of a strain on senior Marine officers, who had no clothing ashore but their rough-and-ready cammies. Colonel Mead, an aviator who properly left the tactical disposition of BLT 2/8 to its commander, was in his element when MNF coordination issues and related social events claimed his attention. Mead was a very tall man with a booming, friendly voice, and he felt particularly at ease and effective in the social settings to which he was regularly invited. His huge frame, gregarious nature, and authentic concern for the Lebanese people made a crowd stopper of him as he constantly roamed the city, inspecting Italian, French, and LAF contingents and simply mingling with the kids.

Mead noted from the outset an unrestrained atmosphere of rebirth throughout the city. Whereas the PLO evacuation had been a bleak affair conducted in bleak surroundings, the first days of October were marked by the noise of new construction throughout the battered city. Bathers crowded the beaches wherever there was a stretch of mine-cleared sand. Restaurants did a thriving business, and thousands of private vehicles—all white Mercedes sedans, it seemed—fought chaotically or quixotically for space on the teeming thoroughfares. Wherever he went, Big Jim Mead was singled out as a savior of the city.

A professor at the American University in Beirut said of the Marine presence, "I can't believe it! It's hard to believe we're finally outside, out of our houses, no longer in fear, and that things are returning to normal."

Bob Johnston noted an understandable dichotomy within the officer corps of the LAF. During the course of the few social events he had time to attend, the BLT commander was treated to some serious anti-Israeli sloganeering by Moslem officers, but also sensed that even they were relieved to be rid of the PLO and Syrians. Indeed, several senior Moslem LAF officers pointedly identified the Syrians as having posed the most serious threat to Lebanese sovereignty. Withal, they averred, the Begin government could become an equal threat. Christian officers were naturally even more inclined to place the burden of Lebanon's tragic civil war upon Syria, and they saw the Israeli occupation as a boon in that it would provide the LAF with an opportunity to reconstitute itself. Both Moslem and Christian officers were reasonably certain that the IDF would leave, but neither expected the same of the Syrians. Further, both groups recognized that the strong IDF presence was about all that was keeping the lid on Beirut.

That the IDF was the dominant force in Beirut was absolutely unmistakable. The Israelis were utterly ruthless in dealing with even the most minor acts against them. Marines at the BIA would note over succeeding months that a single sniper round aimed anywhere near an IDF convoy would result in minutes of all-out firing in every direction by gunners and infantry aboard tanks and armored personnel carriers. In time, the town of Ashuefat was literally flattened by Israeli patrols moving up and down the Sidon Road. Any vehicle parked along the Sidon Road when an Israeli column drove through was simply blown to smithereens by the lead Israeli tank's 105mm gun. Marines never could figure out why anyone in possession of his or her faculties would park along the thoroughfare, but there were always plenty of targets.

The only real danger in October arose from a number of LAF sweeps into Moslem townships just to the north of the BIA. Moslem refugees—mainly Palestinians—who had built a shantytown were given notice that they would be forcibly evicted, and LAF bulldozers threatened to flatten their living quarters and business establishments with graceless brutality. This led to a serious demonstration, about the only outlet open to the 15,000 souls who were in danger of being dispossessed. A mosque just to the north of the northernmost Marine position was the focal point of the rally and, when minor gunfire erupted, stray rounds sent a number of onlooking Marines scrambling for cover behind their low sandbag blast walls. Most of the gunfire was felt to have originated with LAF or nearby IDF soldiers, none of whom were exactly passive observers. That was about as bad as it got in October.

The average member of 32d MAU faced interminable boredom relieved by mundane work parties and what soon became routine patrolling through the Shiite town of Hay-es-Salaam, which was soon known to the American contingent as Hooterville. There was not enough to do and not enough places to do it. The ennui was crushing once routines were established and it was too soon to risk time out on the town both because of the real danger of terrorist incidents and, perhaps to a greater degree, the likelihood that hundreds of horny young Marines might deeply offend the morality that clearly prevailed in the Moslem neighborhoods to which they would have ready access.

But it was over in a month. Thirty-second MAU was relieved on October 29 by the identically configured 24th MAU, comprising BLT 3/8 and air and support units. No member of 32d MAU was particularly unhappy to leave Beirut, for he faced a straight run home, having been gone for the requisite six months. Still, Bob Johnston felt that all hands had a real sense of accomplishment, both for getting the PLO safely away from Beirut and for contributing to the salvation of the city and, perhaps, of Lebanon. The only casualty, a death, had been the result of an accident. On that score alone, there was everything for which to be thankful. And proud.

Jim Mead, who was under consideration to become a brigadier general, had passed his first great hurdle. For the time being, however, he would have to prepare for his second tour as a MAU commander in under four months. Bob Johnston, who had been selected colonel nearly a year before, returned home to receive his eagles and be given command of 8th Marine Regiment, which would keep him in close touch with the developing Marine presence in Beirut. About half the officers and troops of 32d MAU were scattered to the far corners of the Marine Corps, while BLT 2/8 and the air and support units took new people aboard to begin the one-year cycle of training and retraining that had been going on in the Fleet Marine Force for over thirty years.

Whatever happened in Beirut, BLT 2/8 was reluctantly, but safely, out of it.

6

Twenty-fourth Marine Amphibious Unit (MAU) departed More-head City, North Carolina, on August 24, 1982, the day before 32d MAU went ashore to oversee the Palestine Liberation Organization (PLO) evacuation from the Port of Beirut. Though the MAU's official duty station was with the U.S. 6th Fleet in the Mediterranean, it took part in North Atlantic Treaty Organization (NATO) exercises in Denmark and Germany. Such things had been going on for the thirty years that the MAUs and similar amphibious groupments had been "cruising the Med"; in recent decades, Marine amphibious units had been tasked to NATO Northern Command as part of the force that would seal northern Norway against Soviet invasion. In accordance with a plan drawn up long before the Multinational Force (MNF) commitment had even been conceived, the fresh 24th MAU would reach the Mediterranean just as 32d MAU was due to rotate back to the United States in October. Indeed, 32d MAU had replaced

24th MAU in June, just as the Israel Defense Force (IDF) crossed into Lebanon.

So 24th MAU undertook the scheduled exercises in northern Europe, with time off for liberty in Denmark. Mediterranean Amphibious Ready Group (MARG) 3-82 then sailed for Rota and an updated set of orders: either replace 32d MAU in Beirut or "cruise the Med" with routine stopovers and exercises. The smart money, of course, was on deployment ashore in Beirut.

Col Tom Stokes was a peppery, silver-thatched senior parachutist and reconnaissance enthusiast on his second and final cruise as 24th MAU commander. He had made his mark in 1960 when, as a young captain, he had been the only American to jump with Belgian commandos at Stanleyville in the heroic, tragic rescue of European civilian hostages during the Congolese civil war. He had led a quietly distinguished career in the quarter century since, winning his share of professional laurels during and after Vietnam.

Stokes and several of his senior officers flew into Beirut International Airport (BIA) on October 17 to receive a complete briefing from Col Jim Mead and his staff. Unlike Mead, who was an aviator with some schooling in ground operations, Stokes was a highly skilled professional infantryman who was bound to have strong ideas of his own with respect to defining the loosely termed "presence" mission and the deployment and use of his force.

The mission directive under which 24th MAU was to operate called for Stokes to "establish [an] environment which will permit the Lebanese Armed Forces [LAF] to carry out its responsibilities in the Beirut area, and [to] be prepared to protect U.S. forces and conduct retrograde and withdrawal operations from the area."

As soon as Stokes completed his briefing sessions with the 32d MAU staff, he returned to Rota to oversee the fine-tuning of his combat units, chiefly Battalion Landing Team (BLT) 3/8.

The most important result of Stokes's advance trip to the BIA was his instant grasp of the potential for mayhem that could result from even an innocuous exchange of fire between his Marines and the factional militias that appeared to be returning to the relatively lawless environs of the BIA. Thus he contrived a simple set of guidelines, known collectively as the Rules of Engagement (ROE). These would endure, with little change:

- In every possible case, local civil/military authority will be used.
- Marines will use only the degree of military force necessary to accomplish the mission or reduce the threat.
- Wherever possible, avoid injury to noncombatants or damage to civilian property.
- Response to hostile fire will be directed only at the source.
- Marines will act in self-defense only.

The discomfort Stokes and his fellow senior officers felt over their unprecedented and vaguely stated mission is clear from a reading of these general principles. The Marine Corps, as an institution, was thrilled to have been selected for the Beirut deployment, though it was clearly understood that the Corps was the second choice of the Joint Chiefs of Staff, entirely the result of the long-standing success of the amphibious ready group concept coupled with the Army's inability to launch even a battalion-size force onto a foreign shore without months of logistical preparation. The Marine Corps found itself facing in Beirut a mission that was early proving to be antithetical to its stated doctrine, which is active rather than passive, aggressive rather than defensive. Marines have always been trained to shoot to kill, to wreak havoc upon an opposing force, to defend only where attack is obviated. While an incredibly high level of discipline is the source of all that goes into the Marine Corps philosophy, Stokes's Rules of Engagement clearly imposed commonsense restrictions that he felt had to be stated in simple, unheroic terms to attack-minded combat infantrymen who had been told every day of their careers, beginning from training-day one, that they were thoroughbreds. The principles embodied in this first version of the ROE were repeated to all the troops and their officers time and again during the quick passage from Rota to Beirut.

The relief of 32d MAU began at first light, October 29, when the medium composite helicopter squadron attached to 24th MAU dropped the leading elements of the BLT 3/8 command group and two rifle companies at the landing zone at the southwest corner of the BIA. BLT 3/8's third rifle company put on a spiffy mock amphibious assault at Black Beach. Each unit was immediately guided to its position by members of the corresponding element of BLT 2/8. The task was completed by noon, and 32d MAU completed the arduous process of backloading onto its own five-ship MARG. Colonels Mead and Stokes shook hands just before sunset to signify the change of command. Except for Mead, who remained on the beach for two additional days, and elements of the special units flown to Beirut from Camp Lejeune a month earlier, 24th MAU was on its own among strangers in a strange land.

And strange it was. The thoroughly psyched troops happened to get to the BIA just as the first waves of Lebanese tourists were finding their way out of the country for vacations in Europe. It came as something of a shock for armed-to-the-teeth Marines to run into lavishly dressed young Lebanese ladies toting skis and other oddments through the terminal buildings.

The MAU's official introduction to the growing factional pressures in the city occurred on October 31 in the form of a bungled car-bomb detonation near Black Beach, where Marine logistical units worked to control the flow of food and supplies from the MARG circling between five and ten miles offshore. One Marine was superficially injured in the defective low-order thirty-kilogram blast, but the warning was well taken. The commander of MAU Service and Support Group 24 happened to be on the beach at the time of the blast, and he immediately obtained permission from the local LAF commander to clear the area of rubberneckers and the ubiquitous street vendors Marines had dubbed "heyjoes" (after their typical cry, "Hey, Joe!"). The Marines also expanded the beach security zone in the direction of the four-lane coastal highway.

In the end, the bombing was seen as such a dud that wags throughout the MAU jokingly accused Colonel Stokes of having it set just to get everyone's attention.

The routine of patrolling that had been established by 32d MAU was adhered to by 24th MAU. These ventures into Hay-es-Salaam (Hooterville) were seen as a good way both to keep the troops occupied and to show the concern of the American people for events in Beirut. There was little tactical knowledge gained, beyond the seasoning of the troops and the patrol leaders, because there was little going on in Hooterville besides the normal flow of commerce and traffic.

The scope of the original mission order was modified within the first week, however, to include active American "show-the-flag" patrolling in Christian East Beirut. This aspect of the evolving mission was achieved largely through exchanges with the commanders of the French and Italian MNF contingents, who felt that all the good that could be accomplished by the MNF would be the result of a sense of security yet to be fully instilled in the large but vulnerable Moslem populace of the western portion of the city. In its way, this sentiment derived from the true, if largely unstated, reason the MNF had been reconstituted in the wake of the Sabra and Shatilla massacres. It was felt by the three MNF commanders that an American presence in East Beirut would convince the Moslems in West Beirut that the MNF was prepared to stem any aggressive intentions by the dominant Christian Phalange militia or other Christian forces operating under IDF sponsorship. Indeed, bowing to pressure exerted by Moslem leaders, President Gemayel had himself forced through a cabinet proposal calling for the LAF to patrol East Beirut, just as they had been patrolling the Moslem half of the city in search of potential troublemakers. The MNF decision, really a consensus among coequal commanders, was seen in both quarters as a fair parallel move by the MNF to underscore its impartiality.

The first Marine patrol in East Beirut was launched with great international press fanfare on November 4, when fourteen Marines in four jeeps drove off amid smiles and shouts of "Hello!" from Christian residents. The patrol leader had orders to simply report any sightings of armed militiamen or Israeli soldiers to BLT 3/8's command post. What the Marines saw was a city largely untouched by the wars they had been led to understand had ravaged the whole of Lebanon.

Nothing of note happened for the next two months. In the interim, the Marines got comfortable and almost totally bored. In addition to patrols and work details, which were often described as "chickenshit," several day trips were organized to places on the coast north of Beirut, a gorgeous and secure Christian area totally untouched by the strife that had replaced government in most of Moslem Lebanon.

There were nightly "fireworks displays" in the Shouf, but no one gave them a lot of thought; gunplay in the mountains was the IDF's problem. And the daily patrolling up the Sidon Road, through Hooterville and on into East Beirut, was virtually without incident. If anything, the civilians were embarrassingly cordial.

On December 6, Colonel Stokes tried on his command prerogatives by ordering his artillery battery, which had been ashore from the start in an infantry capacity, to bring its six 105mm howitzers to the beach and establish a permanent position near the north end of the BIA. Word went out to curious representatives of the press that the tubes were coming ashore simply because training artillerymen aboard ship was impossible. No one in authority made much of an issue of the move and the brief press brouhaha passed quickly. The plain fact was that Tom Stokes and his senior infantry officers had never felt comfortable with the 105s tucked away aboard ship. Unnoticed but even more important is the fact that the MAU landed its platoon of five M-60A1 main battle tanks right behind the 105s.

The decision to honor the Lebanese Ministry of Defense's request to help train and upgrade the sadly deficient and largely impotent Lebanese Armed Forces was casual, an attempt by a MAU commander concerned over the effects of garrison life on his highly motivated troops, an effort to allow Marines largely trapped within the BIA to kill time by doing one of the things Marines do best: training.

Though a U.S. Army training mission was already in place in Lebanon, it had received little notice or attention in the world press or, indeed, in the U.S. Congress. Tom Stokes's accession to the LAF request to provide Marine trainers, however, was in its way among the most crucial decisions taken during the entire Marine experience in Beirut, for it inextricably linked the intentionally visible Marines to the fate of the LAF and, by extension, identified the Marines and their government completely with the fate of the Gemayel government.

Colonel Stokes bucked the welcomed job to BLT 3/8, which formed a select staff of career noncommissioned officers, many with experience as drill instructors, and directed the creation of a three-week training syllabus. The Marine trainers moved into an LAF training camp at the northern end of the BIA compound and got right to work.

The Marine NCOs took on the job with their particular brand of gusto. Lebanese lads were seen and heard at all hours jogging in formation, chanting Marine marching chants, sporting the "high-and-tight" haircuts that Marines proudly wear as a symbol of their manhood and discipline. Pugil-sticks, padded two-

57

handed punching batons, were borrowed from the Marines' own training stores, and slender Lebanese youths were soon pounding one another into the dust amid bloodcurdling oaths and general pleasure.

The first three-week course, begun around the first of the year, was still under way when the Gemayel government fired its army commander and replaced him with LtGen Ibrahim Tannous, a veteran hard-line infantry officer of considerable national repute. This was a crucial appointment, for Tannous, a Christian, had long publicly avowed that he was married to the concept of a united Lebanon and not to any confessional loyalty. If nothing else, the rabidly efficient Tannous ordered everyone who was anyone in the LAF to get to work on time and get their assignments completed. There were too many political considerations in the workings of the LAF to give Tannous any serious authority to hire and fire, but he quickly and forthrightly performed miracles within the limitations of his mandate. American officers on the scene felt as though a stiff, fresh breeze was blowing from the Ministry of Defense, and they did everything in their power to support the new LAF commander.

The infantry course under way at the BIA was immediately and enthusiastically expanded to include artillery, armored, helicopter-assault, and amphibious training, which, from Tom Stokes's standpoint, had the potential for involving many, many members of his idle MAU.

The first company-size class to graduate from the Marine course—about eighty recruits led by two dozen NCOs and company-grade officers—was designated the 1st Air Assault Battalion and was treated and outfitted as an elite unit. In time, as the 1st Air Assault Battalion grew, it would include Lebanese Air Force crews trained by Marine helicopter crews, though the Lebanese had no assault helicopters. The first graduation ceremony, attended by General Tannous, Colonel Stokes, and their respective staffs, was highlighted by a mock vertical assault and helicopter extraction. Experienced eyes noticed that the Marine-trained LAF noncoms took direct leadership roles in the program, a trait that had hitherto been markedly absent in the ethos of the LAF.

Succeeding courses brought the very best officers, NCOs, and troops the LAF had to offer from throughout the country. The emphasis soon shifted subtly to the training of infantry and artillery trainers who could raise the general standard of military aptitude throughout the LAF. Senior Marines noted, with considerable pleasure, that their trainees were drawn in reasonable proportions from all the confessional constituencies that constitute Lebanon, even some outwardly hostile to the Gemayel government. It was obvious that General Tannous was doing everything he could to deliver on his pledge to forge a national army that might one day serve as a unifying institution within the faction-fractured nation. Meantime, the Marine trainers continued to churn out Lebanese soldiers who looked and sounded at least a little like Marines.

The first serious outside challenge to the MAU commander's authority and military expertise took place on December 24, when Colonel Stokes was ordered by higher headquarters to stop patrolling along the Sidon Road. He considered this an unfortunate turn in that access to the vital link and adjacent areas gave him a clear idea of what was going on in proximity to his isolated defensive positions at the Lebanese University. He was, nevertheless, bound to obey, though he well knew the reasoning lay in a potential perception that Marines were helping to secure the road for the Israelis and because there were renewed efforts afoot by the Reagan administration to pressure Israel to withdraw from Lebanon. The directive took no cognizance of Stokes's operational needs.

The order arrived through the military chain of command, but Colonel Stokes was certain it had originated with the U.S. ambassador to Lebanon, Robert Dillon. This was the first incident of political perceptions impacting directly upon a MAU commander's ability to exercise military prudence. It would not be the last.

Interestingly, Christmas Day, 1982, marked the first serious breach of an uneasy and unstated truce along the Sidon Road. Israeli patrols were ambushed several times, perhaps by Shiite or Palestinian gunmen, but just as likely by Syrians or Iranians. In accordance with long-established policy, the IDF resorted to draconian measures to quell the fire.

No direct link can be established between the decision to terminate Marine patrols along the Sidon Road, the ambushes of Israeli patrols, the Israeli reaction, and a deteriorating relationship between the MAU and the IDF, but these factors seem to form a straight line when they are examined in context.

The draconian measures that the commander of the Israeli mechanized battalion based at Khalde was apparently ordered to take had the effect of endangering Marines manning positions to the west of the road and around the Lebanese University. The Israelis, who were absorbing an increasing number of killed and wounded along their main supply route (MSR), had an understandable tendency to shoot first and ask questions later. However, from the Marine standpoint, the shooting they did was not in the least bit discriminating. No Marine was ever hit by Israeli fire, but there were enough close calls to justify at least part of the reproachful attitude that quickly blossomed between the two forces. It is interesting to note that, until meeting in Beirut, the Marine Corps and IDF had shared a strong mutual admiration. Many Israeli officers, including, in fact, the then-incumbent Israeli chief of staff, were graduates of various Marine Corps schools, and many Israelis are of American birth. Marines have long identified with the IDF's winning ways. Beginning in January 1983, however, each force found great fault with the other. The Marines found Israelis in the field to be slovenly and apparently undisciplined. Israelis found Marines in the field to be overly concerned with appearances and, in a word, naive. These minor antagonisms were, unfortunately, nurtured by the American political requirements of the day, which had a definite anti-Israeli bias, at least insofar as it was important for the U.S. MNF contingent to show no favoritism toward the mission or aspirations of the IDF.

As a result of the clear divergence of the missions of the two forces, there were several ludicrous exchanges, some muscle-flexing by both forces, and, alas, the creation of a powder-keg mind-set that was very nearly detonated.

The key Israeli player was LtCol Rafi Landsberg, the arrogant and aggressive commander of the Israeli mechanized battalion based at Khalde and responsible for patrolling the Sidon Road each day. Landsberg was undoubtedly acting under orders of BGen Amnon Lifkin, the Israeli regional commander. Landsberg's aims are not quite evident from his actions, but it appears that, in the wake of the Marine withdrawal from the Sidon Road, he was to at least try to create the impression that Israelis and Americans were working in concert, as allies. He cannot be faulted for trying, but his exasperating methods and his personality were a bit much for American temperaments.

The first contacts came directly in the wake of the first ambushes along the Sidon Road, when Israeli ordnance fired at the ambushers impacted within Marine positions. A carefully worded message was sent from MAU headquarters up the chain of command and back down through political channels. Marines in the threatened positions, however, let their actions speak louder than words; they made threatening gestures with their—unloaded—weapons. This led to exchanges of sign language of the one-finger variety.

A third set of players quickly emerged: the LAF units securing the BIA. While Tom Stokes was not allowed to speak directly with Landsberg or Lifkin, the LAF security-guard commander, a brigadier, was allowed to act as an intermediary. The Israelis, however, attempted to ignore the LAF's authority—an under-

standable impulse, since they were occupying a piece of an os-
tensibly sovereign nation. Tom Stokes stuck to his basic premise
that the MAU was bolstering the LAF and not vice versa.

Rafi Landsberg took his first intentional action by simply approaching a jointly manned Marine-LAF checkpoint on the airport perimeter and demanding access to the BIA for his two
Centurion tanks and an American-built M-113 armored personnel carrier (APC). The Lebanese soldiers manning the post responded by jumping into their bunkers, leaving a Marine corporal and the other three members of his fire team to stand their
ground. The Israeli battalion commander backed off following
a brief, businesslike exchange.

Within minutes, however, Landsberg crashed his two Centurion tanks and APC through the BIA perimeter fence and roared
off along the airport perimeter road until stopped by a jeep
manned by Colonel Stokes himself. The Israeli battalion commander climbed off the lead Centurion, scowled a bit, and
claimed, with a straight face, that he was lost and merely seeking
a shortcut through the BIA compound. Stokes told him, "The
rules of the game are that we can have no contact," that the
Israeli column had entered LAF territory and should return the
way it had come. Landsberg countered by asking if he could, this
once, continue on his way. Stokes obliged, but lectured the
Israeli on the need to coordinate his movements with the proper
authorities, the LAF airport security force.

A few days later, an Israeli jeepborne patrol approached one
of several jointly manned LAF-MAU checkpoints near the
northern end of the airport complex and the patrol leader asked
to speak directly with the senior American officer. The Marine
captain had definite orders requiring him to speak only with
officers belonging to other MNF contingents, so he refused the
request. The Israelis left without further ado.

Within days, an Israeli bulldozer guarded by an APC plowed
a berm to interdict vehicular traffic on a main thoroughfare
connecting Marine positions at the BIA and the Sidon Road.

This move was countered by the immediate creation of a new jointly manned checkpoint in the vicinity of the railroad embankment, on the far side of the new berm. To further underscore his displeasure with the Israeli move, Colonel Stokes regularly stationed one or two amtracs at the new post, along with from four to thirteen Marines.

Next, on January 17, two jeeploads of IDF soldiers approached a joint checkpoint near the Lebanese University and demanded access to the university grounds, claiming they were in pursuit of terrorists and wanted to sweep the area between the checkpoint and the railroad embankment. The Lebanese sector commander and Capt Chuck Johnson, commander of the Marine rifle company stationed at the university, rushed to the checkpoint. The LAF officer refused the Israelis passage, and the Israelis left. Unfortunately, a wire-service reporter who happened to be interviewing Marines at the university witnessed the exchange and filed a report. This was the first public inkling that there was tension between Israelis and Marines, and it caused something of a sensation in the United States. A false impression of serious mutual antagonism was created and, because the effects of mass communications are so far-reaching, Marines in Beirut who heard the reports from afar for the first time became truly alarmed at the possibilities.

These things have a way of taking on a dynamic of their own, well beyond the gentle prodding or jockeying for position that is the original intent of people who pull strings from lofty heights. Hundreds of frustrated, bored, and well-armed soldiers, bolstered by the conviction that their mission is the only right mission, can easily be led to the brink of havoc.

This nearly occurred on February 2, 1983, when Capt Chuck Johnson observed a trio of Centurion tanks moving on the LAF checkpoint outside the Lebanese University at what he took to be battle speed. Johnson, who was known for deliberate, carefully considered action, surprised everyone by immediately interjecting himself between the Israelis and the Lebanese, forcing the three Centurions to stop within inches of where he stood.

The Marine captain looked up at the turret of the lead Centurion and saw that he was facing an Israeli lieutenant colonel—Rafi Landsberg. Johnson politely informed the Israelis that they were headed directly for an LAF position through which they were not allowed to pass and requested that they leave the area. Landsberg responded with a sneer, stating that he would indeed pass. Johnson simply informed Landsberg that he would do so only "over my dead body."

The lead tank revved its engine and Chuck Johnson drew his heavy .45-caliber service automatic, pushed home an eight-round magazine, cranked a round into the chamber, and pointed the cocked weapon skyward. Landsberg spoke rapidly into his throat mike, awaited a response, and then ordered his driver to back away from the confrontation. Johnson walked along beside the tank track.

Without warning, the two trailing Centurions roared past Johnson and bore down on the checkpoint to which they had been denied access. Chuck Johnson leaped to the turret of the Israeli battalion commander's tank, grabbed Rafi Landsberg by the collar, and demanded that he order the other two tanks to stop. Landsberg immediately complied.

Both officers reported details of the confrontation to their respective higher headquarters and the situation was defused. Chuck Johnson was sure he had seen the last of his career in the Marine Corps. However, Secretary of Defense Caspar Weinberger chose to make public at least some of the details of the incident, and Chuck Johnson was catapulted to brief national fame, though he honestly felt he had somehow screwed up. The resulting press attention had the opposite effect of Weinberger's avowed intention; it further exacerbated the tensions between the IDF and 24th MAU by leaving Marines with the impression that force was the best solution and by forcing the proud Israelis to seek justification for Landsberg's provocative act.

When Tom Stokes realized that Marine-IDF relations had deteriorated to the point where there was a very serious chance of an exchange of ordnance, he pointedly decided to disobey his orders and contact BGen Amnon Lifkin to agree to the face-to-face meeting Lifkin had been requesting for weeks. Stokes's decision was firmed up by a very serious confrontation following close upon the heels of the Landsberg-Johnson blowup.

Israelis manning a checkpoint near the Lebanese University turned a .50-caliber machine gun mounted on an American-made APC onto a Lebanese civilian bird-hunter in a nearby field. In fact, every open field throughout the city was the preserve of Lebanese civilian men in quest of birds for their tables. The target of the egregious Israeli marksmanship this evening, as were most such hunters, was armed with an ancient muzzle-loaded bird gun of absolutely no danger to an Israeli APC. The wild five-minute Israeli fusillade scored many hits on the university library building, in which the Marine company was housed. More important, the bird-hunter fled in the direction of Hooterville, and the Israelis wanted to give chase. It could be argued that Hooterville was in the Israeli sphere, but the road the Israeli convoy leader chose was the Marine MSR from the BIA to the Lebanese University—definitely off-limits to the IDF.

The Israelis—manning three Centurion tanks and an APC— were stopped by a Marine guard detachment. The Israeli patrol leader said he was going through the checkpoint. The Marine squad leader told him he was not. The Israeli armored infantry squad dismounted from the APC and the Marines locked and loaded their infantry weapons and M-60 machine gun. The Israeli officer restated his determination to pass through the checkpoint. The Marine squad leader told him again that he could not.

By this time, Tom Stokes was present at an observation post about 250 meters to the east with a full complement of riflemen, snipers, and TOW wire-guided antitank missiles. These Marines were, in their own vernacular, "good to go."

Lebanese guards, who had earlier evaporated, swaggered back to the checkpoint, all set to begin a fight they knew would be won by their Marine sponsors.

If no other Marine realized the gravity of the confrontation, Tom Stokes surely did. So, fortunately, did the Israeli patrol leader, who motioned his troops to back off, then told the Marine squad leader, "We're coming back."

A very relieved Tom Stokes, aghast at the possibility of trading fire with people he authentically considered friends and allies, decided then and there that it was now time to have a one-on-one with his chief antagonist. He placed a direct call to BGen Amnon Lifkin and offered to meet at 0900 the next morning at the railroad embankment that officially marked the IDF-MAU boundary. Both men realized that a nervous tank gunner or Marine rifleman could upset the legitimate if mutually exasperating policies of their respective governments by applying just a shade too much pressure with an itchy trigger finger. The two agreed, in Stokes's plainspoken words, "to knock this crap off." The issue was finally resolved over Stokes's and Lifkin's heads a week later, when a more senior Israeli general met with an American general representing the Joint Chiefs of Staff at the Lebanese Ministry of Defense.

There were a few further incidents between the IDF and Stokes's Marines, but it was made abundantly clear to the troops that the tension had been alleviated and a Marine-IDF engagement was beyond possibility.

And, indeed, it was beyond possibility for 24th MAU, for it was to be relieved on February 14 by a fresh MAU commanded, once again, by Col Jim Mead.

7

Twenty-second Marine Amphibious Unit (MAU)—simply 32d MAU redesignated—landed at Beirut International Airport (BIA) on February 14, 1983, and quickly assumed complete responsibility for the U.S. "presence" in Beirut. Little had changed since the MAU headquarters had left Beirut in October, but the scenes and responsibilities were entirely new for LtCol Don Anderson's Battalion Landing Team (BLT) 2/6 and most of MAU Service and Support Group (MSSG) 22 and helicopter squadron personnel now constituting 22d MAU. The weather was wetter and brisker, a Middle East winter rainy season, and the patrol responsibilities facing BLT 2/6 had been radically expanded during 24th MAU's stay. But, in the main, the situation in and around the Lebanese capital had not been much altered since 32d MAU had left in October.

The situation remained stable for five days, until February 19, when BLT 2/6 widened its patrol sector into an area northeast of Beirut. The Israelis immediately challenged the new patrol mission, perhaps because it was to be run in conjunction with the Lebanese Armed Forces (LAF). When the American embassy intervened to say that the Marines would indeed participate, the Israel Defense Force (IDF) threatened to obstruct.

For the time being, however, this new area of Marine-Israeli tension went unexplored. A serious deterioration in the weather brought unprecedented low temperatures, high winds, and deep snow to the central Lebanese massif, and both the Israelis and Multinational Force (MNF) turned their attention to helping the Lebanese people.

The initial request for help reached 22d MAU headquarters from the government of Lebanon on February 20, and Col Jim Mead immediately agreed to mount a mission into the mountains about twenty-seven kilometers east of Beirut—behind Syrian army lines. It appeared at first that a simple aerial supply and rescue mission would be run from the BIA and the deck of Mediterranean Amphibious Ready Group 1-83's helicopter carrier, *Guadalcanal.* Two CH-46 medium cargo helicopters were thus launched on February 21, but two attempts to fly to the rescue site had to be aborted because of extreme icing on the helicopters' control surfaces. As a result, the BLT commander, Lieutenant Colonel Anderson, staged nine of his amtracs at the Lebanese Ministry of Defense, in Baabda, in the event a surface mission was approved. (Earlier in the day, an Italian column of jeeps and trucks was stopped about ten kilometers short of the rescue site, but it was unclear if this was a result of weather conditions or Syrian intervention. French columns in the mountains northeast of Beirut accomplished their mission with great difficulty.)

As Don Anderson was seeing to last-minute preparations at the ministry compound, LtGen Ibrahim Tannous, the LAF commander, noted that villagers living approximately forty kilometers northeast of Baabda were in extreme need of heating fuel, food, medical care, and, in some cases, rescue. The Syrians had not yet given approval for a column to enter the area, so the MAU command decided to continue to get helicopters through on February 21 and to get Anderson's amtrac column on the road toward the threatened areas.

The nine amtracs and several wheeled vehicles got under way from the BIA before dawn, February 22, headed toward Jubayl, sixty kilometers north of Beirut on the coastal highway. There they were to link up with Lebanese Red Cross and civil defense officials. The meeting was accomplished without incident and the Marine relief column turned east, into some of the craggiest mountains in the country. The objective was Qatarba, a Christian regional center about twenty kilometers inland—as the crow flies.

While Anderson's roadbound column crept toward the first ridge line, a Marine Huey helicopter made a precarious touchdown at Dahr al Baydar, 5,000 feet above sea level. The mission commander, LtCol Dick Kalata, noted on his cockpit array just prior to touchdown that a nearby fire-control radar had locked onto his bird. This was the focus of extreme concern for about a half instant, by which time the crew had hands and minds completely absorbed in getting down in one piece because of the extreme weather conditions. A check of the console upon landing revealed that the gunnery radar lock had disappeared. Five poorly dressed Syrian soldiers met the crew as it clambered to the snow-covered ground. The leader offered the Marines hot coffee and indicated that there were Lebanese civilians—some alive, some not—stranded about a kilometer from the landing site. It was also revealed that about one hundred vehicles were stranded along the road. The very first of these vehicles, a civilian car that had been trapped in snowdrifts for three days, contained the frozen corpses of two civilian men. A CH-46 arriving right behind the Huey made another precarious landing and immediately picked up four shivering Lebanese. In all, the Marines counted over one hundred civilian dead and rescued barely enough people to fill the two helicopters, which returned immediately to the Ministry of Defense compound.

The amtrac column was fortunate in one respect: the boat bows and wide tracks of the amphibious assault vehicles (AAVs) can displace high snows almost as easily as they displace water. Forward progress was thus of little concern. What did concern Don Anderson and the amtrac crews was the sideways progress on the icy stretches.

Because he had been taught for over twenty years and believed firmly that a commander's place is at the head of his troops, Don Anderson insisted upon riding tall in the commander's hatch of the lead amtrac as it painstakingly negotiated the endless series of sharp, improbable switchbacks leading up into the Metan cordillera toward the regional center of Qatarba. Often, Anderson was almost overcome by vertigo as he stood, seemingly without support, over chasms 1,500 feet deep. High winds and driven snow did not add to his precarious sense of stability, nor did the ominous grinding of treads upon the slippery road.

The amtrac drivers, who were relieved at the first sign of slipping attention, were mainly nineteen- and twenty-year-old privates first class and lance corporals. Those from the warmer regions of the United States had little experience driving cars on flat roads in the snow, and not one had ever driven an AAV in anything like the road conditions they met on the way to Qatarba. In some places, the snow was deep enough to drift back into the open hatches of the tall AAVs. Hundreds of thousands of calories were burned off by Lieutenant Colonel Anderson's ninety roadbound Marines and Navy hospital corpsmen in those frightening, exhausting hours.

The column had started off from the BIA at about 0400 and arrived at Jubayl at about 0900. The only break on the way up to Qatarba was at about 2100, at an isolated, snowbound service station, where the BLT commander called a halt for some hot coffee. It took until after 2300 hours to complete the twenty-kilometer run from Jubayl to Qatarba.

It was soon discovered that the reports of egregious conditions in Qatarba that had beckoned the Marines onward on a mission that was something less than prudent were considerably overblown. The plight of the hearty mountain townspeople was not good, but neither was it extreme in most cases. In the morning, Marine patrols moved into the deep snow—sixteen feet in some places—to check on outlying houses near Qatarba. The most severe casualties were painstakingly rounded up and prepared for evacuation by helicopter while members of the road column distributed the supplies of food and fuel they had hauled in at such great peril.

Colonel Mead spent the morning of February 23 airborne over Qatarba, directing ground operations and the young helo pilots, who brought in additional heating fuel and large supplies of milk and pita bread.

February 23 was a beautiful, sunny day, but on February 24 the skies were slate gray and snow-filled. Rather than leaving at noon, as planned, Don Anderson ordered his column to hit the road at about 0800. The last of the Lebanese civilian evacuees —fifteen elderly people whose illnesses might have been exacerbated by conditions in the isolated town, but also a Lebanese woman in an advanced stage of pregnancy—were loaded aboard the AAVs and trussed in for what all hands expected would be a hair-raising ride out of the mountains. It took four enervating hours to reach the coast.

The boredom of earlier deployments was as evident and potent as ever in the wake of the brutal winter weeks of mid-February. Other than performing routine chores in a fairly relaxed if somewhat exotic environment, the troops had little to do during their off-duty hours. No one but senior officers was allowed to spend free time in town (and, most often, the senior officers were merely attending obligatory social functions sponsored by the other MNF headquarters or Lebanese ministries). A schedule of liberty runs to Mediterranean ports was maintained, which alleviated some of the sexual energies generated by 1,800 men in peak physical condition. But time hung heavy for most Marines most of the time.

Most of the precedents set by Colonel Mead on his earlier, very brief deployment, and by Col Tom Stokes on 24th MAU's pivotal deployment, were adhered to during the opening weeks of Mead's second tour in Beirut. One additional duty Mead undertook with gusto was his obligatory presence at biweekly military-political-coordination-committee meetings chaired by President Gemayel or his representative and attended by the four MNF commanders (the British had recently sent a 100-man contingent), General Tannous, at least one of the many U.S. ambassadors who floated through the country, and such other personages who, for one reason or another, had to be invited.

It was as a result of this committee's operations that the new flare-up in IDF-MAU relations was smoothed over. Special Ambassador Maurice Draper, who was overseeing talks aimed at normalizing relations between Israel and Lebanon, put it directly to Israeli Defense Minister Moshe Arens, who had replaced Ariel Sharon in the wake of the Sabra and Shatilla massacres. The spate of challenges to Marine patrols by IDF tanks immediately dissipated, flared up again a few weeks later, then cooled down completely following direct talks between Ambassador Philip Habib and Defense Minister Arens. The stock of the IDF among U.S. Marines, however, had ebbed to a critical low point in Beirut and worldwide.

Training of LAF units by the Marines continued apace, and courses in diesel-engine maintenance and armored-vehicle operation were added to the curriculum. As time passed, the most heartening aspect of the bolstering of the LAF was the growing shifts in the LAF's demographic balance; more Moslems were attaining leadership positions and, in general, all of the confessions were represented in proportions closer to the confessional demographics of the nation. Young Lebanese company-grade officers and staff NCOs borrowed heavily from the ethos of their Marine trainers in matters of troop leadership. Officers appeared to become something more than order givers, and the recently promoted sergeants clearly became something more than their order-passing predecessors. General Tannous had seven undermanned and underworked infantry and artillery brigades to double in strength from 20,000 to 40,000 effectives. He had to eradicate an institutionwide "checkpoint mentality" and bring the army to loyal fighting trim if he was ever to be able to secure Lebanon with Lebanese troops. Marines were certainly committed to doing everything in their power to help Tannous realize his daunting dream. Doing so meant getting out of Lebanon that much sooner.

In addition to supporting routine operations around the BIA, the MAU helicopter squadron was pressed into service flying Ambassadors Draper and Habib between Lebanese-Israeli negotiating tables in Khalde, a southern airport suburb, and northern Israel.

Of particular importance to relations with the Lebanese people—particularly the poor Shiites living in squalid Hooterville—the MSSG-22 medical contingent expanded a health-care program begun by MSSG-24 early in the year. Regular dental clinics were established, and treatment of minor illnesses and injuries was handled by the BLT 2/6 surgeon and BLT and MSSG hospital corpsmen.

All these positive accomplishments raised morale, at least among the MAU senior staffers. The presence mission, whatever it meant to the various players, appeared to be reaping benefits far beyond the commitment in manpower and matériel. The mind-set of the period, despite infrequent setbacks, can fairly be described as euphoric. Indeed, there was little negative news out of Lebanon, and the temper of the American people toward the ongoing commitment was utterly benign.

Beirut was by then the terminus of a whole new junket route for U.S. senators and congressmen and other Western leaders of note or ambition. Most such visitors with no specific political axes to grind—even those who knew whereof they spoke—were laudatory in their comments concerning conditions and security around the BIA. The frequent arrivals and departures severely strained the MAU's mobility at times, for jeeps and security escorts had to be provided at seemingly all hours of the day and evening. Almost none of the VIPs stayed the night, which spoke reams to the troops about the real character of the junkets. Few of the VIPs noticed or cared to notice that a certain impatience with civilians of rank was evident in the exquisitely polite and elaborately contrived responses young Marines and even senior staff NCOs made to questions they felt ranged from the inane to the obnoxious, from the uninformed to the asinine. Most telling was the perception among Marines that virtually no VIP arrived without a press assistant and personal photographer.

On March 16 a dozen Marines on routine patrol in a Palestinian neighborhood in West Beirut were the targets in a grenade-hurling incident. The patrol's point man, Cpl George Fischer, was legging his way along the street past the broken window of a shell-damaged house when he heard a "clicking sound." He looked up in time to see a single hand grenade falling his way. Fischer yelled, "Hit the deck," and moved to do so himself when the blast caught him in the back. Though Fischer escaped injury because his flak jacket took the force of the blast, the five Marines nearest him were superficially wounded, mainly in their legs, by shrapnel from the low-order explosion of a defective Russian-made grenade. All hands immediately locked and loaded their weapons and prepared to "repel boarders." Their assailant fled.

The BLT reaction platoon was immediately dispatched and the five injured Marines were flown in short order to *Guadalcanal*. By that time, the street was filled with armed men: Marines,

Italians, LAF soldiers, Lebanese internal security police, and members of the official United Nations peacekeeping contingent. Anything at all might have set these terribly keyed-up armed men to indiscriminate shooting, but nothing happened.

All five of the injured Marines returned to full duty the following day. A "group" no one had ever heard of placed a call to a local news agency to take responsibility for the incident and to warn Americans to leave Lebanon.

Lebanese internal security police and the LAF swept through the area and rounded up many suspects in the days following the attack. In time, one suspect was brought to trial and sentenced to death.

President Reagan allayed the obvious fears of the government of Lebanon by publicly stating that the U.S. commitment to Lebanon had "no reverse gear."

The President was within a month of having to seriously validate the depth of the commitment he reaffirmed in the wake of a virtually bloodless provocation. The test came on April 18.

8

Maj Fred Lash, 22d Marine Amphibious Unit's (MAU's) joint public affairs officer, was happy over the steady, positive progress of the press conference that had begun on time at noon, April 18. The subject of the gathering, which included the usual contingent of Beirut-based bureau chiefs and stringers as well as a few international media superstars, was the first known incident in which a Marine, Pfc Kenneth Simpson, had fired back at his assailants after being fired on. The international press, starved for anything but routine activities in Beirut, was all set to make a major event out of the very minor incident in which, it seemed, no blood had been shed. Simpson gave a quick account of the incident and Col Jim Mead delivered a well-worded address aimed at defusing any problems that might arise as a result of the shooting. It was coming up 1300 hours and the principals and the press were milling around in anticipation of the denouement, an international phone call to the young Marine from his girlfriend.

Events were proceeding as well as or better than could be expected when Fred Lash heard a low, distant sound, like thunder. He gave it little thought; artillery rounds impacting in the hills and mountains above Beirut were so common as to have become merely background noise. An instant later, however, the duty officer manning the MAU's combat operations center (COC) stuck his head in to tell Colonel Mead that "the embassy just got hit by some kind of a bomb." That was at 1310. Minutes later, the COC watch officer returned to say, "It might be the French embassy; I'm not sure." He made a final appearance a moment later and said to the hushed gathering, "It's definitely the American embassy."

Colonel Mead headed out the door after ordering LtCol Don Anderson to mount out for the embassy with his Battalion Landing Team (BLT) 2/6 combat reaction platoon.

At about 1300 hours, a nondescript pickup truck laden with an estimated 2,000 pounds of explosives had entered the moderately restricted American embassy compound overlooking the sea beside the Corniche (the four-lane coastal highway) in a busy, fashionable quarter of Moslem West Beirut. No one took particular notice of the vehicle and, indeed, observers were uncertain whether its driver left the scene before the detonation of the explosives or went up with the truck. What is known is that the force of the blast collapsed the central portions of seven stories of the eight-story embassy building, reportedly killing the entire Central Intelligence Agency Middle East contingent, a Marine security guard, several Army trainers, a number of high- and medium-rank State Department officials, and nearly two dozen Lebanese nationals who either worked for the embassy or were in the building on business. Ambassador to Lebanon Robert Dillon was in his front office on the eighth floor when the entire structure beneath his feet was turned to rubble. He was pinned by debris shaken loose from the ceiling of his office and had to be helped up by Chargé d'Affaires Robert Pugh and his secretary. The three climbed through the shattered building to the street, where their minor cuts were bandaged as they attempted to impose order on the chaotic scene.

French marines who regularly patrolled the vicinity of the embassy (an area that incorporated in its immediate environs the British embassy and the American University in Beirut) were on the scene before the dust settled, as were Lebanese Red Crescent teams. So adept were the Lebanese paramedics that battered and bleeding victims were plucked from the rubble and dispersed to hospitals and aid stations throughout West Beirut before identification arrangements could be completed by embassy personnel still capable of functioning. French medics soon arrived at the embassy compound as did, later in the day, Navy doctors and hospital corpsmen from the MAU and the Mediterranean Amphibious Ready Group (MARG).

A phone call to an Arabic-language newspaper by a man claiming to represent an Iranian terrorist group called Islamic Jihad (Islamic Holy War) took credit for the bombing. However, in the confused aftermath of the incident, fingers were pointed at a confederation of local Shiite Moslem groups (Iranians are also Shiite Moslems) known collectively as the Shiite Amal (Shiite Hope). Unfortunately, this error was given additional credence by the fact that Islamic Jihad is the military arm of an Iranian group known as Islamic Amal. Islamic, Shiite, Amal: it all sounded the same to nervous Americans.

Almost unnoticed by the surviving, functioning embassy personnel and French marines, a well-disciplined force of Druse Progressive Socialist Party (PSP) militiamen commanded by "Saleh," a pro-American officer, established an impenetrable cordon well beyond the hastily contrived French lines. No civilian passed through Saleh's checkpoints without good reason.

Lieutenant Colonel Anderson had almost zero information when he jumped into his waiting jeep and led his reaction platoon out of the Beirut International Airport (BIA) compound.

The battalion commander and troops were understandably nervous, for it crossed their minds that the bombing might have been a ploy to suck a Marine force pell-mell onto the streets of Beirut in order to score another telling blow against Americans. All weapons were locked and loaded and pointed outboard as the tiny column sped northward toward the smoky remains of the blast.

It took about thirty minutes to negotiate the typically anarchic streets of downtown Beirut. The reaction platoon passed quickly through the blocking positions manned by Saleh's PSP unit and the French marines, then dismounted and fanned out to man vital interior checkpoints. Don Anderson's practised eye immediately took in the scene, and he called the BLT to get the designated reaction rifle company on the road; every man would be needed to secure the many classified papers and devices that lay on the ground or within the exposed building and to provide convincing round-the-clock protection against further lethal incidents. Crowd control was another key objective, for Beirut days were nothing without some random act of violence to draw out crowds of well-wishers, haters, and rubberneckers.

With a platoon from Echo Company and the whole of Fox Company pulled north to the embassy, Anderson had to face the troubling fact that the BIA was exposed to terrorist attack. One complete rifle company, Golf, had to remain vigilant at the exposed Lebanese University. That left two-thirds of Echo Company and various ad hoc units to guard the BIA perimeter. There was no reasonable alternative.

The young Marines dug right into the rubble, though most of them were facing dead bodies—and parts of dead bodies—for the first time. All the "what-ifs" with which they had been grappling for months were put behind them.

Within hours of the bombing, a young Fox Company corporal manning a checkpoint proved out all the theories on discipline when he brought an approaching limousine to a halt at riflepoint. The sentries had been told to let no one through the cordon, but the driver protested: "This is the President of Leba-non." Not good enough: "I don't give a fuck who he's the president of; my orders say nobody's coming through."

BLT 2/6's massive commitment to securing the embassy would stretch to three weeks, following which a tactical force of seventy to a hundred Marines was permanently drawn from the BIA to the embassy. Within hours of the blast, the area to be covered expanded to the British embassy (the British ambassa-dor offered his American colleagues office space within literally minutes) and the Durafourd Building, an apartment block hous-ing many American officials and residents of Beirut, which was turned into an embassy annex within hours of the bombing. Separating the various buildings that had to be secured by the Marine tactical unit was the open, politically active campus of the American University.

Just three days after the bombing, at 1115, April 21, Lebanese Armed Forces (LAF) soldiers manning a checkpoint near the British embassy fired two rounds at a civilian car that failed to heed their order to stop. Dozens of Marines hit the deck, rifles, machine guns, and grenade-launchers at the ready.

The first postbombing shooting incident involving Marines occurred at about 0220, April 28, when a light green Mercedes raced toward a barbed-wire barrier near the British embassy. Marines manning an amtrac at the nearest checkpoint called a curt warning, then one of them pumped three of six rounds into the vehicle. The first Marines on the scene pulled two totally inebriated men from the crumpled Mercedes and turned them over to Lebanese internal security police. One of the two turned out to be a Syrian national carrying fake Lebanese identification.

The trouble escalated over the next few weeks. On May 5 a Huey helicopter carrying Colonel Mead was hit by a single ma-chine-gun bullet as it flew over the Shouf. No one was injured.

Next day, at about 1450, five rounds traced to a Druse artillery battery in the Shouf plunked into the water near *Fairfax County,* one of the MARG 1-83 transports on station off the BIA. Two more rounds impacted near Black Beach.

Though no one was injured in any of the shelling incidents involving Americans, President Gemayel alerted the tiny, obsolete Lebanese Air Force to prepare to mount air strikes against the Syrian-supplied Druse gunners.

Gemayel's gesture had less to do with the violence directed against Americans than with the rising crescendo of artillery duels taking place between Druse and Christian Phalange gunners in the Shouf and Metan escarpments overlooking Beirut. The hitherto quiescent Druse, somewhat tolerant of the Israeli occupiers of their Shouf homeland, had been increasingly favored by upstart Syria in her recent massive distribution of Soviet-supplied arms.

Perhaps Amin Gemayel would have responded less firmly to the new round of artillery exchanges had not his own official limousine, with him in it, been the near target of a Druse barrage in recent days.

Whatever the truths and perceptions haggled over or shared by the fragmented Lebanese people, there was little doubt in Jim Mead's mind that a Marine helicopter, with him in it, had been the intentional target of a Druse or Syrian machine gunner.

The embassy bombing, the mysterious shooting incident that preceded it by a day, the gunfire brought to bear against the MAU commander, the rounds hitting the sea close to an American warship and Black Beach, the constant eruption of fresh violence around the American and British embassies in late April and early May, pitched artillery duels between Christians and Druse in the mountains during the same period, shell fire hitting East Beirut and killing civilians on the streets of that part of the city—all these things, and more, sent adrenaline coursing through the veins of essentially bored and frustrated young Americans, armed to the teeth, who had little to do but indulge their imaginations with lengthening dreams of getting even.

A spate of so-called accidental discharges—shooting incidents with no provable causes and no known lethal results—brought about firm, positive orders requiring all but a very few designated Marines in the most exposed positions to remove bullets from their rifles.

Col Jim Mead's 22d MAU was due for relief on May 23 by a completely refurbished 24th MAU. Progress in key areas of a slowly evolving agenda for rebuilding the LAF had been deemed successful. A few Marines had been slightly injured, problems with the Israel Defense Force had been minimized, BLT 2/6 had reacted superbly to the embassy bombing and had by many actions ingratiated itself with Lebanese of all confessions and most political persuasions. Still, Beirut seemed to be slipping toward anarchy. An odor of generalized hostility now permeated the Lebanese capital and its environs. New forces and new options had somehow been unleashed.

President Reagan held a televised news conference on May 17, 1983, the day the United States–sponsored accord normalizing relations between Lebanon and Israel was signed. During the course of answering questions, Reagan seriously misstated the original purpose of the Multinational Force (MNF), but, in so doing, reaffirmed his administration's emerging philosophy with respect to maintaining the American outpost in Beirut: "The MNF went there to help the new [*sic*] government of Lebanon maintain order until it can organize its military and its police to assume control of its borders and its own internal security."

Thus, according to the President, the Marine presence was no longer merely a symbolic act of solidarity with a reemergent Lebanese national entity. Instead, the President of the United States announced to his nation and friends and enemies around the world—and particularly in Lebanon—that Marines were based in Lebanon to take an active role in policing borders and *providing for internal security.* President Reagan thus positively identified American servicemen with the beseiged Gemayel government.

The reconstituted 24th MAU had been relieved of all previously scheduled exercises in the Mediterranean and northern Europe. It had trained hard for months with the single expectation that it would deploy in Lebanon for a full six-month tour, roughly from late May to early November. The troops and their officers had nothing on their minds except Lebanon and what had come to be called, simply, "The Mission."

PART III

To the Brink

9

Marine amphibious units (MAUs) are air-ground administrative bodies, parts of larger air-ground teams called Marine air-ground task forces (MAGTFs). The next largest MAGTF unit after a MAU is known as a Marine amphibious brigade (MAB), which in turn is part of a Marine amphibious force (MAF). The MAGTF components exist outside the formal battalion, regimental, and divisional structures in that, at each step, they incorporate a battalion landing team or BLT (in a MAU), a regimental combat team (in a MAB), and a Marine division (in a MAF).

There was nothing to distinguish the 1st Battalion of the 8th Marine Regiment—the core of BLT 1/8—from any of the other Marine battalions that cruised the world's oceans in 1983. The battalion comprised the usual three rifle companies of about 180 men each; a 200-man weapons company (a platoon each of eight 81mm mortars and twelve Dragon wire-guided antitank rocket teams); and a headquarters and service (H&S) company of about 200 staffers and specialists such as communicators, Navy medical personnel, snipers, cooks and bakers, motor transport troops, and the like. Directly attached to the battalion, completing the formation known as a BLT, were several special and service detachments drawn from the service and support battalions that, together with three infantry regiments and one artillery regiment, constituted 2d Marine Division. These attachments included a platoon of amphibian assault vehicles; a platoon of heavy main battle tanks; a platoon of jeep-mounted TOW wire-guided antitank missiles; a platoon of combat engineers; a battery of six 155mm howitzers; and an amphibious reconnaissance platoon. The units so assembled were known as BLT 1/8, the ground combat component of 24th MAU.

Another component of 24th MAU during the mid-1983 deployment was Marine Medium Helicopter Squadron (HMM) 162. When not deployed with a MAU, HMM-162 was a CH-46 squadron specializing in delivery of troops and cargoes to landing sites in support of any sort of Marine ground or amphibious unit. When a component of a MAU, a core CH-46 squadron such as HMM-162 expands to include a pair of AH-1T Cobra helicopter gunships, a pair of UH-1N Huey utility helicopters, and four CH-53 cargo helicopters. In the case of HMM-162 in the spring of 1983, the new CH-53E was deployed because the artillery battery attached to BLT 1/8 was equipped, for the first time, with a newer, heavier, and longer-range 155mm howitzer that required the extra lift capability built into the upgraded "Echo" model. In addition to pilots and aircrewmen, HMM-162 deployed with its own maintenance and service personnel and its own medical team consisting of a Navy surgeon and corpsmen. When afloat, a helo squadron works from an LPH, a helicopter carrier that also carries a large component of the MAU ground force. Each of the five ships in an amphibious ready group has at least a small helicopter flight deck.

The last large component of 24th MAU was a 380-man "company" comprising about one-half of MAU Service and Support Group 24 (MSSG-24). The two MSSG-24 detachments generally alternated floats of 24th MAU. There were two Mediterranean MAUs and two Mediterranean MSSGs, 22 and 24. Thus there were a total of four Mediterranean MSSG detachments, which deployed in turn. Each detachment drew its personnel from service and support battalions constituting the 2d Force Service Support Group (2d FSSG). The MSSG comprised a headquarters platoon, a maintenance platoon, a supply platoon, a construction engineer platoon, a motor transport platoon, a shore-party platoon, a communications platoon, and a medical platoon headed by a pair of dentists.

Each component of a MAU—the MAU headquarters, the BLT, the HMM, and the MSSG—is built to stand alone. Duplicate systems, such as combat operations, command, and communications, exist in each component in the event there is a breakdown at a higher level that needs to be rapidly replaced or in case a component must indeed operate independently of the whole.

The MAU rates a full colonel as commander. Each colonel and his MAU staff usually deploy twice, alternating with the sister MAU. Though the schedule varies, a MAU commander and his key staffers usually spend eighteen to twenty-four months together, from the time the former commander and his staff turn over responsibility at the conclusion of their second float until the next commander and his staff come aboard at the conclusion of the current commander's second float.

When Col Tom Stokes returned from Beirut in February 1983, he turned over command to Col Timothy Geraghty, a handsome, athletic, brown-haired forty-six-year-old reconnaissance specialist who had achieved a flawless and distinguished career as a combat troop leader, trainer, and planner. Until succeeding to the command of 24th MAU, Tim Geraghty had been 2d Marine Division's Operations Officer, one of the best positions a Marine infantry colonel can hope to hold short of a command of his own. Geraghty had been a career Marine since 1959.

The BLT 1/8 commander was LtCol Howard (Larry) Gerlach, who had enlisted in the Marine Corps in 1961 and who had been commissioned in 1966 following his graduation from college under the auspices of the Naval Reserve Officers Training Program. Larry Gerlach had two Vietnam tours to his credit—as a rifle-platoon leader and an adviser to the Army of the Republic of Vietnam. He had been severely wounded just two months into his first tour. Aged forty-two, Larry Gerlach had twenty-three years in the Marine Corps in mid-1983. This was his first float as a rifle-battalion commander, a job most Marine infantry officers consider the pinnacle of their professional careers. That the battalion was bound for a specific mission in a potentially hot environment was icing on the cake. BLT 1/8 was Larry Gerlach's outfit; he had trained it, he had molded it into his image of what a Marine rifle battalion should be, he would lead it wherever events in Lebanon led him.

While the MAUs are technically subordinate to higher Marine Corps headquarters, the truth of the matter is that they are *operational* components of the fleet to which they are attached. In the case of 24th MAU, and 22d, the operational fleet is 6th Fleet. The MAU and MARG commanders (the latter is a Navy captain with the honorific of "commodore") are technically co-equals, but tradition places the landing-force commander—the colonel commanding the MAU—in a subordinate position to the transport group commodore while the MAU headquarters is aboard ship. Technically, then, Tim Geraghty reported to and received orders from the commander of 6th Fleet or his designated subordinates, whether he was embarked or ashore. The 6th Fleet commander, a vice admiral, reports directly to the Commander in Chief, U.S. Fleet, Europe (CINCNAVEUR), who is a four-star admiral subordinate to the Commander in Chief, U.S. Forces, Europe (CINCEUR), a four-star Army general responsible directly to the Joint Chiefs of Staff (JCS).

The Marine chain of command leading upward from the MAU

to the MAB to the MAF to Fleet Marine Force, Atlantic (FMFLant) really only served as a conduit for training aids and orders, supply, and some personnel assignments. Also, BLT 1/8's technical chain of command through 8th Marine Regiment and 2d Marine Division (which also led to FMFLant) was administrative and logistical rather than operational.

There was no direct link between any operational Marine unit in Lebanon and Headquarters, Marine Corps (HQMC) except insofar as HQMC could provide training, logistical, or manpower support back down through FMFLant and its subordinate chains.

The political crossover between the State Department representatives who, in fact, controlled the Marine presence in Lebanon was technically achieved by way of the President of the United States, who is also the Commander in Chief.

The Reagan administration dealt with events in Lebanon through two cabinet departments, Defense and State. The former provided guidance downward through the operational military chain of command—that is, from JCS to CINCEUR to CINCNAVEUR to 6th Fleet and ultimately to Colonel Geraghty and his subordinates. The latter provided guidance to Ambassador to Lebanon Robert Dillon as well as the bevy of special presidential envoys (beginning with Philip Habib and Maurice Draper) in whose hands was placed the responsibility for controlling the U.S. Multinational Force contingent—once again, Col Tim Geraghty's 24th MAU. In a very real sense, the White House controlled the parallel chains of command, both of which impacted directly upon ongoing changes in the initially very loose "presence" mission directive. So, while all trails led back, eventually, to the Oval Office, there was and would remain some question for whom, precisely, Tim Geraghty was working.

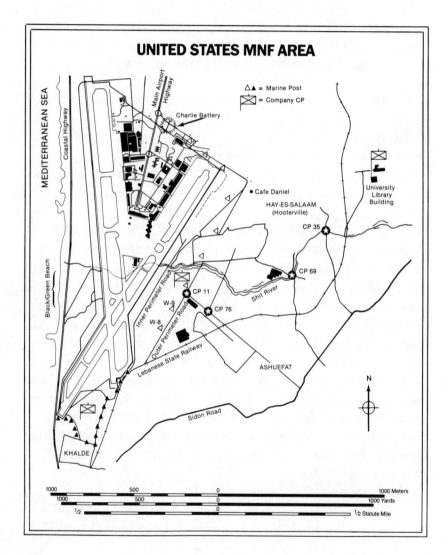

UNITED STATES MNF AREA

MEDITERRANEAN SEA

Coastal Highway

Black/Green Beach

Main Airport Highway

Charlie Battery

△▲ = Marine Post
⊠ = Company CP

Cafe Daniel

HAY-ES-SALAAM
(Hooterville)

University
Library
Building

CP 35

CP 69

Shit River

Inner Perimeter Road

CP 11

W-9

CP 76

W-8

Outer Perimeter Road

Lebanese State Railway

ASHUEFAT

N

Sidon Road

KHALDE

1000	500	0	1000 Meters
1000	500	0	1000 Yards
½		0	½ Statute Mile

10

Mediterranean Amphibious Ready Group (MARG) 2-83, embarking Col Tim Geraghty's 24th Marine Amphibious Unit (MAU), made direct from North Carolina to Rota, where a small advance party was flown off to Beirut to arrange the changeover with 22d MAU. The five-ship troop convoy, plus escorts, arrived off Beirut International Airport (BIA) on May 28 and the MAU landed the next day.

The first reactions of the troops to "The Root" were mixed. To Capt Monte Hoover, Battalion Landing Team (BLT) 1/8's assistant operations officer, the gleaming white high-rises along the shore made the rumors of war in the city seem greatly overblown. He changed his mind when he peered through his ship's big-eyes binoculars, for he could see the hundreds of thousands of scars on the faces of battered and burned-out concrete buildings. "It didn't seem like the place to be; it was so devastated." First Lieutenant Ron Smith, a CH-46 pilot, did not expect to find the city as torn-up as it was, but he still found it a beautiful place. HM3 Avery Chester, a rifle-platoon corpsman serving with Charlie Company, was immediately taken by the kids, who flocked around him as soon as they saw his medical bag; Chester knew he was in a foreign place, but the kids made him feel at home. Some Marines and corpsmen were just surprised that Beirut was so built-up and modern-looking, while others who got out on the first jeep and foot patrols were mildly shocked to find life going on pretty much as they had imagined it would in an Oriental city at peace.

It was indeed true in late May 1983 that there was a peace of sorts in Beirut. Perhaps the Multinational Force (MNF) and the Lebanese Armed Forces (LAF) were having some impact in that regard; the Israel Defense Force (IDF) certainly was. In the hills and mountains overlooking the BIA, war seemed to be the natural state of affairs, for the fireworks display was incessant.

The fact of the matter was that many of the troops and most of the younger officers were severely let down. There was no action in Beirut in late May or early June, and that was just plain frustrating in view of the dedication the troops and troop leaders had shown during the hard months of training. First Lieutenant Brent Smith had vowed to keep a detailed diary of his Beirut experiences, and he did—for about a week, after which he never opened his diary again.

Tim Geraghty's response to what he perceived as unsettling surroundings was to put the troops to work on strengthening existing defenses and building new ones. This was partly a reflection of a common command syndrome—when you relieve another unit, change what it has done to keep the troops busy, to heighten awareness, and to make clear to everyone that your unit really knows how to get the job done. That, and Tim Geraghty's natural caution. Maj Fred Lash, who stayed on briefly to head the MAU public affairs bureau, sensed from the outset that the relatively "relaxed atmosphere" stressed by Col Jim Mead was to be a thing of the past under his relief.

That caution was at least in part justified. While there was no one overtly out to get Marines in the immediate wake of the changeover with 22d MAU, early briefs and intelligence summaries indicated that the U.S. MNF contingent was becoming less and less welcome to many of Beirut's poorer residents, mainly the Shiite Moslems who lived close to the BIA compound. Any Marine walking patrol felt that.

The first great shock came three days after 24th MAU landed: a mild earthquake shook Beirut and destroyed some of the equanimity of the troops.

The character of life in the lawless Lebanese capital was driven home to 1stLt Brent Smith, of Alpha Company, during one of his frequent motorized patrols. Smith's jeep and a truckload of Marines were suddenly stopped in a huge, formless traffic jam, and Smith was casting about nervously for an exit when the streets were suddenly filled with heavily armed Phalange gunmen. Smith snicked back the bolt of his driver's M-16, chambering a round. So did the two men riding shotgun in the rear of the jeep. It was a considerable relief when the Phalangists passed down the column without paying any attention to the Marines. As the sense of imminent danger passed, Smith noticed that the traffic jam had been caused by a head-on collision. Several civilian men were standing by the smashed cars, cursing up a storm, flailing their arms, pacing off their intense anger. At that moment a Phalange fighter decked out in a khaki tiger-striped uniform walked up to Lieutenant Smith and told him he would clear a path through the tumult. As he was driven off, Brent Smith realized that he had witnessed the Lebanese analogue to Americans battling out their grievances in court. These Lebanese were quite prepared to reach full settlement in public, on the street. The Phalange gunmen had arrived on the scene to see that the process did not get completely out of hand.

Training and working with the LAF was fraught with frustrations and dangers as well as the warm glow of success. The training camp that had been erected in the northern reaches of the sprawling BIA compound was churning out recruits and retrained Lebanese regulars, but all of the trainers well knew that they could accomplish nothing beyond teaching the rudiments to Lebanese who were being sent into action, most of them, within weeks of first arriving at the camp.

First Lieutenant Chuck Dallachie, the battalion legal officer, was engrossed in a conversation in his first-story office of the BLT headquarters building when his train of thought was interrupted by a dramatic crash against the outside wall. As all hands in the room and adjacent rooms sprawled on the floor behind desks and other, flimsier, cover, a sound like "a manhole cover flipping across concrete" could be heard from the macadam parking lot below. There was no explosion, so Dallachie made his way to the window in time to see a large-caliber artillery round come to rest at the edge of the parking area. Word came up a short time later that it was an American-made 155mm round of the type provided to LAF artillery. The shell was a dud because the Lebanese gun crew had neglected to insert the detonator in its nose before firing.

Sometime later, a Bravo Company squad leader testing a new night-vision scope he had just attached to his M-16 decided to track two nocturnal joggers trotting along the BIA perimeter road, a favorite exercise ground of Marines and many of the Lebanese soldiers who wanted to be like Marines. A single round left the M-16 and felled the two runners. The first American officers and corpsmen on the scene found two young Lebanese soldiers writhing in agony. The two had been running in perfect cadence, and each had been shot by the same round, squarely through his right thigh; one was lightly injured while the other had had his sciatic nerve severed. What really surprised and shocked the Marines was the attitude of the first batch of Lebanese officers on the scene. A Lebanese lieutenant colonel actually apologized on behalf of the runners. "I understand," he averred over the embarrassed protests of the Marines. "Our soldiers were in a place they should not have been, and your sentry shot them. It is really very good shooting, you know. I understand." The Marines attempted to take the blame, but the LAF officer won the claim. The Marine sharpshooter was court-martialed and transferred to another company.

The incident that really drove home the nature of the LAF and of Lebanese society to 24th MAU began at the Marine-staffed LAF training camp in the BIA compound. A young LAF sentry grounded his new M-16 rifle a bit too boldly and jarred loose a round into the head of an LAF recruit on his way to get a cold soda. Marine instructors scrambled to the sound of the shot amid the screaming of both Lebanese boys. A corpsman took one look at the head wound, realized he was out of his depth, and ordered up transport to the battalion aid station for the grievously wounded soldier. The first vehicle on the scene, a jeep, received the bloody cargo and highballed right up the main runway to the BLT building. The battalion combat operations center (COC) had been alerted within seconds of the shooting, so a crowd of Marines and corpsmen was on hand to greet the jeep. The Lebanese soldier, awash in a deepening pool of bright red blood, had already expired. When the fearful, blubbering soldier who had done the deed was brought in a few minutes later, quick-witted Marines actually had to protect him from the rain of blows delivered by LAF officers who had by then joined the incredulous throng. When 1stLt Greg Balzer, one of the COC watch officers, asked an LAF officer what would happen to the shooter, he was informed that the youth would be "tried and executed" within a few weeks. Indeed, that is precisely what came to pass.

Fun and games with the Israelis, though milder than they had been, continued throughout the first months of the deployment. Bravo Company had been on duty guarding the northern approaches to the BIA for only one day when the company weapons chief, GySgt John Gentry, received word from the observation post (OP) atop the city's Pepsi-Cola plant that an Israeli tank and armored personnel carrier (APC) had crossed the battalion boundary and were headed directly for the plant. Gentry ordered the troops there to go to full alert and headed out to see for himself what was going on.

When Gentry got to the OP, he chided the Israeli tank commander: "Don't you know you're not supposed to be here? We have an agreement."

The Israeli allowed as he knew about the agreement, then added, "I just want to take your picture."

This was not the response for which Gunny Gentry had bargained. "Okay. Take it and turn around."

The Israeli snapped one frame and turned his minuscule armored column for home.

Alpha Company spent its first weeks in Beirut hunkered down along the southern BIA perimeter. Each night during that period, Marines standing watch noted the passage of an Israeli patrol as it waded through the muddy bog fronting the 2d Platoon sector.

One night about two weeks into the deployment, 2d Platoon was electrified by the call, "Corporal of the guard!" which was taken to mean that intruders were approaching or already within the platoon area. Cpl Tom Megna ran out toward the post with SSgt Michael McCorkle.

The platoon leader, 1stLt Brent Smith, was sound asleep in his tent and had to be awakened by his radioman, LCpl Ron Medeiros, who had heard of the disturbance on his radio: "Sir, they're up there with guns, and they're laughing. Sir, it doesn't look good!"

Lieutenant Smith rubbed the sleep from his eyes. "Huh? Who? What are you talking about, Medeiros? What's going on?"

"The Israelis, sir. They're out there, making a lot of noise."

As Smith tried to calm his radioman's frazzled nerves, he climbed into his boots and threw his holstered .45 over his shoulder on the way out of the tent.

The first authority on the scene was Corporal Megna, who lapsed into a form of Pidgin English when confronted by the Israeli patrol leader. He experienced no end of embarrassment when the Israeli officer introduced himself as a graduate of Washington State University and responded to Megna's questions in flawless American English.

Lance Corporal Medeiros, who became separated from the platoon leader when Lieutenant Smith went around the far side of a tent that barred their way, encountered Pfc Robert Black running back to the platoon area from his outpost. Black was so agitated that Medeiros could not understand the rapid-fire twists and turns of his one-sided conversation. Before Medeiros could do anything to calm Black, he was severely shaken when an intense beam of light was shone directly in his face. The radioman instinctively reached toward the source of the light and swung aside a flashlight in the hand of Staff Sergeant McCorkle. Right behind McCorkle was Corporal Megna, whose M-16 was at the ready. As Medeiros's eyes reacclimated themselves to the dark, he saw in the bright moonlight that many people were lying on the ground all around him. All seemed to be ready to conduct a close-quarters gunfight.

When Lieutenant Smith arrived, Staff Sergeant McCorkle explained that an eleven-man Israeli patrol had cut the wire and come right up to the 2d Platoon line.

The Israeli patrol leader joined the five standing Marines to explain in his slangy English that he was certain he was well within his patrol area.

"You can't go through here," Lieutenant Smith cautioned.

"Why not?" the Israeli countered.

"Because this is our perimeter. You don't belong here."

Then Smith thought to himself that he was not required to explain anything to the Israeli. Indeed, he quickly concluded that he was well within his rights to order the Israelis to depart, which he did in a businesslike and cordial manner: "Take your people and get them out of here before something happens."

The Israeli agreed to leave, so Smith and his command element led him and his men back through the wire. As the Israeli patrol leader turned to leave, he asked Smith how to avoid the swamp. Bemused, Smith told him he did not know, thus closing the conversation and, he hoped, the entire incident.

No sooner did Lieutenant Smith and Lance Corporal Medeiros return to their tent than an amtracker manning a checkpoint in the 2d Platoon area sang out, "Halt! Who goes there?"

There was no question at the 2d Platoon command post (CP) but that the Israelis were back. Smith, McCorkle, and Medeiros grabbed their flak jackets and weapons and headed back out.

One of Smith's junior NCOs offered the Israeli patrol leader a simple solution to the growing nonsense. "You fuckin' guys," he shouted, "if you don't fuckin' stop comin' through our fuckin' lines and fuckin' leave now, we're going to have to fuck you up."

The amused Israeli patrol leader singled out Lieutenant Smith and claimed that he had again become lost in the swamp bordering the platoon sector, that his men were wet and cold, and could Smith please let them pass through the platoon sector to spare them the discomfort of another walk through the swamp. Smith took Staff Sergeant McCorkle, Corporal Megna, and Lance Corporal Medeiros aside and told them to lead the Israelis out to the main road through a jointly manned checkpoint about a mile away; Medeiros was to walk point, Megna was to walk rear, and McCorkle was to walk in the middle of the Israeli column.

Medeiros halted the column about 300 meters short of the jointly manned checkpoint and told Staff Sergeant McCorkle that he wanted to go ahead alone to brief the LAF soldiers and Marines there. At first, the Lebanese post commander refused to believe that a Marine was guiding an IDF patrol through the area: "You mean you are leading an *American* patrol?" "Uh, no, sir. I mean I'm leading an *Israeli* patrol." The LAF officer responded with a statement of bravado Medeiros was sure he did not feel: "I want to kill some Israelis." One of the Lebanese privates even went so far as to lock and load his weapon. Lance Corporal Medeiros coolly pulled that soldier aside and called for McCorkle and Megna to bring the column forward. True to form, the battle-hardened Israelis were laughing at the irate Lebanese and incredulous Americans as they passed from sight.

The next afternoon, while Brent Smith's platoon was putting out tripflares and noisemakers all along its frontage, word arrived from an adjacent platoon that an Israeli foot patrol had cut the perimeter wire and entered the company defensive zone.

Though they had been on edge the night before, these young Marines had no problem with the obvious testing the Israelis were undertaking; most agreed that they would do the same. As time passed, Marines came to understand the challenges and dangers faced by the IDF. When the daily morning Israeli mechanized patrol shot up cars and buildings on the Sidon Road adjacent to the Marine lines, some Marines found themselves in full sympathy with the IDF's plight. This sense was considerably heightened when stray bullets, rocket-propelled grenades, and mortar rounds meant for the Israelis impacted with increasing frequency within the BLT perimeter.

Higher headquarters continued to make much of the Israeli tendency to conduct "recon by fire," but Brent Smith, who was, after all, in a position adjacent to the Israeli main supply route, had the distinct feeling that the Israelis were highly selective as to which buildings they fired into; he felt they fired most often when they had reason to suspect that their fire would be returned. Often as not, Smith noted, they did draw return fire and, indeed, suffered casualties in the engagements that ensued.

Intramural athletic events with other MNF contingents and the LAF had been standard almost from the start of the Beirut deployments. They were great monotony breakers. In time, however, national pride reared its ugly head. A common joke for a few weeks anticipated the arrival of Howard Cosell to officiate at the increasingly lavish affairs.

The spiral reached a sublime plateau when 1stLt Bill Zimmerman, who doubled as the BLT training officer and BLT special services officer, casually invited some of the Lebanese officers whose units he was helping to train to participate in the BLT's usual Sunday cookout, to be followed by a basketball game behind the BLT building.

Something got misinterpreted somewhere in the chain of command, for Zimmerman and his roommate, 1stLt Greg Balzer, wound up overseeing the construction of a "real" basketball court to replace the informal hoops-on-poles arrangement that had served the MAUs to that point.

When Balzer and Zimmerman recruited the BLT's combat engineer platoon, SSgt John Bohnet, the engineering platoon sergeant, drove off into town with two of his troops, then showed up hours later with a truckload of "commandeered" telephone poles to be sawed into planks for the court. He also had his engineers set the steel backboard poles in concrete. Lieutenant Balzer went to the Lebanese University library in search of a set of official international basketball rules. All he could find was a French-language version. Second Lieutenant Maury Hukill, the engineer platoon leader, worked with Balzer to decipher the placement of markings, which he had flawlessly painted. A scoreboard was constructed and referees were trained from Greg Balzer's imperfectly translated notes.

Come the day of the big game, LtGen Ibrahim Tannous, the LAF commander, arrived with his entourage. He was seated, as was Colonel Geraghty and other senior American officers, at a table bedecked with a colorful Heineken patio umbrella, the better to shade the Marine retainers detailed to see that the commanders and their staffs were well stuffed with steak and hamburgers and, of course, ice-cold beer.

A good time was had by all. The Marine team creamed the Lebanese, who complained bitterly that the Americans kept reverting to the American rules they knew rather than adhere to the translated international rules. The interlude provided weeks of incautious merriment. The basketball court was never again used for organized play.

There was surprisingly little unofficial fraternization with Lebanese civilians—at least insofar as the various unit commanders ever learned.

One celebrated case involved four members of Charlie Battery. For reasons never fully clarified, two teenaged Lebanese girls who apparently lived in a two-story house across the road from the BIA took to parading bare-breasted in front of their bedroom windows at night. Naturally, the gunners indulged in no end of speculation regarding the intentions of the young ladies. By the end of June, after months at sea or restricted to all-male activities, the four gunners in question could no longer control their impulses, so they decided to find out what the Lebanese lasses had in mind. The four slipped the leash late one evening, but were grabbed as they approached the house wherein their dreams resided. The four were court-martialed for offenses ranging from disobeying a lawful order to wrongfully wearing physical-training gear outside the perimeter. All were reduced to the rank of private, forfeited two-thirds of a month's pay, and confined at hard labor for thirty days. The last punishment made little impression on most Marines; they had already been confined at hard labor for six weeks by the time the verdict came down.

Able to get around town more easily than the Marines, MAU Service and Support Group (MSSG) 24 corpsmen picked up large supplies of beer and whiskey whenever possible, which was often. Usually, the liquor was consumed within hours of its arrival at the MSSG bunkers reserved by the corpsmen for their almost-nightly parties.

It would be hard to believe that no one in the MAU compound partook of the local hashish, known worldwide as Lebanese Red.

The constant passage of VIPs through the BIA wore thin in no time. Dog and pony shows were incessant and drew extremely negative reviews from the troops and junior officers. If a Marine on post happened to be caught in the act, for instance, of picking his nose, or if the area for a hundred meters around a checkpoint had not been completely policed for trash, the offender and his officers took no end of abuse from above.

An explanation of the MAU's mission delivered by a tough-looking combat Marine dressed in starched cammies might have been good, heady stuff for the person who listened to it only once, but the people who regularly delivered such briefs could soon be singled out by virtue of the fact that their eyeballs were poised firmly against the roofs of their eye sockets.

The MSSG-24 corpsmen were particularly incensed at the level of make-work generated by the VIP visits. It all seemed so pointless. For example, the docs repeatedly swept a few yards of hallway in the MSSG building basement despite the facts that, first, an unrepaired broken window admitted a steady trickle of fine dust onto the newly cleaned floor and that, second, almost none of the VIPs ever visited the basement aid station.

One of the great causes for alarm among Marines in the know was the tendency for congressional and administration VIPs to think and speak mainly in terms of the national leaders they perceived as holding the strings to the Lebanese situation, the Gemayels, the Begins, the Assads. Marines who had been out in "the ville" (Hooterville) on patrols had come to think routinely of the factions they saw represented in the streets, the Druse Progressive Socialist Party, the Shiite Amal, the Christian Phalange, the score of splinter groups routinely lumped under these broad headings. But no one from the higher reaches of the U.S. government deigned to ask these camouflage-bedecked soldiers of the sea to validate their preconceptions. And no Marine thought to breach etiquette and tradition by speaking up or speaking out.

Perceived dangers around the edge of the BIA perimeter were slow in coming and slower in registering. At the isolated Lebanese University position, 2dLt Bill Harris, a Charlie Company platoon leader, noted over the first eight weeks that the young men were coming home to Hooterville. Coincident with their arrival, Harris noted, streets and buildings in the quarter were soon plastered with handbills depicting the Ayatollah Khomeini.

The honeymoon was drawing to a close.

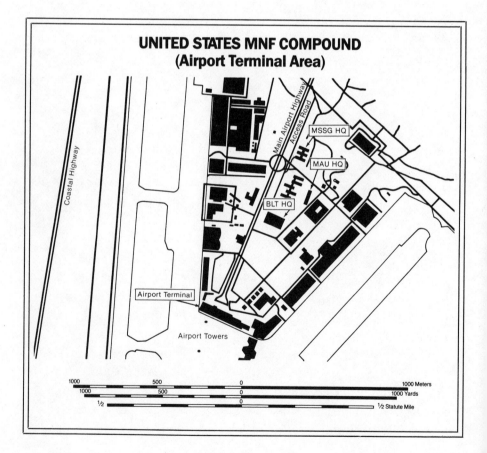

UNITED STATES MNF COMPOUND
(Airport Terminal Area)

Coastal Highway

Main Airport Highway

Access Road

MSSG HQ

MAU HQ

BLT HQ

Airport Terminal

Airport Towers

1000	500	0	1000 Meters
1000	500	0	1000 Yards
½		0	½ Statute Mile

11

Mixed with the fun and games, the enervating VIP tours, the thousands of tried-and-true and highly original methods the troops employed to relieve their crushing boredom, was a slow, at-first-barely-perceived deterioration of the general peace that had for months enfolded the teeming city beyond the fence around Beirut International Airport (BIA).

HM3 Avery Chester, of Charlie Company, was on the very first Battalion Landing Team (BLT) 1/8 patrol out of the Lebanese University. The patrol, comprising mainly staff NCOs who had to familiarize themselves with the neighborhood, was conducted by a BLT 2/6 corporal who had stayed behind to help the newcomers settle in. Everything went well until the patrol passed six teenagers lounging in a corner. The Lebanese youths muttered, "Ah, Americans" and some words in Arabic, then one ran up and grabbed the arm of the BLT 2/6 corporal, who wordlessly punched out the Lebanese teenager. Doc Chester was totally stunned, more than a little fearful, and really happy to drag himself to the end of the seven-mile walk. The corporal did not tell the patrol members why he had decked the obnoxious Lebanese; he left them to learn for themselves.

Capt Jay Farrar, the Marine Amphibious Unit's (MAU's) assistant public affairs officer, was heading through Hooterville by jeep to take care of some routine business at the Lebanese University when he and the other occupants realized that a foreign object had been tossed into the vehicle by a young boy standing in the shadows of the narrow street. There was absolutely no hesitation among the four green Marines; though each dimly perceived that the foreign object was just an empty soda can, all jumped instinctively to the road and ducked for cover. The jeep slowed to a crawl and thudded gently into a wall. As Farrar stood to assess the damage to the jeep, he was greeted by gales of laughter from the many residents who had turned out to see what the commotion was about.

First Lieutenant Greg Balzer, the battalion assistant operations officer in charge of scheduling and routing Marine patrols, was out with a jeepborne patrol commanded by SSgt Duane Richardson when he spotted a great crowd of shouting, crying civilians running up a hilly side street on what appeared to be a converging course with the jeeps.

Running women and children: this was one of the deeply ingrained danger signals, so Staff Sergeant Richardson sounded an immediate alert—"Get the fuck out of the jeeps!"—over the squad tactical radios carried in each jeep. The troops had anticipated the order and immediately cleared the vehicles and sought cover behind a knee-high retaining wall beside the road. Machine guns were set up and all rifles and grenade-launchers were at the ready.

After seeing that the men around him were settled in, Lieutenant Balzer cautiously walked forward to find Staff Sergeant Richardson, whom he had seen ducking around the corner of a nearby building. The officer could not see the patrol leader's position because the mass of civilians blocked his view, so he continued to advance along the edge of the road to within fifty meters of the obstructing building. The air was positively electric with tension.

Staff Sergeant Richardson ambled into view, right in the center of the road. His head was cast downward and Balzer thought he saw a sheepish sort of look on the NCO's face. The lieutenant popped the magazine out of his .45-caliber pistol and strode up to Richardson, who was laughing quietly to himself.

Just as Balzer joined Richardson, a white-clad Lebanese lady stalked into view and shouted, "No shoot! No shoot! Is only wedding." She was the bride, who, along with her new husband, had left the church just as the Marine patrol hove into view. The Marines had mistaken the wedding party and all the celebrating neighbors, on their way back to a line of cars arrayed behind the wall that the main body of the patrol was using for cover, as a telltale sign of the ambush every Marine truly believed would seal his fate.

Kids between the ages of eight and thirteen were the bane of many patrolling Marines. If they were not trying to sell something, they were testing the reflexes of the Marines, tossing debris such as soda cans and treats of food with equal glee. Most Marines took the mild testing well, but a few reacted to the hostility that edged these childish confrontations. One combat engineer who was hit by a stone as his jeep passed a small knot of youngsters jumped to the street and grabbed his assailant by the throat in preparation to striking a blow for law and order with his beefy fist. The youth cowered, but so did the Marine, who looked up in time to see a knot of stern-looking men heading his way. The young Marine released his grip on the collar of the Lebanese boy and stalked back to the waiting patrol, where he found his comrades all locked and loaded and peering anxiously at the rooftops and second-story windows dominating the narrow road.

In numerous similar incidents, Lebanese youngsters hurled taunts like "Khomeini good; America no good," then dared a response by punching on the Marine walking rearguard as the patrol passed along the narrow streets. One patrol's corpsman was next to last in line when a kid darted out of a crowd of well-wishers. Startled, the doc looked at the last man, who motioned with his rifle that he was covering the action. The Navy man turned back and found the intruder right on top of him. He reflexively decked the Lebanese teenager, then stepped over him to accept a handful of flowers from a little girl.

The most sobering cause of reflection among the officers responsible for mounting and briefing the patrols was the tendency for very young boys to push the barrels of real-looking cap pistols into the faces of patrolling Marines. It was a positive miracle that a jumpy Marine did not let fly with a lethal response to this truly childish form of terrorism.

On the other hand, volunteers from MAU Service and Support Group (MSSG) 24 went to the poor Moslem suburb of Bourj-al-Bourajniah, just north of the BIA, to install playground equipment that had been built or collected and rebuilt by volunteers from the departed MSSG-22.

In time, the local residents became less forthcoming with the gifts of fruit, cakes, and cool drinks they had once showered on the passing patrols.

The first reported incident of BLT 1/8 taking fire of any sort came at 0030, June 8, when Pfc Mike Stringent, of Charlie Company, was on duty on the rooftop observation post (OP) at the Lebanese University's library building. It was dead quiet until an unidentified attacker fired what Stringent guessed was a rocket-propelled grenade (RPG) at a nearby Israeli position.

The RPG had no sooner detonated than Charlie Company Marines throughout the building tumbled out of their racks and headed for their firing positions. A second RPG round, fired within minutes, drew Israeli .50-caliber-machine-gun fire around a 360-degree arc. Several of the half-inch-diameter Israeli bullets tore through Charlie Company's sandbagged defenses, behind which young Americans crouched in tight, little bundles of pure nerve and sweat. The gunfire raged for ten minutes, then the Israelis fired illumination rounds, some of which landed within seventy-five meters of the library building. The .50-caliber fire erupted again until the Israelis settled down or tired of the sport.

In the morning, while Charlie Company Marines worked feverishly to improve their firing positions, HM3 Avery Chester and several other corpsmen were called out into one of the fields near the library building to assist a Lebanese family. LCpl Jeff Boulos, a Lebanese-American Dragon antitank gunner, went along to translate. The father's story emerged slowly: three of the family's children had been killed in the night, literally blown out of their home during the gunplay. That's when the situation in The Root struck home with Charlie Company.

The first shells to strike the BIA fell in the last days of July. It was perceived then—or, at least, the story was given out—that these were "overs" intended for the Israelis or fallout from the Lebanese intramural fighting that raged in the Shouf and Metan almost every day.

The first rounds were three 122mm Katyusha rockets, which slightly injured a pair of enlisted Marines and blew up a civilian grocery truck that had just delivered goods to the BLT.

The first night shelling to hit the BIA compound arrived within days. It caught MSSG-24, closest to the detonations, completely unprepared.

LCpl Ken Spencer, an eighteen-year-old truck driver, was sitting in his tent listening to the radio when he heard the first rocket whistle through the still night air. The truckers reacted to the explosion with complete confusion: where do we go, what do we do, let's get the hell out of here!

There was a plan. All the MSSG's heavy equipment was to be

driven out of the congested central parking area and dispersed in the open to lessen the chances of mass destruction. But the troops were not psychologically prepared to carry out the elaborate plan that had been communicated verbally just once.

The Truck Platoon commander ordered his Marines out of their tent and to the truck park. Everyone grabbed his helmet, flak jacket, and weapon and headed for the trucks. Lance Corporal Spencer grabbed a handful of photos he would regret losing and was rolling through the darkened compound within five minutes of the first detonation.

All the vehicles hit the one-lane gate at the same time, creating a traffic jam of unprecedented complexity. It took endless sweating and swearing to get the trucks and heavy equipment moving again.

It was dead silent once the trucks had been spaced out along the far edge of the runway. All Lance Corporal Spencer could hear was the loud baying of frightened dogs—to which a Marine vented his spleen by shouting, "Shut up!"

Nothing else happened. In the morning, after the Truck Platoon commander did some fancy verbal tap dancing, the MSSG was given a new plan in the event of repeated shellings.

The first clearly *intentional* shelling of the BIA occurred on August 10 as part of a general rocket bombardment against targets throughout Beirut by Druse gunners in the Shouf.

SSgt Charlie Garcia, of Bravo Company, was walking from the BLT to his company area when he heard what he assumed to be two detonations from the Lebanese Armed Forces (LAF) grenade range, north of the Marine command compound. He even told a sentry to ignore the explosions. Garcia's arrival at the next post was accompanied by another pair of detonations, so he told the sentry there that he thought it was noise from the grenade range. However, as Garcia reached his platoon command post, he distinctly heard a rocket being fired from the hills beyond the Bravo Company sector.

Capt Keith Arthur, the MSSG-24 exec, was in the Maintenance Platoon machine-shop van speaking with SSgt Mike Isajewicz and Sgt Kim McKinney when he noticed that the van was gently rocking by itself. McKinney told the captain not to worry, that the shock waves from artillery fired in the nearby Shouf always sounded close to whoever was in the van. Not ten seconds elapsed before the first rocket detonated in the BIA compound, less than 200 yards from the machine-shop van. Captain Arthur, who had been raised in a Marine Corps family (his father had been BLT 3/8's sergeant major in Beirut and was at that moment the 8th Marines regimental sergeant major), looked around through popping eyeballs before commenting that the distant shelling really did sound closer. Staff Sergeant Isajewicz had to tell Arthur that he had never heard one *that* close. The three then went outside to see what was going on. They were joined by the Maintenance Platoon commander, CWO-4 George Allen, who told them that Condition I, the highest state of alert, had been sounded and that all hands were required to get into bunkers with overhead protection.

All hands not directly involved in the defense of the BIA were in the aboveground bunkers or accounted for within minutes. All any of them could do was wait and worry.

The fifth round—the one heard by Staff Sergeant Garcia—hit dead on the BIA control tower. There was little more than superficial damage, but the panicking Navy air traffic controller on duty "spazzed out," filling the airwaves with pleas to rescue him.

First Lieutenant Neal Morris, BLT 1/8's Headquarters and Service Company executive officer, was the only Marine injured in the brief shelling. He was just exiting the officers' head beside the BLT building when he was hit by a few shrapnel pieces in the back of the right thigh. This notorious piece of bad luck (everyone on the beach seems to have harbored a deep, dark fear of being blown away while using the head) earned Morris a medevac flight to helicopter carrier *Iwo Jima* and a few days in the sack.

The Condition I alert at the BIA lasted an interminable thirty minutes.

The rocket barrage, which also nearly hit Ambassador Robert McFarlane, a former Marine lieutenant colonel and President Reagan's latest special Middle East envoy, was apparently a sort of Druse calling card, an effort to tell the Gemayel government and other interested parties that the Druse desired a place at whatever bargaining sessions everyone had in mind. In addition to the rocket attack, the Druse kidnapped and held hostage for several days three Lebanese cabinet ministers who had ventured into the Shouf to demand the removal of several hundred Syrian-supplied Druse artillery pieces which could easily dominate the coastal plain and which had for several months been arrayed against Phalange positions in the neighboring Metan.

Claiming responsibility for the shelling and kidnapping was Druse chieftain Walid Jumblatt. The three ministers—a Maronite, a Shiite, and a Druse—were released unharmed following some concessions from the Gemayel government.

No one then knew it, but some interesting battle lines had been drawn and some interesting precedents set. Chief among these were two. Ambassador McFarlane responded to the violence by cutting off all negotiations with Walid Jumblatt and the Druse. Second, the Druse attack, which killed five and wounded twenty-nine people throughout Beirut, went unanswered, least of all by American artillery or naval gunfire.

PART IV

First Blood

12

The factional hostilities that had been simmering in and around Beirut finally erupted on August 28, 1983, a Sunday.

The flashpoint was reached only after Israel Defense Force (IDF) units precipitously turned a number of their checkpoints in East Beirut and the northern Shouf over to Lebanese Armed Forces (LAF) units.

Without the heel of the IDF firmly planted upon their necks, local warlords moved their militia forces into the power vacuum created by the limited IDF withdrawal. Their target was the LAF, for any defeat suffered by that weak force would serve to undermine the Gemayel government and, it was assumed, enhance the positions of the disparate Moslem groups seeking to gain increased power within and without the state structure.

Early on Sunday, August 28, 1stLt Mark Singleton, the artillery forward observer attached to Alpha Company, led a small contingent of Marines and French foreign legionnaires into the foothills east of Beirut International Airport (BIA) to conduct a cross-training exercise. Everyone got to fire everyone else's weapons amid exchanges of compliments and the good-natured spinning of elitist tall tales. Several of the Marines were surprised to discover that the legionnaires were not Frenchmen but *foreigners!*

As the Marines and legionnaires were returning to Alpha Company to participate in the scheduled weekly cookout and basketball game, Lieutenant Singleton and others noted that the city was, well, "a little too quiet." The traffic flow was unusually light for a Sunday, which was a Moslem workday even if it was the Christian sabbath, and there did not seem to be the usual numbers of pedestrians on the streets.

First Lieutenants Greg Balzer and Chuck Schnorf, of the Battalion Landing Team (BLT) staff, were jogging on the perimeter road near Alpha Company when Balzer heard several rounds crack overhead.

"Chuck, I think someone is shooting at us."

"Nah! Keep running."

Balzer heard several more rounds crack overhead as the two continued through the Alpha Company sector and turned up a dirt road detour past a construction site.

"Chuck, I *know* they're shooting at us."

"No, no! Keep running. No problem."

The two kept going and finally reached Rock Base, the helo control area just north of the Marine Amphibious Unit (MAU) and BLT headquarters buildings. It came as no great shock to Balzer that all the air-wingers were hiding behind every bit of available cover.

Two rounds pinged off the pavement and the two lieutenants dropped in unison to the roadway.

"Jesus Christ," Schnorf bellowed, "they're shooting at us!"

"No doubt, Chuck," Balzer replied. "They are definitely doing that."

While most of Alpha Company spent the early afternoon embroiled in intramural sports and a cookout with the legionnaires, Cpl Terry Moore was on the streets of Hooterville, trying to conduct a routine patrol in the midst of unfettered chaos. Amid shouted gutteral warnings of "There's going to be a fight," hundreds of people were running back and forth along the narrow streets, including numerous young men armed with rifles, submachine guns, and rocket-propelled grenades (RPGs). The farther the Marine patrol walked, the greater the unrest it encountered. At length, Corporal Moore opted to change the patrol's projected route and head for home.

No sooner had Moore's vulnerable patrol cleared the built-up area to walk across an open field fronting the Alpha Company position than nine mortar rounds passed overhead, undoubtedly on their way to LAF positions near the BIA.

The reinforced squad reflexively deployed in the field, setting up its M-60 machine gun and pausing tensely to see what might befall it. There was no additional fire, so Corporal Moore hurriedly led his Marines back into the company position and reported his observations to the company command post (CP).

LCpl Frank Orians, an Alpha Company M-60 gunner, was supposed to have had the Sunday off but had been ordered to replace one of the company's star basketball players on guard duty. He arrived at his post at exactly 1600, just as the first mortar salvo was passing over Corporal Moore's patrol.

The sergeant of the guard ordered all hands into their bunkers to await developments. When nothing happened for many minutes, he allowed his Marines to stand down. Lance Corporal

Orians was greeted on the outside by a fresh salvo, which, though it was not close, was nonetheless unsettling.

The indirect overhead fire was unnerving enough, but Alpha Company and the legionnaires were really put on edge by the whispered *whee, whee, whee* of small-arms fire from the east as it transited the company sector only ten or fifteen feet overhead.

There was a rush to don helmets and flak jackets—and finish off the last of the beer. Then the legionnaires headed home. Capt Paul Roy, the dark, athletic Maine-stater who commanded Alpha Company, ordered his troops into their bunkers, at full alert. Marines throughout the BIA complex were ordered into Condition I, the attack-imminent combat status.

The Alpha Company combination command/observation post was situated on a tiny isolated knoll overlooking the three main platoon positions and numerous posts and checkpoints throughout the company's sector. The post, which had been inherited from all the previous companies of all the previous BLTs, was more ceremonial than real, for it offered no overhead protection and was, in fact, shielded only by a knee-high sand-bag blast wall.

Most of the troops were initially willing to buy the official line that they happened to be situated between the bolder militia factions and the intended target, the LAF. But while mortar and rocket fire continued to pass overhead long into the night, small-arms fire passed overhead at between eight and ten feet. Many bullets fired from adjacent Hooterville dinged into squad tents throughout the company sector.

Alpha Company's 2d Platoon was closest to Hooterville and most of the small-arms fire directed from the town against Alpha Company struck the dirt berm around and the tent tops within the platoon sector. The disciplined troops took it for hours, but a noticeably rising volume of unanswered fire led the platoon leader, 1stLt Brent Smith, to request permission to return fire. The message was sent up the command chain, and permission to engage in limited form came back at about 1800: designated shooters could return fire if they had clear targets, if those targets were actually initiating or returning fire, and if the return fire did not spill over onto civilian targets.

The 2d Platoon shooters were closely supervised. Because they felt it was imperative to demonstrate their will and ability to dominate the battlefield, the NCOs in charge of the return fire directed several shooters against each confirmed target. It was, however, extremely hard to spot the Moslem fighters; survival of the fittest since the start of the Lebanese civil war, eight years earlier, had taught snipers to fire through open windows two or even three buildings back from the line of structures facing Alpha Company. It was thus extremely difficult for the Marine shooters to confirm even the sighting of clear targets, and the very close supervision by Lieutenant Smith and his NCOs prevented a wholesale venting of frustrations.

No one in 2d Platoon had ever fired at live targets, nor had anyone ever been one. One of the truly surprising bonuses for the troops was the general rush of power, danger, and fear that they found easy to swallow.

The militiamen's marksmanship, if it was intended to kill or maim Marines, was egregious.

The fire tapered off after midnight and stopped altogether by 0200. Condition I was lifted and three Marines out of every four were released to get some sleep in their bunkers.

The gunfire began again at about 0400, rousting 1st Platoon and the company command group. It was light fire, perhaps typical of the general mayhem Alpha Company had endured for weeks. No one did much about it. It woke HN Victor Oglesby, the 1st Platoon corpsman, who lay listlessly on his cot for a few minutes before reaching for his helmet.

The overhead fire heated up at about 0700, when elements of the LAF 1st Air Assault Battalion performed a helicopter landing operation on the main BIA runway directly behind the Alpha

Company CP. The commander of one of the LAF companies joined Captain Roy to learn what he could about known militia positions across the way in Hooterville. While the helo assault and briefing were still under way, gunners in the Shouf and around Khalde fired medium artillery, 82mm mortars, 106mm recoilless rifles, and 122mm Katyusha rockets against Air Assault troopers and the nearby LAF encampments. The fire really got heavy as the Air Assault platoons moved through Alpha Company's lines and on toward Hooterville to reinforce LAF units already embroiled in battles with Shiite Amal militia units. Several rounds landed around the airport hangars, and a near miss cleared the control tower of air traffic controllers. The Air Assault companies continued eastward toward the jointly manned checkpoint at Combat Post 76 and then swung northward through Hooterville.

Capt Bob Funk's Charlie Battery, 10th Marine Regiment, had been fairly innocent bystanders in the widening circle of violence engulfing the adjacent Alpha Company position. Located on a hill several hundred meters to the west of Alpha Company, Charlie Battery Marines had seen and heard small-arms fire and had even counted 106mm recoilless rifle rounds as they whizzed overhead on their way to the nearby LAF training camp. A few small-arms rounds nicked tents and five-ton trucks within the battery's hilltop compound, but damage was negligible and no one was hit.

At 0730, the Charlie Battery exec took it upon himself to order the guns manned and prepared to fire. The level of small-arms fire steadily increased.

The fire through the Alpha Company sector suddenly intensified at about 0800. All hands who were not already underground headed to the bunkers and trenches, where they stayed for about an hour. Then corporals and sergeants drifted into the open to carry out their duties. Soon, most of the troops simply left their bunkers to make head calls, get food, or do the things they wanted to do.

Captain Roy and 1stLt Andy May, the temporary company exec, drew the particular attention of one militia sniper as they went about their business at the isolated company CP. Beginning at about 0800, one or the other drew fire every time he popped his head over the sandbag blast wall. The two tested their paranoia a few times and came away convinced the fire was meant especially for them. There was not a great deal of danger, for the sniper was on lower ground and had a tendency to fire high. There was no telling, however, if he might improve. The two victims shared some weighty advice ("Keep your head down"), then invective ("I can't believe this bastard"), and finally relief every time the terrible marksman missed.

Shooting at gunmen who were not actually firing their weapons was forbidden; all the Marines could do was watch as groups of three or four Moslem fighters walked with their personal weapons slung into buildings or bunkers fronting on Alpha Company's positions. Everyone knew that these men would fire on the company until they ran out of ammunition or grew bored. And everyone knew the militiamen would then sling their weapons and walk in plain view—unmolested by Marine gunfire—to a café (Café Daniel) or what was assumed to be their armory. It was not unusual for militiamen in the open to point their fingers at the Marines and shout, "Bang, bang" amid general group laughter. All the Marines could do in response was "flip them the bird," which simply didn't do the job.

As the intensity of the gunfire picked up at about 0900 in the face of 2d Platoon's continued response, 2dLt George Losey, the 1st Platoon leader, ordered all hands to take cover. Then he and his platoon sergeant, SSgt Alexander Ortega, split up to check the trenches and bunkers, agreeing to meet back at their own hooch, the middle of three sandbagged tents covering most of the platoon compound.

Second Lieutenant Losey had been the last of the Alpha Company officers to come aboard before the deployment. He was different from the other lieutenants in several respects. He was, at twenty-eight, a few years older. He had also accepted a commission in the Marine Corps following an enlisted hitch as an Army Ranger. He was a quiet, self-reliant man of deep religious convictions. The junior lieutenant, Losey had first commanded Weapons Platoon, then had been moved with Staff Sergeant Ortega to 1st Platoon, whose commander was filling in for the detached company executive officer. Of all the Alpha Company officers, George Losey was the best liked among the enlisted Marines. Though Losey was scrupulous in avoiding any but the routine fraternization that arises out of living with enlisted Marines in the field, his prior enlisted service seemed to afford him a special aptitude for dealing with their problems and concerns. He was a good leader whose soft-spoken orders were the law because the troops wanted them to be.

Capt Bob Funk left the Charlie Battery fire direction center at about 0830 to man a forward post from which he had a clear view of Hooterville, which was just down the hill on which the howitzers were emplaced. Funk watched, incredulous, as a militiaman stood up on top of a building in full view of the Marines manning the bunker and repeatedly fired RPGs into the street below.

Certain that the wild, undisciplined fire from Hooterville would eventually be aimed at the battery, Captain Funk phoned the BLT to request permission to return fire if any was aimed directly at him. He was awaiting a reply—it would be a long wait —when he and the three other men in his bunker were rattled by a mortar round that detonated 100 meters to their front, near Alpha Company's 2d Platoon.

Sgt Robert Galt, of Alpha Company's 2d Platoon, was engrossed in directing return rifle fire at presumed Shiite Amal gunmen in nearby Hooterville when, at about 0915, the first mortar round of the day impacted between his position and Charlie Battery. Galt, like everyone around him, pulled his head into his shoulders and muttered a term of relief once the shock had dissipated. A second round landed in the 400-meter-wide field that separated Smith's 2d Platoon from Losey's 1st Platoon. So did the third round, farther to the east and closer to 1st Platoon. It dawned on Galt that the 82mm rounds were being walked straight toward the neighboring platoon, but there was no time for anyone to get on the horn and voice a warning.

WO Charlie Rowe, the MAU assistant public affairs officer, was on the roof of the BLT, escorting Associated Press photographer Don Mell on a routine shoot. Their vantage point was the best available to the Marines manning the BIA; it offered virtually unrestricted vistas of the entire MAU compound and most of the surrounding Moslem hamlets. Only a few frames had been shot when the first mortar round impacted just north of the main runways—in the field between Charlie Battery and Alpha Company. While the wire service photographer coolly followed the action through his viewfinder, Gunner Rowe held his breath and watched the mortar rounds walk eastward across the field. Rowe had been an infantryman for nine years before being selected for warrant officer and, though unblooded, his years of training nagged a warning into the deepest recesses of his mind: Alpha Company was well and truly in "deep shit."

Moments before the first mortar round impacted near Charlie Battery, Cpl Bruce Dudley, of 1st Platoon, had ordered his squad from its tent and deployed the troops behind the waist-high sandbag wall that ringed the three platoon tents. After setting in his men, Dudley looked back in time to see the lieutenant and platoon sergeant enter their hooch. This struck Dudley as extremely odd because Losey had been explicit in his instructions that everyone get down behind the best cover available.

Dudley was just getting comfortable on the ground between

the blast wall and the command hooch when the third mortar round blew off in the open just the other side of the sandbags. That was only registering when the fourth round impacted right on top of the center tent.

Mortar rounds are equipped with extremely sensitive point detonators. The round that hit the 1st Platoon command tent exploded the instant its nose touched the taut canvas.

LCpl Joe Thorpe, a fire-team leader, was killing time playing chess with his squad leader when a huge *BOOM* erupted almost on top of him. HN Victor Oglesby's ears were ringing when he reflexively left his bunker and headed for a better-built structure nearby. He had not yet settled in when he heard Marines outside yelling, "Doc!" and "Corpsman up!"

Corporal Dudley emerged from a momentary blackout and felt a sharp stinging in his head and right arm. As his ears cleared from the blast, he heard other Marines complaining about their injuries. There was great confusion along the squad's line. Dudley quickly calmed down, carried out a body-function check on himself, found he was still intact, and reached to his belt for his first-aid packet. His first priority was patching the nicks in his head, which, though superficial, bled heavily. Another squad leader knelt down for a look-see and told Dudley that he had not been badly hurt, which was a relief. As soon as he had his head patched, Dudley decided to forgo treatment of his arm wound, which was fairly serious, in order to run around to the front of the striken tent.

When Doc Oglesby left his bunker, he found five bleeding Marines arrayed in the open. A quick pass through the group revealed that none of the wounds was life threatening. All of the injured were being helped by other Marines, who were patching wounds and muttering words of encouragement through their own profound fears. Oglesby was called into the command tent.

There were shouts outside Lance Corporal Thorpe's bunker, so he ran into the open, where he saw a small crowd standing by the command hooch. Thorpe stuck his head in and saw

George Losey and Alexander Ortega sitting up in their chairs. There was an awful smell of blood. Thorpe ran back to his fire team and ordered his troops to lock and load and, above all, stay under cover in the trench. That done, he returned to the command tent to help if he could.

Staff Sergeant Ortega had died instantly. He was sitting upright in a canvas chair, bleeding profusely from head and neck wounds. Doc Oglesby took just one quick look at the platoon sergeant, then turned his full attention to the platoon leader.

George Losey was still alive. He had also sustained numerous head wounds, a three-inch gash on his leg that was fully two inches deep, and a bloody nose. He was unconscious.

Corporal Dudley joined Doc Oglesby in lowering the officer gently to the ground for treatment. Losey was an extremely large man, a prodigious bodybuilder, so getting him safely to the ground was a monumental feat. Oglesby was checking the grievously injured man when someone suggested that aid be administered in a less-vulnerable setting. Oglesby, Dudley, and Lance Corporal Thorpe took it upon themselves to carry Losey from the tent to a nearby dirt berm, another prodigious feat, particularly in light of Dudley's untreated, bleeding arm wound.

Capt Paul Roy could just make out the mortar rounds hitting his 1st Platoon area; there was a pillar of dark gray smoke to mark each detonation. He knew Alpha Company had been hit by the indirect fire, but he could not quite bring himself to believe it. He asked his executive officer, 1stLt Andy May, to place a call and find out if there were casualties. Before May could respond, however, Roy saw through his binos that several people were being carried or helped across the open platoon area to a secure bunker.

Sgt Donald Williams, the 1st Platoon guide, came up on the tac net. Captain Roy and the others heard only the exec's end of the conversation: "Roger, I copy. Staff Sergeant Ortega dead, Lieutenant Losey seriously wounded."

Roy stared in disbelief, then called out his company corpsman, radioman, shotgun, and driver and headed for his jeep.

The crowded company commander's jeep bounced out of the command post and hit the dirt road at top speed. Mortar rounds were still impacting near 1st Platoon. As soon as the jeep left, Lieutenant May took it upon himself to call the BLT and request that several amtracs be sent to evacuate the wounded under fire.

Within minutes, Captain Roy strode into the 1st Platoon CP tent, where he found Staff Sergeant Ortega's body. After only a moment's hesitation, Roy headed for the platoon's aid bunker. The scene inside the bunker was utter chaos. First-aid kits, offered by shocked Marines who wanted to do something to help, kept arriving through the low entryway. The wounded were brought in, and fellow Marines treated their injuries while Doc Oglesby turned his full attention to stabilizing George Losey. Captain Roy's arrival imposed a sense of order that had thus far eluded the grieved gaggle of Marines that was 1st Platoon. The company corpsman joined Doc Oglesby in patching the wounded.

WO Charlie Rowe was staring in disbelief at the impact area from atop the BLT, trying to convince himself that Alpha Company had weathered the storm, when a column of three hogs rolled past the building and headed north up the perimeter road. There was no official word around the BLT yet, but Rowe knew beyond a doubt that there were injured out there. He hoped there were no dead.

George Losey was placed aboard the first amtrac and Corporal Dudley and the other injured 1st Platoon Marines went out aboard the second vehicle. By then, Staff Sergeant Ortega had been placed upon a stretcher and covered tightly with a blanket. He went in the third amtrac, escorted by several of his uninjured troops, who insisted upon providing an impromptu honor guard.

First Lieutenant Greg Balzer was sitting in the BLT just outside the combat operations center (COC) when he heard Captain Roy's cool, professional voice over the small tac-net loudspeaker: "One KIA, one WIA serious, and five WIA not critical."

An immediate hush descended over the general hubbub of activity within the confined, crowded work space. The flow of work missed barely a beat, but there was a palpable feeling, often discussed among members of the battalion staff, that there would be hell to pay if an American serviceman died in Lebanon. It seemed that now was the time to pay.

Scores of Marines turned out to meet the amtracs. Gunner Rowe had his heart in his mouth as he watched their progress. The first hog arrived and stretcher-bearers carried George Losey into the lobby of the BLT. Then the next hog disgorged the bandaged ambulatory wounded. Not great, but okay. Then, as Associated Press photographer Don Mell leaned over the parapet of the roof and snapped pictures as fast as he could, Gunner Rowe watched the blanket-covered stretcher bearing Alexander Ortega being carried into the lobby. He fought back tears and rage and, perhaps, allowed a stifled moan to escape. The dozen or so other Marines on the BLT roof were tense and quiet.

Lt Lawrence Wood, Marine Medium Helicopter Squadron (HMM) 162's six-foot-five Navy surgeon, did not want to be on the beach. He had joined the Navy simply because it offered him a medical residency in his specialty, ophthalmology. He had no idea why he had been selected to work with the Marines. Though Wood was normally based with the helo squadron aboard *Iwo Jima,* he had assented to do a two-week tour at the battalion aid station while the BLT 1/8 surgeon toured Greece with his wife. It had taken Wood some time to get used to life on the beach. The thing he liked least was using the open-air piss tubes and insubstantial heads. But he had done his best to fit in.

On Sunday afternoon, the enormously tall doctor had joined in a game of grab-ass basketball at the weekly cookout. He had finally allowed himself to relax, to get into the group high. Distant gunfire seemed like no big deal at first, but the noise grew in volume, and there was definitely more of it. If this made Lawrence Wood extremely nervous, the Condition I alarm nearly unhinged him: "I knew absolutely nothing about war." Being on the float with air-wingers for three months had done little to enlighten him.

Dr. Wood sweated through Sunday night and most of Monday, and was just getting his nerves under control when the first mortar rounds set him off again as he sprinted with his corpsman from their third-floor rooms to the basement aid station.

The name of the game in combat medicine is triage. The job of the doctor and his senior corpsmen in a mass-casualty situation is to stabilize and attempt to save the men with the best chances while passing the grievously injured to more-distant aid stations or setting them aside.

George Losey arrived at the BLT well beyond any help that the aid station's limited facilities could offer. All the BLT headquarters staffers who were free were standing on a balcony overlooking the atrium lobby of the BLT building to watch George Losey being prepared for transport. He was in such poor condition and the need for him to be flown to *Iwo Jima* was so apparent that he was treated right on the floor of the lobby.

Dr. Wood assigned a team of corpsmen to keep the brutally battered platoon leader alive and stable, and ordered him to be medevacked to *Iwo Jima* as soon as a bird could be brought in. As the onlookers gazed mutely at the scene below, George Losey was stripped of his clothing, checked for hidden wounds, and given a shot in the thigh to help fortify him against shock. While a pair of corpsmen forced Losey's jaws open with a screw

(Col R. B. Johnston)

LtCol Bob Johnston

(Col Thomas Stokes)

Col Tom Stokes

(Official Marine Corps Photo)

LEFT TO RIGHT: **Col Jim Mead, Col Tim Geraghty, and Gen Robert H. Barrow during turnover at the BIA in May 1983**

(Official Marine Corps Photo)

Gen Robert H. Barrow and other senior Marine officers inspect the U.S. Embassy building following the terrorist bombing of April 18, 1983.

LtCol Larry Gerlach *(left)* **and SgtMaj Frederick Douglass**

Showing the Flag: 24th MAU Marines foot patrol on tracks of Lebanese State Railroad in June 1983

(Official Marine Corps Photo by SSgt Robert E. Kline, USMC)

Showing the Flag: 24th MAU mobile patrol drives through Hooterville in mid-August 1983.

(Eric Hammel)

Capt Paul Roy

(Eric Hammel)

1stLt David Hough

(Rodney E. Cliff)

Aerial view of encampment of Alpha Company's 1st Platoon. 2dLt George Losey and SSgt Alexander Ortega were killed in the center of the three tents.

M-60 machine gun at CP 69. Post 1 can be seen atop building in left background. The gunner is LCpl Gordon Hickman.

Firefight at CP 69; standing with rifle, Cpl Rod Cliff; kneeling, with glasses, HM3 Mark Hacala

Searching for hostile targets at CP 69. LEFT TO RIGHT: **LCpl Edwin Douglas, 1stLt David Hough, Cpl Rod Cliff**

Capt Mike Ohler napping in the Library Building observation post

CP 35, June 1983

Dr. Gil Bigelow, the MSSG-24 senior dentist

**Sgt Steve Russell, Sergeant-of-the-Guard at the BLT
Headquarters on the morning of October 23, 1983**

device, Dr. Wood unwound the head bandage that Doc Oglesby had applied at the 1st Platoon bunker. Losey immediately stopped breathing, but a good punch in the chest administered by the surgeon got him going again. The corpsmen started an IV and carried him outside to the waiting helo.

If there had been any question among the onlookers as to what a Marine's mission or possible fate might be, it was eloquently answered during George Losey's brief stay at the BLT.

Alexander Ortega, who needed no help, was flown out with his barely breathing platoon leader.

The five other wounded Marines were checked, given supplementary treatment, and likewise flown to *Iwo Jima.*

After the amtracs left, HN Victor Oglesby returned to his bunker to replenish his medical kit. He thought of staying, but decided to hunker down with the main body of the platoon in a stronger bunker about thirty feet away. He drew heavy fire from Hooterville when he ventured into the open alone.

The indirect overhead fire and the direct small-arms fire continued in waves, rising and falling for no apparent reason and with no apparent purpose. No more Marines were hit.

First Lieutenant Brent Smith was at the 2d Platoon CP when word arrived from Captain Roy that Ortega was dead. Smith, who had been having the time of his life during the controlled shooting undertaken by his troops, said nothing for a few moments, then looked at his radioman, LCpl Ron Medeiros, and said in a low voice, "This shit's for real."

The amtracs carrying 1st Platoon's casualties to the BLT passed 2d Platoon just then, and they drew fire "big time" from the waiting militia fighters. Much of the fire had passed around the amtracs to strike 2d Platoon's positions. A pair of 2d Platoon lance corporals manning an isolated post found the limits of their nerves and discipline. Though they had no specific targets, the two agreed to fire into a gutted building fifty meters away

from which the incoming seemed to be originating. The militiamen across the way took the response to heart and really started
throwing rounds at 2d Platoon.

Most 2d Platoon Marines, whether designated shooters or
not, had long since chosen targets they wanted to fire at if
ordered or allowed to do so. When the two lance corporals
opened up and drew heavy return fire, everyone in 2d Platoon
who could bring a weapon to bear reached out for his prese-
lected target. The sense of accomplishment was considerably
enhanced when many of the troops saw one of the machine
gunners drop his target in the open. The Lebanese was not
killed and was quickly retrieved, but blood had been drawn.

There was no going back; Alpha Company's 2d Platoon was
"good to go" from that moment on.

Not coincidentally, the swaggering gunmen who had so often
appeared in the open throughout the day did not appear during
the late afternoon of August 29.

When Capt Bob Funk, of Charlie Battery, heard the first radio
reports of Staff Sergeant Ortega's death he knew beyond mere
certainty that the battery's six brand-new M-198 155mm howitzers would be fired for the first time in combat that very day. He
ran with his first sergeant from their forward bunker to the
battery exec's bunker and ordered the howitzers readied, then
switched on the BLT tac net, where he heard that George Losey
had died aboard the helo on the way to *Iwo Jima*.

First Lieutenants Andy May and Mark Singleton, at the
Alpha Company CP, had gone to work trying to locate the lethal mortar as soon as they heard of Staff Sergeant Ortega's
death. It was no easy task, for all they had to go on, barring a
really lucky break, was divining the approximate direction
from which the fire was coming. The tac net almost blew a fuse
because of the traffic from the other companies, which were
also searching for the mortar as well as artillery and rocket
emplacements that were dropping rounds throughout the BIA

complex. May and Singleton could not find the mortar, but they did agree on a probable grid for an obnoxious rocket battery and called it into the battalion COC. This was followed a few moments later by approximately the same grid from Charlie Company, which was occupying positions along the southern edge of the battalion sector. The Target Acquisition Battery shot its radar beam to fix the spot and called the COC with its set of ten-digit coordinates, which matched those from Alpha and Charlie companies.

As the brass was deliberating about what to do with the confirmed target grids, an 82mm mortar round impacted in a tree about fifteen meters to the left of the Alpha Company CP. Lieutenant Singleton took a solid hit in his right calf and two little slivers in his right thigh. His map had a hole blown in it and a handful of gravel scoured his teeth and tongue.

There was a moment of stunned silence, which Lieutenant May broke: "Mark, are you all right?"

"Well, I'll be damned," Singleton drawled in a stunned voice. "They got me." He had no idea what else to say until an attempt at movement brought an exquisite pain, like a red-hot poker, to the oozing gash in his calf. "Well, holy shit!"

May was trying to control Alpha Company, but he had time to ask, "Are you all right, Mark?"

"Yeah. I think so."

It is an axiom of military medicine that the injured man never be told the extent of his injuries. The Marine assigned to patch Singleton's leg blurted out, "Holy shit! Look at that hole in your leg, sir!"

Well, it did look pretty nasty. May chimed in, "Damn, that is pretty big." The tiny crowd that had gathered concurred.

All the wounded were gathered in the more secure of the two CP bunkers and patched. These included Lieutenant Singleton's radioman and scout-observer and a cook. Lieutenant May's helmet had taken a piece of shrapnel, which was deflected down through the back of his flak jacket, but he was untouched.

Much later, Maj Andy Davis, the battalion operations officer, called Charlie Battery with a fully confirmed target grid. As the battery fire direction officer plotted in the data, Captain Funk notified the gun line that "A fire mission is coming down." The gunners were really excited, though they became somewhat subdued when they received the order to fire six *illumination* rounds over an opposing rocket-battery position.

The fire mission was carefully calculated by Col Tim Geraghty to avoid heavy Moslem bloodshed—and retribution—if possible. The MAU commander reasoned that a warning in the form of a precisely plotted six-tube salvo of illume would provide a clear message to the Moslem (probably Druse) gunners that the Marines could fend for themselves but chose not to kill many of them. Besides, plenty of high-explosive (HE) ordnance was on hand if the benevolence of the response was not divined.

The illume burst directly over the target, about 3,000 meters to the south, near Khalde, but the shelling of the BIA continued. Word reached Charlie Battery that it was to fire a full six-gun salvo once again. The load was to be shell HE.

When the battery exec advised the gun line that shell HE was to be fired, the cannoneers erupted in rebel yells, cheers, catcalls, and whistles. Sgt Craig Waterhouse, the Gun 6 section chief, hurriedly scrawled a message across his HE round just before turning it over to his loader for delivery: "Payback is a motherfucker."

The guns were fired at 1155. The target was the same.

On the little hummock supporting Alpha Company's CP, Lieutenant Singleton stood up and shook his fist as the salvo impacted. "Motherfuckers," Singleton yelled, "this is for George Losey." The others punctuated the epitaph with a solid "Oorah" Devildog grunt.

Charlie Battery came up on the net and asked Lieutenant

Singleton if he had observed the fires. "Roger. Target destroyed. Over."

"Target destroyed," the battery talker confirmed in an even, professional voice.

"Good shooting. Pass that to the gun line."

The second batch of Alpha Company wounded caught Dr. Wood on a roll, on full automatic. He quickly assessed their injuries, ordered treatment, and stood back to allow his corpsmen to work while he supervised.

When the aid station had been cleared, Dr. Wood was simply staggered by his coolness and aptitude. And mightily relieved to hear that the liberty run to Greece, with the regular battalion surgeon aboard, was due back in the morning.

Three of the five Marines injured by the round that killed Losey and Ortega returned to duty within the week, as did the three enlisted Marines injured at the company CP. Two of the wounded were evacuated to the States. Mark Singleton spent two weeks away from Beirut, escorting George Losey's body home for burial.

On August 30 a disbelieving nation first heard the news as it was offered by the press and the explanations as they were offered by stunned Reagan administration spokespeople. The only thing that really frosted Alpha Company was news of its having been caught in a "crossfire" on August 29.

There was a full-blown war in The Root, and the MAU was part of it.

13

The strangest and, in its way, the most troubling Marine action
at the start of the generalized unrest throughout Moslem Beirut
involved the guards at the American embassy provided by the
Battalion Landing Team (BLT).

Marines of BLT 1/8 were never particularly fond of the embassy guard assignment because, quite simply, usually about
seventy of them were isolated miles away from the main body
of the Marine Amphibious Unit (MAU) and stationed around
dispersed buildings that had already been the target of a serious
bombing. There were compensations, to be sure, but, on the
whole, the enlisted Marines on embassy duty would generally
have preferred to be elsewhere. Indeed, about the only thing
besides a direct order that gave the young enlisted Marines any
motivation to go willingly was the persistent rumor that there
was an opportunity to find "some action" with young Lebanese
ladies.

The paranoia that developed within the BLT embassy guard

detachment—a result of seeing daily the wrecked eight-story monument to the consequences of letting one's guard down— was at least in part justified. The embassy was not a fun nor a particularly safe place to be. The guard detachment had to be divided into shifts (six hours on and twelve hours off) and the shifts had to be dispersed over about 1,300 meters, from the Durafourd Building in the east to the British embassy and El Dorado apartments in the west. In addition, the East German embassy sat directly between the old American embassy and the Durafourd Building, an apartment complex now housing some embassy offices. No one expected trouble from the East Germans, but no one trusted them, either.

The terrain behind the buildings rises, which meant to Marines that their positions could be totally dominated by gunmen bent upon their destruction. There was always a certain amount of gunplay going on in the background, which both kept the Marines on their toes and lulled them into a false sense of security as long as it did not spill over in their direction. There was heavy vehicular traffic along the Corniche, from right beside the ruined American embassy to the British embassy, which was worrisome in a city where car bombs were detonated daily.

The greatest perceived threat lay in the 600-yard stretch between the two embassies, where stood the campus of the simmering American University in Beirut. If there is civil unrest loose in the capital of a Third World nation, leave it to students to become involved.

The American dean of the American University walked a fine line between Moslem and Christian sensibilities, and it was in the cards that he should slip once in awhile. Where such gaffes would produce harmless high jinks in most places, the form of retribution in Beirut was certain to be literally explosive. Only two weeks into BLT 1/8's deployment, Marines later learned, the dean had inadvertently taken sides with Christian students following a campus demonstration.

Corporal Scott Lockley, of Alpha Company, was in charge at

the post nearest the university. He was just accepting a bottle of fruit juice from a student when a terrific blast went off nearby. As the dust settled, so did the juice—all over Lockley and everyone around him.

First Lieutenant Pete Ferraro and SSgt Manasamua Fiame of Alpha Company's 3d Platoon were inspecting a guard post in front of the British embassy, wherein worked American embassy staffers, when the earsplitting explosion reverberated off the nearby high-rise buildings. Ferraro naturally assumed that one of his posts had been hit, and he and Staff Sergeant Fiame rushed to the nearest door. Ferraro, a bodybuilder, was extremely wide at the shoulders and fairly short of stature. So was Staff Sergeant Fiame. The two ran to the doorway and collided. Neither could get past the other. They ran in place for long seconds until the platoon leader ordered a truce and proceeded through first.

An investigation revealed that a disgruntled student, presumably a Moslem, had vented his frustrations by detonating a stick of dynamite beneath the dean's car, which was parked in the lot adjacent to Corporal Lockley's post. Fortunately, no one was hurt, but the dean needed new wheels.

When Alpha Company was relieved by Charlie Company at its original position at the southern end of the Beirut International Airport (BIA) compound, the Alpha Company embassy detachment was replaced by a similar Charlie Company group under the command of the Charlie Company exec, 1stLt Jerry Walsh.

In conjunction with Druse and Shiite attempts to separate the MAU from collocated Lebanese Armed Forces (LAF) units manning installations around the BIA, other Druse and Shiite forces were moving against the LAF throughout greater Beirut. One such Druse Progressive Socialist Party unit was commanded by Saleh, who in April had voluntarily helped secure the American embassy grounds in the wake of the bombing. Since then, Saleh had been on excellent terms with the embassy staff and had, in fact, provided assistance and substantial information during the intervening months.

On Tuesday, August 30, Saleh arrived at the guard post in front of the American embassy building and asked to speak with Chargé d'Affaires Robert Pugh, a former Marine captain. Lieutenant Walsh, who was called to the guard shack, heard Saleh's cordial-sounding request and called Bob Pugh to the gate.

Saleh was quite simply on an errand of mercy. He had been ordered to attack the LAF unit bivouacked near the Cadmos Hotel, a building several hundred yards from the embassy that housed about seventy U.S. Army Special Forces trainers assigned to the LAF. Saleh saw no reason to involve the American "Marines," as he called the Green Berets, and asked that Pugh remove them from the hotel.

Pugh was nonplussed by the request and needed time to brief his superiors. He asked Saleh to be patient, and Saleh agreed. The two had worked together before, trusted one another, and conducted themselves in a cordial, even friendly, manner.

Within moments of Saleh's departure from the main embassy gate, a troop-carrying helicopter with LAF markings landed right in front of the bombed-out embassy building and let out a squad of LAF air-assault riflemen. The air-assault troopers briefly opened fire on suspected Druse emplacements in the old American embassy building with rifles and a machine gun, and then marched off in the direction of the Cadmos Hotel, near the beach.

Saleh was back a short time later, and he was extremely angry. He had not seen the gunplay, but he had seen the helo land and armed men march off to reinforce the detachment guarding the Cadmos. He naturally assumed that Pugh had issued an alert and called in an American helo and American reinforcements. Saleh told Pugh that he felt betrayed and then threatened to kill everyone at the Cadmos in the course of a direct assault. He said he would be back soon to receive Pugh's answer, then departed in a huff.

Pugh knew that the Green Berets were virtually unarmed, a normal state for training advisers in a host country. He also felt responsible for the escalating misunderstanding, even if only because he was unable to calm the raging Druse officer. Jerry Walsh, who had seen all and heard all, quietly ordered his guard contingent to prepare for a fight and recommended that Pugh and all other civilians get indoors and under cover.

As soon as Saleh left, Pugh was on the phone to his State Department superiors and Lieutenant Walsh called Battalion.

Two hours crept by, then Saleh returned. He was still quite angry and issued a peremptory demand that the "Marines" leave the Cadmos since his direct assault on the place was imminent. He made it clear that he did not want to hurt Americans but that he was willing to do so if that's what it came to.

Bob Pugh stood his ground. He and Al Bigler, the State Department–appointed regional security officer, tried to explain to Saleh that the government of Lebanon was an ally of the United States and that the policy of the United States was to assist and support the LAF under all circumstances. The conversation became extremely heated and Saleh again proclaimed that he had an objective to seize and he would do so even if American blood had to be spilled.

It was then about 1530. No sooner was this threat enunciated than two gray-painted American ships appeared on the horizon. The *thud-thud-thud* of high-speed rotary-wing aircraft caused everyone to look up. The MAU's two Cobra helicopter gunships were hovering just off the water about 400 meters from the Cadmos. Their multibarrel 20mm cannon and Zuni rockets were aimed in the direction of the hotel.

Pugh never missed a beat. He pointed to the warships—two lightly armed Mediterranean Amphibious Ready Group (MARG) transports—and the Cobras, and asked Saleh what he intended to do against this array.

The Cobras remained on station for only about five minutes, just enough time to back Pugh's rhetorical question. One was hit by unobserved gunmen and both flew off to land on one of the ships. This diminished their usefulness and, indeed, might have given the impression that they had been *driven* off, but the threat of a massive retaliation was implicit. Saleh had no idea how many Marines there were aboard the two warships. In fact, neither did the embassy staff nor Jerry Walsh.

Saleh reached a decision. After a few more rounds of heated conversation, he agreed to give Pugh just one chance to evacuate all the Americans from the Cadmos. He would personally guarantee the safe passage of a vehicle convoy from the embassy to the Cadmos and back.

It was by then quite late. Indeed, it took until after sunset to assemble a small fleet of cars and utility vehicles with barely sufficient space for the sixty-plus Green Berets trapped at the Cadmos. The column set off through city streets and the Marines and embassy staffers held their breaths.

Soon after the column reached the Cadmos, the night air was split by the sound of artillery fire. Air bursts erupted over the streets between the Cadmos and the embassy, and Jerry Walsh ordered his troops to prepare to repel boarders. Within moments, however, it was determined that the artillery was being fired by the LAF, whose leaders apparently wanted to give the Americans reason to stay at the Cadmos. The reasoning: Saleh would bellow and threaten, but he would not attack the Cadmos as long as there were Americans trapped there. The air bursts, which drove the residents indoors were more dangerous to vehicular traffic and pedestrians than they were to buildings, so the risk of killing or maiming housebound Lebanese was minimal and, in Moslem West Beirut, acceptable.

The rescue column drove back through the artillery fire, but the result was less than anticipated by Bob Pugh, Al Bigler, Jerry Walsh, and Saleh. To the extreme chagrin of all, less than half the Green Berets billeted at the Cadmos were in the vehicles. Though there had been sufficient room, barely, for all the Special Forces trainers, the first contingent had opted to carry out its gear and, to the amazement and ire of the Marines, their personal effects and souvenirs—including a man-sized teddy bear that took up one whole seat.

The LAF artillery fire and Saleh's aggrieved impatience prevented the convoy from returning to pick up the remainder of the Green Berets and their junk.

As soon as the rescued Green Berets were moved inside the ring of armed Marines, Lieutenant Walsh spoke to Capt Walt Wint, the battalion intelligence officer, with whom he had been in direct contact from the moment Saleh first approached the embassy. Over the next twenty or thirty minutes, Walsh was patiently questioned about every conceivable bit of information he had regarding the layout of the area between the embassy and the Cadmos, the beach and the Cadmos, the strength and disposition of Saleh's militia, the strength and disposition of the LAF, Pugh's attitude, Saleh's attitude—everything the BLT staff would require to mount a relief. As Wint completed his questioning, LtCol Larry Gerlach came up on the net and said in a reassuring tone, "We will help you."

The scheduled August liberty run had carried about 150 Marines and Navy medical personnel to Greece for a two-week vacation. Great fun was had by all, particularly a few men whose wives and families were able to fly from the United States to join them.

The run back to Beirut had been, in a word, uninteresting. But the arrival of the liberty ship on August 29 was, in another word, unusual, for Green Beach (the new name for Black Beach) and the BIA were under intermittent artillery, rocket, and mortar fire, some of which reached out toward the slowly circling MARG. It was decided that the liberty detail would have to remain aboard until a safe landing by air or landing craft (LCU) could be accomplished. The wait went well into August 30, for the intermittent shelling continued.

The transport was joined by another MARG ship in midafternoon and sent around the nose of Beirut to stand off the embassy and, as it turned out, the Cadmos Hotel. The few Marine infantry officers aboard the transport were sketchily briefed by the ship's captain.

The senior Marines were Capt Paul Hein, the battalion headquarters commandant; 1stLt Chuck Dallachie, the battalion legal officer; and 1stLt Miles Burdine, the Bravo Company exec, who had seen his six-week-old daughter for the first time in Greece. Dr. John Hudson, the battalion surgeon, and Lt(jg) Danny Wheeler, the battalion chaplain, were also on hand.

Soon after the Cobras returned from their threat-run to the beach, the ship's captain called the Marine officers to the wardroom. He announced that the Marines would be equipped from the ship's armory with M-14 rifles, flak jackets, and helmets, divided into several landing parties, and sent to the beach after dark to rescue the American occupants of the Cadmos Hotel.

The groan that passed from the lips of the Marine officers was barely audible, but it was heartfelt. Lieutenant Dallachie heard the captain out with the impression he was having his leg pulled. Captain Hein asked for confirmation, and the captain of the ship obligingly radioed his superior, the admiral commanding the amphibious squadron of which MARG 3-83 was a part. The response requested that the Marines submit a detailed plan of action, which worried the Marines a great deal.

The incredulous officers added up their assets. In the first place, the offer by the ship's captain to arm the Marines with M-14 rifles was worrisome. The M-14 had been purged from Marine Corps stocks a full decade before Captain Hein, the oldest of the officers, had entered the Corps. Three of the staff NCOs aboard had been trained with M-14s, so it became obvious that the hundred-odd Marines would be divided into three groups, each staffed by an NCO who could fire an M-14.

The Navy also proffered old-style flak jackets, which are hot as well as cumbersome, and gray-painted steel helmets, the like of which Marines had scorned years before in favor of lighter plastic-lined metal pots; wearing a steel helmet in action takes getting used to. There were no automatic weapons except for a few M-14s which could be fired on automatic. Indeed, as far as the Marines were concerned, there was no gear worth taking into a fight. There were no usable maps aboard, and the only intelligence matter was what Captain Wint relayed from Lieutenant Walsh. A request to send a party to the BIA to collect adequate weapons and "deuce gear" (packs, ammo belts, etc.) was denied through Navy channels on the same grounds as the liberty party's return had been denied: too dangerous. The only remotely positive news was that the Marines would be augmented by a Navy SEAL team. The members of this highly skilled air-amphibious commando unit were about as thrilled with their proffered immolation as were the Marines.

It was decided that Lieutenant Dallachie would land his team first to establish a base of fire at the seawall separating the four-lane Corniche from the beach. Captain Hein and Lieutenant Burdine would command the main body, which would advance quickly to the Cadmos and guide the Green Berets to the beach. A mobile reaction team under SSgt Charlie Garcia, of Bravo Company, would remain at the seawall with Dallachie for use as required. The LCUs would drop the Marines and then circle offshore to provide .50-caliber-machine-gun support if needed, though the state of communications was so basic that Dallachie decided to forgo the support unless he was actually being overrun. The LCUs would return to the beach to extract the Marines and, it was hoped, the Green Berets.

The plan was approved at several higher levels. Then all hands were assembled on deck and briefed. The unanimous reponse was mirth. None of the enlisted Marines believed the plan was real. In time, as preparations got off to a shaky start, the air of mixed merriment and incredulity was replaced by one of daring. It became an exercise in machismo, and certainly not of intellect, to prepare for what all agreed was a suicide mission. Several Marines stated, flat out, that they were not going. Peer pressure was applied and even these sane souls were sucked in.

The troops filed below to the landing-craft bay and began climbing aboard their LCUs. All hands were orderly and subdued. At the last minute, the landing was canceled.

Saleh had decided to postpone his attack indefinitely. The Green Berets would remain hostage at the Cadmos until the situation resolved itself days later. The liberty party was flown ashore the next morning. While several groups had to dismount under fire from moving helos, the volume of complaints was minimal.

Only upon the arrival of the liberty party at the BIA did LtCol Larry Gerlach and his BLT staff learn that their troops had been readied for the aborted landing.

14

As nearly as any of the American servicemen who were directly involved could tell, the August 28 fighting in and around Beirut was precipitated by the desecration of a Maronite Christian church with posters depicting the Ayatollah Khomeini. This seemed a clear enough message that the Shiite Amal was throwing down the gauntlet. So Phalange militiamen riposted by plastering a mosque in Hooterville with posters depicting the martyred president-elect and Phalange chieftain, Bashir Gemayel. Later, the story went, two Shiite youths were caught with posters by several Phalange gunmen, who shot the teenagers and left them to the tender mercies of a Christian Lebanese Armed Forces (LAF) officer. The officer did not chase off the Phalange gunmen, but he did kick and punch the two injured Moslems.

These incidents are reputed to have taken place on the morning of August 28, a Sunday. If they really did occur, it is understandable that both the Christians near Hooterville and the Shiite Moslems in Hooterville were deeply insulted. Given the hair-trigger temper of the times, it is no wonder that both factions vented their dismay in the streets. The LAF was called in to quell the disturbances. That placed the Amal militia in direct confrontation with the LAF.

The American servicemen most threatened by the disturbances in Hooterville were serving at and near the isolated Lebanese University: Capt Monte Hoover's Bravo Company, 8th Marines.

The main body of Bravo Company was exercising its usual Sunday prerogatives, a cookout and some intramural games in the lower levels of the library building. The barbecue was in full swing when news arrived via the company tac net that a Bravo Company patrol was being menaced in the ville, caught between Amal fighters and LAF soldiers who were exchanging fire. It appeared that all the Marines in the street had hit the deck.

The atmosphere was strained to the limit as everyone at the library clamored to hear the news as it arrived. An Amal officer moved into the open and asked the Marine patrol leader to leave the area before any of his troops was injured. The young Marine NCO gladly obliged; the patrol eased out of the area and returned to the university as the crescendo of gunfire throughout Hooterville escalated. As the afternoon wore on, and more and more stray rounds crackled across the university compound, Bravo Company moved to an elevated state of alert.

Adhering to a pattern established early in the Lebanese venture, the main body of Bravo Company remained at or adjacent to the university library building. However, one rifle platoon reinforced by machine-gun squads from the company Weapons Platoon was divided up to man three isolated positions east of the main company area. On August 28, 2dLt Dave Hough's 2d Platoon was rounding out what the troops thought would be an eight-day outpost assignment. Second Squad was in the hills, at Yardze, guarding a radio intelligence installation manned by a detachment of 2d Marine Radio Battalion. Third Squad was at Checkpoint 35 (CP 35), a jointly manned post in a built-up area of Hooterville. The reinforced 1st Squad was at CP 69, another jointly manned post two kilometers southwest of the library. CP 69 was considered the most vulnerable of the Bravo Company positions, so 1st Squad was overseen by Lieutenant Hough.

Combat Posts 69, 35, and 76, to the southwest, had been established months before by another Marine amphibious unit (MAU) to deter the Israelis from firing into Hooterville and Beirut International Airport (BIA). The posts were manned by LAF contingents; Marines manned sandbagged positions near the LAF posts in order to demonstrate the will of American diplomacy and not necessarily to support or aid the LAF directly.

Second Platoon had rotated out from the library on August 21 and was due to be relieved on August 29. The troops began packing on Sunday and were looking forward to showers, hot food, and the reasonable comfort they would find at the university.

The LAF sergeant commanding the post adjacent to CP 69 kept telling Lieutenant Hough that the Moslem militias were preparing to mount attacks to sweep the combat posts. This was chilling news because, whatever else the failings of the LAF as a viable military force, its field intelligence was generally accurate.

CP 69—a sandbagged compound just eighty meters by forty meters in size—was in the open about 150 meters south of the edge of Hooterville and close enough to the areas vacated by the Israelis during the night of August 27–28 for Lieutenant Hough to observe groups of nattily dressed gunmen as they moved from the Shouf to the cultivated areas and townships around his end of Hooterville. The Israelis swept the edge of Khalde very early in the morning of August 28 and prodded the militias back into the hills, but the militias soon returned. All this was duly reported, and Lieutenant Hough and his splintered platoon were told to sit tight.

The first seven bullets arrived from the northeast and hit in and around the LAF portion of CP 69 at about 1400 hours, August 28. When a round *cracked* over the Marine compound, LCpl Gordon Hickman, a machine gunner, refused to believe that he was being targeted by hostile fire; he insisted for some minutes that the *crack* and *thonk* of bullets were merely the fluttering of birds' wings. He held to this line for only a minute longer, until a "bird" nearly tore off his ear.

The troops were not so much astonished by the fire—they had been hearing stray rounds crack overhead all week—than nonplussed by the crystal-clear realization that it was intended for them.

The gunfire in nearby Hooterville intensified steadily over the next two hours. The most ominous sign came at 1600 hours, when civilian workers fled from sight across a field in which, minutes earlier, they had been peacefully harvesting mint leaves. The first Amal machine gun opened fire at 1610. Then CP 69 became the target of rocket-propelled grenades (RPGs), mortars, and 106mm recoilless rifles. Most of the fire, however, came from four or five AK-47s on full automatic.

Lieutenant Hough was soon beset by requests from his troops to be allowed to return fire. A committed professional officer with prior enlisted service, Hough was considered one of the battalion's outstanding junior lieutenants. He was not about to engage a Lebanese civilian force without clear authority from his superiors. On the other hand, the troops were certain that once ordered or authorized to engage the opposing force, Dave Hough would do his duty and more. The extremely popular lieutenant, a tall, blond twenty-six-year-old, had graduated from the Army Ranger School just before leaving North Carolina and

149

was one of the most motivated troop leaders in this first-rate battalion.

Hough's radioman, LCpl Jeffrey (JJ) Firda, was minding his own business, just standing radio watch, when a round clipped off the end of his radio's antenna. Firda knew the Rules of Engagement (ROE) by heart and had no trouble identifying the round that clipped his antenna as "direct fire," to which he could respond. He called the company command post (CP) to say he had taken direct fire and was told if this was so—and if the squad had clear targets—they should "Fire 'em up." Lance Corporal Firda left his bunker to give Lieutenant Hough the message. Hough asked Firda to contact Captain Hoover and confirm the instruction. Firda returned to his bunker and spoke to the company commander's radioman, heard the response, rogered the information, and went to tell Hough the fire could be returned subject to the ROE.

The biggest impediment to dominating effectively and, thus, controlling incoming with return fire was a scarcity of small arms ammunition. There had been no real demand for such ammunition during the relatively tranquil Marine deployments of the preceding year. There were only 175 rounds per man for the M-16s. Hough and Sgt Bob Davis, the platoon guide, carefully selected targets and had designated riflemen prepare to shoot at the walls of the buildings from which most of the fire was coming. It was Hough's intention to demonstrate to the opposing gunmen that he could suppress their fire if he had to.

The lieutenant demanded the honor of being the first to fight. He aimed in on the wall beside an Amal gunman, squeezed the trigger of his M-16, and placed his round exactly where he wanted it. Then Hough turned the job over to his subordinates, who aimed and fired as directed by Lieutenant Hough and Sergeant Davis. The message, however, did not get through. Hough authorized his riflemen to take more direct action.

Sgt Bob Davis, a superb marksman, planted rounds from his

M-16 with telling effect. Though even Davis could not be certain that he was actually drawing blood, it was generally agreed that he and the other marksmen were quelling the incoming fire from the windows and doorways they were targeting.

Cpl Rod Cliff, the machine-gun-squad leader at CP 69, had only one of his two M-60 teams at the post—the other was at CP 35—but he was sure he could use it to excellent effect. He offered to fire at a target he could easily reach from atop the machine-gun bunker at the northeast corner of the post. Lieutenant Hough told him to go ahead.

The brand-new gun was set up atop the bunker, in full view of the Moslem snipers, and Lance Corporal Hickman squeezed off what he intended to be a marking burst. Only two rounds flew from the muzzle, then the gun jammed. Hickman, Cliff, and Hough, all standing in a row, groaned. Hickman yanked back the bolt and extracted the jam, then fired again. One round only flew from the gun. This jam was quickly cleared and the sights were again set on the target. The gunner squeezed the trigger. One round erupted. The frustrated machine gunners went to work, stripping the weapon, looking for the cause of the problem. Onlooking Marines felt sorely abused and considerably more vulnerable than they had before the M-60 went into action. As it turned out, the gun had been equipped with a defective bolt and only single rounds could be fired, which was not worth the effort. The nearest replacement bolt was at the university, beyond reach.

For all the concern about ammunition shortages and the care exerted in selecting targets to suppress, the Marines knew they had to maintain a level of fire sufficient to tell the attackers that CP 69 could be adequately defended. It was a precarious balance between two opposing kinds of prudence. The worst realization was that the intense fire would prevent the landing of a helo with ammunition and reinforcements.

Another shock arrived at about 1830, about four hours after the Marines at CP 69 began returning fire. Lieutenant Hough could not imagine why Captain Hoover had not called in for a situation report, so he called the company CP and asked to speak to the captain. After Dave Hough had laid it all out for the skipper, there was a strained silence, then the choked Hoosier vowels of the usually unflappable captain erupted on the net. "You *what!* You're doing *what* to them? How long have you been shooting? How many rounds have you expended?"

This was Dave Hough's first indication that he did not, in fact, have clearance to return fire. He was certain he would be court-martialed if he survived the fight.

As soon as Hough got his worried company commander off the line, he stalked over to LCpl JJ Firda and confronted him with the bad news. Firda claimed total innocence, explaining that he had received positive intructions to suppress the militia fire from Captain Hoover's radioman. Of course, Firda averred, he had no way of knowing whether the company commander's radioman was actually speaking on behalf of the company commander.

The gunfire stopped at dark. When Dave Hough was certain it was safe to stand erect, he pulled his penknife from his pocket and pried several smashed slugs from trees in his compound. He was sure he would need them for evidence at his trial.

The reinforced 3d Squad of Bravo Company's 2d Platoon had had a ringside seat to the excitement in and about Hooterville on August 28. Combat Post 35 was a sandbagged two-story building facing directly down a narrow alley in the middle of a crowded Shiite neighborhood in Hooterville. A similarly vulnerable LAF post was located a few yards away, on the same narrow street.

The Marines tensely listened to gunfire during the night of August 28 and heard tales the next morning of confrontations between Shiite Amal fighters and Phalange and LAF units throughout the eastern suburbs.

At first light, a cowboy on the street opened fire at the wall of the building, nearly hitting several Marines on the roof. The 2d Platoon sergeant ordered all hands to get behind the concrete wall on the second deck and the sandbagged blast walls on the roof as he sat in the rooftop radio bunker to provide the company combat operations center with a running commentary.

Unknown to the platoon sergeant, the 3d Squad leader, Cpl Mike Clepper, using the platoon sergeant's authority to check on the troops, had placed himself in the thick of the incoming. It was the platoon sergeant's understanding that Clepper and the M-60 team leader, LCpl Guy Fortier, were preventing the troops from returning fire until Captain Hoover authorized them to do so. On the contrary, Clepper and Fortier were actually telling the men to "take out anybody who points a weapon in our direction."

There was so much noise from the incoming, that the platoon sergeant had no inkling his Marines were firing back. When authorization finally arrived by radio hours later, the gunner manning the rooftop M-60 (which had not yet fired) spotted a gunman about 120 meters down the alley and cut loose. The Lebanese man fell through a spray of blood and bone and lay still. The M-60 gunner held his fire as rescuers bravely dragged the fallen gunman around the corner. All hands agreed that the Amal warrior was probably dead. Upon reporting the incident to the Company CP, the platoon sergeant was ordered to hold his fire.

The next confirmation these Marines had that they were being drawn into the rising tempo of violence arrived in the form of fifteen armed Amal fighters who stood at the end of the alley for a few moments before one raised a bullhorn and asked the Marines to leave peacefully, since the Amal had no quarrel with Americans. The fifteen then offered to leave while the Marines conversed with higher headquarters. There was, of course, no question but that Corporal Clepper's reinforced squad would remain at CP 35.

A good deal of strangeness ensued.

Tantalizing targets—teenagers carrying RPGs and AK-47s—kept flitting back and forth across the head of the narrow alley. It was assumed by all that the Lebanese were both daring the Marines to fire and reconnoitering the Marine building, trying to locate firing positions and heavy weapons with which they and their fellows might have to contend.

When Amal fighters were not indiscriminately shooting at CP 35, they were waving at the Marines there. Women were sent into the streets to reconnoiter the Marine and LAF positions. The most blatant of the scouts was a heavyset middle-aged woman—or a large man dressed in a woman's clothing—who made trip after trip across the end of the alley. One of the Marine riflemen reached the end of his tether late in the afternoon and dropped her in her tracks with one M-16 round. An Amal gunman who was duck-walking on the woman's ample hidden side scuttled for a nearby building when his cover fell to the street.

Next, a small boy appeared at the end of the alley and cut loose with an RPG that struck the building in which the neighboring LAF squad was holed up. That did it: every time anyone appeared at the head of the alley, the Marines and LAF soldiers opened fire. Four more RPGs were fired, but all were high. The sixth RPG detonated in the air right over the Marine position, but no one was hurt. And the seventh impacted in a tree right beside the Marine-held building, which was amply sprayed with shrapnel. The squad grenadier popped an M-203 round into the intersection and the nonsense with the RPGs ended.

Sporadic fire struck CP 35 throughout the remainder of the day, but the Amal made no serious attempt to overrun the building. It was feared, however, that they might try to do so at any time.

The day's action ended at CP 35 when a pair of machine guns opened up at dusk from the end of the alley. Lance Corporal Fortier's M-60 team suppressed that fire, perhaps injuring or killing the Amal gunners.

When the Marine platoon sergeant moved among the troops that night, he learned that most had fired twenty or more times during the day, and that the squad's two grenadiers had each expended ten M-203 rounds, all they had. He was surprised, hurt, and furious, and he took Corporal Clepper to task for the unauthorized firing. Clepper and Lance Corporal Fortier explained that the M-203s had been fired to eliminate an Amal RPG position. This calmed the platoon sergeant somewhat. (Months later, he saw that Clepper and Fortier were decorated for taking the initiative.)

The tiny Marine garrison at CP 69 began taking fire from both north and south at about 0430, August 29. The fact that fire was arriving from the Druse-controlled areas to the south was ominous, for it marked a serious escalation in what had appeared only hours earlier to be the settlement of Shiite-Christian and Shiite-LAF disputes. The Druse were then the most politically active of the Moslem factions within and around Beirut, and their participation in the fighting was seen as being primarily of a political nature.

The gunfire continued until 0700, then abruptly stopped. An Amal officer escorted by several gunmen walked right up to CP 69 and asked to see the commander. Dave Hough obliged. Astounded Marines heard the Shiite leader ask Hough why he was shooting at buildings in Hooterville. Hough tried to remain calm, but he was really put off by the implied disclaimer and told the Amal officer exactly why his troops were firing. The Shiite started waving his arms: "We not shoot. You shoot." So Hough offered an obvious deal, "Well, if you don't shoot, we won't shoot." To which the Amal officer replied, "Good. We not shoot." That settled, the Amal gunmen walked back to Hooterville.

A pair of soldierly and battle-hardened Druse lieutenants arrived from positions south of the Marine compound at 0710. These two demanded that Hough surrender and turn over all his weapons by 0730 or face annihilation in a direct assault. Hough summarily ordered the Druse to leave, then sent word to the adjacent LAF squad that he had no intention of abandoning his compound. The LAF sergeant commanding the post voiced a desire to leave because "there are too many of them." Hough told the man that he would call Captain Hoover and "get the big guns to fire if there is any more trouble," that all the Amal and Druse fighters would be killed. Only then did the LAF sergeant tell Lieutenant Hough that he would remain.

The deadline came and went. Minutes dragged by, the pressure built. Nothing ever came off on time in Lebanon, but the promised assault was near enough. Gunfire erupted from the south and east at 0745 and rapidly built up all around the tiny sandbagged perimeter as Shiites joined in with machine guns and RPGs. Soon Druse artillery rounds and 122mm rockets were impacting in the fields adjacent to the Marine and LAF compounds. An incredible amount of choking, blinding dust was stirred up by the incessant detonations.

The Marines at CP 69 were in a pretty bad place. In addition to their meager supply of 5.56mm rifle ammunition, they had only ten M-203 rifle grenades, no hand grenades, and three LAAW antitank rockets.

The Lebanese, all members of Battalion 31, an "old army" unit of moderate repute, were doing just so-so. The battalion officers were Christians, but the squad leader and all the troops manning CP 69 were Moslems. Battalion 31 was not a particularly well-trained or well-equipped unit, and the Moslem riflemen were really undecided how they should react to gunfire put out by brother Moslems. One of the Lebanese riflemen voted with his feet, leaving the LAF compound as soon as he could get away. Fortunately, he neglected to take his German-designed G3 assault rifle, which Lieutenant Hough secured from the LAF squad leader. The G3 rifle was a major find because it could fire 7.62mm rounds meant for the defective M-60. HM3 Mark

Hacala was forbidden by law to aid combatants except as a medical practitioner, but he took it upon himself to unbelt the M-60 ammunition and load G3 magazines; he had as much at stake in the outcome as any man in the compound. Lieutenant Hough tried the G3 first, liked it, and kept it for himself.

The incoming went on and on and on into the afternoon.

The cavalry arrived in the form of three Marine helos—a Huey and a pair of Cobra gunships—that flew west to east along the foul waterway ("Shit River") separating the Marine and LAF compounds. The Huey passed low overhead, apparently to spot targets for the Cobras, then veered away sharply as it drew fire from the ground. The lead Cobra also took .50-caliber fire from a particularly troublesome Druse bunker about 200 meters south of the combat post. The pilot of the second Cobra, Capt John Kerr, passed directly over the bunker and reported in to *Iwo Jima,* which ordered him to clear out. Kerr, who later swore that he never heard the order, roared across the Marine compound at treetop height and stopped right over the center of the sandbagged perimeter.

There was a great flash and roar, and a stream of smoke shot out from beneath the Cobra. Dave Hough was certain that the Cobra had been hit and severely damaged until he saw that the trail of smoke was going away from the helo. Captain Kerr had fired one of his Zuni air-to-ground missiles at the hostile emplacement, waxing it, the gun, and the gun crew. Hundreds of Americans at the university and all across the BIA had tears of pride in their eyes. The helos circled and drew heavy fire from other Druse machine guns, which severely damaged Captain Kerr's Cobra. The helos skied out to *Iwo Jima,* where Kerr barely made it aboard.

Shortly after the helos left, the excited LAF sergeant reaffirmed his decision to remain at his post. Asked if he had called the Cobras, Hough lied and said he had. He was certain that Battalion had sent them in response to an earlier request for an 81mm-mortar fire mission against the very bunker Captain Kerr had blasted. It turned out that Kerr just happened to spot the target on his own and had decided on the spur of the moment to take it out because it was firing on him.

GySgt Danny Evans, the Bravo Company gunny, arrived at CP 69 at dusk with a jeep and a truck manned by volunteers. The minuscule convoy had driven from the university right into Hooterville, where it was intercepted by an Amal political functionary who escorted it to CP 69. The troops who had been manning the post were exuberant until it was learned that Evans had not brought one round of ammunition—either because he had misunderstood an earlier radio conversation with Lieutenant Hough or because it had been forgotten. The food and water were welcome, and the soda was especially appreciated even if warm. Corporal Cliff was delighted to receive a new bolt for his defective M-60, and everyone appreciated the attachment of a two-man Dragon antitank rocket team, albeit without launcher or missiles. In fact, the two Dragon gunners carried only seventy-five rounds of 5.56mm ammunition apiece, another severe disappointment.

Though Gunny Evans's convoy was escorted by the Amal political officer, the return trip was fraught with danger. No one shot at the vehicles, but the Marines were threatened by numerous gunmen as they barreled through the narrow streets of Hooterville.

Despite the loss of life within Alpha Company's lines, the plight of the tiny garrisons manning combat posts 69 and 35 were uppermost among the concerns of the MAU and BLT staffs. No Marine positions were as isolated or as vulnerable as the two Bravo Company combat posts. Col Tim Geraghty and LtCol Larry Gerlach spent a good deal of time working out a solution for the rescue of the combat post garrisons if the need arose: an armored force was kept manned and ready to thrust through the Moslem townships from the BIA. However, given the very ticklish political realities of the day, both senior Marines knew that the armored rescue force could be unleashed only as a last resort. If things became desperate, however, there was no way Geraghty and Gerlach were going to leave Marines "out there to be overrun."

On the morning of August 30, an LAF armored force comprising three armored personnel carriers (APCs) carrying infantry and supported by tanks, armored cars, and jeep-mounted 106mm recoilless rifles, staged into the university compound and then moved into Hooterville to relieve CP 35. Many Bravo Company Marines at the university assumed that the outbreak in the ville would be snuffed.

The few Marines manning CP 35 who dared to sleep were awakened early to the strains of .50-caliber fire hitting nearby Amal-occupied buildings. The LAF had brought their APCs into the street, sealed the Amal fighters in, and commenced to pour out an incredible volume of fire. The LAF gunners were really quite casual about it, calmly pausing to change overheated and worn barrels and reload depleted ammunition cans. Bricks and stucco and shards of concrete endangered human flesh as much as the half-inch bullets that splintered them.

BOOM!

All the firing immediately stopped as everyone turned to see what that was about. An LAF tank had rolled in and fired a 90mm round directly into a school building from which Amal snipers had continued to pepper CP 35. Eight 90mm rounds were fired in all, then the tank moved on. In its wake, however, some serious-looking LAF soldiers stalked up the street, kicking down doors and spraying M-16 rounds all over the place.

Several of the newly arrived LAF soldiers appeared at the door of the Marine post and asked for water. The Marines had expended about 40 percent of their ammunition, so they swapped several canteens of water for a can of 5.56mm rounds.

There was plenty of action on the fringes of the jointly manned post, but CP 35 was not threatened again that morning.

The Word was that better than sixty Amal fighters died during the LAF morning sweep through Hooterville. However, the armored assault galvanized Amal fighters in nearby neighborhoods, and they went to work to stop the progress of the LAF force.

As Marines at the library looked on, the three LAF APCs attacked between fifty and a hundred armed Amal men and women who were firing at the armored formation from along a narrow thoroughfare. To everyone's utter amazement, all the LAF soldiers manning the APCs dismounted and chased the militia fighters. Two of the abandoned APCs were destroyed and the third was remanned—by Amal warriors, who drove it off while lavishly spraying the vehicle's .50-caliber machine gun at its former owners.

The surviving LAF armor returned to the university with an ample contingent of injured LAF soldiers. The casualties were evacuated in short order, but the tanks, Panhards, and jeep-mounted 106mm recoilless rifles deployed within the university grounds. This brought down artillery fire from the Druse-held hills that dominated the Lebanese University and, indeed, all of Beirut. The fire the Marines at the university were taking at this point was undisputably fallout from the internecine struggle that was being waged by the Moslem militias against the LAF.

First Lieutenant Lee Marlow, the Bravo Company Weapons Platoon commander and supporting arms coordinator, was on the battalion tac net throughout the morning, relaying news of the LAF assault and the subsequent militia shelling from the company commander and observers on the library roof to the battalion combat operations center. Whenever a Marine was able positively to identify a hostile target, Marlow relayed Captain Hoover's request to return fire. Hoover, a man of unflappable goodwill and calm, started small, first requesting authority to use his company's three 60mm mortars. To this request, he received a negative. He next asked for support from the battalion's 81mm mortars. Another negative. Finally, Hoover asked for Charlie Battery's 155mm howitzers. The support was routinely denied. Bravo Company Marines wanted to know why Charlie Battery was not trying to take out the Druse artillery that was firing in their direction.

The answer was quite simple: neither the BLT nor the MAU had the authority to fire the 81s or 155s, nor even to direct Bravo Company to fire its own weapons in defense of the LAF, which is what most officers on the ground saw as a reasonable solution to the threatening gunfire all across the BIA. Quelling Druse and Shiite fire was not politically expedient.

Bravo Company Marines at the library were not motivated by anything like political convictions or by a desire to aid the LAF, nor even because, as Marines, they were up for a little shootout. They were being shot at, which, in their minds, constituted a sufficient grievance. The fire was low and, though no one was hit, it seemed to be intentional.

If the Marines could not return the militia fire, the LAF could, with several tanks, armored cars, and APCs staged in and around the university compound. Lieutenant Marlow was approached during a trip through the Moat—a concrete trench that surrounded the library—by a machine gunner, who complained about one particularly menacing sniper: "Sir, we have to do something about that fire before someone gets hurt."

Marlow agreed, but he knew he could do nothing. As he looked around, however, he saw an LAF tank commander sitting peacefully atop his tank, which was parked between the library and the next building. "Corporal, do you see that guy sitting on the tank over there?"

"Uh, yes, sir."

"Why don't you tell him about it?"

The corporal strode over to the tank, and Marlow returned to his office on the second floor of the library to reman his radio. His mind had long since drifted off the subject he had broached with the corporal in the Moat when he was literally felled by the loudest explosion he had ever heard. The LAF tank had tracked the sniper and fired one round. The report of the 90mm tank gun had been trapped between the concrete buildings. It lifted many Marines right off their feet and blew out several windows on that side of the library building and across the face of the adjacent university administration building. When he regained his feet, Lee Marlow looked out the window. Looking up from the open turret hatch was the broadly smiling Lebanese tank commander, his right thumb raised in salute. "No more sniper," he reported.

Some time later, one of the Marine snipers manning the library building's rooftop observation post watched an exchange between LAF infantrymen and the crew of a six-wheeled Panhard armored car. With more-than-useful advice from his comrades, the gunner swung his 90mm tube on the proffered target, a building overlooking CP 35. The round sailed clear across the Sidon Road—a "miss by a mile."

A knot of LAF officers surrounded the Panhard and screamed at the man in the turret, who was ordered to the ground and shown, by exaggerated gestures, where his target lay. He nodded his comprehension, climbed back into the turret, and relayed the gun. The next round sailed well across the Sidon Road and impacted about 100 meters to the right of the first round. The officers returned to the Panhard, the commander was again ordered to the ground, and there was again a great deal of yelling and arm waving. The third round was pretty much on line with the target but high. The frustrated LAF soldiers surrounding the Panhard cut loose with .50-caliber machine guns, RPGs, and rifles, and they obliterated the building. Whether or not the Amal snipers who were in the building at the start of the action had remained long enough to be killed is fairly moot.

August 30 at CP 69 dawned hot and clear. Snipers located all around the sandbagged compound opened fire at first light.

The gunfire, sporadic at first, quickly built up around CP 69. The Marines asked the LAF squad to provide support, but the

Battalion 31 Moslem riflemen were not inclined to kill brother Moslems this day. They put out hundreds upon hundreds of rounds but deliberately aimed high. At length, LCpl Edwin Douglas, the squad's M-203 grenadier, was asked if he thought he could hit a machine gun set up in an old shack about 150 meters to the northeast. Douglas had only ten rounds but said he would try the shot. Lieutenant Hough told him he had just one chance. Douglas estimated his range and angle of fire and, to his everlasting amazement, placed the first round through an open window, destroying the shack and the machine gun. Most of the onlookers cheered, but LCpl Gordon Hickman refused to be impressed. "Hell," Hickman sneered, "he just done his *job.*" Thereafter, any feat, no matter how spectacular, was met with an echo of Hickman's uncharitable professional assessment.

Heavy .50-caliber fire continued to menace CP 69 through the rest of the day.

Lieutenant Hough was on the tac net bright and early on the morning of Wednesday, August 31, requesting ammunition. He was told that it was too dangerous to send a helo, so he offered to lead a retrieval party if the Huey crew chief would just kick out a case of 5.56mm ammunition from any height anywhere near the post. The request was firmly denied.

As if in answer to everyone's fervent prayers, the gunfire all but stopped at about 1000 when an Amal officer approached the compound and asked to speak to Lieutenant Hough. Hough came forward, saying with body language that he really did not want to waste his breath.

"Brave Marines," the Amal warrior sneered, "you kill little girl in the town. You maybe stop shooting now?"

Hough leveled a cold blue-eyed stare at the posturing Shiite. "How many Amal warriors did we kill?"

"You kill no warriors."

"Bullshit," Hough spat.

The Amal officer stalked off.

Sgt José Lopez, the 1st Squad leader, and Pfc Michael Horne had volunteered to establish a firing position atop a small building thirty meters northwest of the Marine compound and adjacent to the LAF compound across Shit River. Lopez was going to try to pinpoint the APC that had fallen into Amal hands the day before; it was reported by observers to be firing at CP 69. The two set up a machine gun on loan from the LAF, climbed into the tiny sandbagged bunker, and opened fire on targets along the southern edge of Hooterville. They must have done some damage, for Lopez soon came up on the net to report that the APC was peeking around a corner at the southern edge of Hooterville.

HM3 Mark Hacala was manning the squad radio when the squad leader reported sighting the APC. The next thing he heard on the net was the slow *dut-dut-dut-dut* of .50-caliber rounds impacting near the open mike in the squad leader's hand. "Lopez," Hacala screamed into the handset, "talk to me, goddamnit!"

Lopez and Horne were hopelessly outclassed by the APC's .50-caliber machine gun and others that opened from bunkers and buildings nearby. Before they could react, the sandbags in front of the bunker were shredded by a corrosive stream of half-inch rounds; the wall puddled lower and lower as the pair flattened themselves against the floor of the too-small fighting position. Lopez was kicked in the head by a round that failed to penetrate his helmet.

Dave Hough grabbed Pfc Carmelo Ortiz and one of Ortiz's three LAAW antitank rockets and the two sprinted into the open during a lull, hoping to live long enough to get off a clear shot at the distant APC. They were not menaced, but Ortiz was unable to sight the armored fighting vehicle, which abruptly pulled back around a street corner. The lieutenant used the lull to check on Lopez's position and was absolutely amazed to find the squad leader doubled over in laughter generated by what he thought was lousy Lebanese marksmanship. Hough returned to the compound, but Ortiz remained in case the APC returned.

It did, menacing Lopez, Horne, and Ortiz with such heavy .50-caliber fire that they could not fire back. Despite it all, however, Ortiz came up on the net and reassured Doc Hacala with a brave, "Boy, we're going to kick ass." He could do no such thing, but this was one of those times when the thought really counted. The three were manning the best vantage point at the combat post, so they risked quick peeks from time to time to help the main body of the squad find targets. It was hair-raising business, but it was the best they could do to save themselves.

At length, the Moslem gunners abuptly ceased fire, leaving three very shaken but unscathed Marines clinging to little more than hope and life atop the perforated building. Sergeant Lopez opted to remain at the post with Private First Class Horne, but he ordered Private First Class Ortiz to return to the main compound because there was no longer room in the bunker for three. Ortiz climbed down from the roof and crossed the exposed Shit River bridge, ending his breathless run with a magnificent head-first dive over the compound's hip-high sandbag wall.

The APC returned several times over the next hour to snipe at the Marine compound from long range, then it disappeared altogether. The firing wound down from that point and the militia fighters had all withdrawn by about 1500 hours.

The reinforced squad was eating a late lunch hunkered down behind the post's sandbag walls when Corporal Cliff, who was manning the northwest corner of the compound, sang out a warning. A man dressed in Marine-style cammies had just stepped out of Shit River from beneath the footbridge connecting the Marine compound with the LAF compound. The man was reeking of the effluvia of the entire township.

"No shoot, Marines. No shoot. I Lebanese army."

Dave Hough ran to the wall for a look. The man was festooned with belts of ammunition and had hand grenades hanging all across his chest. He seemed to be on the level, so Hough motioned him forward. Before moving, the man motioned with his arm and an entire squad of similarly burdened soldiers decked out in Marine-style cammies emerged from the liquid shit.

These 1st Air Assault Battalion troopers had come to repay a debt of gratitude, both for the training they had received from Marines and for Hough's having stood by the LAF troops from Battalion 31.

On comparing professional notes, the two lieutenants discovered that each had been trained at Fort Bragg. The LAF lieutenant was scheduled to go to the U.S. Army Ranger School as soon as he mastered English. Hough, a recent Ranger School graduate, was so impressed and so appreciative that he allowed his Lebanese colleague to set in his own troopers along the western and northern flanks. When Hough later inspected the way the LAF lieutenant had set his people in, he was impressed with the Air Assault's high state of training, particularly as it contrasted with the readiness of the Battalion 31 soldiers.

The Druse and Amal resumed firing late in the afternoon and kept it up until dark. The only real mistake any of them made came at dusk, when a particularly dangerous machine gun that the Marines really wanted to take out kept on firing. The militia crew's exuberance was its undoing, for alert Marines quickly spotted the muzzle flashes. The gun was taken out cleanly by Lance Corporal Hickman's accurate M-60 burst. Strangely, several other militia gun crews also allowed themselves to be wasted under identical circumstances later that evening. Next day, Hough's troops noticed that the Druse machine gunners had pulled the tracer rounds out of their ammunition belts, a mixed blessing for the Druse gunners in that it prevented Marines from immediately locking on targets but also prevented the Druse gunners from immediately finding where their fire was going.

More of the same occurred on September 1. As usual, an Amal officer approached CP 69, and Dave Hough and the LAF lieutenant met with him. As usual, nothing was accomplished, but the LAF officer told the Amal officer, "If you shoot at us, we shoot back and kill plenty." That was heartening.

The Shiite and Druse units arrayed against CP 69 appeared to have had about enough. Though snipers continued to pester the jointly manned position, no serious threat was made.

Capt Monte Hoover called CP 69 on the morning of September 2 to order Hough's reinforced squad to abandon the post and turn over some of their supplies to the air-assault squad. The news dismayed the air-assault lieutenant, who begged the Marines to stay. Hough commiserated with the lieutenant but said that his orders could not be ignored, though he personally wished to remain. The Lebanese officer asked Hough to delay his departure for awhile, then got on his radio to talk with his superiors. Hough walked back to his tent to begin packing but was immediately called to the radio. A senior officer at Battalion was waiting on the line: "Lieutenant Hough, you're being reinforced and resupplied. What do you need?"

Hough ad-libbed a shopping list: 5,000 rounds of 5.56, 5,000 rounds of 7.62, 50 hand grenades, 150 M-203 HE rounds, Dragons, and another M-60 machine gun. He got it all, just like that; Captain Hoover was instructed to reinforce and resupply combat posts 35 and 69. While 2dLt Andy Prichard moved two reinforced squads of his 3d Platoon to CP 35, 2dLt Steve Sekellick's 1st Platoon humped in all the supplies and returned to the university. Hough's platoon sergeant led Cpl Mike Clepper's 3d Squad, a second machine-gun team, and a second Dragon team to CP 69, thus doubling the 2d Platoon contingent there.

After two more quiet days, a reinforced squad from Prichard's platoon was sent out on Sunday, September 4, to relieve Hough's contingent.

The troops who came out of CP 69 with Dave Hough were in desperate need of showers, hot chow, and a good night's sleep, but most of them expressed a willingness to stay if called upon to do so. Few of them discussed it openly, but these young troops were charged up by their experiences of the previous five days. They had encountered a level of excitement—the sheer physical pleasure of living on the edge—that none had ever dreamed he might achieve. None of Hough's troops knew for certain, but few doubted they had wasted many Druse and Amal warriors.

For all the good feelings about personal accomplishments and the brotherhood that had been forged at CP 69, the troops were generally dismayed over the lack of support they had received. Their lives had been in serious jeopardy for a week, but they had seen help just once, the helo attack on August 29. When the troops pieced it all together, they realized that the LAF had provided more support than had the MAU.

LtCol Larry Gerlach made a special trip to the university and warmly congratulated Dave Hough for a job well done. Gerlach vowed to back the decisions of the man on the spot, a fundamental principle of command that would be sorely tested by political requirements in the weeks to come.

It was not yet obvious, but the Moslem militias had established a pattern that would rarely be broken over the next several months. Henceforth, Sunday would be the day the shooting began in earnest each week, followed by steadily decreasing attacks through the week. Fridays would usually be quiet, for Friday is the Moslem sabbath and Saturday is the second day of the traditional Lebanese Moslem weekend (and the first day of the Christian weekend).

PART V

The September War

15

First Lieutenant Greg Balzer was Battalion Landing Team (BLT) 1/8's combat operations center (COC) watch officer when news of heavy vehicular movement on the Sidon Road began arriving over the tac net at about 0230, September 4, another Sunday. The news was only minutes old and mounting when the thunder and whine of jet aircraft resounded overhead and to the west, out over the sea. There was no doubt in Balzer's mind that the final Israel Defense Force (IDF) withdrawal from Beirut was under way, so he had the entire battalion combat operations staff roused from its sleep. Unlike August 28, when confusion and shock had prevailed, the COC was busy but orderly from the instant the alarm sounded. Officers and Marines who had been manning their desks for hours were revitalized by the activity and excitement and were almost too busy to think of possible consequences.

As numerous Israeli air force jet fighter-bombers ranged all across Beirut to protect the roadbound columns from any form of attack, Charlie Company Marines near the Sidon Road passed along counts of 300-plus vehicles per convoy, and the convoys were lined up nearly end to end.

Capt Walt Wint, the BLT 1/8 intelligence officer, had been trying to predict the date of the IDF pullout for weeks. In fact, he had been running a pool in which participants guessed the day the Israelis were going to pull out from the area around Beirut International Airport (BIA). There was no question that they would be going, for they had been packing and shipping gear since mid-August. By the time the Shouf and northern Beirut suburbs were abandoned on the night of August 27–28, IDF troops around the southern end of the BIA were sleeping under the stars and in their combat vehicles, and they were all eating combat rations, sure indicators that a move was afoot. Of course, there was just the slightest chance that the Israelis would be attacking rather than withdrawing.

Israeli preparations for the final withdrawal from Beirut were accompanied by an ironic reversal of strident American foreign-policy pronouncements. The Reagan administration had appealed directly to the government of Israel to keep IDF units around Beirut to prevent the dissolution of the fragile peace there. But the IDF had been amply bled—"nickeled and dimed to death"—and it was long past time to leave. The partial pullout on August 27 had resulted in the instantaneous eruption of factional fighting. Two Marines lay dead and a score had been wounded in the wake of the partial withdrawal. By the night of August 29, any Marine who knew anything about anything dreaded the final departure of the IDF.

The Israeli withdrawal from the Shouf and the northern Beirut suburbs on the night of August 27–28 had deeply and directly affected the security of Alpha and Bravo companies, located in the northern and central sectors of the BIA. However, powerful IDF armored and armored-infantry units had remained in possession of Ashuefat and Khalde, thus partially screening Charlie Company. This did not exempt the entire BIA from indirect mortar, artillery, and rocket fire, but it did mean that Charlie Company took far less small-arms fire than did its sister rifle companies. Of the three rifle companies, Charlie was the weakest, for the unit securing the south end of the runway provided about one-third its total strength for duty at the American embassy. Thus it was fortunate that the balance of the company had an extra week to dig in and acclimate itself to the sounds of war that had engulfed its sister companies.

Charlie Company's relative good fortune ended the morning of September 4. Ironically, the Lebanese Armed Forces (LAF) hastened the change. The BLT and Marine Amphibious Unit (MAU) staffs fully anticipated an LAF move to secure key IDF checkpoints, as had occurred in the wake of the partial withdrawal a week earlier. In fact, Captain Wint predicted that the LAF would mount a thrust southward along the coastal highway to secure Khalde. The only problem was that—as on so many occasions that bloody week—the LAF did not bother to alert the MAU as to its intentions.

SSgt Joe Curtis rousted Charlie Company's 1st Platoon early instead of letting the troops sleep in an extra hour, as had been customary on Sunday mornings. Curtis had been worried about the platoon's bunkers, which appeared weak in light of the previous week's fighting, so he put the troops to work filling sandbags. There was no end of bitching and moaning and muttering about what an asshole the platoon sergeant was being, but that was music to Curtis's ears, for he had learned that the worst bitching accompanied the best work.

The first Druse artillery round of the day struck Khalde at about 0930, a little too close to 1st Platoon for comfort. Everyone looked up in unison and broke for the platoon's tents to collect helmets, flak jackets, and arms. Staff Sergeant Curtis got on the tac net in time to hear that the LAF was massing some sort of armored formation near the BLT.

A solid mass of LAF tanks and armored cars rolled out of the LAF training camps and armored-vehicle parks at the northern end of the BIA after 0930, just as the tail of the last IDF convoy cleared Khalde. As the armored fighting vehicles—tanks, Panhards, and jeeps equipped with 106mm recoilless rifles—moved down the northwest-southeast airport runway, a second column —armored personnel carriers (APCs), trucks, and jeeps— moved farther west before turning south onto the four-lane coastal highway. While the LAF armor rolled out, a quick check through liaison channels indicated that it was slated to sweep into Khalde and then northward along the Sidon Road to secure Ashuefat and Hooterville. The solid mass of armor appeared inelegant to the hundreds of Marines observing it, but many were gratified to see the LAF out in force, showing itself, making the effort to secure a grip on the environs of its own capital city.

First Lieutenant Leo Lachat, MAU Service and Support Group (MSSG) 24's Shore Party Platoon commander, was at his command post (CP) on Green Beach when word of the anticipated LAF sweep reached him from MAU headquarters at 0900. At about 1000, Lachat spotted the head of an LAF armored-infantry column about four miles north of the beach, heading down all four lanes of the coastal highway at ten to fifteen miles per hour. He reported in to the MSSG-24 COC and prepared his shore party personnel and the Navy Beachmasters and Seabees to weather incoming fire of virtually any sort. The beach units had been hardening their bunkers for days in anticipation of an upswing in the fighting once the IDF pulled out. It was clearly time.

From Lachat's perspective, "What had previously been an extremely quiet Sunday morning suddenly turned into hell on earth. Almost simultaneously, .50-caliber fire from several guns south of the airport sprayed the beach and highway to our front. Air-burst artillery rounds exploded overhead, and multiple volleys of 82mm and 120mm mortar rounds impacted in the sand behind us. Rounds which impacted on the highway sent shrapnel slicing through our tents and ricocheting off our vehicles."

The lead elements of the LAF column halted and remained motionless right in front of Green Beach. The fire immediately intensified to the point where Lieutenant Lachat "could not hear messages coming in over my radio, and I had to yell into the handset to be heard." Lachat well knew that the destruction or immobilization of the lead vehicles would result in a clogged road and endless incoming. Thankfully, the convoy rolled south again after ten or fifteen minutes. The incoming also shifted south, along with the lead vehicles. Over the next ninety minutes, while indirect .50-caliber rounds continued to shower the beach, some sixty-five LAF APCs, tanks, trucks, and jeeps passed on their way to Khalde.

The progress of the twin LAF phalanxes was closely monitored at the battalion COC. Lieutenant Balzer, who was still manning the watch desk, heard directly from the Charlie Company commander, Capt Chris Cowdrey, at about 1015 that the head of the eastern LAF column was directly behind Charlie Company, on its way to the back gate of the BIA. This seemed to confirm the news from the liaison officers, but the sense of ease was short-lived. Cowdrey was back on the net within two minutes to say that the armored column had *stopped* right behind his 1st Platoon.

Captain Cowdrey and 2dLt Bill Harris, the 1st Platoon leader, stalked toward the gate leading from the BIA to Khalde to have a talk with the LAF force commander. The two officers were concerned that Moslem gunners in the hills might deduce, incorrectly, that the Marines and LAF were working together in the assault on Khalde. It was immediately apparent to the two Marine officers that the LAF Panhards were not ready to move.

An LAF officer, who spoke little or no English, responded to Captain Cowdrey's entreaties with "Infantry, infantry." The two Marines assumed he was waiting for the APCs, which had not yet reached the gate.

The lead Panhards were stopped for only a few moments before they tried to move away from the Marine positions. But events were moving too rapidly for a solution as simple as getting the armored force realigned and back on the move. An LAF Panhard fired its 90mm gun into the hills overlooking the southern end of the runway. Other Panhards opened with their .50-caliber machine guns. No sooner done than four 120mm mortar rounds impacted near the back gate. Others fell across the BIA.

It was 1020.

The LAF was utterly incapable of mounting a large, albeit amateurish, armored thrust on short notice. Obviously the Israelis had prepared the Lebanese for their pullout. On top of that, the instantaneous response by Moslem batteries indicated that someone—undoubtedly Moslems within the LAF—had warned the militias that the armored thrust was to take place.

Druse gunners were not about to withhold fire simply because the LAF armored force was partially screened by Charlie Company. Druse and Shiite Moslems had already spilled American blood and perhaps as many as five or six dozen had already died at the hands of Alpha and Bravo companies and Charlie Battery. While rockets, mortars, and artillery were fired into the BIA, Druse and Shiite riflemen within range of the LAF force fired at it and at the Marine force that appeared to be screening it.

Chris Cowdrey came up on the tac net with a calm, reasoned, and highly detailed report of the .50-caliber-machine-gun and heavy-caliber fire his company was taking. The company commander then requested permission to return fire. There was no hesitation at the COC; the battalion commander authorized Cowdrey to take appropriate action as long as he remained within the guidelines set down in the Rules of Engagement. By then, Charlie Company was taking an increasing volume of fire

—including rocket-propelled grenades (RPGs) aimed at several amtracs in the company sector and 106mm recoilless rifle fire aimed at bunkers and the company CP. Anything Charlie Company could dish out was considered fair.

Permission to fire came a bit late for 1st Platoon. The heavy fire falling around the back gate had convinced Staff Sergeant Curtis that his company commander and platoon leader had been killed. (They were not even touched.) Curtis had already told the troops they could return the fire.

Perceptions are everything. Marines had trained the LAF and the United States had provided much of its equipment. Now, as the return fire spread all along the Charlie Company line, Druse and Shiite militiamen facing the BIA must have assumed that the LAF and Marines were conducting a coordinated combined operation. From the hills to the east of the BIA and from Khalde, it would certainly have appeared that Charlie Company was establishing a base of fire in direct support of an LAF armored assault directly through the Marine lines.

As soon as Charlie Company opened fire, the LAF armor moved out toward Khalde. The men in the hills saw two things: the assault and Marines supporting the assault. The Marines saw two things, too: the gunfire coming in and the LAF going out.

While Marines on the scene were tracking targets and ducking intense fire, Capt Mike Haskell, the battalion Weapons Company commander, took firm control of the MAU's supporting arms assets. Marine Medium Helicopter Squadron (HMM) 162's two Cobras, under the direct control of the air liaison officer, Capt Vinnie Smith, were ordered to orbit just off the coast. Charlie Battery, under the control of the artillery liaison officer, 1stLt Chuck Schnorf, was ordered to a high state of readiness. The Marine Target Acquisition Battery was already at work plotting possible targets, mainly artillery and rocket batteries firing on the BIA. All eight 81mm tubes were kept on target, ready to fire at an instant's notice. The MAU's naval gunfire assets, in the hands of Navy Lt Jim Surch, were trained out on appropriate targets. And all five Marine tanks were ordered to prepare for action. Busy as he was keeping track of his assets, Captain Haskell managed to keep up a running string of one-liners designed to take the edge off the tension that built in waves as an increasing volume of bad news arrived over the loudspeakers. Captain Wint and his clerk worked furiously to plot in the targets on the intelligence map overlay, and Maj Andy Davis, the battalion operations officer, ran it all through the computer of his mind, balancing the numbers and locations of the troops and weapons available against all the possible scenarios that might befall Charlie Company and the rest of the MAU. First Lieutenant Joe Boccia, the ace battalion communicator, and his comm chief and two radiomen fretted over the viability of the various communications nets running through the COC circuit, for vital information or orders might be lost and men might die if any of the lines went down. Some of the heaviest pressure was on Lieutenant Balzer, who, despite a sleepless night, had to keep track of every incoming message and every outgoing order; it was Balzer's job to know precisely what was going on every step of the way. The COC functioned with precision despite the tension and pressure.

One of the factors that undoubtedly preserved a great many Marine lives was the inability of the Druse gunners to mass their fires. There were over 600 artillery tubes located in the Shouf. Most were aimed northward to counter Phalange artillery in the Metan, but an ample number of guns could be pointed down at the BIA at any time. The Druse appeared incapable of coordinating massed fires and, in fact, of laying and firing more than one gun at one target at one time.

Moreover, small-arms fire directed by the Moslem militiamen was notoriously and, to Marines, laughably inaccurate. Following the week of shooting between the militias and Alpha and Bravo companies, the opinion around the BIA was that "aimed" fire could not be deadly; the only way to die at the hands of Moslem marksmen was to be in the path of a round meant for someone else.

It was a good thing, too, as far as the Charlie Company Marines were concerned. For, despite all the coolly conceived preparations going down at the COC, no supporting arms were fired. All the artillery, Cobra gunships, tanks, 81mm mortars, and naval gunnery in the world is of no value unless someone puts it to use. Though they yearned to order massive retaliation, Col Tim Geraghty and LtCol Larry Gerlach could do nothing; they were paralyzed by orders from the highest echelons of government to avoid appearing as a hostile participant in the civil war. The men of Charlie Company were bitter. It was evident to them that, despite high-level debates to the contrary, the civil war had already engulfed them.

The troops were really placed in a quandary when, after an intense hour of combat, they were ordered to cease firing. It turned out that the LAF column attacking into Khalde was being endangered by the Charlie Company fire, so the company had to shut down until the LAF armor moved to safety, an exercise that used up an hour and during which the militia fighters were not equally hampered by the niceties of even forced alliances.

Sgt Foster Hill, of 1st Platoon, took advantage of the "lull" by having his men low-crawl around the platoon area to get needed ammunition and something with which to counter a trio of 106mm recoilless rifles firing from atop a nearby hill.

Pfc Victor Rollins plotted the 106s in on his map and called in an eight-digit grid coordinate, about as good as it gets from eyeballing a target. The requested artillery fire mission was denied. So was 81mm mortar fire.

Second Lieutenant Bill Harris was having trouble from snipers occupying a small concrete building near the 1st Platoon sector, so he contacted SSgt Richard Smith, commander of the only Marine tank in the company area, to ask him to fire the tank's .50-caliber coaxial machine gun at the snipers. Smith was awaiting permission to fire his main gun when a 106mm recoilless rifle round passed overhead. As the tank commander continued to wait, five more 106mm rounds passed the tank. Finally, permission to fire was granted. Smith already had the .50-cal coax aimed at the recoilless rifles. Since the machine gun was optically linked to the tank's 105mm main gun, it was nothing to send a high-explosive (HE) round on its way. The first round was over and the second round was short. Staff Sergeant Smith ordered up a beehive round, a wicked antipersonnel concoction filled with thousands of barbed steel flechettes. The 106mm crewmen were obliterated. The turret then whirred softly as Staff Sergeant Smith brought the machine gun to bear against the target first suggested by Lieutenant Harris. Minutes later, RPGs fired from atop a nearby building forced the tank to withdraw, for a direct hit by an RPG can kill a tank.

When Sgt Foster Hill was ordered to get the Moslem grenadiers, he turned loose three M-203 grenadiers. They each fired five rounds of HE and took out all the snipers.

Farther up the platoon line, SSgt Joe Curtis was standing outside his bunker, observing fire, when an exploding RPG knocked him flat on his back. One of the troops within the bunker yelled, "He's hit! The staff sergeant's hit!" Curtis thought he was, too, but he was not. A second RPG struck a few meters down the road, setting the brush afire. As Curtis got up to return to the bunker, a third RPG impacted just ten meters behind the bunker. The concussion dropped the platoon sergeant onto his face. He was amazed to find he had yet to be scratched. No sooner had Curtis entered the bunker than the structure took a direct hit by the fourth RPG. Heavy rifle fire also hit the bunker; it was coming from nearby and was unusually well aimed.

Keen-eyed Pfc Victor Rollins suddenly sang out, "It's coming from that building, right there!" All eyes followed his pointing finger to a small concrete building just twenty-five meters distant. All the riflemen fired their M-16s, but they did no good; the hostile gunfire continued to impact on the bunker.

Staff Sergeant Curtis asked for a LAAW, a shoulder-fired antitank rocket encased in a disposable plastic launcher. He opened the launcher to its full length, settled in, braced himself, sighted, and let go—the first time a LAAW had been fired by a Marine in combat since Vietnam. The snipers in the concrete building did not fire anymore. Curtis immediately became known in Charlie Company as "the LAAW man," which was soon changed to "Sheriff." When, a short time later, snipers from another nearby building harassed Staff Sergeant Curtis's bunker, he slammed a second LAAW into it, with precisely the same result.

A pair of men dressed in civilian clothing but carrying AK-47s ran across an open field in full view. Sgt Foster Hill was certain the two militiamen felt they would be given free passage, and was on the verge of saying he did not believe what he was seeing, when the nearest M-60 gunner swiveled his weapon's barrel, eased back on the trigger, and turned the two into "sausage meat." Then the gunner turned his attention to three snipers who kept popping up from behind a building to snap off rounds at the Marines. Two of the three went down in a spray of blood and bone, but the third kept at it. Private First Class Rollins stood up in the open and brought his M-16 rifle to the offhand position. The next time the sniper popped up, Rollins dropped him with a single round.

Capt Paul Roy, of Alpha Company, was monitoring the progress of the LAF armored column through Khalde from his company observation post well to the north when he saw about fifteen militiamen mount the upper stories of an uncompleted skeletonlike building several hundred meters north of Khalde. It appeared to the company commander that the militia fighters would be able to hit the LAF column from the building, so he called Battalion and received permission to support the LAF by laying down some screening fire.

The closest Marines to the building were two squads of 1stLt Pete Ferraro's 3d Platoon, Alpha Company, which were manning CP 76, several rooftop fighting positions at a road junction on roughly the same northeast-southwest outpost line that included combat posts 35 and 69. Ferraro already had the building in question plotted in as a major feature on his map of the area. The range was known, and it was a clear shot.

Captain Roy passed along explicit, detailed orders. Third Platoon was to establish a squad-size base of fire at CP 76, and one or two designated shooters were to fire into the left-hand portion of the open four-story building in such a way as to herd the militiamen there away from positions from which they might hit the LAF column. Lieutenant Ferraro responded that he understood and would comply. He called CP 76 and gave the same explicit instructions to SSgt Manasamua Fiame, a combative Samoan whose command of English was sometimes tenuous.

Captain Roy watched and waited as the head of the LAF column crept toward the zone that could be reached from the skeleton tower. He got back on the horn and cautioned, "Just a few rounds. Are you people ready to go?"

Staff Sergeant Fiame came up on the company net. "Roger dat. Dees ees Hotel Two. Roger dat."

"Open up." Roy expected to hear a few rounds pop off and see the militiamen scatter for cover.

The entire Marine squad opened fire at the open steel latticework. Immediately, the LAF squad at CP 76 saw what was happening and opened fire, really "cleaning house." Roy cringed as he saw people on the building "flying in every direction."

The open building was thereafter known as Checkpoint Samoa.

The most frustrated men in the Charlie Company sector that day were the sixteen Dragon antitank gunners attached from

Weapons Company. The Dragon is a large-caliber wire-guided-rocket launcher, ideal for work against bunkers. Unlike artillery or mortars, the Dragon is a surgically precise weapon whose only fault is that the gunner must expose himself to hostile fire in order to acquire and maintain a target in his sights. The gunners were willing to risk the incoming, but Battalion refused to unleash the awesome power of the four Dragon launchers. The gunners were advised to conserve their ten rounds in case the militias mounted a direct assault supported by tanks or APCs captured or stolen from the LAF.

That night, the Dragon bunker took a direct heavy-caliber hit and three gunners were slightly wounded. The entire section headed up the line, taking care to stay in the system of shallow communications trenches the Marines had earlier excavated between the bunkers. They found a corpsman, who patched wounds and led the casualties to the rear, from which they were evacuated. Meantime, a 120mm mortar barrage impacted around the bunker in which the balance of the Dragon section had found haven. Sgt Foster Hill, commanding the next bunker up the line, raised his voice over the blasts, "Goddamnit, Dragons, get the fuck outa there." The gunners humped their bulky gear into the open, where they were picked up by a militia .50 cal. Sergeant Hill's squad laid down a base of fire, then Lieutenant Harris ordered the entire platoon to cover the Dragon section, which headed for the rear amid the clatter of small arms and booms of exploding RPGs and mortar rounds.

First Lieutenant Leo Lachat, who had watched what he could of the day's fighting from his vantage point at fire-swept Green Beach, was most taken aback by the number of automatic weapons possessed by the militia forces. Almost every building he could see in Khalde was alive with winking muzzle flashes. As the day wore on toward dusk, "thousands of tracer rounds, the wiggling tracks of RPGs, and the flash of numerous rocket and artillery exchanges blazed through the sky." Incoming around

Green Beach slowly dissipated as the LAF brigade built up its combat power around Khalde.

LAF vehicles driving at high speed began evacuating dead and wounded and carting in ammunition resupplies along the coastal highway at about 2000 hours. Militia artillery opened on the roadway, and many rounds impacted in front of Green Beach. The shellings, punctuated by brief lulls through the night, petered out around 0500, September 5. Miraculously, no one at Green Beach was injured or killed in the nineteen hours of free fire in their direction.

After a day and a night of begging for artillery or mortar support to take out the distant 82mm and 120mm mortars, 122mm rockets, and medium artillery that constantly walked fire up and down the company sector, Charlie Company was supported at about 0400, September 5, by a salvo of 155mm illumination rounds. One Charlie Company Marine stated the feelings of the company with just one word, "Whoopie." The insult was compounded when, with the help of official briefers, the media carnival that had become Beirut deduced and announced to the world that Charlie Company was taking "spillover" and "stray rounds" meant for the LAF.

16

Capt Paul Roy was awakened at about 0300, Tuesday, September 6, by a salvo of incoming 122mm rockets and medium artillery. It was the sort of random barrage that had been striking in and around the Alpha Company sector for over a week. Indeed, it was the sort of shelling that had inflicted the first two deaths and a score of injuries upon Alpha Company on August 29. Unsettled by the continued violence that was reaching out at their company, Roy and his exec, 1stLt Ron Baczkowski, manned the company observation post (OP) to observe additional incoming. For the time being, however, it remained quiet.

Most of the Marines who had been manning sentry posts at that time had not been relieved, as expected, at 2000 because of the flurries of incoming artillery and rocket fire. It was coming up 0400 when all three of the Alpha Company rifle-platoon leaders called Captain Roy on the company tac net to see if they could relieve their posts. Roy was all for that. It had been fairly peaceful for the better part of an hour, and experience and prudence dictated that the activity be carried out while it was still dark. Roy told the platoon leaders to "make it quick."

Cpl Bryan Criste, an Alpha Company fire-team leader, awoke just before 0400 to relieve himself. When finished, he realized he was not tired enough to return to sleep, so he ambled over to the 1st Platoon guard shack to see what was going on.

Criste had been scheduled to take the duty that night, but Cpl Pedro Valle, a fellow team leader, had offered to take his place. Criste found Cpl Marcus McNelley alone in the shack and asked where Valle was. McNelley replied that Valle was on his way to post the relief at Checkpoint 11.

At about that time, Captain Roy and Lieutenant Baczkowski heard Marines from 1stLt Andy May's 1st Platoon approaching across the rear of the company command post (CP). It was Corporal Valle and two sentries crossing a bridge across Shit River on the way south to Checkpoint 11. Lieutenant Baczkowski left the OP position and met the three when they stopped briefly to pick up canteen cups of coffee from a vat can that was sitting on a sandbag wall adjacent to the dirt path they were using. The three 1st Platoon Marines continued on toward Checkpoint 11, and Baczkowski returned to the OP with coffee for himself and Roy.

As soon as Corporal Valle reached Checkpoint 11, he changed the guard and started back to 1st Platoon's compound with LCpls Randy Clark and G.A. ("Iceman") Davis. Captain Roy spotted them as they entered the company lines and stopped at the coffee vat. At that moment, however, Roy's attention was diverted northward, where several rounds impacted in front of and on the runway behind 2d Platoon. Valle, Clark, and Davis stayed at the coffee vat, talking with HM3 Darrell Gibson, the company headquarters doc, until things quieted down, then they headed north again. Captain Roy heard them cross the Shit River bridge.

It was about 0420 when another sudden barrage impacted somewhere out toward 1st Platoon, the unit that had taken the bulk of the previous week's casualties. Moments after the blast, Captain Roy heard a voice yell out in English, but the words were indistinct. He asked Lieutenant Baczkowski if he had heard anything, but Baczkowski had not. Roy heard the voice again, but he could not determine how far it was from the OP. Fearful that more of his Marines had been hurt, Roy asked Baczkowski to call Lieutenant May to find out what had happened. May, who had been placed in command of 1st Platoon following George Losey's death, was farther from the point of impact than Roy, so he had to cross the platoon area before he heard shouted pleas for help. He ran back to his platoon CP and called Captain Roy to say he could hear the yelling and would send help. Roy instantly jumped up and called out for his radio operator, Cpl Donald Giblin, and HM3 Gibson. The three headed toward the Shit River bridge.

The salvo of rockets and artillery impacted close enough to the 1st Platoon guard shack to shake the earth. Corporals Criste and McNelley were still exchanging exclamations when the phone rang. It was Company, with news that someone had been injured by the incoming. Criste did not have his combat boots on, so he offered to stand radio watch while McNelley ran out to get help for the injured.

LCpl Shawn Gallagher was adrift between dreams and reality. The big, gravel-voiced Alpha Company M-60 gunner knew he should be sleeping because he had just come off the midnight guard shift, but the poking was insistent and he had to lift his heavy eyelids. Sgt Donald Williams drifted into view.

"Come on, Gallagher. You're on for Post 5."

"Uh, uh. I just came off Post 5 at midnight."

"Well, who's on?"

Before Gallagher could respond, the two Marines unconsciously leaned over toward the wall of the trench in which Gallagher had been sleeping. Only then did it register that a salvo of artillery rounds and 122mm rockets had struck in the fields around the Alpha Company sector. Neither thought much about the incoming any longer. There had been deaths just eight days earlier, but the impact of losing the platoon leader and platoon sergeant had receded into the memories of the resilient young men who had survived the first ordeal. If Gallagher or Williams, or any other Alpha Company Marine, took the time to think about the dead lieutenant and staff sergeant, there would be tears and a sense of loss. But life in the fast lane at Beirut International Airport (BIA) placed survival at the forefront of everyone's mind; there was literally no time to dwell on 1st Platoon's loss.

As Gallagher and Williams concluded their exchange, Corporal McNelley loomed out of the darkness and yelled, "Someone's been hit between us and the company CP!" McNelley then darted out of the trench and headed south down the road.

A single 122mm Katyusha struck the field between the 1st Platoon area and the company CP. Corporal Criste, on radio watch at the platoon guard shack, reflexively hunched his head into his shoulders and said out loud, "Damn, I hope no one got hit by that one!" He called Lieutenant May to suggest that Battalion be asked to provide medevac, then ran out of the guard shack in his stocking feet to find the platoon corpsman, HN Victor Oglesby.

LCpl Joel Montgomery was returning from Post 5, hoping for some sleep, when the Marine with whom he had shared his watch stopped by the side of the path to urinate. The two had been standing idle for only a moment when they heard Corporal McNelley shout, "Someone's been hit."

Montgomery joined McNelley and Pfc John Lux as they ran toward the company CP. Cpl Preston Luke cut across their path, on his way to collect his helmet, flak jacket, and rifle. He would be right behind Lux, Montgomery, and McNelley, who ran only a few dozen meters before coming upon what Montgomery thought was a pile of tree limbs and part of a tree trunk beside the path. It was too dark to be sure what the debris was until they got right up to it.

Montgomery looked off to the edge of the path and saw the body of Corporal Valle. The fire-team leader had taken a virtually direct hit by the single 122mm rocket.

Montgomery took only an instant to recover. He turned toward the platoon area and shouted, "Corpsman up!"

Immediately, a single Katyusha slammed into the ground only a dozen meters from where Montgomery, Lux, and McNelley knelt over Corporal Valle's body. The three shared a wordless thought about leaving to get help, and then put the thought into action, retracing their steps toward the platoon area, about 200 meters to the north. They came upon Corporal Luke, who had donned his combat gear and raced to catch up. He had run right into the detonation of the last Katyusha and was bleeding from two deep holes in the back of his left thigh. His left arm was covered with blood where it had been abraded by dirt and debris. Pressure bandages were applied by nervous but agile fingers, then Lux and Montgomery scooped Luke up and jogged toward the platoon area. Lance Corporal Montgomery decided that the two-man carry was too slow, so he simply swung the injured corporal onto his back and trotted down the road beside Lux and McNelley. They ran into a milling crowd of curious, worried Marines.

Cpl Bryan Criste had been joined by LCpl Antoine Serena, another fire-team leader, and the two rousted Doc Oglesby.

Then all three headed up the road, passing Lux, Luke, Montgomery, and McNelley, who were on their way back to the platoon area. No words passed between the groups, but Criste had a deep sense of forboding. They came upon Corporal Valle's corpse, and Doc Oglesby instantly confirmed that the man was dead. Then they rushed on in the direction of the company CP, where, Criste knew, there was at least one casualty.

The first injured man on the dirt trail that Doc Oglesby treated was LCpl Iceman Davis. The corpsman, who had had more than enough on-the-job-training eight days earlier, when 1st Platoon suffered two killed and five wounded, quickly checked Davis's body and found that the worst wound was a hole in the lower abdomen. He applied a sterile pressure bandage to the injury, then went looking for someone else to treat.

They found LCpl Randy Clark unconscious in a pool of blood. He had been severely injured throughout his upper left torso and neck, and his chest was full of holes. It seemed to Corporal Criste that the nineteen-year-old assaultman had a broken arm and two broken legs. Doc Oglesby dropped to his knees and went to work. Criste hunkered down beside the doc to help.

Lance Corporal Serena stayed beside Iceman Davis, who asked about other injured Marines: "Why don't you go check them out?"

"They're okay," Serena smoothly lied. "Someone's up with them now." He had the impression that Davis did not know the extent of his own injuries, which were severe but not life-threatening.

"I'm okay, too," Davis argued. "Go on and help the others."

"Davis, you'll be all right and they'll be all right. Don't worry about it. Don't worry."

"No, I don't think so."

LCpl Frank Orians, an M-60 gunner attached to 1st Platoon, and LCpl Richard Watson, a machine-gun-team leader, were a little late arriving because they had been asleep when the first

Katyusha detonated. They had run off into the night as soon as they could pull on their boots and arm themselves. They found Pedro Valle beside the path, saw that he was beyond help, and ran past him. When he arrived, Frank Orians knelt beside Randy Clark's head and asked, "What's wrong with you? You all right?"

Clark answered tiredly that his legs and one arm hurt, that he thought they were broken. Orians did not confirm the surmise, but he agreed with it. He realized that Clark was dazed and probably beyond great pain. Orians, who was called "Shaky" because of his nervous disposition, paused for a few moments to regain his composure, then pulled Clark's aid kit from his web belt and went to work assisting Doc Oglesby. Through the fog of his rampant imagination and the struggle to provide aid, he was only vaguely aware that other hands were helping his own and Oglesby's. Orians helped tilt Clark on his side, as he had been taught, in order to prevent him from aspirating blood or vomit into his lungs and, possibly, drowning. Marines kept up a light banter, but the exchanges were inconsequential, simply the words of extremely frightened youngsters. Unknown to Orians, Captain Roy arrived with Doc Gibson. The company commander had seen Valle and knew he was dead, and he concluded that Iceman Davis was strong and had a good chance of surviving. Roy knelt silently beside Clark, who by then had slipped into unconsciousness.

A tank rolled into the field beside the trail, providing a barrier between the Americans and the denizens of Hooterville.

When many more 1st Platoon Marines had arrived to share the load, Corporal Criste and Lance Corporal Serena headed back up the path to where Corporal Valle lay. They reached the body just as a pair of amtracs arrived. Criste and Serena gingerly collected Valle's remains and laid them gently on a poncho. The resulting package seemed too small to be a man.

When Criste and Serena carried the poncho aboard the hog,

one of the crewmen blurted out, "What are you doing! Bringing your fucking trash aboard my vehicle!" Though the amtracker could not have known the truth, his bellicosity struck a deep, resounding chord in both mourning Marines. "This is Corporal Valle," Serena yelled. The amtracker became apologetic, then broke into tears.

Corporal Criste immersed his profound grief in the whirlwind of activity that had carried him this far. He left Valle to Serena's tender care and returned to help with Randy Clark. The thing that impressed Criste more than anything that impressive night was the size of the injured man's eyes, for they were wide, wide open, as if drinking in sights to be remembered through eternity. "It's going to be okay," Criste soothed the wounded man, "it'll be fine." Clark dazedly lifted his head every few moments and turned slowly back and forth to fix an unfocused and distant stare upon Bryan Criste and his other friends.

Willing hands lifted Iceman Davis and Randy Clark into the thundering amtrac. Doc Oglesby climbed aboard to provide aid, and Lance Corporal Orians followed to provide comfort. The amtrac's steel ramp slowly lifted and the huge vehicle roared off in a cloud of dust and tears. Helpers and rubberneckers— mourners all—shambled back to the platoon area in a mood of shocked disbelief.

As soon as Lance Corporal Orians helped place Randy Clark on the steel deck of the amtrac, he removed his own cammie blouse and folded it beneath Clark's lolling head. Then, as Doc Oglesby worked to keep the man alive, Orians lifted the pillow and Clark's head into his lap and tried to absorb the road shock with his knees. As Orians the man did all this with exceptional tenderness, Orians the Marine screamed into Clark's ear to keep him conscious or bring him back when he drifted off. The amtrac bucked and leaped so much that Doc Oglesby had to abandon his efforts to stabilize Clark, who had slipped into deep shock. It was all he and Orians could do to keep the grievously injured man from bouncing across the steel deck.

The ride was an eternity.

The ramp dropped and Frank Orians was dragged back to reality by a rush of men who lifted Randy Clark and bore him off.

Doc Oglesby accompanied Clark into the Battalion Landing Team (BLT) headquarters. His hand was on the injured man's arm; he could feel Clark's body temperature drop as Clark drifted deeper into shock. This was the first time Oglesby allowed himself to think that Clark was going to die. Corpsmen rushed by to help Lance Corporal Davis from the amtrac. Captain Roy's jeep arrived minutes later, carrying Corporal Luke's stretcher.

Frank Orians found himself alone, unable to work off his grief and shock. The amtrac carried him back to Alpha Company.

Most of the men living in the BLT were in the basement, suffering through another Condition I alert, when the wounded were brought in. First Lieutenant Chuck Dallachie, the battalion legal officer, left the communal hideaway in the basement when he heard a bloodcurdling scream of pain. He knew that badly injured Marines were being carried down to the basement, but there was nothing he could do. Dallachie, who had been a platoon leader on BLT 1/8's previous float, felt like crying, like doing something, but his training as an officer compelled him to act out his grief and frustration in private, away from the troops.

The screaming man was Iceman Davis. As dozens of grim-faced Marines in the rooms adjacent to the aid station stared past one another, Davis yelled, "I don't want to die." Nearby, Dr. John Hudson, the battalion surgeon, did his best for Randy Clark, but the young Marine slipped into a coma and stopped breathing.

Lance Corporal Orians was met by Lieutenant May when the amtrac arrived at the 1st Platoon CP. May had been working hard, trying to control events, so had not gotten out of the platoon CP to be with Pedro Valle or the badly injured Marines.

He was, therefore, a bit too businesslike for the profoundly shaken machine gunner. He informed Orians simply, "Clark's bought it."

Orians did not want to believe the implication of May's words. The son of an Army major on active duty, Orians bit back the answer that stood on the tip of his tongue: "Damn, sir, give the man half a chance!" But he knew in his heart that May was right.

The lieutenant let the shattered nineteen-year-old pass without another word.

The support Orians gave and received when he rejoined his comrades was silent; there was nothing anyone had left to say.

Doc Oglesby hung around at the aid station long enough to help carry Iceman Davis to the helo that would evacuate him out to *Iwo Jima*'s superior medical facility. Then, his work finished, he climbed aboard a jeep and rode home with Captain Roy, who had stood in grieved silence as he learned that Randy Clark had died just minutes after reaching the aid station.

Luke and Davis were evacuated to the United States. Doc Oglesby was transferred to the battalion aid station the following week; he had had his share, and more, of attending dead and wounded comrades. Pedro Valle, aged twenty-five, was flown home to Puerto Rico for burial. Randy Clark, aged nineteen, who had grieved openly following the deaths a week before his own, was buried in Minong, Wisconsin, following services in the gymnasium of the high school from which he had graduated two years earlier.

17

The generalized random violence that ebbed and flowed across Beirut International Airport (BIA) and West Beirut following the deaths of George Losey and Alexander Ortega became known to Marines as the September War.

The deaths on August 29, the isolation of combat posts 35 and 69 through that week, and the Lebanese Armed Forces (LAF) attack that somehow engulfed Charlie Company on September 4 were part of the larger Lebanese civil war, for each incident initially involved fighting between the LAF and the Moslem militias. The objective of the attacks was to somehow separate Marines from the LAF. On the other hand, the shelling that killed Randy Clark and Pedro Valle on September 6 was random, simply part of a program of harassment aimed at fracturing American resolve or, in many instances throughout September, to simply inflict pain and suffering upon Americans.

There were powerful forces loose in and around Beirut in September 1983, and not all of them were directly concerned with the plight of Lebanon or the Lebanese. Where Americans were involved in hostilities, there would always be some question as to the motives—indeed, as to the identities—of the attackers or harassers. No party then actively at war in the Beirut area was entirely exempt from the impulse to manipulate the United States through force of arms. In the case of the Cadmos Hotel incident, the LAF had itself directed its own artillery to fire air bursts over a section of Beirut in the hope the danger would dissuade the Marines from evacuating fellow American servicemen from a position manned by a threatened LAF contingent. Again, on September 4, by design or as a result of incompetence, the LAF had maneuvered the Marines into hostile action against both Druse and Shiite militia units. The dispatch of a reinforced squad of the 1st Air Assault Battalion to CP 69 was not much different, for the reinforcement and resupply had been authorized by the LAF chain of command only after the tiny American garrison had been ordered to clear out.

Beginning on August 28, Marines throughout the BIA were subjected to random shellings of varying intensity and to both random and carefully orchestrated small-arms fire. Except in a few locations, the violence built and subsided in waves. No one was ever quite certain if his position would be targeted or, if it was, for how long it would be subjected to hostile fire. There appeared to be no real focus to the attacks; the messages were mixed and, at best, vague. If the Marines were being goaded by one faction or another, it was often unclear whose hand lay behind the goading or to what purpose the pressure was being exerted. To this crippling uncertainty—for men in danger at least like to dream that their deaths might serve a useful purpose —was added the unflinching rigidity of the Marine Amphibious Unit's (MAU's) outmoded mission concept and the unrealistic Rules of Engagement.

Thus, faced with threats whose intent they could not clearly perceive and hobbled by rules that reflected not one whit of compassion for their plight, the Marines of BLT 1/8 did what servicemen in combat have done since war was invented: they sought and found solace within the groups in which they lived, they shifted loyalties downward from "Corps and country" to "life and limb." By September 1, 1983, all the elements—all the individuals—of BLT 1/8 had found a purpose: payback. Until the mixed messages from above could be made cogent once again, the troops would fight simply for the sake of survival.

Cpls David Baldree, Jonathan Crumley, and Tom Rutter had been at the Lebanese University from the start. All were members of the battalion Surveillance and Target Acquisition (STA) Platoon, a sixteen-man team of highly trained, highly skilled scout-snipers attached to the battalion intelligence section. There had been some talk, early in the deployment, of rotating the STA sections around the various company positions, but the snipers themselves had dissuaded their superiors, though doing so meant long hours and few breaks. The snipers reasoned that their well-honed powers of observation would be most useful if the basic teams specialized in particular locales, got to know the rhythms and people of the particular neighborhoods over which they watched.

Baldree, Rutter, and Crumley built a bunker high atop the library and fashioned several blinds through which they might observe the comings and goings through Hooterville without being seen. When the crunch came on August 28, Crumley had been able to see most of the activity around Combat Posts 35 and 69 and had had a bird's-eye view of the LAF's ignominious loss of three armored personnel carriers.

The task of observing was not without its risks. As soon as the ragtag militiamen in Hooterville figured out why the Americans were able to pinpoint their bunkers with such startling accuracy, they tried to neutralize the observers. The militiamen did not realize, when they selected the STA snipers for targets, that they could not win what quickly became a private war.

The main event began one morning when a dozen ill-clad

Amal militiamen with mismatched weapons and independent inclinations manned a bunker facing the library building. Baldree and Rutter, who were manning the observation post (OP) while Crumley tried to get some rest after being on duty all night, felt sorry for the militia fighters because it was evident at the outset that their chances of drawing blood were nil—they were not good shooters and had a tendency to spray rounds in long, useless bursts. In fact, the highly skilled STA snipers sneered at the militiamen, though they knew that a stray could be as deadly as a well-aimed round. The rounds Rutter and Baldree put out were calculated to inspire fear, not to draw blood.

As the exchange continued, several Amal snipers manned a new position to the west that had not been previously spotted. The eagle-eyed corporals on the roof could not locate them. Corporal Crumley was awakened and sent down to the Moat in the hope of finding the new bunker from ground level. Crumley could not pinpoint the new Amal bunker so he climbed to the roof with his hand-tooled sniper rifle, one of only eight such perfect weapons in the battalion.

The break came when Crumley spotted a rifleman running in the open. The man was wearing a green sateen uniform and a helmet, perhaps clothing he had been wearing when he deserted from the LAF. Incongruously, he was shod in tennis shoes. Crumley watched where the man went and, suddenly, the whole Amal layout became evident. Trained to use all his patience, the corporal watched long and hard before taking any sort of action. Killing was easy, but learning was the crux of the job. Besides, the bullets the Amal fighters were putting out were passing way over the bunker; the shooters were too close and the angle of fire too steep to endanger the Marine snipers.

The sateen-uniformed militia fighter became obnoxious. He had an automatic weapon Crumley could not identify, which he constantly threw atop the dirt berm next to the Amal bunker and fired right at the STA OP. Enough got to be enough, and Crumley was sufficiently bored to make an example of the cowboy.

The STA sniper carefully placed his scoped sniper rifle on the bunker's sandbagged wall and pointed it in the direction of the dirt berm. He had only a few seconds to settle in before the sateen-clad shooter ripped off another burst. He was going to make Crumley work for the kill. When the firing stopped, Crumley stood up and hurriedly sighted down the barrel of his weapon. The shooter was hiding by then, but the Marine was sure he knew where. Then he had to duck as his target sprayed more rounds at him. When the shooting stopped again, Crumley stood up and perfected his aim. He was not quite ready, so he hunkered down to allow the Amal warrior to squeeze off another burst. He sensed the man was growing impatient, something he would have to watch. The meticulous process of refining the shot continued. There was a growing sense of humor among the Marines in the STA bunker, and more than a little bravado, for it would be a difficult 600-meter shot if the Amal warrior stayed around long enough. Duck and aim, duck and aim.

Finally, Crumley announced, "I'm going to get him this time." He had become bored; it was time for the payoff.

The Amal gunman popped up, then hesitated before firing—the first time he had done so.

CRACK!

The sateen-clad warrior slumped behind the earth berm. Crumley knew he had his kill. The others thumped him on the back. It had been quite a shot despite the long preparation.

Amal gunmen nearby were mad enough to risk everything. The whole line of them stood up behind the berm and ripped off countless rounds while the Marines in the OP huddled laughing behind the sandbag wall. There's no warning some people.

September 8 was marked by a visit to the trenches by BLT 1/8's favorite general, MGen Al Gray, the rough, gruff commanding general of 2d Marine Division, 1/8's parent unit.

Al Gray was known in the Marine Corps as a "troop"—an officer who genuinely enjoyed the company of enlisted Marines.

He had been one himself, before receiving his commission from the ranks in the mid-1950s. An intellectual with less formal schooling than most American officers, Gray had served three consecutive tours in Vietnam and had been the chief architect of the rescue of the American ambassador to Vietnam in 1975. Al Gray's visits were always considered special, but his inimitable style this day made it thoroughly memorable for the grunts.

Druse forward observers must have had little trouble selecting the general's party as a target on September 8. There is something about large batches of brass in spit-shined boots and tailored, starched cammies that draws the eye.

Gray was visiting with Alpha Company when he eased up and clapped his hand on the shoulder of Sgt Robert Galt, a favorite pose. "Sergeant, what problems are you Marines having out here?"

"Sir," Galt replied, "we can't get any chew."

The general pulled a foil bag of Red Man from his pocket and pressed it into Galt's hand.

As Gray mingled with the troops, the first Druse rounds reached toward the Marine lines. The division commander stood with the troops, but his entourage milled about in confusion, the faces of many senior officers dead white from the strain. Gray stood tall for a few moments, then decided it was time to leave. The squat white-haired man with the goggles on his helmet and the two stars on his collar walked upright through the dust toward his helo while the officers behind him strained every inch of the way to remain a discreet distance to his rear. There was definitely a different style at work right then.

Perhaps because a general had been involved in the Druse shelling, perhaps for reasons of state, the Navy unleashed the guns of destroyer *Bowen* against the Druse batteries. This was the first time an American warship had fired on Moslem positions.

One day in early September, a medevac helo had to be dispatched to the university to pick up a slightly injured Marine. As the helo approached, the voice of one of the STA snipers came up on the S-2 net at the battalion combat operations center (COC) to say that a militiaman standing next to an air-conditioning unit on the roof of a nearby building was tracking the CH-46 with a rocket-propelled grenade (RPG).

As the CH-46 flared out for its landing, the sniper came up on the net again. "The RPG's on his shoulder." Then, "He's tracking the helo. Should we take him out?"

Inside the COC, 1stLt Greg Balzer picked up his handset: "Waste him."

The calm, professional voice of the STA sniper came over the net one last time: "Scratch one raghead."

One day when the shooting was slack at the university, Cpl Jonathan Crumley paid a little back to a cowboy the snipers had dubbed Wheelchair Willie, an older man who was wheeled out to man a street-corner checkpoint.

Willie, who was clearly not a deep thinker, had one day blown off a whole AK-47 magazine at a passing truck. The driver had stepped down and pumped a whole AK-47 magazine right into the ground around the wheelchair. Willie had been too frightened to wheel off, so he had scrunched himself into the chair. The lesson held; the STA snipers never saw Willie fire at another truck.

On the day in question, Willie met with a group of Western journalists, many of whom took his picture as he sat with the university at his back and his favorite AK-47 cradled in the crook of his arm or brandished in the air. As soon as the reporters walked from view, Crumley popped up from behind his sandbag wall and aimed his scoped sniper rifle right at Willie. He had no intention of firing, but Willie knew what the STA snipers could do if they wanted to. He was last seen that day scorching the skin off his palms as he madly whirled the wheels of his getaway wheelchair.

Naturally, because a joke is only a joke and all things except blood feuds are eventually forgiven in the land of Lebanon, Wheelchair Willie was back on duty the next day.

The really weird part of looking into Hooterville and the other embattled suburbs was seeing the way the Moslem fighters treated one another. It was evident that they were members of a large number of factions and splinters that did not always see eye to eye. In fact, on balance, the Moslems spent more time and bullets fighting one another than they did fighting the LAF or Marines. That was during working hours. Everyone knocked off for long lunches and at quitting time, around 1700 each day. The STA snipers were sure they saw men who had been fighting one another all day relax together at outdoor cafés, sharing food and cooling beverages before going home to be with their families. After a hard day's fighting between Marines and Moslem gunmen, it was nothing for the gunmen to wave good night to the Marines when it was time to leave. Of course, the Marines waved back.

As more Marines were learning every day, the journalists who crossed between the Marine sectors and the Druse and Amal areas carried news of deaths and injuries. In this way, the STA snipers, and others, were able to confirm their scores and, in general, most of their observations.

It was a toss-up whether the press was worth having around. Most post commanders would have preferred avoiding the responsibility of escorting them and seeing to their safety, but they could provide some needed diversion.

First Lieutenant Pete Ferraro was at an old general store, one of several buildings constituting CP 76, during a rare quiet day when a whole slew of press folks escorted by LtCol Larry Gerlach arrived for a briefing and a look around. The visitors included James Webb, a former Marine combat company commander and author of several popular books on Vietnam and the Naval Academy, who was on assignment with a Public Broadcasting System camera team working for the "McNeil-Lehrer News Hour"; Maj Bob Jordan, the MAU joint public affairs officer; and about twenty print journalists.

There were altogether too many people in the crowded compound, and all that activity inevitably attracted the attention of Moslem gunners, who otherwise might have taken the day off. Most of the newspeople quickly moved on, but several remained on the roof. Pete Ferraro was standing beside the general store with Lieutenant Colonel Gerlach and Jim Webb, pointing out known militia positions. Suddenly, the quiet was shattered when small arms opened an impromptu orchestration. Then heavier stuff started impacting around the building.

Gerlach, Ferraro, and Webb headed up to the roof for a better look and so Ferraro could run his platoon. Nearly all of the half-dozen newspeople there had been in Beirut long enough to know what to do; they all hit the deck. Pete Ferraro took it in stride; he was long past worrying about incoming, had reached the point of fatalism that everyone who has experienced hostile fire reaches. He didn't know how used he had become to the incessant danger, however, until he turned and saw the look on the face of a young lady reporter who had just arrived in the city that day and was on her very first outing. The woman's skin was pallid, and she was trembling from head to foot. Ferraro spoke to her in what he hoped was a soothing voice, telling her to relax, that she would be escorted to safety as soon as the fire subsided.

Ferraro's platoon had good, clear targets in a building in an orchard just 200 meters away. A nearby Druse checkpoint straight up the road from CP 76 was also firing, as were militia emplacements in a large building known as the Chocolate Factory. Bullets of all sizes and RPGs were ripping across the rooftop.

Alpha Company's 3d Platoon took it in stride, though everyone felt the added pressure of the battalion commander's presence and the added responsibility for the newspeople. Pete Ferraro had become so inured to the whole concept of combat and the specter of personal injury that it took a direct order from the battalion commander to get him beneath the protection of his helmet, which he forgot to put on when the firing started and which he was too busy to think about as the fight intensified.

LCpl Eugene Lopez, an M-60 gunner, managed to bag at least one militia marksman firing from a window across the way. And most of the rest of Ferraro's troops were able to bear on firm targets. LAF soldiers manning an APC at Checkpoint 11, just to the rear, sprayed .50-caliber rounds right down the road at the Druse checkpoint while a British-made LAF Centurion tank joined in, firing its 90mm main gun from time to time. LAF soldiers at Checkpoint 11 and the adjacent LAF CP 76, fired their rifles, machine guns, and RPGs. An LAF jeep mounting a 106mm recoilless rifle was hit and set afire by the Druse. This forced Pete Ferraro to move the Marine nearest the jeep because he felt it might explode.

As the exchange continued without sign of letup, it was decided that the newspeople would low-crawl to the rear of the roof and climb down the ladder to the street, from where they would be whisked away at the first lull. The young newslady, who was visibly quivering, did not seem to want to go, but she gamely set out on her hands and knees, following along with the pack, which included combat vets Larry Gerlach and Jim Webb.

The firefight raged for hours. The militias even brought up a 23mm antiaircraft gun at dusk and hosed explosive rounds at CP 76. Ferraro's troops learned a whole new meaning of the word "fear" as the 23mm rounds burst right over their heads. One of the Marines was wounded and evacuated.

The fight lasted until the wee hours, then petered out. In all, Ferraro's platoon expended about eight hundred 7.62mm M-60 rounds, about seventy 40mm M-203 high-explosive (HE) rounds, and nearly five hundred 5.56mm M-16 rounds. Lebanese ambulances were seen around the militia positions in the morning, a sure sign that Ferraro's platoon and the LAF had drawn blood. On the other hand, the LAF suffered one killed and six wounded, and Ferraro had one Marine wounded.

Following the intense September 4 actions, the militias became content to pound Charlie Company with indirect fire from mortars, artillery, and mobile rocket launchers. The root of the militia fighters' action, of course, was the heavy losses they had sustained at Charlie Company's hands. For their part, the Marines were not satisfied simply with sitting in fixed positions and hitting back; the troops wanted to leave the airport and kick the Moslems clear into the Shouf, beyond small-arms range. In fact, the grunts wanted to *occupy* the Shouf, a daring desire but an impractical one.

Charlie Company's troubles with the indirect fire really began when the LAF armored column succeeded in securing a former Israeli checkpoint on the edge of Khalde, across from the Marine sector. The Druse and Amal units responsible for most of the mayhem in the area had to fire over Charlie Company to reach the LAF post, and much of their fire had a tendency—perhaps an intentional tendency—to fall into the Marine lines.

The southernmost position in Marine hands was CP 39, an isolated observation post manned by members of the Target Acquisition Battery. The tiny position consisted of a bunker and an aiming circle, an instrument used to shoot a radar cross-azimuth on hostile positions. Several small-arms rounds whizzed over CP 39 at about 1500 hours, September 7, a Wednesday. All hands had just ducked down into the bunker when an earthshaking noise erupted right overhead. Great gouts of sand and gravel blew into the bunker, convincing everyone that the shelter had sustained a large-caliber direct hit. When the noise died down, after everyone had had an opportunity to inventory limbs and heads, the post commander led the way to daylight. They found that the aiming circle—only ten feet from the bunker—had taken a direct heavy-caliber round. The troops at CP 39 spent days trying to collect the components of the direction-finding equipment, but all they found was its travel case.

By far the most satisfying confrontation between Marines and Moslem gunners occurred one dark September night when, as often happened, the unguarded radio net of a Druse battery bled over into the BLT tac net. An interpreter was called into the COC, and he related the gist of a conversation between a Druse forward observer named Abdul and his battery commander. As the Moslems spoke, Capt Mike Haskell ordered his radio-direction-finding gear into action, and he soon had a rough coordinate on the forward observer. This was relayed to Charlie Battery, which received permission to "fire up" the forward observer, who had been calling fire down on the BIA.

The Marine battery fired one round in the hope an observer would be able to adjust fire. No one saw the round land, but the Druse battery commander came up on his net: "Abdul, are you okay? They just fired at you."

"I am okay. They were short 200 meters."

Captain Haskell heard the translation and nearly jumped for joy. He put his handset to his lips and told his contact at Charlie Battery, "Crank it up 200. Battery, three [rounds]. Fire for effect."

No sooner said than eighteen 155mm HE rounds were fired.

There was a long silence, then the Druse battery commander asked, "Abdul, are you okay?" There was no answer, nor were any of the battery commander's entreaties answered for an hour, at which time a new voice was heard, "Abdul is no more."

SSgt Joe Curtis, of Charlie Company's 1st Platoon, was on his way to the platoon piss tube when he heard the distinctive *pop!* of a Russian-made light mortar hurling a round in his direction. He waited a few minutes after the round impacted, then set out again. *Pop!* Another light-mortar round landed a few moments later. Curtis returned to the bunker, waited a half hour, then headed out a third time. He really had to go now, so he ran to the piss tube and started urinating. *Pop!* The fourth round impacted and Curtis charged back to the bunker. The game had gone on long enough. The platoon sergeant grabbed his binos and scanned the front in search of the forward observer who had been playing him for a fool. *Pop!* The next round landed within ten feet of Curtis, fortunately in a large pile of filled sandbags that had not yet been emplaced. Curtis was thrown clear across the bunker by the concussion.

The big joke around Alpha Company for a few weeks in September was tossing rocks at the head when someone was using it. It seemed like great fun to see a fellow Marine erupt into the open, holding his helmet down with one hand and pulling up his cammie trousers and skivvy drawers with the other.

Corporal Jack Ruffner, of Alpha Company's 3d Platoon, was just leaving the head at CP 76 when a medium-caliber round hooked over the nearest Marine-manned outpost and dropped just ten meters behind the tiny building. Ruffner was blown several feet into the air and landed in a heap, dazed but unhurt.

Working within the confines of the BLT's COC during this period was less dangerous than grappling with the cowboys at the university or on the BIA perimeter, but the pressure was intense. Any incident that could be made lighter became the object of some sort of joke by restless men in peak physical condition who were forced to work off adrenaline while seated.

The coordinates of Druse artillery impacts being fed to the COC during one intense night bombardment in mid-September made absolutely no sense to the officers on watch, so 1stLt Greg Balzer queried one of the observers on the BLT roof for a visual description of the target. The news arrived a few moments later that the target was a construction site at the rear of the nearby BIA baggage terminal.

This made no sense at all, so Balzer turned to Capt Mike Haskell, who was hugging the floor next to him, and said, "Well, sir, they must be using scab labor on the site."

Haskell's eyes brightened and a weird thought popped into

Balzer's head. As the COC staff bounced lightly to the tune of the incoming, both officers sang, "Look for the union label."

Combat Post 76 was dominated on three sides by higher buildings manned by Moslem militia units. One day in early September, LCpl Dan Kovach and Pfc William Oyler, of Alpha Company's 3d Platoon, were on the roof of one of the post buildings when a hitherto undisclosed militia .50-caliber machine gun suddenly burst into life, sending them and their fellow Marines in the compound between the buildings scuttling for cover. Kovach and Oyler located the hostile gun on a rooftop only 200 meters away. When the incoming pierced the tin roof and tin door of the rooftop bunker, Oyler raised his M-203 and blooped out four quick HE rounds. The militia machine gun ceased firing. Next day, an LAF patrol discovered four dead gun crewmen.

A few nights later, Lance Corporal Kovach was standing radio watch at a desk protected by a six-foot-high sandbag wall. A sudden storm of machine-gun rounds flew through the building, lodging in the walls and streaming out through windows facing away from the Moslem positions. First Lieutenant Pete Ferraro stuck his head into the office and said, "Where'd that hit?" Then he saw Kovach sprawled beside the desk, unhurt but severely shaken by a .50-caliber round that had passed inches from his face, narrowly missing the radio.

And then there was the quiet night when three 122mm rockets fired from the Shouf impacted on top of one another all through CP 76. No one was hurt, but each of three positions was rearranged and the troops manning them were severely shaken. Everyone at the combat post "spazzed out" and were only pulling themselves together when, less than a minute later, a fresh 122mm rocket salvo hit home. The rest of the night was dead quiet.

Another rocket salvo hit as six 3d Platoon Marines and corpsmen were crowded into a tiny room mixing a stew from their ration packs in a helmet on the deck. When they heard the rocket whistle in, they all headed for the door together, realized they would not make it, and hit the deck, which was far too small for six men. In the morning, they found the casing of a dud 122mm rocket stuck in the ground right outside the door.

In addition to its positions at CP 76, Alpha Company's 3d Platoon deployed a reinforced squad at posts Whiskey 8 and Whiskey 9, both on the outer perimeter road a few hundred meters south of Checkpoint 11 and fronting the platoon compound.

Each post comprised three trench-connected bunkers set on high berms just west of the road. Only Whiskey 8, the southern-most Alpha Company position, had a machine-gun bunker. Ten Marines, including an M-60 team, usually manned Whiskey 8 and seven usually manned Whiskey 9.

First Lieutenant Pete Ferraro was at Whiskey 9 every night to observe activities in the 3d Platoon sector. One night, several rounds hit the machine-gun bunker at Whiskey 9. Ferraro reported the incident to Company, adding that he had observed the fire as it left a narrow two-story building about 300 meters to the southeast. Only a minute had passed when Ferraro saw another burst fired from the lower left side of the same building. He called a report to Company, which instructed him to fire one M-203 illume round over the militia position to warn the hostile gunners that they had been spotted. Ferraro's grenadier popped the illume, which was answered by bursts of fire from the same building and another Moslem bunker located in a three-story building, also about 300 meters away.

Ferraro reported to Company yet again. He was given permission to return fire, but cautioned to remain within the Rules of Engagement. Marines at both Whiskey 8 and Whiskey 9 opened with M-16s and the M-60. The machine gun concentrated on the two-story building while the riflemen fired at it and the three-story structure. Far from suppressing the incoming, Ferraro's response brought on an increased volume of fire. He reported to Company, which recommended that he use M-203 HE. Three HE rounds were fired, and all were seen to impact on the target, which was silenced for only a few moments.

Capt Paul Roy next suggested that Ferraro fire only M-203 illume. Ferraro complied. The *pop* of the grenade launcher brought the incoming to a halt because the militia gunners no doubt ducked to evade HE.

The incoming started again as soon as the illume flared overhead. Ferraro repeated the tactic, and the Moslems stopped firing. When the illume died, however, they returned even heavier fire. A third militia position located in a chicken coop 150 meters directly across the outer perimeter road joined in.

Pete Ferraro got on his squad radio and told the troops manning Whiskey 8 to open fire on the chicken coop on his signal, then cease firing as soon as his M-203 popped the next illume. The M-60 was to hit the long three-story building. When the platoon leader received an acknowledgment from Whiskey 8, he told the Marines manning Whiskey 9 to fire everything they had at the two-story building. The two M-203 gunners were each to fire three HE rounds.

Ferraro passed the order, and everyone fired as directed until the lieutenant was certain he had suppressed the targets. He ordered up the M-203 illume, and all hands ceased firing.

The militiamen manning the bunker in the lower left portion of the two-story building immediately resumed firing at the Marine posts. Ferraro had several more illume rounds fired, but they did no good. He called Company, which told him to fire only M-203 HE.

Cpl Jack Ruffner aimed in with his M-203. Right behind him was Pete Ferraro, ready to reload the launcher as soon as the first HE round was away. Ruffner fired once, twice . . . five times in rapid succession. All the rounds were right on target. Nothing more was heard from that bunker, or any of the others. Pete Ferraro proudly told Company, "We got that SOB!"

And so it went.

18

Col Tim Geraghty had seen the changes coming, and he had reported his observations and opinions through the chain of command. Not much had come back. Beirut had long been quiescent; it was possible for the people with the strings in their hands to believe that the Multinational Force (MNF) contribution to peace in Lebanon was real and lasting; they chose to make that observation; the messages of unease emanating from 24th Marine Amphibious Unit (MAU) were largely discounted.

Geraghty was a busy, busy man. Not only did he have responsibility for monitoring the day-to-day activities of his command, he had to meet regularly with the senior naval officers who were his superiors in the 6th Fleet chain of command; he had to meet with his fellow MNF commanders and with representatives of the Lebanese Armed Forces (LAF); he had to sit before so many news cameras that there was a brief joke about his being asked to join the American Federation of Television and Radio Announcers; he had to inspect the troops; and he had to spend an enormous amount of time with VIPs ranging from the Vice President of the United States to foreign heads of state, senior military officers, and congressional junketeers. It took all of the colonel's considerable powers of concentration and energy to keep his attention on the mission and the situation in and around Beirut.

It was easy for Geraghty to immerse himself in the most important and potentially most rewarding assignment of his career until, in mid-July, the Israelis announced their intention to withdraw from the Beirut area.

The Israeli announcement was a major blow to the people overseeing the security of the city for, no matter what political pronouncements were made in world capitals, it was known beyond doubt that the Israel Defense Force (IDF) was the force that made peace work in Beirut—that everything else was essentially window dressing.

The incongruities of the situation became evident when the Reagan administration publicly demanded an Israeli withdrawal while it privately asked the government of Israel to keep the IDF in Beirut for as long as possible.

Geraghty and his fellow MNF commanders spoke openly about this and other inconsistencies in the foreign policies of their respective governments each Tuesday and Friday, when they and their political counterparts met at the presidential palace.

Until the initial Israeli withdrawal on August 28, Tim Geraghty's job was exhausting but largely routine. The spilling of American blood on August 29 decisively changed the mission of 24th MAU—whether or not the Reagan administration, the U.S. Congress, or the military chain of command agreed. The problem was that Geraghty could not adequately *react* to the coming of general war to Beirut in a manner that he considered prudent. He was the man on the spot, but it was evident from the start that no one at higher levels and removed from the scene really cared to hear what he was saying. Solid military professional that he was, Tim Geraghty publicly went along with the public charade, but he was also a seasoned player, and he used his knowledge of the system—and allies within it—to try to leverage an adequate response from above. However, Geraghty was an apolitical officer; he had no leverage with the political people and institutions that mattered.

There had been no time when 24th MAU was ashore that Colonel Geraghty did not feel a sense of unease over the open, "permissive" nature of his compound. He made guarded entreaties through the chain of command in the hope of being allowed to dig in deeper, but each request was rebuffed with a warning that Beirut International Airport (BIA) could not be fortified. Not digging in went against everything Tim Geraghty had learned and lived by for a quarter century, but he obeyed —though he was not without the savvy to test the limits of the directives by which he was hobbled. He knew that any step he took over the vague line drawn in his mission directives would be slapped down, so he either fostered a program of finding what was considered to be an overstep or he turned a blind eye while his subordinates stretched the rules. The results, and the messages, were mixed, but Geraghty was grateful for any step in what he thought was the right direction.

Frankly, everyone in authority—both military and political— appears to have known precisely what was going on, and everyone was kept abreast of what might happen. But political considerations—some domestic, some foreign—prevented the MAU commander from taking many prudent steps that might have saved American and Lebanese lives or, indeed, kept the lid on the BIA and its immediate environs.

One of the things that made Geraghty really nervous was his dependence upon the LAF and other Lebanese agencies for securing the BIA. Marines could not stop inflowing traffic, nor even stop suspicious-looking pedestrians at or near the BIA. The job had to be left to the Lebanese, many of whom shared dubious leanings in the midst of what was, after all, a civil war sparked by legitimate political and confessional grievances. No one knew what particular security guards might be allowing to pass, nor were Marines thrilled by the standards of the Lebanese security agencies in the selection of their operatives. Colonel Geraghty was turned down every time he tried to wrest more control of airport security, so he had no effective control over his own compound. The charade was carried to a dangerous extreme when Marine sentries were ordered to remove magazines from their weapons and prevented from using those weapons until after a presumed hostile act was already under way.

Somehow, despite misperceptions and power plays within and between the departments of State and Defense, the United States managed to maintain at least a facade of neutrality through the end of August. It had been impressed upon Tim Geraghty, and by him upon his subordinates, that the United States was a neutral player in Lebanon, and that all parties to the civil war were to be treated equally. However, one of the parties, the Gemayel government, was the only one officially recognized by the United States, and one organ of the Gemayel government, the LAF, was largely trained and equipped by the United States. While it could be stated that neither the government nor its armed forces was a creature of the United States, nor vice versa, such arguments evaporated forever on August 28, when the Marine contingent at CP 69 was drawn into the civil war on the side of the LAF, and again on September 4, when the LAF assault on Khalde was inadvertently supported by Battalion Landing Team 1/8.

By the end of the first week of September, the MAU was essentially isolated at the BIA, the Lebanese University, and the American embassy—three fortresses without adequate fortifications. Marines could no longer get around town to "show the flag" nor even adequately supply their outposts. What had been a ten-minute walk from the BIA to the university became a dangerous and circuitous forty-five-minute drive for supply trucks. The MAU contingent at the embassy had to be resupplied by boats from the Mediterranean Amphibious Ready Group on days that fighting in West Beirut closed all the roads from the BIA. Thus, despite monumental efforts to show the opposite, the MAU was placed in de facto fortifications, isolated by events if not by barbed wire and sandbags. Very quickly, the Marines developed a defensive, fortress mentality, which was about all that was allowed them in that regard by higher authorities.

Tim Geraghty's personal pain and suffering resulted when his desire to react forcefully to Marine casualties had to be balanced by his acute understanding that short-term solutions would obviate the potential long-term benefits of U.S. neutrality in the conflict.

The placement of illumination rounds in proximity to hostile Moslem batteries, for example, was a painstakingly conceived response aimed at showing the power of the United States in a benign fashion. However, American minds did not grasp Lebanese realities. Force met with less than equal force was no force at all; a weak response was a sign of weakness, and the weak were put on earth to be beaten. Stronger responses, from meeting snipers with heavy fire to blasting militia batteries with 155mm shells, were invariably taken seriously by the posturing militias.

The MAU's perceived weakness was codified under three basic principles: first, Marines were to initiate no gunplay; second, any hostile displays were to be terminated in the shortest possible time; and third, the American response would remain in direct proportion to the threat. Once it was realized that Marines would not raise the ante, the United States ceased to be a serious player in Lebanese internal affairs; the objective of the Lebanese players became the neutralization of the MAU and the manipulation of the organs of American democracy.

Despite Colonel Geraghty's obvious concern over the impact of the September War upon the MAU, he realized at the outset that the war was essentially between Lebanese. A typical September afternoon saw the expenditure of 6,000 or more 155mm artillery rounds by LAF or Christian Phalange forces against Druse or Shiite positions, and at least an equal response by Druse and Shiite mortars, rockets, and artillery. Whatever fire fell upon the Lebanese University and the BIA was minor by comparison, a mere sideshow in as total a war as Tim Geraghty had ever seen. There was no doubt, however, that the sideshow was intentional.

Geraghty had no difficulty seeing that the civil war was between Lebanese, but he was having a great deal of difficulty understanding why he was saddled with an outmoded and emasculated mission directive in the face of so radical a departure of the real from the ideal. Tim Geraghty wondered what purpose the MAU was serving in Lebanon, and he was not at all happy with assurances that there were essential considerations to which he could not be made privy.

The turning point arrived on September 9, when LtGen Ibrahim Tannous formally asked Special Ambassador Robert (Bud) McFarlane to provide direct U.S. support for an LAF force fighting in the Shouf market town of Suq-al-Gharb.

On September 5 Druse infantry had destroyed a Christian militia force in Bhamdoun, overlooking Christian East Beirut, and it became imperative that a retaliation of some sort be mounted against the Druse. The LAF 8th Brigade, an American-trained, Moslem-Christian formation, was ordered to attack into the Shouf. The advance was hotly contested, but 8th Brigade attacked with uncharacteristic vigor and managed to achieve an unprecedented success. Suq-al-Gharb was not the final objective, nor even a particularly important one, for it was dominated by Druse positions farther up the cordillera. Suq-al-Gharb just happened to be the place where the LAF assault ran out of steam and the Moslem defenses coalesced.

Bud McFarlane had given up a promising Marine Corps career after serving for several years as a military aide to Secretary of State Henry Kissinger during the Ford administration. He had retired as a lieutenant colonel and had entered the State Department hierarchy as a Kissinger protégé. His career flourished during the early Reagan years, and his assignment as special presidential envoy appeared to confirm Henry Kissinger's discerning eye for talent. Nevertheless, McFarlane was plunged into an arena for which, on balance, he seemed woefully unprepared.

General Tannous's request appears to have been sparked by a September 9 report from Suq-al-Gharb that powerful contingents of the Syrian-backed Palestine Liberation Army, with some Druse, Palestine Liberation Organization, Iranian, and Syrian support, were massing in the hills overlooking the town. An attempt to reinforce 8th Brigade was halted by Druse artillery. According to Tannous, Suq-al-Gharb was in danger of being overrun and at least one LAF artillery battalion had fired all its ammunition supporting 8th Brigade.

The essential fact from General Tannous's standpoint appears to have been the initial success of his relatively untried army. Contrary to all expectations, 8th Brigade had not split along confessional lines but had stuck together. And Christian and Moslem officers and noncoms had been killed or injured in forward positions while *leading* their troops in battle. So, quite aside from the dubious value of Suq-al-Gharb as an objective, the LAF was in the process of forging a new ethos, and Tannous believed that neither it nor the concept of a united Lebanon would survive a defeat there.

Once McFarlane had the LAF request and had been apprised of the reasons for it, he asked for permission to support the LAF. It was his surmise that a defeat at Suq-al-Gharb could very well result in the fall of the Gemayel government. He was also deeply concerned with the emergence of Syrian forces as active participants in an effort to dislodge 8th Brigade. The request passed from McFarlane's boss, National Security Adviser William Clark, to President Reagan. A meeting between Reagan, Clark,

Secretary of State George Shultz, and Secretary of Defense Caspar Weinberger was held on September 11. Though Weinberger opposed Clark and Shultz, President Reagan authorized a bombardment of the forces attacking Suq-al-Gharb by U.S. warships—but only if the commander on the ground felt that Suq-al-Gharb was "in imminent danger of falling."

Upon hearing from Washington, Ambassador McFarlane asked Colonel Geraghty to formally request the use of naval gunfire in support of 8th Brigade at Suq-al-Gharb.

Although Geraghty felt that abandoning the LAF troopers at Suq-al-Gharb would have been unconscionable, he refused to request the naval gunfire support. If the U.S. MNF contingent was to remain neutral in the civil war—if he was denied access to prudent measures to protect his Marines in the name of that neutrality—he was not going to be a party to actively siding with the LAF in the civil war. More to the point, Geraghty attempted to dissuade McFarlane from pursuing the matter. Information from intelligence sources to which the MAU commander had access indicated that 8th Brigade was not in nearly the difficulty portrayed by the Lebanese army commander; he asked McFarlane to at least obtain complete information. Geraghty's immediate concern, however, arose from his knowledge that the Druse had amassed about 600 medium and heavy artillery tubes in the Shouf and that these could be turned upon the BIA at any time. Tim Geraghty was quite simply concerned that the MAU would be ground to dust by Druse artillery if warships at the MAU's disposal attempted to destroy Druse positions overlooking Suq-al-Gharb.

Faced with Geraghty's refusal to request the mission, McFarlane went back up through his own hierarchy in the hope that either convincing pressure could be applied through the military chain of command or that a more pliable military officer could be talked into making the necessary request. When the message traffic reached the Pentagon, however, senior military officers interpreted President Reagan's initiating order as enabling Colonel Geraghty to block the request if he thought the naval fire mission might bring harm to his troops. Since Geraghty had stated that so clear a stand on the side of the LAF would probably cause the Druse to smother the BIA in artillery fire, McFarlane's effort was stymied.

The Reagan administration was then coming under mounting pressure at home to end or at least reassess the Lebanon involvement. On September 8—the day *Bowen* first fired to suppress Druse artillery—Congressman Clarence Long opened a congressional debate on the War Powers Act, the law under which President Reagan had placed troops in Beirut and under which the Congress could demand an active role in future events. Long also warned that funding for the MNF contingent was up for review on November 1 and that the law demanded a formal administration declaration of the mission of American troops in combat.

The congressional attention no doubt caused the Reagan administration great concern. That the deployment was becoming a test of political wills was only then becoming evident. More to the point, however, the War Powers Act prevented U.S. forces from becoming actively involved in a foreign war without congressional approval *or* unless American lives were directly threatened. Unless the naval gunfire could be shown to be an act of self-defense, the Congress was bound by law to scrutinize not only the precipitating incident but the entire background.

So, while the President had allowed the ground commander, Tim Geraghty, some discretion in the matter of supporting the LAF with American naval gunfire, and while Geraghty had good reasons for blocking the mission, Bud McFarlane was under enormous political pressure to get Geraghty to reverse his decision. McFarlane's job was not made any easier by the support Geraghty received from other military officers on the scene, chiefly Capt Morgan France, the amphibious force commodore who was Geraghty's nominal superior. Another key ally was Army Col Tom Fintel, head of the American mission assigned to train the LAF. Fintel had sources of his own at Suq-al-Gharb that revealed that 8th Brigade was holding up well against attacks of considerably less magnitude than were being reported by the Lebanese Ministry of Defense.

Geraghty and McFarlane, who had been near contemporaries in the Marine Corps, are reported to have had several acrimonious exchanges during the next seven days. Indeed, the routine at the MAU communications center was shattered one day when Geraghty received a bit too much pressure from one of McFarlane's associates. "We'll pay the price," Geraghty yelled. "We'll get slaughtered down here."

The colonel and the ambassador agreed that 8th Brigade should be assisted if in extreme danger, but the lengthening argument saw 8th Brigade remain in possession of Suq-al-Gharb. The danger had been real enough by Lebanese standards, and it had been severely exacerbated by a scarcity of artillery ammunition within the LAF. This shortage was repaired by an emergency delivery of American-supplied munitions through Jounieh, the Phalange-controlled port north of Beirut.

By the end of the week, Bud McFarlane had shifted his interest solely from helping 8th Brigade to demonstrating American willpower to Syria and her Soviet backers. Tim Geraghty simply wanted to preserve the lives of his Marines.

Events in Beirut took an ugly turn on September 16 when, by accident or design, several shells fell around the U.S. embassy in West Beirut and the U.S. ambassador's residence in Yardze. No reports indicate who fired these rounds, but the Druse were held accountable, for frigate *John Rodgers* pumped sixty rounds of 5-inch HE into Druse battery positions in the Shouf beginning at about 1100. On the same day, the Lebanese Air Force launched its first air strike in a decade. Five aged Hawker Hunter fighter-bombers hit the ridge lines around Suq-al-Gharb and reportedly destroyed numerous Druse positions and several obsolescent Soviet-built, Syrian-supplied T-54 tanks. One of the Hunters was shot down into the sea, from which its pilot was plucked by a helicopter from U.S. carrier *Eisenhower.* A second Lebanese jet sustained damage and made an emergency landing at the BIA, while two others were hit and flew to Cyprus, where they landed at the Royal Air Force base at Akrotiri. Three Lebanese jets mounted an air strike the next day, September 17. On that day, also, *John Rodgers* continued to fire at Druse batteries harassing the BIA.

In the end, McFarlane prevailed when a U.S. Army officer who had slipped into Suq-al-Gharb reported on the night of September 18 that he could hear tanks being brought up to Moslem staging areas overlooking the 8th Brigade lines. Tim Geraghty well knew that 8th Brigade would probably not weather a tank assault, so he relented and ordered his own officers to plot the naval gunfire mission.

What Geraghty won in his week of stubborn refusal was the arrival of a fresh MAU, the 31st, off the coast of Lebanon, to which it had been dispatched from Hawaii on September 2, and permission to call carrier air strikes against hostile targets. So if the naval bombardment resulted in a massive Druse retaliation, 24th MAU could at least depend on some support.

It is revealing that the military authorities overseeing 24th MAU persisted in publicly minimizing the fighting between Marines and Moslem militias.

Secretary of Defense Caspar Weinberger lobbied long and hard against the escalation of the military role in Lebanon, but he was beaten by Secretary of State George Shultz. Though Marines in Beirut knew better, the Commandant of the Marine Corps, Gen Paul (PX) Kelley, told a congressional panel on September 13 that there was "not a significant danger at this time . . . to our Marines" and "no evidence that any of the rocket or artillery fire has been specifically directed against Marines." Kelley's statement obviated the administration's gambit to support 8th Brigade by tying the naval gunfire support to a threat upon American lives—a major requirement of the War Powers Act.

___

The shredded veil of American neutrality in Lebanon was whipped off on the morning of September 19, when three gray-painted American warships sliced through the waters off the Port of Beirut and trained their guns on Moslem positions overlooking Suq-al-Gharb. The first ship to fire that morning was guided-missile cruiser *Virginia,* which opened at 1004 with her two radar-controlled 5-inch guns. Shortly thereafter, destroyer *Bowen* and frigate *John Rodgers* also fired. The three American warships expended a total of 338 rounds.

The results of the naval gunfire were monitored by F-14 Tomcat fighters launched from carrier *Eisenhower.* And the reconnaissance jets and the BIA were further protected by several divisions of fully loaded fighter-bombers on station in the air over the Mediterranean. This was itself a quantum leap in the role of U.S. forces in and around Lebanon. The reconnaissance flights had been going on for at least a week, but the launching of armed fighter-bombers was something entirely new. Not surprisingly, given Ambassador McFarlane's desire to impress Syria, details were easily obtained by the press.

The Congress acted just two days after the bombardment of the Moslem positions around Suq-al-Gharb by authorizing the Reagan administration to keep up to 1,200 Marines on the ground in Lebanon for up to eighteen months. This was something more than the administration had dared request.

While the Marine commandant, Gen PX Kelley, was telling reporters on September 21 that he thought a cease-fire in Lebanon was imminent, Moslem batteries redoubled their shellings of Beirut and its suburbs. The U.S. ambassador's residence in Yardze had to be evacuated overnight when rounds fell into the compound. Also on September 21, the Durafourd Building, which housed part of the U.S. embassy staff, was struck by a rocket-propelled grenade. In following days, the main Italian MNF ammunition dump was destroyed by a Druse rocket, four French MNF soldiers were injured by an artillery round, and two more Frenchmen were wounded by a hand grenade. On the other hand, the continuing naval bombardment of the area around Suq-al-Gharb added considerably to the tally of dead and injured Moslems.

News reports on September 23 revealed that *New Jersey*, the world's only active battleship, had passed Gibraltar on its way to Beirut. And, on the same day, it was announced that American and Saudi mediators had hammered out a compromise peace plan that appeared to be acceptable to the warring parties. In reality, the plan had to appeal to only two parties, the Gemayel government and Syria. While proposals and counterproposals were by then daily fare in Beirut and Damascus, it was felt by knowledgeable parties that a cease-fire really could be worked out. Eventually.

Despite criticism of the American naval bombardment by the French foreign minister a few days earlier, French warplanes struck Moslem batteries behind Syrian lines on September 24. When news of the air strike—mounted in retaliation for the six French soldiers injured earlier in the week—was heard at the BIA, Marines found the time to be angry; many of them wondered aloud what it would take to move their own leaders to mount a retaliatory air strike in direct support of the MAU— rather than naval gunfire missions in support of the LAF. Incoming injured four Marines that day.

New Jersey arrived off the BIA on September 25. To Marines, she was the loveliest hunk of steel in the world. Her 16-inch guns were reputed to be able to fire one-ton shells as far as Damascus, and she had a dozen 5-inch guns in her secondary battery. Marines at the BIA thought and talked about little more than what *New Jersey* would do to the Moslem gunners.

The first cease-fire accord was announced by Saudi and Syrian mediators on September 26. The time for silencing the guns came and went, but no one had seriously expected the accord to stick on the first try. Everyone knew that no real cease-fire could be implemented until each faction had convinced itself that it had achieved maximum advantage over its competition. This invariably meant a rising wave of violence—until military stalemates or political goals had been achieved.

Nevertheless, this was a period of monumental optimism. Representatives of the major warring factions were meeting secretly in the hope of convening a national reconciliation conference aimed at settling the years-old civil war, and some militia checkpoints were closed down. The BIA was patched and reopened on September 30, hundreds of construction crews were at work around the city, roads were being repaired, shops were reopened—life in The Root made a few halting steps toward "normal."

19

The Bravo Company positions at and around the Lebanese University had received their fair share of the action in the weeks since 2dLt Dave Hough's 2d Platoon had held the line at combat posts 35 and 69, but the intensity of the fighting had been nowhere near the levels achieved during the week before Hough's platoon returned to the university from the combat posts.

Bravo Company's 2d Platoon was rotated to the combat posts once again on September 23, just as the September War was reaching its grand finale.

The situation in Bravo Company's sector did not change much through the third week of September. There was a huge volume of continuous small-arms and heavy-caliber fire, both outgoing and incoming, but there was no direct threat of ground assault. The Lebanese Armed Forces (LAF) inserted a new combat post between 76 and 69 in order to further squeeze off the flow of munitions into Hooterville, but the Marine Amphibious

Unit (MAU) declined to place Marines there. The objective, even in the face of so much incoming throughout September, was to provide as low a profile as possible. Capt Monte Hoover, Bravo Company commander, several times requested that the Marine contingents at the jointly manned combat posts be withdrawn to strengthen the university defenses. However, Colonel Geraghty was not prepared to go quite that far. No one was seriously harassing the posts, the Marine presence seemed to bolster the spirit of the LAF contingents, and the flow of munitions and arms into Hooterville seemed to be under control; there was no apparent or immediate need to evacuate.

If anything, the virtual strangulation of the militia supply routes into Hooterville was the most important aspect of the continuing maintenance of the three combat posts. The LAF attack into the Shouf, to Suq-al-Gharb, had the effect of creating an LAF cordon running from the mountain town to Ashuefat and, by extension, along the line linking combat posts 35, 69, and 76. If the militias in Hooterville were to be adequately provisioned with arms and ammunition, that line would have to be breached. The obvious place was at the most isolated juncture—CP 69.

Second Platoon hiked out of the university compound on the morning of September 23 with the intention of dropping the reinforced 2d Squad at CP 35 and then marching on to 69. Things became tense as soon as the column marched into Hooterville. A squad of Amal gunmen manning a high dirt berm on the right side of the road blocked the path of 1st Squad, which was on the point, and made extremely threatening gestures with their rifles and rocket-propelled grenades (RPGs). As 1st Squad deployed to defend itself against the harassers, Lieutenant Hough trotted forward, identified the Amal leader, and got down to the sort of harsh negotiations he had learned to conduct a few weeks earlier. While Hough spoke, the Marines at his back relieved and resupplied CP 35. When that was done,

Hough told the Amal officer that he would leave, which he did.

The bulk of the reinforced platoon had only just cleared CP 35 when the Amal toughs standing atop the berm again brandished their AK-47s and RPGs. HM3 Mark Hacala had been calm to that point, but he now reached slowly for his holstered .45-caliber automatic and eased a round into the chamber, the first time he had ever been moved to do that. The *snick* of bullets being pushed into the chambers of M-16s provided the corpsman with as much reassurance as he knew he was going to get.

When the balance of Hough's platoon arrived at CP 69, it was packing a heavy wallop. Two thirteen-man infantry squads were bolstered by a three-man Dragon team with six Dragon rounds, a seven-man machine-gun squad, and a four-man platoon headquarters group. There were as many LAF troops at the combat post—a squad each from Battalion 31 and the 1st Air Assault Battalion—but they had far more weapons and ammunition than the Marines. The disparity in armaments was equalized as soon as Hough's force arrived. The lieutenant ordered a rigorous cross-training session so his Marines could avail themselves of the Lebanese weapons and munitions in the event there was heavy action—in which case, all assumed, the Lebanese would either refuse to fire or would waste their ammunition.

There was definitely something in the air around Hooterville. The heaviest shellings of the period had hit the university on the three successive nights before Hough's platoon left the library building for the outposts. There were numerous reports of increased militia patroling and footborne supply deliveries to the ville and known militia positions around Ashuefat. And, most ominous, LAF intelligence operatives were filing reports indicating a final assault by the militias.

As soon as 2d Platoon had relieved 3d Platoon at CP 69, the 1st Air Assault platoon leader approached Dave Hough with news that 250 Druse and Palestine Liberation Organization fighters, bolstered by six T-55 tanks and commanded by four Syrian army officers, were massing in the Chocolate Factory, a large building in Ashuefat southeast of the combat post. It was certain, the Lebanese lieutenant declared, that a ground assault would soon be launched. The LAF officer also informed Lieutenant Hough that the combat post had been rocketed two nights in a row, a definite sign that the place was being softened up.

Light small-arms fire began flitting across the sandbagged compound only two hours after Hough's arrival. Shelling was continuous through the balance of the day. Lieutenant Hough, who had become inured to the effects of artillery bombardment, was using the communal piss tube about ten meters outside the wall when an LAF 155mm round impacted several hundred meters away. The air over the piss tube was filled with madly whirring steel silvers, many large enough to kill a man; some of them landed within feet of the urinating officer.

Welcome back to CP 69.

Just before sunset, fifteen overeager Moslems were spotted as they crossed between several greenhouses just west of the post. Marines could plainly see that the militiamen were carrying heavy loads of weapons and ammunition, but the Rules of Engagement prevented them from initiating a hot contact. The LAF troopers were not burdened by such directives, so they whacked the group with their .50-caliber heavy machine guns, 7.62mm assault machine guns, and M-16s. Ten of the bearers were definitely killed. Within thirty minutes, several white Ford Pinto station wagons flying Red Crescent flags arrived to carry off the dead and dying.

The LAF had been given free-fire orders in response to the Moslem buildup between Hooterville and Ashuefat, and they were actually bragging about drawing large quantities of blood. Indeed, that was the biggest change Lieutenant Hough noted when he arrived at CP 69—the Battalion 31 squad was looking sharp and very much into the business of "taking names," of killing militia fighters. The LAF squads even undertook "recon by fire" every half hour during the night, a technique borrowed from the Israelis that was aimed at achieving maximum random violence with minimum personnel losses. On the other hand, an LAF plan to mine the mint fields around the combat post never came off.

Another significant change pointed out to Lieutenant Hough by his LAF counterpart lay on the outside, where the Druse and Shiite militias had marshaled bulldozers to install a trench system, complete with reinforced bunkers, all the way around CP 69. Hough, who could clearly see sandbagged windows in all the nearby buildings, felt he knew precisely how the French paras had felt at Dien Bien Phu.

Eighteen 122mm rockets impacted around the combat post during the night.

The new LAF combat post between 69 and 76 was struck by Moslem fire at about 1300, September 24—another bloody Sunday. Lieutenant Hough ordered his men to don helmets and flak jackets and man their fighting positions. The alerted Marines could see Moslem militiamen moving into their carefully prepared bunkers and fighting holes, prepping weapons, and taking aim. The Marines could do nothing to prevent what they knew was coming. Unless the Moslems opened fire, the American weapons had to remain silent.

The first RPG flew over CP 69 from out of nowhere at about 1345. Immediately, massive small-arms fire hosed the perimeter, then .50-caliber, 12.7mm, 23mm, and 106mm weapons joined in. There was no question about it: this was the big one.

Cpl Rod Cliff, the machine-gun-squad leader, hit the deck with everyone else, then heard Lieutenant Hough's order to provide a minimal, cautious response. Cliff ordered the crews of his two M-60s to return fire, then settled in to direct his gunners to take out the opposition machine guns. He had to run back and forth across the compound to control the two guns, but the teams were well trained and highly motivated. The system worked like a charm as each gunner had good, clear targets and could easily see his tracers going in. There was no question that militiamen were being killed and wounded.

Sgt José Lopez was hard at work organizing the northern defenses when the first rounds struck the post. Within seconds, as the 1st Squad leader yelled "Fire-team leaders up," one of the hundreds of rounds traversing the compound from south to north hit him solidly in the left buttock. LCpl JJ Firda was only a few feet away, but he had no idea that the sergeant was hit, for Lopez bit back the pain as he was picked up off his feet and flipped onto his back. Firda thought that the sergeant's dropping to the deck in the face of so much fire was a pretty sane thing to do. Only after the nearest rifleman knelt beside Lopez to offer aid did it dawn on Firda that something was amiss, and only then did he see the heavy smear of blood on Lopez's trousers.

"Corpsman up!"

HM3 Mark Hacala was seated peacefully in his bunker, carving a wooden sign that was to read "Fort Apache—U.S." when the first gales of fire struck the compound. He had managed to carve his way to oblivion, answering calls only when someone entered the bunker to request a headache remedy or the like. When Hacala heard the shouted calls of "Corpsman up!" and "Doc! Doc!" he furiously pushed his head through the entryway and yelled back, "What the fuck is it this time? Someone hit, or something?"

"Yeah."

Hacala immediately "hauled ass" across the fire-swept compound, but had to turn back midway to collect his Unit-1 aid pack. When he finally reached the northern wall, he was stunned to find that the casualty was Sergeant Lopez, a hitherto unassailable wildman who had kept everyone's sense of invulnerability operational during the last fight at CP 69.

Pfc Michael Horne was manning the radio when Lopez was hit, so he was the one to report the injury to the company combat operations center (COC). Lieutenant Hough was a real stickler for radio procedure, so the radiomen were careful to get all the call signs in perfect order while transmitting. Thus Horne said, "Foxtrot-2, this is Foxtrot-1. Echo-5-Lima has been wounded in the gluteus maximus." The company radioman came back with, "What?" Horne repeated the message. The company radioman asked, "What the hell are you talking about?" Horne lost all patience: "Be advised that Sergeant Lopez has been shot in the ass."

Sergeant Lopez was the ideal patient. He had served a tour as an Army airborne medic, so he and Doc Hacala had forged a close companionship on the basis of their medical expertise.

The bullet had entered right at the top of Lopez's buttocks and had exited at an awkward spot at the top of the left leg, barely missing the femoral artery. Tiny chunks of meat had been spread across the sergeant's cammie trousers and wads of sub-cutaneous fat ringed both wounds.

Hacala fingered his speed scissors and went to work cutting away the sergeant's trousers. The scissors were designed to cut through a penny, but the doc had a defective pair that would not even damage cloth. The corpsman then accepted Lopez's offer of a cheaply made clasp knife he had traded away from a Lebanese soldier, a blade reputed to have taken the life of an Amal warrior. Hacala forced the fabric and exposed the wound. It was going to be impossible to bandage properly, but at least the wound was not bleeding or, apparently, life-threatening.

Finished with the task of organizing the defense, Dave Hough dropped down beside Doc Hacala to see how Sergeant Lopez was faring. Then Hough asked the corpsman if he thought Lopez should be moved behind the nearby blast wall.

"No, sir. I don't think he should be moved."

Hough stared at Hacala for a moment, then asked, "Doc, where did he get shot?"

"Uh, right here."

"Well, don't you think if they shot Lopez here they could get you here?"

Lopez was rolled into a poncho, carried from where he had fallen in the open, placed upon a stretcher set between the inner and outer blast walls, and made about as comfortable as the situation allowed. But there was one serious problem. The wounded man had such bad veins from low blood pressure brought on by shock that Doc Hacala could not get a proper IV started. Once Hacala had used his only three catheters, he had to repeatedly sterilize and reuse them, a technique that would have been absolutely forbidden under any other circumstances.

It was apparent from the start that this was to be nothing like the battles that had been waged in late August and early September. The opposing force was extremely well armed and had no end of ammunition to fire. On the other hand, the Marines had brought along over 10,000 5.52mm bullets, over a hundred M-203 rounds, fifty hand grenades, numerous LAAWs, and six Dragon rounds. There were over a hundred American Marines and LAF soldiers manning the twin CP 69 outposts, and all were highly motivated. Still, the incoming was so intense that the old olive trees within the Marine compound were splintered, then felled by bullets alone, and sandbags lining the outer wall leaked through hundreds of ragged gashes. RPG rounds, about forty in all, skipped through the compound within the first hour. As soon as Sergeant Lopez was hit, Lieutenant Hough told his Marines to take any action they felt was appropriate; the time for holding back had passed: "Wax the fuckers!"

Militia arms that had initially fired at CP 76 and the LAF post between it and CP 69 were all shifted after the first hour to bear upon 69, a cause for deep concern.

Captain Hoover, who was observing from the roof of the university library, two and a half kilometers away, could see the smoke and hear the fire. He tried to maintain control of his emotions and his radio procedure, but one massive detonation caused him to involuntarily yell, "Lieutenant Hough! Lieutenant Hough!" He literally had his heart in his mouth.

Hough responded in his calmest voice, "Foxtrot-2, this is Tango-1. Over."

Hoover pulled himself together and chirped back in his friendly, high-pitched Hoosier drawl, "Oh, uh, how's it goin' down there?"

"Okay, sir."

"Well,' uh, keep up the good work."

There was that rush again, that incredible, exhilarating, unique, feral excitement of being in life-stakes action. It made time pass quickly and the scenes pass slowly. Everyone had a buzz on, from terror and shock and fast living.

Target acquisition was severely hampered by the uncharacteristic care the militia fighters had exerted in preparing their bunkers. Very few bunkers or reinforced rooms within the numerous nearby buildings could be easily seen, and very few Moslem fighters stood near windows when they fired. The muzzle flashes that had helped Marines identify numerous militia fighting positions a few weeks earlier were quite rare this day, forcing Marines to expose themselves to find targets and bring their weapons to bear. The machine gunners were superb in this regard; when they could find no other way to bring the M-60s to bear, they habitually stood up in the face of incoming rounds to return the fire. LCpl Gordon Hickman was thus nicked in the neck, and he dropped behind the sandbagged blast wall to chill out.

Lieutenant Hough found Hickman in the course of his rounds through the compound and asked the gunner what the trouble was.

"I was shot," Hickman responded. "Do you think I'll get a Purple Heart?"

Hough overcame his initial alarm when he saw how small the wound was. He could sympathize with Hickman's need to get calm, but he needed every available man on the wall. Thus the lieutenant ridiculed the gunner and "ordered him off his ass."

It worked. Less fearful of incoming than of general levity at his expense, Hickman was back manning his M-60 within seconds.

Lieutenant Hough asked for help from the company 60mm or battalion 81mm mortars almost as soon as the shooting started, but the request was denied. That raised a few eyebrows at the embattled compound. The really scary part was that the defenders could see dozens, then scores, then perhaps hundreds of Moslem fighters advancing by means of fire-and-move tactics upon the vulnerable combat post. No matter how many rounds the defenders poured out, it was not enough. Within three hours, the combat post was losing, "big time."

The LAF post commander had been caught at CP 76 by the sudden onset of fire, and the sergeant in charge at CP 69 was uncertain of his authority to fire the jeep-mounted 106mm recoilless rifle under his control. When requests by the Marines that the 106 be brought into the fight went unanswered, Sgt Malcolm Howell, the Dragon team leader, asked Lieutenant Hough for permission to man the weapon himself. Hough told Howell to take a man and engage the Moslem bunker nearest the compound.

Sergeant Howell selected LCpl Donnie Phipps for the mission, but as the two awaited a lull, they were joined by LCpl JJ Firda, a volunteer. When the lull came, the three ran across the Shit River bridge to man the weapon. Howell had trained for years with 106s before the Marine Corps replaced them with Dragons, but his task was not made easier by the fact that the 106's sight was bent and useless. Thus, as he, Phipps, and Firda sat in the exposed 106mm jeep, Howell had to carefully bore-sight the weapon, a time-consuming task in the best of circumstances.

Lieutenant Hough selected targets and relayed information via land line to LCpl Mark Graves and Pfc Anthony Urban, who were manning Post 1, the tiny sandbag bunker atop the building adjacent to the LAF post. Graves and Urban adjusted Howell's first round by simply shouting down from their rooftop position. Howell then scored direct hits on two militia bunkers to the southeast, across Shit River. The first Moslem bunker was so strongly built, however, that it took four rounds, one in each facing window, to collapse the front of the two-story structure. The second bunker also required four direct hits. Sergeant Howell then fired southward in the hope of scoring against the numerous heavy machine-gun bunkers firing from that direction. It was not long before the 106mm ammunition supply, only sixteen rounds, was exhausted, at which juncture Howell, Firda, and Phipps raced back to the Marine compound.

Graves and Urban were desperately low on M-16 ammunition, but there was no way to resupply them from the far side of the Shit River bridge. What really burned the two was the way some LAF troopers blew away their vast store of 7.62mm bullets by firing magazine after magazine downrange while keeping their heads well below the sandbag walls.

Lieutenant Hough, who was wracked by the onset of a bad case of dysentery, was constantly on the move, checking on each and every Marine along the line. Once he settled down behind the wall to fire at targets, but got off only a few rounds before the pain in his gut had him heading for the command tent to relieve himself into a cardboard box. Watching the lieutenant empty the box over the sandbag wall gave rise to several grim jokes. Someone said that Hough was "dashing."

Meanwhile, back at the university, Captain Hoover heard that Lieutenant Colonel Gerlach was prepared to send a large portion of Charlie Company, mounted in amtracs, to relieve CP 69 if it looked like Hough was about to be overwhelmed. Hoover sensed the extreme reluctance at the command level to play that card, but he had no problem with that; the armored force would have to traverse long stretches of open ground exposed to numerous weapons capable of penetrating hog armor.

A tank commander based near the Alpha Company command/observation post took some risks searching for targets for his 105mm main gun, but Battalion denied his request to fire in support of the combat post. In the end, it was pretty much a one-man show—Dave Hough's. Everyone in authority was camped on the same radio frequency, but only Hough could call the shots.

When the fighting got really heavy, Corporal Cliff and Lance Corporal Firda volunteered to cross the fifty meters of open ground to the LAF-manned portion of the combat post and try to scavenge arms and ammunition that might be of use. They happened to catch a lull. The two had to carry off the gleanings of their search through vicious fire, but they reached the Marine compound unscathed.

The LAF troopers at CP 69 were, as usual, a mixed blessing. Since their officer was absent at CP 76, most of them became spectators. However, an older Battalion 31 private who had been on duty at CP 69 during Hough's previous fight fired a .50 cal with great effect from an armored personnel carrier hidden in the bed of the almost-dry Shit River. Another Battalion 31 private left the safety of the main LAF compound to volunteer his services to the Marines. He accosted Lieutenant Hough and asked permission to fire his RPG. Hough obligingly selected a target. The back-blast from an RPG is awesome and can kill a man who is directly in its path. So, as soon as the LAF trooper raised his RPG to his shoulder, Lieutenant Hough and all the Marines near him moved aside. The LAF trooper paused to smile at Hough, then suddenly pivoted. Marines yelled "No!" and "Shit!" as the back end of the tube swung right on them. The trooper squeezed the trigger, and the RPG ignited and took off. Americans were bowled over in a great dusty, camouflaged heap. Adding insult to injury, the gleeful Lebanese ran over to the Marine lieutenant and giggled, "RPG good! RPG good!" To which Dave Hough issued a vile rejoinder.

One covey of militiamen in a building sixty meters to the east evaded direct gunfire for some time, so Hough ordered a LAAW to be fired at them. He had an immediate volunteer, a bespectacled machine gunner who assured everyone he knew how to use the disposable antitank rocket. The gunner retrieved one of the LAAWs from the armory bunker, extended the plastic launcher, took careful aim, and fired. The smoky trail rose and rose over the sixty-meter interval, and the rocket destroyed the water tank atop the militia-manned structure, dousing the building and the men in it in an avalanche of water but injuring no one. The "expert" fired two more LAAWs but hit nothing. He thus became the immediate recipient of some advice on interesting ways to dispose of the empty rocket launchers. Meantime, Lieutenant Hough contacted Post 1 via the land line and asked Lance Corporal Graves to get the LAF to fire an RPG against the target. Graves came back on the land line a few minutes later with news that the LAF troopers were firm in their refusal to expose themselves to the incoming.

In time, as the pressure mounted, the Bravo Company 60mm mortar section was authorized to fire at a staging area several hundred meters to the east of CP 69. All Dave Hough wanted was for the 60s to be able to drop rounds within meters of his sandbags, for he was certain that the small bursting radius would maim numerous attackers, when they came, without hurting Marines.

First Lieutenant Lee Marlow, who was on a high berm surrounding his mortar pits, was surprised to see how very far off target the first round was—something like 600 meters! This was the section's first fire mission in Beirut, so Marlow wanted to turn in an especially good performance. The Weapons Platoon commander ordered a fifty-meter adjustment, but the second round, Willy-Peter (white phosphorus), was still 550 meters from the target. Marlow ordered another fifty-meter adjustment, and yet another, but was still off the mark. Captain Hoover finally stopped the firing and climbed down to the mortar pit to see what the trouble was.

It turned out that the section chief had never been given the correct azimuth. A gunner set an aiming stake in front of one tube while the Weapons Platoon leader climbed a nearby dirt berm to set and align a second stake. Marlow stayed up on the berm to adjust fires, which were on target in just two rounds. No sooner done, however, than the 60s were ordered to stand down.

It was then coming up 1600. Corporal Cliff called the lieutenant from his firing position on the south wall, "Sir, they're getting on line. Looks like they want to come in."

Dave Hough instantly placed a request for an "immediate suppression" fire support mission with Captain Hoover, who contacted Maj Andy Davis, the battalion operations officer, at the battalion COC. When the battalion commander heard "immediate suppression," he gave the nod. Capt Mike Haskell, serving at the COC as both the Weapons Company commander and battalion fire-support coordinator, came back on the battalion tac net and asked Hoover for permission to speak directly with Lieutenant Hough. Hoover complied, and Haskell was patched through on the Bravo Company tac net. Haskell asked Hough for coordinates.

It was then that the two officers learned that their maps were not identical, that Hough's preregistered target list varied considerably from the 81mm Mortar Platoon's.

Sgt Bob Davis, the platoon guide, had trained on mortars during a few years in the Marine Corps Reserve, so he and Lieutenant Hough, who had been a Reserve mortar platoon sergeant while attending college, selected the targets and prepared to adjust the fire. Dave Hough gave Mike Haskell a grid mission, got a confirmation he could not pinpoint, decided it was probably the best he would get, and gave Haskell the fire commands. He wanted to hit the mint field and the olive grove on the south side of the perimeter.

There was a distintive detonation a few moments later, but no one saw the impact. Sergeant Davis, who was on the south wall to adjust fires, called back a correction to Lieutenant Hough, who was near the center of the compound wall, manning the tactical radio. Hough keyed his handset: "Drop 200." The gunnery sergeant working the fire-direction center came back with news that he might have made a small error in computing the grid coordinates, but he would honor the platoon leader's request. The next round dropped in only twenty meters from the combat post wire. Marines on the south wall hit the deck as dirt and debris rained on them.

Sergeant Davis lifted his head and called back to the platoon leader, "Left 200, add 400, fire for effect." Hough relayed the adjustment to the 81mm fire-direction center and prayed the gunny knew where the spotting mortar was aimed. Three other mortars matched azimuths, then the four tubes each fired four rounds into a militia trench system shielded by a line of olive trees 150 meters to the south. The rounds—a mix of air and ground bursts—detonated right over or impacted right on target, spreading olive wood and human viscera all through the grove and stopping the ground assault before it really got going. Marines who had not been able to see the militia fighters massing for the attack certainly saw plenty of them withdrawing at top speed through the shattered trees.

The next adjustment—"Left 100, add 200, repeat"—brought six tubes to bear on a new set of targets. Thirty-six 81mm rounds dropped into the mint field, where five concealed bunkers were playing havoc with the south wall defenses. Several direct hits quieted things down in the south sector. The fire from the east and north remained heavy, but everyone in CP 69 could feel the slack.

Hough's next main concern was the reported 250 Syrian-led and tank-supported militiamen the LAF said were spotted around the Chocolate Factory. He adjusted the 81s and requested "Fuze delay," which would allow the mortar rounds to penetrate the roof of the concrete building before going off. This request resulted in a query from the COC. Hough's explanation was countered with "Have you tried all your other weapons systems on them?" Hough said that he had but that it had come to nothing. Battalion suggested that he fire his Dragons, but the platoon leader replied that he was saving them for the T-55s reported to be at the Chocolate Factory. It was getting quite dark by then, and the fire mission was never cleared. The 81s fired illume through the night, but nothing stronger.

Sgt José Lopez's condition remained in question throughout the long afternoon.

As the hostile gunfire crackled through the air just over his head, Doc Hacala sat by Sergeant Lopez between two sandbag blast walls near the northern end of the minuscule Marine compound. At length, the injured man began muttering Hail Marys, but he never completed one because other matters kept coming to mind. "Hey, Doc, take care of my men" or "Doc, you know what really pisses me off? I never got a chance to shoot back." That last set the sergeant to thinking of ways to redress the imbalance. After a moment, he asked Hacala to retrieve his illegal 9mm automatic pistol. "Doc, chamber me a round; I want to fire just one round. Just so I can say I fired." Hacala complied, asking only that Lopez leave him a round. The sergeant pointed the barrel straight up.

BAM! BAM! BAM! BAM! BAM! BAM! BAM! Click, click, click.

"Thanks, Lopez." But the sergeant just flashed a strained smile and dropped the weapon tiredly onto his chest.

Within the first hour of the fight, Private First Class Horne suddenly sang out, "Doc!"

Hacala jumped out of his skin, certain someone else had been hit. "What?"

"What're his vital signs?"

"Who wants to know?"

"Battalion surgeon."

Hacala rattled off what he knew.

"What's his blood pressure?"

Bullets were pinging into the dirt all around the treatment

site. "Tell them to fuck off. They didn't give me a BP cup."

Minutes passed. "Doc! Come to the phone."

Hacala lifted himself from the wounded squad leader's side and sprinted across the open compound to the radio shack. "This is Dr. Hudson. Tell me about the patient." Hacala was usually inclined to go along with the surgeon, but he could not help feeling that, perhaps, John Hudson had missed the point of this day's exercise. Nervous and excited, Hacala rattled off the facts and described his treatment. He then returned to Lopez, but was unable to get anything done, for Horne called him back to the radio bunker. It was the battalion aid station's chief corpsman, who was informed by a thoroughly upset combat corpsman that responding to phone calls entailed a dash through hostile fire. That was the last time the aid station initiated a conversation with CP 69. The only hard information Hacala had obtained in thirty minutes of exchanges with the aid station was that a medevac flight that day was out of the question—unless Lopez took a turn for the worse.

What Hacala could not discern was how very concerned Dr. Hudson and the battalion staff were regarding Lopez's condition. John Hudson had no time at all for military protocol, but he was a physician who cared so much for his patients that, before floating with the battalion landing team, he had often taken the unprecedented step of making house calls to care for ill Marines and their dependents. All the phone traffic to Doc Hacala was made at Hudson's insistence because he wanted the battalion commander to be absolutely positive that Lopez did not require immediate evacuation. Hudson even had Larry Gerlach talked into mounting a helo evac, complete with gunship escort, if Lopez appeared to be in any danger of succumbing to his wounds. Doc Hacala's unconscious feistiness did a lot to allay the surgeon's concerns.

It was so difficult to get shock-suppressing drugs into Lopez that Doc Hacala became fearful of losing his patient. As the hours crept by, Lopez became increasingly shocky. In an unusual departure from the standard rules, Hacala had been entrusted with a small supply of morphine because CP 69 was the most isolated Marine position and it had earlier been felt—rightly, as it turned out—that prudence dictated the need to have morphine stashed there. The powerful narcotic was available if permission to use it could be obtained. Hacala told the duty radioman to *tell* the aid station that he was going to inject his patient. Then, before an answer could arrive, he had the biggest Marine in the compound demolish the sealed M-60 ammo box in which the morphine had been placed—a long and difficult job—and pumped half a tubex of the drug into the sergeant's arm. Lopez immediately settled down, and his vital signs stabilized within minutes. The one dose was enough to fly him to the clouds for the entire night.

The dark hours were filled with the flash and boom of rockets and the unremitting crackle of small-arms fire. A number of the bolder militia fighters crawled through the network of irrigation ditches that crisscrossed nearby fields in order to probe the combat post defenses. As the battalion 81mm mortars fired illume, the LAF contingent blindly fired its .50-caliber machine guns at odd intervals, but the effects were not observed. Sgt Bob Davis stopped the close-in probers with the aid of his starlight scope, M-16, and steady hands. LCpl Mark Graves, who had been stuck all day atop the building adjacent to the LAF compound, left the protection of his sandbag bunker and popped off part of his dwindling supply of 5.56mm bullets at the intruders he could reach. Voices from the dark proclaimed that Marines would die in the morning. No one slept.

Midway through the evening, and working on the assumption that a medevac of some sort would eventually be launched in behalf of Sergeant Lopez, Lieutenant Hough called Captain Hoover to request an urgent ammunition resupply. Hough's tiny force had expended over 8,000 rounds in three hours on

Sunday afternoon, so an extra 5,000 5.56mm rounds did not seem excessive. Neither did 5,000 fresh 7.62mm rounds, nor another hundred M-203 rounds. Hough also asked if he could send Lopez out via the almost-dry Shit River streambed on the 106 jeep. The request was denied as being too risky.

It was 2300 hours, and relatively calm, when Battalion notified Captain Hoover that a medevac bird and Cobra gunship escort would attempt to fly into CP 69 to pick up Sergeant Lopez at about 0700 the following morning. Hoover passed The Word to Dave Hough along with the medevac frequency and call sign. Hoover had also placed Hough's ammunition request with Battalion, and he was able to tell the combat-post commander that the resupply would be aboard the medevac bird.

The CH-46 radioed CP 69 at the appointed time and asked for smoke to mark the landing site. Hough read from a brief he had prepared during the night, then cleared them to land "hot" and fire, if fired on, to the east, north, and south.

Cpl Rod Cliff and four other Marines moved into the open to take up covering positions overlooking the landing zone while Lieutenant Hough and a half dozen other Marines spread out across the adjacent field. As two Cobra gunships orbited over the area, their pilots itching to eject hot ordnance, Hough popped smoke into a clear area about 100 meters west of the compound.

The swirling mass of red cloud rose with the wind. Lopez was on his stretcher, wearing his Cool–Ray sunglasses and a jaunty green bandana. Still a little woozy from the morphine, he assured Doc Hacala that he was "good to go." Nearby, a small work party was preparing to dash out and unload the ammunition.

Doc Hacala was absolutely certain that this was to be his last hour on earth. He knew in a calm, assured way that he was going to die dragging José Lopez to the helo. He did not fight the realization. He did what had to be done.

There was no fire. It occurred to Corporal Cliff, who had

weathered the first fight weeks earlier, that the militias "did not want to mess with the Cobras again."

The lumbering CH-46 whipped in low, flared out for its landing, and set down in a huge cloud of dust beside the smoke marker. As the helo crew chief dropped crates of ammunition from the hatchway, Doc Hacala and the stretcher-bearers hustled across the open ground with Lopez. Hacala's supertuned senses heard grunting Marines yelling Marinelike things: "Go! Go! Go!" and "Move it!" and "Keep it moving!" and "Come on, fuckhead, get your ass out the way!" Lopez was dragged up the yawning rear ramp and passed to waiting hands in the helo's dark interior. When Mark Hacala realized that he was halfway home, he turned on his heel, but one of those Marinelike oaths sought him out, whipped him around in his tracks, and obliged him to pick up a heavy, heavy case of rifle ammunition, which he dragged through the swirling dust and tossed into the ditch by Shit River.

Shortly after the helo lifted off, Lieutenant Hough was informed by radio that the Marine radio intelligence team at Yardze had picked up messages indicating that a massive assault would be mounted against CP 69 later in the day—and that this time the combat post would probably fall. Lieutenant Colonel Gerlach ordered Captain Hoover to close CP 69, to order Lieutenant Hough to pack everything and prepare to leave within sixty minutes. When the LAF troopers manning the combat post got wind of the Marine preparations, they sent a delegation to beg Lieutenant Hough to stay. This had worked once, early in the month, but the reprieve from above did not arrive, as it had on that earlier occasion. Many of the Marines, particularly those who had weathered their second fight at CP 69, had strongly mixed emotions about "swooping" while the situation was still very much in doubt. In the face of Hough's demurrers, the Lebanese arranged for one of their officers at the library to approach Captain Hoover with a request that the Marines remain at least until the LAF detachments could be reinforced.

Hoover said he would try to get an extension but firmly stated his intention to comply with orders. Whether because of LAF requests or other factors, the execute order was held up for about three hours.

Bravo Company's 3d Platoon arrived at CP 69 under moderate fire at noon with a pair of mechanical mules, upon which the post's tents and other bulky equipment could be piled.

After passing a large quantity of ammunition to the LAF squads in return for the 106mm ammunition used the day before, the Marines speedily abandoned CP 69. However, all hands were too encumbered by all the remaining ammunition, their weapons, food, water cans, and personal possessions to hold out much hope for winning a running fight. The really irksome part of the march out was everyone's inability to manage his cot. The awkward contraptions were simply beyond belief. They unfolded themselves, caught on all sorts of anticot devices on the crowded, narrow streets of Hooterville, and generally made the march hell. Several Amal gunmen had to be dealt with on the way through Hooterville, and bullets constantly impacted against the walls and along the road. The troops were "pissed."

The refugees made a detour to CP 35 to pick up 2d Platoon's reinforced 2d Squad. The cots and some other gear were loaded aboard jeeps, and then the bloated force split into two parts and trudged on toward the university along two separate routes.

HM3 Mark Hacala's group got stalled in the ville, and Hacala, third from the rear, was accosted by a dozen hard-looking teenagers. He parried their questions about where he was going and where he had been by identifying himself as a doctor. One of the Moslem youths pulled up the top of his blue-striped pajamas and yanked off a bandage to reveal a long midline-incision scar. "Phalange do this to me." A few feet away, Lance Corporal Firda set his M-16 on automatic, eased the safety off, and slowly leveled the weapon at the Moslems. The exchange continued until the telescoped column peacefully moved away. Hacala and Firda trudged the last few hundred feet into the university compound through sniper fire. All the men in their part of the column were simply too exhausted to drop to the road.

Dave Hough had a terrible, spiking fever. He dribbled over the last few hundred meters, went to see Captain Hoover for debriefing, had a shower, and then headed straight for his room, where he tried to sleep through a major shelling, too sick or too indifferent to leave his rack.

The LAF soldiers manning CP 35 surrendered to the Amal without a fight the next day. As Marines at the library helplessly looked on, the LAF post was ransacked. Later, nude and nearly nude LAF troopers who had been manning the post walked into the university compound. They reported that their officer had been tortured, murdered, and dragged naked through the streets of Hooterville.

PART VI

Cease-Fire

20

The rifle companies rotated once again, and for the last time, on October 3. The clockwise move brought Capt Paul Roy's Alpha Company to the Lebanese University, Capt Monte Hoover's Bravo Company to the southern end of Beirut International Airport (BIA) runway, and Capt Chris Cowdrey's Charlie Company to the northern and northwestern edges of the BIA runway.

Second Lieutenant Bill Harris's 1st Platoon, Charlie Company, was strung out in a line of sandbagged posts across the northern end of the BIA and for several hundred meters down along the eastern edge of the Marine Amphibious Unit (MAU) compound—roughly the same line that had been held by Alpha Company's 2d Platoon. The 3d Platoon line began over a kilometer away, and 2d Platoon was at Checkpoint 11 and isolated CP 76.

The hotbed of militia activity in Charlie Company's new sector was Café Daniel, just across from Harris's platoon, at the northeastern corner of the BIA compound. This Amal meeting place was under the control of a local warlord known to Marines as Castro, a nickname derived from his martial bearing and heavy beard. Castro was something of a renegade, a man dedicated to achieving his own program of social reform in Hooterville even if that meant going against the policies of Nabieh Berri, the Shiite lawyer who was emerging as the leader of the Amal coalition. Thus, though peace talks were getting under way and the Shiite Amal would be a party to them, Castro exercised his independence by applying almost constant pressure upon the Marines within his reach—Bill Harris's platoon of Charlie Company. The closest Amal bunkers were only 100 meters north of Harris's sector, an easy shot, and Café Daniel was about 400 meters from the nearest Marine position, as was a red-and-white-striped concrete structure known as the Armory, after its apparent chief function. Behind Harris was an LAF training camp, the perfect excuse for the Amal gunfire "through" 1st Platoon.

The sniper fire was intermittent during Harris's first week in the new position, not worth a response that might upset the uneasy peace that had descended upon most of the rest of the BIA. It became ugly one night when a sentry heard a *pop!* and realized that a hand grenade had detonated in an unmanned bunker just beneath his post. Next, three militia riflemen opened fire. The Marine popped a flare and saw several dark forms heading across an adjacent field. Next morning, Capt Chris Cowdrey joined Lieutenant Harris for a walk across the road that divided the MAU from Castro's militia. The two Charlie Company officers found the spoon from a Soviet-manufactured hand grenade in the open field east of the road, but they could find no shell casings left by the riflemen. As Cowdrey and Harris turned to leave, a small boy ran up and showed them a handful of shell casings he had collected at first light. Three different kinds of weapons had been fired during the night, a sure sign that the incident had been perpetrated by the ragtag militia.

The tempo of shooting incidents picked up. Two nights after the grenade incident, four rocket-propelled grenades (RPGs) flew over 1st Platoon outposts, then machine-gun fire cut through the night air. The Marines responded by bringing up two Surveillance and Target Acquisition (STA) Platoon snipers, who located favorite militia firing positions and prepared to make a few examples. Then, with great ostentation, the Marines moved up four Dragon launchers and a tank to positions just behind 1st Platoon. The new weapons were dug in, but they were withheld in the hope that Castro and his subordinates would see the light.

All of a sudden, during the latter part of the week of October 10, some new players appeared in Hooterville. Many of these were hard-bitten, professional-looking soldiers wearing Russian battledress uniforms (BDUs), similar to Marine cammies but colored rust and brown. It was assumed that Castro had made a deal with the Syrian army. In addition, another ragtag group, distinctly different from Amal fighting units, took up residence around Café Daniel. The thing that set this group apart was the white headband with red Arabic letters sported by each fighter. It was presumed that these were members of Islamic Amal, Iranians from the Syrian-sponsored training camp at Baalbek in the Beqa'a Valley. Immediately, the number and quality of bunkers that could be observed by Marines increased, as did the accuracy of incoming small-arms sniper fire.

Adding to the growing sense of discomfort and isolation along the northern BIA perimeter was news that large numbers of Hooterville residents were leaving town. Soon, Charlie Company Marines could see flag-festooned buses picking up whole families from nearby neighborhoods. It was axiomatic that the sudden departure of noncombatants presaged a big fight.

————

SSgt Dennis Allston had been in Beirut longer than any other Marine—nearly 400 days since he accompanied the first explosive ordnance disposal (EOD) detachment sent to the BIA to clear unexploded ordnance for Battalion Landing Team (BLT) 2/8 in October 1982. The twenty-five-year-old Philadelphian had seen it all and had come to have mixed feelings about the city in which he had spent two birthdays—loved the city and its diverse peoples, hated what those people did to one another in the name of religion and politics.

On October 15, 1983, a Friday, Allston was temporary NCO in charge of the EOD detachment. He and his good friend, SSgt Allen Soifert, a twenty-five-year-old Canadian-born professional Marine, had decided to respond personally to a routine call by a Lebanese Armed Forces (LAF) unit in Hooterville that had discovered what appeared to be an unexploded RPG round. The two left MAU Service and Support Group (MSSG) 24 headquarters and drove out along the perimeter road to Hooterville, where they found the casing of a defective RPG that had apparently detonated without actually blowing up. The reasonably intact steel casing was thrown into the back of the EOD jeep and the two staff sergeants climbed aboard for the ride home.

Between the time Allston and Soifert passed 2dLt Bill Harris's platoon on the way to the RPG and the time they approached the corner on the way home, the BDU-clad Syrian snipers stationed around Café Daniel had begun taking potshots at passing American vehicles. The first such shooting occurred as a MSSG-24 dump truck lumbered past the corner. A few rounds *spanged* off the heavy-gauge steel frame of the truck before the driver realized that he was in danger. As he pushed the truck into high gear and ran from the area, the shaken youngster mouthed a hurried warning into the handset of the vehicle's radio. Several other vehicles that happened to be passing at that time were also the objects of sniper fire from the vicinity of Café Daniel. One of them, a jeep, was under the control of LCpl Bill Riddle, of

Weapons Company, who was taking his military driving test. Riddle was shot through both legs as he passed Café Daniel. Other vehicles on the outer perimeter road highballed out of the area as the radio waves crackled with blunt warnings. A Marine backhoe operator was forced to pull over and hide behind the rear tire of his vehicle as Charlie Company Marines engaged the Moslem riflemen—Syrians and, by then, Iranians. MAU headquarters ordered the outer perimeter road closed to all traffic. Bill Harris's platoon was placed on full alert, ready to battle the snipers if they could be pinpointed.

The EOD jeep, with Staff Sergeant Allston driving, was neither halted nor apprised of the closure of the road. Allston and Soifert were bantering to pass the time until they got back to the MSSG, just a few minutes away. Moments before the jeep arrived in the vicinity of Café Daniel, the Charlie Company sentries assigned to block the road to vehicular traffic had been forced by heavy Moslem gunfire to seek cover.

It was about 1000 hours. As the jeep headed south toward the corner opposite Café Daniel, both staff sergeants involuntarily leaned back, then exclaimed their surprise when they simultaneously realized that several rounds had passed in front of them, between their faces and the windshield. It dawned on Allston that the gunfire was coming from a treeline about 100 meters to his right. As Allston turned his head to pinpoint the source of the fire, other weapons along the route opened on the jeep. He instinctively thumped his booted foot hard upon the accelerator, hoping to run the gauntlet.

"I've been hit," said Staff Sergeant Soifert in a calm voice. "In the chest." Allston then felt his passenger slump down beside him.

The jeep was rapidly approaching an intersection where Lebanese workers had been building a culvert. This was the path to safety, so Allston started the jeep into a tight right turn. At that instant, Allston sensed that Soifert was slipping out of the right side of the jeep. Without thinking, the driver took his right hand from the steering wheel and grabbed his tottering partner. This action prevented Allston from completing the turn. The jeep turned wide and both left tires bounced across a low berm shielding the newly emplaced culvert. The jeep turned over and Allston was thrown clear over a distance of about ten feet.

There was just time to duck and roll, then Allston came up running, under continuous fire, back to the jeep, which had turned over, driver's side up. The only good fortune was that the jeep now formed a substantial barrier between the two Marines and the direct fire.

Allen Soifert's right foot was beneath the side of the jeep, and the laces of his left boot were entangled in the framework of the passenger seat. He had landed on his buttocks, his head was scraped or cut by the lip of his helmet. Or perhaps he had been grazed by a passing bullet when the snipers—most likely Iranians now—first opened fire.

Soifert was fully conscious. He spoke to Allston in a very calm voice. Allston had the feeling that the wounded man was more in control of himself than he, Allston, was in control of himself. Soifert reaffirmed that he had been shot in the chest, but when Allston probed beneath Soifert's flak jacket, he could find neither an entry wound nor any blood. In fact, Soifert had been shot just beneath his right nipple. The round had penetrated his sternum, cut through his trachea and lungs, rearranged vital organs, and lodged near his left kidney.

Allston reached into the jeep's cargo compartment for their squad radio. It was not there. As he cast about for the missing radio, he spotted a lone gunman in the treeline. Allston drew and cocked his .45-caliber automatic pistol and fired several rounds without hitting the man. As he ducked back behind the jeep, however, he saw the radio, which had been thrown clear when the jeep rolled over. It was now in the open, about where he had earlier landed. Allston screwed up his courage and darted into the open. He was lucky, for no one fired directly at him, though he had heard rounds passing overhead since landing on the ground. Allston pulled the radio back to the lee side of the jeep and keyed the handset. Nothing.

As Allston thought about his next move, he saw some movement about 300 meters away, on the BIA side of the road. Marines were pouring M-16 and M-60 fire at the Moslem positions and nearby rooftops in Hooterville. Staff Sergeant Allston shouted at them in the hope they would send help, but he knew that their doing so would likely result in additional casualties. Allen Soifert, who was fully cognizant and who had a very keen sense of the severity of his injuries, verbalized Allston's feelings of desperation, actually announcing that he did not want other Marines risking their lives on his behalf. There was no need to worry. Lieutenant Harris's heart went out to the two men trapped in the open, but he knew he would take dead and wounded if he sent any of his riflemen to help them. His decision to keep his troops under cover was confirmed within minutes in a message from Captain Cowdrey, Charlie Company's commander.

Soifert next chided Allston for his failure to get through on the radio, suggesting in a bantering voice that his nominal superior had forgotten to turn it on or failed to key the handset or improperly set the antenna. This was typical of Soifert's well-honed sense of humor. Allston was not feeling the wounded man's mirthful energy, so he responded in less than charitable manner, which caused Soifert to respond in a humorous fashion.

Continued efforts by Allston to work the radio were unsuccessful. At length, Soifert said that he would try to get through. Allston obliged him, but it was by then apparent that the radio had been damaged in the accident or, indeed, had not been working at all that morning.

As the two sat tight, Allston thought he heard a tank moving nearby. In fact, SSgt Richard Smith was attempting to maneuver his heavy tank to the roadway, to either provide direct fire support or, if the opportunity arose, to dash out and snatch the two EOD noncoms. The racket from the tank drew the attention of militia fighters on the opposite flank, and several of their RPGs passed close enough to the tank to force Smith to reconsider his boldness. He well knew that an RPG could destroy a tank.

Next, a jeep bearing 1stLt Nick Nanna, of Charlie Battery, and two enlisted Marines pulled up right beside the overturned jeep. Nanna stepped out behind the damaged vehicle just as heavy fire from the Moslem-held tree line whipped by overhead. He grabbed a small radio, ordered the jeep to get clear, and hunkered down next to Soifert to see if he could help.

Lieutenant Nanna took charge, forcing his way onto the battalion tac net with a report on his arrival and Soifert's injuries. The radioman on the other end of the conversation was infuriatingly dense, getting the message completely fouled up three or four times. Dennis Allston's simmering frustration grew to overt ire, and he yelled at Nanna to "stop playing word games" with the idiot radioman and order up some help. Nanna requested that corpsmen be dispatched with an ambulance jeep.

Second Lieutenant Mike Murphy, the MSSG-24 communicator, was incensed by the events unfolding on his tactical net. An extremely motivated young officer who had, perhaps, grown frustrated with his indoor duties while fellow Marines had been engaged in combat for a month, Murphy volunteered to lead the rescue. He was turned down, but he could not be kept down.

HMC B. C. Miller and HM3 Ken Boyer were on duty at the MSSG aid station when a runner arrived to announce that a member of the MSSG had been shot on the outer perimeter road. Miller and Boyer grabbed their Unit-1 medical kits and headed upstairs to get the platoon ambulance. They discovered that it was on a run elsewhere. The two corpsmen next headed for the BLT motor pool, intent upon borrowing the battalion aid station ambulance jeep. Their request was turned down. Boyer and Miller cursed up a storm, applied a liberal dose of guilt, and won the day. As Boyer started the engine, he and Miller were joined by HN Gary Cooper and 2dLt Mike Murphy.

The roadway was blocked at a Marine checkpoint by a dump

truck, perhaps the one that had earlier been hit by militia gunfire. As the corpsmen and Lieutenant Murphy fretted, the driver and the sentry chattered away. Murphy yelled "Hey, Marine!" several times before the truck driver looked up. When Murphy identified himself, the dump truck pulled out of the way, but the sentry moved to bar the road. "Hey! We got sniper fire down there."

"Yeah," Boyer called as he passed, "we're going to pick up the guy who got shot."

As Boyer pulled up behind a dirt berm, Murphy, Cooper, and Miller jumped out, grabbed a backboard, and headed for the roadway. Boyer was out of the vehicle but decided to turn off the jeep's engine. He was just about to lean back in when the windshield on the driver's side was blown out by a high-velocity bullet. He left the engine running.

Sgt Foster Hill, one of Lieutenant Harris's squad leaders, was watching the corpsmen tear across the open ground to the overturned jeep when he was asked for an up-to-the-minute report by LtCol Larry Gerlach, who had arrived at his elbow without warning or entourage. Hill gave his report, then turned back to watch the unfolding drama.

By the time Murphy, Miller, Cooper, and Boyer reached Soifert's side, the EOD staff sergeant was sinking. He had remained in a jocular mood until then, realistic about his condition, but very much in control of his emotions. As potshots continued to fly overhead, Soifert got into an argument with the corpsmen over his condition. He knew he had been hit in the lungs, and he said so, but the docs initially thought he had not, for he was not coughing blood. He also felt himself becoming shocky and offered advice on how the corpsmen might treat him. Doc Boyer ran his hands down Soifert's torso to feel for wounds. When he reached back to the wounded man's kidneys, a 7.62mm round fell into his hand. This he handed to Staff Sergeant Allston, then he applied a battle dressing.

As Chief Miller continued to treat the wounded Marine, who

was by now drooling blood from between bluish lips, Boyer and Cooper went to work getting Soifert's foot untangled from the seat. It was clear that the ankle had been broken by the twisting fall, so it was decided to keep Soifert's boot on if possible; at least it was providing some support. The laces were so badly entangled that Boyer decided to disassemble the seat. He twisted nuts and bolts and worked a set of oversized wire cutters where they could do their job. At length, as Soifert's eyes began rolling back and a pink froth appeared on his lips, the seat was pulled from the jeep and the wounded man was stretched out on the roadway. A little shove on the jeep itself by all hands freed the trapped right foot. Doc Boyer knelt over the declining wounded man to administer mouth-to-mouth resuscitation.

SSgt Richard Smith briefly returned with his tank to traverse his main gun in the direction of the Moslem-held buildings, but he was again threatened by RPGs and ordered to withdraw. This time, at least, the Marines and corpsmen behind the overturned jeep could see the attempt, and that was mildly heartening. An amtrac rolled up behind a nearby berm and everyone grabbed the backboard on which Soifert had been placed and ran up the ramp into the lighted interior.

Charlie Company's 1st Platoon opened on Moslem fighters, forcing many of them to seek cover in the Armory. Then Lieutenant Harris unleashed his grenadiers, who volleyed their M-203 high-explosive (HE) rounds into the building's thick concrete walls. It is doubtful that any Moslems died, but they were certainly bounced around.

Allen Soifert finally lost consciousness as the amtrac driver pivoted the huge vehicle and headed directly up the roadway to the battalion aid station, where a litter team was standing by. Dennis Allston stood by the door of the BLT for a moment, then heard himself called to the MSSG building. He reluctantly tore himself away, knowing that he would be put to work to get his mind off the morning's trauma.

Maj Doug Redlich, the MSSG-24 commander, had been at

Green Beach when he heard of the shooting. He arrived just as the amtrac pulled up at the main entrance. Redlich had been exec of the MSSG on its previous deployment in Beirut, and Soifert had been attached to EOD then. In fact, Redlich had submitted Soifert's application to the warrant officer program the last time out. He knew Soifert well and liked him. Soifert seemed to be groggy, but nothing Doug Redlich saw was particularly alarming. He touched Soifert on the arm and said, "Now you're an official Beirut vet." Soifert was carried off and Redlich turned to get the details from the BLT S-3, Maj Andy Davis.

First Lieutenant Chuck Dallachie had been on duty in the combat operations center (COC) during the rescue. He was at the bottom of the stairway on his way outside for a breather, when the litter team thundered into the BLT lobby. Dallachie tried to move aside, then saw that he would have to back down the stairway, which he did as quickly as possible. The crush of bodies swept him right into the operating room, where an unconscious Allen Soifert was placed on the table. Unable to press through to the door, Dallachie squeezed into a corner and stared wide-eyed at the drama unfolding before him.

Dr. John Hudson was in the Navy for just one reason: he had run out of tuition money midway through medical school, and the Navy had paid his way. He was a good, caring doctor, but he either had no sense of military discipline or superbly resisted the growth of an officerlike veneer. Tales of his military ineptitude were legend in the battalion, and he went out of his way to put on weight, his way of bearding the slim-trim Marines with whom he served. This day, the games were left at the operating-room door. John Hudson simply wanted to save a life.

Grim-faced Danny Wheeler, the battalion chaplain, stripped off Allen Soifert's flak jacket and cammie blouse. The surgeon probed the bloodless wound beneath the right nipple. At first, Hudson was certain that Soifert's heart had been nicked, and he was ready to open the staff sergeant's chest, but he decided within seconds that the heart was not involved. He also determined that Soifert was as good as dead. But as good as isn't the same as already, so the overweight Georgia country doctor worked to stabilize his patient, who would not survive surgery of any sort if his shock could not be controlled.

The wisdom and curse of a battalion aid station is that complex and sophisticated equipment is reserved for medical facilities farther up the line. All a battalion surgeon is supposed to do is patch the wounded who might live and pass them along to better-manned and better-equipped surgical teams. Most often, the system works. Large numbers of surgeons are not risked in the close combat that is the fare of rifle battalions but are available in safe places, where they can better serve the majority. Marine battalions facing the hardest combat in Vietnam each drew just one surgeon, a team of under twenty aid-station corpsmen, and limited equipment. This is hard-nosed wisdom, but where John Hudson and Allen Soifert were concerned this October noon hour, it was a curse. Treating Soifert was simply beyond the capabilities of the battalion aid station, and Soifert was in no condition to be moved. Hudson did what he could, but it was not enough. Within minutes of his arrival, Allen Soifert slipped into a coma and then stopped breathing. John Hudson got Soifert's heart pumping, but it failed again. And again. Then there was no bringing him back.

Chaplain Danny Wheeler, a Lutheran, administered last rites, a Catholic ritual, to the dead Marine, who was Jewish.

Dennis Allston was told an hour after he arrived at the aid station.

Allen Soifert, who had become a U.S. citizen in 1968 at age ten, was buried a week after his death in Beirut at age twenty-five in the Jewish cemetery in Nashua, New Hampshire.

When news that Allen Soifert had died reached Charlie Company on the afternoon of October 15, some members of 2dLt Bill Harris's 1st Platoon decided to "get some."

M-203 rounds were accurately placed just behind many of the

walls the Moslem snipers were using for cover. Some of the grenadiers became so adept at this sort of fire that they were soon bouncing their HE rounds off buildings to get them into hard-to-hit Moslem emplacements. The platoon's M-60 machine guns were used to suppress the militia automatic weapons.

Word arrived that night through the news reporters who daily traveled between Hooterville and the BIA that women and children had been hurt by the Marines, so Harris was obliged to order his men to withhold their general fire.

Though MAU headquarters was loath to allow Harris's platoon to undertake a general firefight, it sanctioned the use of STA snipers to begin a routine of careful, aimed target suppression the next day. When Lieutenant Colonel Gerlach heard the news, he sent four additional snipers to Harris's sector, bringing the total to six. In addition to their own specialized equipment, the STA snipers were to make use of the optical range-finding equipment aboard SSgt Richard Smith's heavy tank, a terrific plus for pinpointing targets in the built-up areas opposite Harris's positions.

Fearful that his platoon's teeth had been unfairly drawn, Sgt Foster Hill put forth a plan aimed at achieving a balance more favorable to the Marines without endangering the lives of noncombatants. In Hill's opinion, it was not worth the expenditure of a great deal of ammunition to go after five or six militia fighters here and five or six there. Instead, grenadiers could force the small groups toward the alley fronting Café Daniel and the Armory, and the STA snipers could pick them off, almost at their leisure. Harris felt it was worth a try.

When militia warriors opened fire on Harris's platoon on the morning of October 16, Harris had his grenadiers draw extra ammunition, and then he put them to work.

Sergeant Hill did the honors. His M-203 gunner dropped several rounds right on top of the Armory. The smallish rounds could not penetrate the concrete roof, but the deafening noise forced the gunmen hiding inside to run into the alley.

Aided by spotters, the STA snipers had a field day. With the full concurrence of higher headquarters, Lieutenant Harris simply reread the Rules of Engagement and decided that, as long as there was shooting going on, anyone caught with a weapon in his hands was fair game. This slight shift in the rules caught many hitherto untouchable militiamen off guard. Militia cowboys exiting the Armory with weapons were dropped without warning in the alley between it and Café Daniel.

Five Amal warriors were definitely killed this day, and at least ten others were severely wounded by high-velocity bullets.

At length, however, Colonel Geraghty arrived with news that the Amal leadership had asked for a cease-fire. It was clear to the troops that the MAU commander was uncomfortable with his role, but Harris's Marines understood and immediately complied. They knew, at least, that the Moslems would not have asked for a cease-fire if Charlie Company's fire had not been effective.

As soon as word was passed to Castro's militiamen that the company of Marines would honor the cease-fire, there appeared in the alley beside the Armory a large yellow truck. Moslem gunmen strode bravely into the open and were soon loading large quantities of munitions onto the truck. When it was full, the vehicle drove off through Hooterville, heading east, toward the Lebanese University. Many of the Moslem gunmen followed in its wake.

21

Cease-fire or no cease-fire, life at the Lebanese University was fraught with danger almost from the moment Alpha Company relieved Bravo Company on October 3. When the company received fire that very night, Capt Paul Roy requested a .50-caliber machine gun from Charlie Battery. Three nights later, LCpl Peter Bellair was shot in the shoulder while walking post in the Moat. Cpl Mickey Cumbee, an M-60 gunner, fired his borrowed .50-caliber machine gun at the source of the fire, a location known as Hole-in-the-Wall. Later that night, observers saw a half dozen bodies driven from Hole-in-the-Wall by an Amal Ford Pinto ambulance. The militia units around the university kept the pressure on, initiating "mad minutes" every two or three days during a period that was supposed to be quiet.

It was all nickel-and-dime harassment until the night of October 14, when scores of militiamen manning bunkers from 100 to 600 meters out along the east, south, and west sides of the university sent uncountable rounds into the library building.

Alpha Company doled out a measured response for three or four hours, until the militia gunmen ceased firing.

October 16 was a Sunday, Beirut's traditional day of war.

Captain Roy, Alpha Company commander, and Capt Mike Ohler, the forward air controller assigned to the university, spent many hours manning the library's rooftop observation post (OP) that day. The two captains and other observers on the roof could hear and see the gunplay at the corner of Beirut International Airport, where 2dLt Bill Harris's Charlie Company platoon was winning a few for the visiting team, and they had a clear view of the Moslem neighborhoods to the south, east, and west, where numerous armed civilian men were stalking the streets. What made Captain Roy nervous was what he could not see; there were no women or children on the streets of the Moslem neighborhoods.

Contrary to the Alpha Company commander's expectations, the fight that erupted was between armed Moslem fighters to the south and battle-hardened Phalange units to the east. Nearly all the rounds skimmed the university grounds, but only a very few strays impacted now and again around the library building. Captain Roy ordered Cpl David Baldree and his Surveillance and Target Acquisition (STA) team to monitor the firing positions that occasionally sprayed the university, but neither the snipers nor Alpha Company Marines returned the fire. Later in the afternoon, however, aimed fire from the west—Hooterville—drew a calculated fifteen-minute response from the Marine company. Then the fighting to the south and east petered out, and so did the incoming from the west.

Just before sunset, Captain Roy finally gave in to a nagging feeling, a compelling sense of danger that arrived without a lot of thought, no doubt as a result of his weeks of combat.

As soon as Alpha Company had moved into the Lebanese University library building on October 3, the troops had gone to work changing portions of the tactical layout. This was natural and, indeed, expected; no company commander worth his salt was going to admit that another man's company had achieved tactical perfection. But Roy's nagging doubt went beyond mere competition or even prudence. Roy ordered all hands to evacuate the two aboveground floors of the library building and spread out through four levels of underground library stacks. There was the requisite bitching and moaning, but the troops carried out the order with alacrity. No one ever messed about with an order from Paul Roy and, besides, Alpha Company had been to the wars; the troops were themselves uncomfortable in the new surroundings.

When the furious activity died down, the only Alpha Company troops outside the library stacks were 1stLt Pete Ferraro's reinforced 3d Platoon, manning the Moat, and several 1st Platoon fire teams, manning reinforced sandbag bunkers on the two floors that had just been evacuated. The rooftop OP was continuously manned during the early evening by Captains Roy and Ohler, Corporal Baldree, and four other STA snipers, an 81mm forward observer, and Captain Ohler's radioman.

It was about 1830 hours and nearly dark. Only thirty minutes had passed since the troops had cleared out of the exposed aboveground floors. Corporal Baldree, who was manning the rooftop OP, saw a small explosion, about the size of a 60mm mortar round, near an Amal bunker. It was obvious who the Amal fighters manning the bunker thought had fired the round, for they immediately fired on the library building. Baldree and four other STA corporals fired at clear targets while Captain Ohler spotted for them. The firing soon subsided, but another small explosion soon rocked the same Amal bunker.

A single rocket-propelled grenade (RPG) passed the OP bunker on the library roof and impacted on the building itself. Suddenly, the library was hit by RPGs, small arms, and machine guns from the south and west. Several RPGs whooshed through windows into rooms that had just been evacuated, starting several fires and forcing the 1st Platoon fire teams manning the interior bunkers to evacuate. As the sky darkened, Marines in fighting positions in the Moat and at five two-man outposts only 100–200 meters from Hooterville returned the heavy fire. As it became clear that the library building was the focus of a spreading funnel of fire, the company's three 60mm mortars and several M-203 grenadiers fired illume over the areas from which the heaviest incoming seemed to be originating, emplacements from 100 to 600 meters across open ground. Alpha Company's borrowed .50-caliber machine gun tore at those positions with its half-inch rounds, and M-203 high explosives scattered Moslem machine-gun teams. The company M-60s were assisted by the STA snipers, who marked targets with single tracer rounds fired from their rooftop vantage point.

Captain Roy had only just settled in when he heard the dreaded cry, "Corpsman up!" He immediately swung down out of the rooftop OP, through the escape hatch, and climbed down an exposed ladder on the south side of the building. He learned that a machine-gun bunker had been hit by an RPG and that several Marines were down.

LCpl Shawn Gallagher, an M-60 machine gunner, was working out in the company weight room when he heard the distinctive *pop-pop-pop-pop* of incoming .50-caliber machine-gun fire. The husky, gravel-voiced Philadelphian, who was just three days short of his twenty-second birthday, dropped what he was doing and grabbed his gear, dressing on the way to his bunker. By the time Gallagher arrived, however, his gun was manned by his squad leader, Cpl Robert Robey, who would not relinquish the weapon. Gallagher had never fired in anger, so he fussed at Robey, who finally sent him to relieve LCpl Edwin (Junior) Newcom in the next bunker down the line, which was located on the southeast corner of the Moat.

Just as Gallagher eased the stock of the M-60 into the angle of his shoulder and pressed his cheek against the warm wood, 1st Lt Pete Ferraro, the 3d Platoon leader, ordered his riflemen to cease firing while the M-60s sought targets spotted by the STA snipers on the roof or selected by the gunners in the glare of 60mm or M-203 illume. The grenadier beside Gallagher's bunker popped an illume over a known Amal position about 550 meters out. Gallagher thought he saw someone aim right at him. He squeezed off fifteen 7.62mm rounds, waited, then fired again.

Gallagher soon lost track of time. At length, Lance Corporal Newcom asked if he could "get some." Gallagher agreed to relinquish the gun the next time he had to change belts. The moment soon arrived, and Gallagher bent down to retrieve a fresh bandolier of ammunition.

Corporal Cumbee was in the next machine-gun bunker with Corporal Robey when he saw a man stand up in the field on his front and fire an RPG. Certain that he was the target, Cumbee yelled "Duck!" in Robey's ear and tucked his head in. He lifted it just as the RPG impacted.

LCpl Sonny Rando, a rifleman, screamed, "Get down!"

CRACK!

Gallagher found himself sprawled in the corner of the bunker. Gouts of blood were pouring from the right side of his head. He had staggered out of the bunker and simply collapsed. Lieutenant Ferraro and Lance Corporal Rando were at his side. Shouts of "Corpsmen!" were echoing through the Moat.

The RPG had scored a direct hit on the M-60 machine gun, which was severely damaged. Junior Newcom, standing just behind the bunker, was hit. He was covered with puncture wounds of the head and neck, and the chest portion of his flak jacket was chewed to pieces. He must have seen the incoming round, for his right hand had a large hole in it, no doubt acquired when he instinctively lifted it to ward off the blow. Gallagher had one shrapnel wound in the head and his right eardrum was blown. Cpl Richard Mathews, a Dragon gunner, was just stepping into the bunker with fresh ammunition when he was caught in the blast. He was hit in the left arm by shrapnel.

BOOM!

A second RPG hit the corner of the bunker and Gallagher went into shock. The blast caught LCpl Antoine Serena, of 1st Platoon, as he was ducking into the bunker to help. He received a superficial wound in the right forearm and was unconscious for over five minutes. Pfc John Wright was stung in the right hand.

While Captain Ohler placed a call for a medevac helo, Captain Roy arrived as Gallagher, Mathews, and Newcom were being staged outside the wrecked bunker. Ohler sent word down that the medevac could not land because of the incoming. Roy thought of sending them by jeep to the battalion aid station, but it was too far and the fire was too heavy. The three were sent down to the tiny company sick bay, where they were stabilized and prepared to depart at a moment's notice.

As soon as Captain Roy had seen the wounded safely to the sick bay, he returned to the Moat, where he found the firing on both sides to be more intense than when he left. Even utilizing all the company's weapons, Roy was having a great deal of difficulty maintaining fire superiority and taking out hardened militia bunkers.

Captain Roy finally decided to give in to the incessant requests of the Dragon gunners attached to his company. He called Battalion for the requisite permission to fire and, while that was in the works, allowed the Dragon team to select a target for their wire-guided antitank rockets. The gleeful gunners scuttled through the Moat to get set. Meantime, Battalion radioed an affirmative.

The Dragon is an awesome weapon, propelled by booster rockets that kick off in pairs every few seconds; its noise alone can dominate a battlefield. Powerful enough to destroy a tank, the charge in the nose of the Dragon can take down a building. The big problem is that the gunner must expose himself to hostile fire in order to acquire a target and guide the rocket to a successful hit. Firing and guiding a Dragon requires superb reflexes and the heart of a lion.

To help the Dragons acquire their target with accuracy, Roy ordered all hands to put out "max fire" to suppress militia weapons. Illume was lofted to light the targets as the Dragon gunner settled into a nearly supine position and adjusted the bulky launcher on his right shoulder.

It was about 1930.

The first Dragon missed, an understandable occurrence given the volume of incoming and the pressure to succeed that had been placed upon the gunner, who insisted upon another chance. It took another five minutes to get set, then Alpha Company opened again with max fire, popped illume, and waited.

The target was confirmed destroyed, though incoming from other bunkers continued almost without letup.

The spotters manning the rooftop OP bunker were busy but exhilarated. They did not work without opposition, however, for RPGs kept detonating over and around the post, forcing the snipers constantly to interrupt their work to duck. Captain Ohler took it upon himself to find the men firing the RPGs.

Mike Ohler was a very special man. A deeply religious 1977 Naval Academy graduate, he carried out his duties with superb discipline, but he was also a dedicated family man who spent many of his limited free hours reading books and articles about raising his three-year-old daughter and the newborn son he had not yet seen. He consulted with officers and enlisted Marines with children about the many fine points of educating and raising kids, and he jotted down notes whenever he heard something new. Whenever an enlisted Marine serving with Mike Ohler had a problem of any sort, the gentle, blond, blue-eyed helicopter pilot found the time to provide words of encouragement or simply a ready ear. When the troops filled sandbags, Mike Ohler filled sandbags. So enamored with the idea of being a full-time family man had Ohler become that he had actually turned in the papers necessary to separate himself from the Marine Corps, which simply demanded more time than he felt he could give. Ohler was naturally cautious; he even wore goggles on the *back* of his helmet because, he explained, a sniper might lose a crucial moment deciding whether the captain was coming toward him or going away. Despite his natural caution, Ohler constantly risked exposure to hostile fire on the night of October 16 as he looked for militia machine guns and grenadiers in the fire-swept streets.

At about 2100, Ohler found the bunker from which most of the RPG fire was hitting the south side of the building. Corporal Baldree moved in and marked the bunker with tracer, certain that the M-60 teams in the Moat would react. As Baldree fired, Captain Ohler moved to assist Cpl Jonathan Crumley, who was observing fire from a Moslem machine-gun bunker about 570 meters to the west. When Ohler came up, Crumley moved beside the captain and fired several tracer rounds into the Amal bunker. All movement around the hostile bunker ceased, so Crumley lowered his rifle and stood up for a better look. Nothing happened.

Crumley instinctively crouched. Ohler lowered his binos and opened his mouth to speak. A stream of 7.62mm machine-gun bullets burst across the top of the waist-high sandbag wall. One round passed beneath the rim of Mike Ohler's helmet and hit him above the left eye.

Crumley was sprayed with blood. Certain he had been shot in the ear, the corporal twisted away to the left and dropped to the deck. He was not yet aware that the man beside him was down.

Corporal Baldree was on his knees just to the rear, checking on a metal sliver that had just been driven into his hand by an explosive bullet. He heard Ohler let out a gasp and watched him slump slowly into a fetal position at Crumley's feet. Baldree had trained as a paramedic before enlisting in the Marine Corps, so he crawled to Ohler's side, decided that the captain was beyond any help he could provide, and turned his attention to Crumley, who said he thought he had been hit. Baldree reached out in the dark to grasp his partner's shoulder. He felt the blood and assumed that Crumley had been hit by at least several rounds. The two talked briefly and became convinced that Crumley was either very lightly wounded or untouched.

Cpl Lee Norton, who was firing his night-vision-scoped M-16 just to Ohler's right, was not aware that Ohler had been hit until he heard Crumley and Baldree gabbling away about Crumley's possible injuries. Norton saw that Ohler was hunched over and asked, "Are you okay?" Then he saw the captain had been hit in the head. The stench of raw blood hit Norton's nostrils as the reality of death at his left shoulder was sinking in.

Corporal Norton waited for a lull and slid down the exposed ladder. When he reached the hatchway to the top floor of the library he shouted, "Anyone down there?" Someone shouted back, and Norton yelled, "Corpsman up!" He heard the shout as it passed through the building. Two corpsmen arrived within minutes, and Norton led them up to the OP bunker.

The Navy men took one look at Mike Ohler and told the snipers and communicators what they already knew but did not want to hear. As the other snipers lowered Ohler to his back and Corporal Norton spread his poncho liner over the recumbent form, Corporal Crumley submitted to a cursory medical examination. When the docs found that Crumley was uninjured, Corporal Baldree, now the senior man on the roof, ordered everyone to clear out. It was obvious that the OP was a major militia target and that continued attempts to spot targets would result in more fatalities. Baldree stayed alone with Mike Ohler.

Captain Roy was in the Moat speaking with Lieutenant Ferraro when an RPG detonated against a ferroconcrete beam right above them and blew the two off their feet. After the two officers checked their bodies for wounds, Roy decided that it was time to head back up to the rooftop OP. The company commander tried to buck the tide of men descending from the roof, but the exceptional volume of fire prevented him from mounting the exposed ladder. Once he was certain he could not go up, Roy climbed back to the Moat to direct the defense.

The intense fight ended at about midnight. When the Alpha Company Marines compared notes, it was discovered that a Lebanese Armed Forces unit stationed at the university had not fired a single round in support of Alpha Company. Those stalwart allies were religiously adhering to the official armistice.

Shortly after the fighting stopped, Captain Roy turned his attention to organizing an evacuation of the three wounded Marines. The big worry was Junior Newcom, who was in critical condition. Roy arranged to send Newcom, Gallagher, and Mathews northward to the Lebanese Ministry of Defense, in Baabda, which was only twenty minutes away by jeep. Roy knew that a CH-46 medevac helo could be sent in the dark. The British Multinational Force contingent, located several hundred meters away and untouched by the war raging around the university, dispatched a pair of Ferret armored scout cars to ride shotgun for the evacuation. Second Lieutenant Mark Brilakis, the artillery forward observer attached to Alpha Company, led the tiny convoy of jeeps out the back gate of the university. Soon a sniper fired at the jeeps. LCpl Donald Beach turned his stanchion-mounted M-60 on the source of the fire and proceeded to chew up the building as the column gained speed and hurtled past to the ministry of defense.

The CH-46 medevac piloted by recently promoted Capt Ron Smith was covered all the way to the ministry of defense by a pair of Cobra gunships. The helos were fired at during most of the trip over Moslem territory, but Ron Smith was so intent upon finding the ministry compound in the dark and getting down safely that he was utterly unaware of the tracking fire. The wounded were loaded without incident and Smith took off. Just as it cleared the harbor area the CH-46 experienced a shuddering jolt. The aircrew was certain their ship had taken a direct hit, and all available hands turned to find the damage. It turned out that the clamshell hatch over the front transmission had popped open due to the incessant vibrations running through the entire helo whenever the engines were turning. Captain Smith's crew chief, Sgt Mike Clancy, swung out of the crew door on a gunner's belt and held the flapping hatch steady until Smith brought the medevac home to *Iwo Jima*.

As soon as Junior Newcom arrived aboard the carrier an emergency tracheotomy prevented him from choking to death.

When the casualty convoy cleared the back gate of the library compound, Paul Roy ordered SSgt Michael McCorkle to gather a team to carry Mike Ohler's body from the roof. McCorkle selected three of the company's leading bodybuilders, who followed Captain Roy up the exposed ladder on the southeastern edge of the building to the rooftop OP. The stench of blood within the OP was overpowering. Someone found Mike Ohler's helmet thirty feet behind the position he had been manning when he was shot, thrown there by the impact of the killing round. The dead captain was strapped onto a stretcher and lowered by rope over the side of the roof to the Moat, then carried to the basement sick bay, where a four-man fire team was detailed to stay with him in the candle-lit room for the rest of the night.

Ammunition was inventoried and redistributed, and hot coffee was passed out to all hands. The level of vigilance was not diminished one iota during the rest of the long, sad night. The evacuation convoy was hit again by small-arms fire on the way back from the Ministry of Defense, but this was quickly suppressed by M-60 machine guns emplaced at the library, and no Marine was injured.

Lance Corporal Gallagher came to aboard *Iwo Jima* late Monday morning with a throbbing headache and very sore ears. He asked how he was, heard some good news, and then asked after

Junior Newcom. The news was bad; Newcom was not expected to survive severe injuries to his head, neck, and shoulder. He had been on the operating table for six hours. Gallagher demanded to see his friend and was helped to the intensive-care compartment.

Gallagher was severely shaken by what he saw, but he walked over to the comatose figure and bent down beside Newcom's ear. "Hey, Newc, how ya doin'?"

The severely injured Marine's eye fluttered open. Everything in the room came to a dead halt.

"Hey, Newc, how ya doin'? How ya feelin'?"

Lance Corporal Newcom lifted his uninjured left hand and raised his thumb: Okay!

Shawn Gallagher and Richard Mathews were returned to duty on October 19, Gallagher's twenty-second birthday. Junior Newcom was evacuated to the United States.

Michael Ohler, aged twenty-eight, was buried by his parents, wife, daughter, and the son he had never seen in Pensacola, Florida.

22

It was the home stretch.

A new 22d Marine Amphibious Unit (MAU) left North Carolina on October 18, and the relief was set for the second week of November, less than a month away. Nonessential equipment was already being backloaded, staged at Green Beach, and carried back to Mediterranean Amphibious Ready Group (MARG) 3-83.

There remained some unfinished business. Castro, the renegade Shiite Amal warlord whose fighters occupied the Hooterville neighborhood opposite Charlie Company's 1st Platoon, had imported Syrian soldiers and Iranian Revolutionary Guardsmen, and these new arrivals were understood to be behind the deaths of Allen Soifert and Mike Ohler. On a trip to 1st Platoon's sector within a few days of the Marine deaths, LtCol Larry Gerlach discussed Castro at length with 2dLt Bill Harris. It was noted that Castro was always surrounded by a team of bodyguards and that he never handled a weapon.

Technically, Castro could not be made a target of Marine snipers because he was not, strictly speaking, a combatant. On the day the battalion commander spoke to Harris, the older man ended the discussion of Castro by using his forefinger to point quickly and emphatically at the center of his forehead. To Bill Harris, the meaning was quite clear. Though snipers were set to work tracking Castro, no one could ever get a clear shot. One of the more galling aspects of the task was presented to Harris in the form of a late-week safe conduct for Castro through 1st Platoon's lines to meet with Amal chieftain Nabieh Berri, who wanted to bring the renegade into the mainstream of the Amal coalition.

The matter of Marines sniping at targets in Hooterville became something of a press football that week, also. Amal officers found that they could simply tell some of the reporters that Marines were taking down women and children in order for stories to appear in Western newspapers. This infuriated a lot of Marines, who felt that their story was being neither adequately nor fairly covered.

There had been a simmering hostility between Marines and the press since the Vietnam War, and it had been allowed to get a bit out of hand at times. There was, however, a nugget of accuracy in the Marines' position, and it carried over into press relations in Beirut. On the other hand, and simply stated, some Marine briefers intentionally obscured the level of hostilities faced by Battalion Landing Team (BLT) 1/8.

Free access to Beirut International Airport (BIA) and Hooterville by the press was definitely a two-edged sword. Intelligence picked up from news reporters was often valuable, but having open mikes and prying eyes and ears around was considered by most Marine officers to be a definite liability. For example, it was often more expedient to yell orders and information during a contact with the militias than it was to use the secure radio nets. Thus the few reporters who could be coaxed to Marine line positions during a fight often heard things said in the heat of battle that Marines would rather have kept to themselves. Few reporters comprehended military jargon or had an understanding of even rudimentary offensive or defensive tactics, so they were generally apt to report some events incorrectly. On the whole, however, the Marines were irked because the press was reporting things the Department of Defense did not want the world to know.

The Marines' tendency to mislead reporters derived in large part from the Department of Defense's desire to minimize the American public's potential alarm over the daily heavy combat faced by Marines on the BIA perimeter line. The policy that had been transmitted to the Joint Public Affairs Bureau (JPAB) from above backfired a bit when news of the deaths of women and children at the hands of Marines was widely reported in the United States. The reports were erroneous, but the impact was heightened because the American public had not been adequately informed as to the full extent of the combat the Marines in Beirut were weathering. The news of the sniper kills, real and alleged, was beyond the comprehension of an American public long lulled into a sense of well-being through what seems to have been a program of calculated misinformation or deliberate omission. The reports pierced a contented vacuum: sniper kills were in context, but *reports* of the killings were not. The press was itself largely to blame because many of its representatives had long settled for misleading or incomplete information spooned out at JPAB briefing sessions.

Many Marine junior officers could not figure out what MAU and Battalion had in mind. They knew that they had to keep their mouths shut, but they were faced most days with inquisitive newspeople escorted out to their sectors by members of the JPAB. They had to both accommodate questions and attempt to bolster the officially sanctioned image. And they had to look out for the safety of the many press people. The Amal and Druse fighters across the way cooperated in this last to a remarkable degree, for it was not in their interests to pick a fight when reporters were around.

The younger Marine officers were members of a generation that had been told ad nauseam by Vietnam veterans that the press was antimilitary, anti-Marine, and, above all, un-American. However, the keenness of this acquired mistrust was amply tested by the unexpected insistence of a few stirling news professionals to inform Marine families in the States of upcoming TV reports involving their loved ones in Lebanon.

The allegations that women and children were being targeted by Marine snipers were countered in a forthright and effective manner. Representatives chosen by the press corps were taken to the snipers' firing positions and encouraged to peer through the powerful scopes used to sight in on targets. In this way, the press was convinced that no Marine sniper could misidentify his target, for anyone using such a scope could literally count the hairs in the target's beard.

The long-awaited peace talks were stalled before they quite got under way. The problem lay in Damascus, where the government of Hafez al-Assad withheld its blessing. Inasmuch as Syria controlled Walid Jumblatt, the Druse Progressive Socialist Party chairman, realistic negotiations could not begin. Jumblatt wanted to state his case within a national forum—his destructive bent over the past months had, in its way, been his contribution to a serious dialogue with the Gemayel government and the Phalange—but Syria was holding his cards, his cash, and his life.

At one point, on October 18, it was mooted that the national reconciliation talks might be convened at the BIA, in which case 24th MAU would provide security for the warring factional leaders and their deputies. This did not sit as well with those factional leaders as someone in Washington apparently thought it would, and the tender came to nothing.

Also on October 18, it was announced in Washington that the Rules of Engagement would be reviewed by the Joint Chiefs of

Staff. The effort of placing the story in the national media was largely wasted; most Americans had no idea why a change might be warranted. A related story out of Washington on the same day indicated that President Reagan was personally reviewing a proposal that Marine snipers be allowed to fire on hostile targets. Clearly, the Defense Department and White House press secretaries were backlogged with several weeks' work.

Finally, on October 18, the National Security Council met to consider, among other things, a recommendation made by Secretary of Defense Caspar Weinberger—acting on behalf of the nation's most senior military officers—that the U.S. contingent in the Multinational Force (MNF) be *immediately* withdrawn from Beirut and placed in readiness aboard the relatively safe ships of the MARG. Weinberger noted that the entire MAU could be off the beach within twenty-four hours.

Weinberger's proposal culminated several busy days of briefings and reports from both the Joint Chiefs of Staff and the Central Intelligence Agency. Everything pointed to an increased terrorist threat and, following the Suq-al-Gharb affair, a serious diminution in Lebanese eyes of American neutrality. Weinberger argued that the military situation on the ground in Beirut had become untenable in the face of the administration's continuing inability to state a clear or cogent foreign-policy goal with respect to Lebanon.

The details are not now known, but it is clear that others attending the meeting prevailed upon Weinberger during a break to drop his proposal. The Secretary of Defense did so, and President Reagan thus avoided the necessity of making a decision one way or the other on the specific withdrawal proposal or on any of the information and recommendations supporting it.

Col Tim Geraghty was just taking it all in. He had no difficulty tying the appearance of Syrian professional soldiers and Iranian Revolutionary Guardsmen on his doorstep with the policy decisions of Bud McFarlane—who, incidentally, had been called back to Washington to take a job with the National Security Council.

The MAU commander keenly felt the impact of the decision to bombard Suq-al-Gharb in the increasing tempo of violence against his Marines—there was no longer the charade of even thinking that the Marines were taking spillover fire meant for collocated Lebanese Armed Forces (LAF) contingents—and the virtual isolation of the components of the MAU.

No Marines had been "present"—as in "presence" mission—on the streets of Beirut or its suburbs for nearly two months, unless heavily escorted resupply convoys could be called a suitable presence for a force of so-called peacekeepers. Even that appellation was inaccurate; except for misstatements by the President of the United States following the May 17 signing of a Lebanese-Israeli peace accord, no one had ever officially given 24th MAU a mission to "keep the peace."

Attempts by Colonel Geraghty and Lieutenant Colonel Gerlach to bolster their defenses at the BIA and beef up security around the MAU, the MAU Service and Support Group (MSSG), and the BLT command posts met with resistance along the civilian chain of command, which seemed to have won whatever power struggles it had gone through leading up to the naval bombardments around Suq-al-Gharb. Overt security arrangements that appeared to acknowledge that 24th MAU was involved or even might be involved as a direct player in the fighting were slapped down as soon as word of them reached higher authority. Men who had never set foot in Beirut issued orders that prevented the MAU and BLT commanders from sanctioning adequate responses to attacks and potential attacks. Politicians who had acquired a direct stake in the successful outcome of the upcoming national reconciliation talks continued to cast blind eyes at the reality of the situation in which their fellow countrymen—expendable lance corporals—found themselves.

Officially, the LAF was charged with the security of the MNF.

That had been the official line from the start, and it remained the official line. The fact that LAF troops in the vicinity of the Lebanese University had not come to the aid of Alpha Company on the night Mike Ohler was shot was not surprising to Marines, but it certainly revealed the sentiments of the Gemayel government, which did not want to rock the ship of state when a chance of legitimization was so close at hand.

They almost got Tim Geraghty on October 19.

Security on the streets of Beirut had become so iffy that Geraghty had taken to removing his eagles and riding shotgun in the jeeps in which he traveled. A casual observer or an assassin who did not know the MAU commander by sight could easily mistake him for a trooper. There was sufficient intelligence information to warrant the precautions.

Colonel Geraghty's jeep had just passed the Kuwaiti embassy, right outside the gates of the Sabra and Shatilla camps and well inside the Italian MNF zone, when a car bomb detonated beside the road. The colonel's jeep was missed by a minute, and the bomb went off as it was being passed by a Marine supply convoy on the way back from carrying a meal to the Bravo Company contingent guarding the American embassy.

Cpl Gene Siler, a Dragon-team leader who was on a break from months of duty on the lines with Charlie Company, spotted the white Mercedes just before the explosion, but he thought nothing of it. Cars had been able to park anywhere they wanted since the Israelis had pulled out.

The point jeep gunned past the Mercedes and on up the long slope outside the camp gates. The single truck in the four-vehicle convoy slowed slightly as the driver downshifted, then *WHOOM!* The car blew up just as the truck came abreast.

The truck took most of the impact and thus shielded the second jeep, which was right behind it. The third jeep, with Corporal Siler aboard, was caught in the powerful blast and thrown against a telephone pole. The two gunners manning the stanchion-mounted M-60 in the tiny rear compartment were all mixed together and Siler was shifted from the front passenger's seat into the driver's seat. He disentangled himself from the driver and yelled, "Get the hell out of here!" The driver threw the jeep into reverse but could not move. The front bumper had been bent into the front tires.

Light gunfire was passing overhead, but help was on the way.

First Lieutenant Mark Singleton, who had been wounded on August 29 and sent back to the States as George Losey's escort, was commander of the BLT 1/8 reaction force, an ad hoc platoon drawn from Charlie Battery and mounted aboard three amtracs stationed permanently at the battery. The car bombing outside the refugee camps was Singleton's first call.

The artillery lieutenant was given no details, just a location and a heads-up. He called his amtrac commanders and squad leaders together while waiting for a wrecker to arrive from the MSSG, told them he knew as much as they did, and ordered them to stop for nothing. Then the force raced across the BIA and turned north onto the Sidon Road.

Sgt Steve Russell, a TOW-squad leader, was in charge of jeep patrols that day. At about 1605, the Dragon Platoon sergeant stuck his head into Russell's hooch beside the BLT building and asked if he had an escort accompanying the daily supply run to the embassy.

"Yes. Why?"

"They been hit."

The two NCOs ran to the battalion combat operations center, where they heard a captain speaking with one of the escorts by radio. Sergeant Russell listened for a few moments, then headed out to his hooch, where he found several TOW gunners playing cards.

"Myself and three others, get your shit on. Our convoy escort's been hit."

Russell and three armed Marines were in a jeep and on the move within a minute. They were joined by another jeep carrying Lieutenant Colonel Gerlach and SgtMaj Frederick Douglass as they pulled in behind Lieutenant Singleton's amtracs on the way out the gate.

The react force was rounding a turn on a narrow street when an old Lebanese man drove his ancient pickup truck across the roadway. Lieutenant Singleton was sure the truck would clear the area in time, but as the amtracs approached to within 100 meters at a speed of forty-five miles per hour, Singleton saw the old truck driver step to the road and stare at the oncoming vehicles. The obvious thought passed through Mark Singleton's mind: car bomb.

SSgt Jim Inglett, the amtrac chief, looked at Lieutenant Singleton. "What do we do, sir?"

"Ram it!"

The hulking tracked amphibian crunched into the pickup and spun it off the road.

They raced along the road and topped the hill overlooking the scene of the bombing—and found a carnival in progress.

The street around the blast site had quickly filled with a dozen bloody-minded Marines, who organized a 360-degree defense and prepared to "repel boarders." Someone spotted an automobile engine some eighty feet from the site of the blast. Nearby was an automobile front-drive train. The only Marines in the tiny perimeter were those who had emerged from the truck and the two chase jeeps, and they all assumed that the debris was from the point jeep, which was, in fact, atop the nearby hill. There was nothing to identify the streetful of scrap as a Mercedes.

The street filled with civilians, LAF soldiers, and armed Italians. Newsmen were only moments behind, taking pictures and jotting down notes. A Lebanese civilian offered to tow the shattered truck but was turned down. Another local offered his tools, so Corporal Siler asked him to fetch a sledgehammer for straightening the bumper of the rear jeep. The truck was going nowhere: the hood was jammed back against the blown windshield, the brakes were gone, the tires were losing air, the radiator was full of holes.

An LAF major sidled up to Corporal Siler with some reassuring words: if anything happened, the LAF would take care of it. Siler coolly responded that his Marines would take care of their own security until help arrived from the BIA.

The lead amtrac roared to the top of the hill, about 500 meters from the entrance to the refugee camps, stopped, and dropped its rear ramp. Sergeant Russell, who was in the last vehicle in the column, watched with his heart in his mouth as fifteen combat-equipped artillerymen charged into the open and quickly established a 180-degree covering position on the high ground. It was the first time Russell, or nearly anyone in Beirut, had seen Marines use live combat assault tactics. The second amtrac repeated the performance halfway down the hill and the third amtrac stopped right beside the camp gate, where it pivoted completely around on its tracks and dropped its ramp. As twice before, fifteen combat-ready Marines charged out and covered the entire area with their leveled weapons. Sergeant Russell heard a few bullets pass overhead, so he motioned his driver to stop. He and his three companions joined the artillerymen and scanned the rooftops and streets all around. The wrecker hooked the damaged truck and everyone was gone within twenty minutes.

There would always remain the question of whether the car bomb was meant for Tim Geraghty or the meal truck.

Somewhere in the hills overlooking Beirut, Iranian Revolutionary Guardsmen were perfecting a new kind of bomb.

PART VII

The Bomb

23

It is 0600, Sunday, October 23, 1983.

Most members of 24th Marine Amphibious Unit (MAU) are asleep or otherwise dormant in their racks and sleeping bags. It has been thus on Sundays since the MAU arrived in Beirut; the troops and their officers are given an extra hour to sleep in. Only those Marines on critical duty—guarding or monitoring—or those who cannot or will not lie still are up and about.

First Lieutenant Bill Zimmerman, the battalion training officer, has the combat operations center (COC) watch this morning. Normally, Zimmerman's friend and roommate, 1stLt Greg Balzer, would be on duty, but Balzer has been temporarily assigned as the MAU liaison officer to the Lebanese Ministry of Defense. Bill Zimmerman is on the radio, placing routine calls to the line companies. It is 0622, and Zimmerman has just completed a conversation with the Marine manning Charlie Company's command radio. His last words to the radioman are, "Have a nice day."

Cpl Denny Palmer is asleep in the battalion aid station, which is located in a pillar-supported room in the basement of the Battalion Landing Team (BLT) building. Palmer is a Bravo Company rifle-squad leader who has injured his foot in a basketball game. He will remain on bed rest for a few days longer, then return to Bravo Company.

LCpl Scott Schultz, also of Bravo Company, is up and about. He has pulled mess duty at the BLT, which is a kind of reward the staff NCOs give deserving troops: a little time away from the lines.

LCpl James LaRocque, a communicator, is late for his shift at the BLT galley. LaRocque walked to the galley earlier, but he was adjudged to be out of uniform because his cammie trousers were not properly bloused. He returned to his quarters 150 meters away and put on the proper blousing garters. He is now ready to return to work.

Sgt Kim McKinney, a MAU Service and Support Group (MSSG) Maintenance Platoon squad leader, is awake in his rack, trying to decide if he should enjoy the added moments of lazy rest or begin preparing to leave his tent to eat a leisurely breakfast at the BLT field mess hall.

SSgt Randy Gaddo, a Joint Public Affairs Bureau (JPAB) photographer, is up because he has work to complete this day, and he wants to get an early start. Sunday is a great day for completing chores put off by the crush of business during the week, for the JPAB usually receives and escorts no representatives of the press on the day of rest. Gaddo shaves and cleans up, noting how very still it is this day, unusual even for a Sunday. The sounds of war that are always in the background seem distant today. About all he can hear is the warbling of the birds who populate the stately trees that surround the MAU headquarters. The JPAB noncoms are scheduled to waterproof their bunker today, and Staff Sergeant Gaddo wants to develop eight rolls of film before that. He is thus anxious to get to the photo lab, which is located on the second deck of the BLT headquarters building, just 250 meters or twenty-three seconds away from Gaddo's tent. But it is so peaceful this morning that Staff Sergeant Gaddo decides to delay his trip, to suck up some rare solitude. He draws a cup of coffee from the JPAB's perpetual pot and sits at his desk to list all the things he will do at the lab. Gaddo completes his list at 0622. He pushes his chair back and prepares to stand, but he is stopped from completing this simple act by a disturbing noise.

LCpl Richard Bailey and Pfc Carl Hancock, both members of the 81mm Mortar Platoon, are on guard duty at Post 2, several hundred meters north of the BLT building. They have been manning the post during the 0400–0800 shift for several days and have frankly lost track of what day it is. It would be time for breakfast during the week, so Hancock offers to man the post alone while Bailey goes to the BLT mess hall for some coffee and food. Bailey declines, telling Hancock he ought to go first. They haggle on until a sound from the south draws them sharply from the conversation.

First Lieutenant Leo Lachat, commander of MSSG-24's Shore Party Platoon, has been up since 0530 preparing for a heavy day's business. If everything goes according to plan, a great deal of the MAU's nonessential equipment will be sent to the Mediterranean Amphibious Ready Group (MARG) via Green Beach, which is Lachat's domain. As he does every morning, Lachat joins the Navy warrant officer commanding Beachmaster Unit-2 and visually checks the entire beach for mines or ordnance that might have floated in during the night. As Lachat finishes his visual sweep of the beach, he continues to turn so that he can see the entire Beirut International Airport (BIA) compound. His eyes are passing the dominant BLT building but are arrested by a sight he cannot quite place. There is a strange noise as well.

Cpl Joe Martucci and LCpl Bob Calhoun are in the open sandbagged forward air control (FAC) bunker at the southeast corner of the BLT roof. They had to haul their radio gear to the roof late on Saturday to direct a medevac operation and did not want to shut down completely because they knew they would only have to haul it up again on Sunday, the day the fighting usually boils over around the BIA. Their decision was vindicated during the night when Condition I was sounded, for, while everyone else heads for the basement, the FAC team has to be on "the high ground" to direct helo operations or—dream on—jet air strikes. The two communicators are pulled from their sleep by the crackle of gunfire. Then they hear something large impact against something solid. Finally, they both hear someone yelling, but neither can make out the words. Calhoun begins to climb out of his sleeping bag.

Cpl David Wilcox, the battalion classified materials clerk, has slept for about six hours this night in his tiny room on the east side of the first deck. Wilcox had planned to spend three days aboard ship getting ready to backload for the float home, but he finished a day early. During the night, Wilcox spent several hours in the basement during the Condition I alert and finally got to sleep at 2330. He is awakened at 0530 by his roommate, LCpl Bruce Hollingshead, who has pulled morning duty in the COC. Unable to get back to sleep, Wilcox begins preparing for an inspection that will be run later in the day. When he hears shots fired nearby, Wilcox grabs his automatic pistol and heads for the door.

LCpl Burnham Matthews, a member of the reconnaissance platoon attached to BLT 1/8, has just returned from an early-morning security sweep around the BIA. He is standing beside a window on the second deck of the BLT building. He hears a loud crash and turns to the man next to him. "There's something going on," Matthews says. "Wake everybody up!"

Sgt Steve Russell is the battalion sergeant of the guard (SOG), a grueling twenty-four-hour duty requiring him to man a plywood-and-sandbag post the size of a theater ticket booth at the southern entryway to the BLT building's atrium lobby.

Steve Russell is a Marine with a future, a small, wiry, and

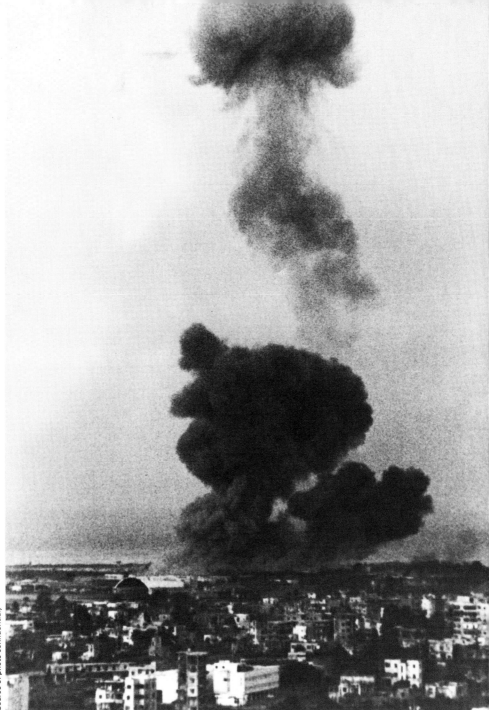

Sunday morning, October 23, 1983: At approximately 0622 and 31 seconds, an Iranian photographer heard the sound of the bomb and released the shutter of a 35mm camera he had set up before sunrise on a hill about four kilometers from the Beirut International Airport.

The Rescue: October 23, 1984

(Official Marine Corps Photo by SSgt Robert E. Kline, USMC)

Marine sentry on guard October 23, 1983

habitually precise man of twenty-eight with clear eyes, a neatly trimmed mustache, and the flowing movements of a man in complete control of his physical being. He first enlisted in the Marine Corps in 1974, upon his graduation from a Boston-area high school, and he succeeded in graduating as his recruit platoon's honor man, number one of seventy-two. He later graduated number two of 169 from the Noncommissioned Officers Leadership School, then left the Marine Corps in 1977 to take an automotive assembly-line job. He also joined the Massachusetts National Guard, which seemed tame compared to the Marine Corps. The failing economy and uncertainty over his future on the assembly line brought him back to the Marine Corps in August 1982. He became a TOW-squad leader that October. That is his regular job, a squad leader with the TOW antitank missile section attached to BLT 1/8. Steve Russell has spent most of the last five months on patrol around Beirut and providing escorts for convoys and many of the VIPs who inhabit Beirut between crises.

Other than the shellings, which have been going on since July, Steve Russell's most exciting experience in The Root took place only four days ago, when he responded to the car bombing of the Marine supply convoy outside the Sabra and Shatilla refugee camps. He remains deeply impressed by the way the reaction platoon conducted itself in establishing security around the site. He has never seen Marines at such a perfect pitch.

Steve Russell usually catches duty as SOG on the twenty-second of each month. His October duty was delayed, however, because of the October 19 car bombing. Russell's intimate knowledge of the streets of Beirut resulted in his being detailed to prepare a new patrol-route map overlay and lead a convoy to Alpha Company's positions at the Lebanese University. The extra convoy duty lasted from 0530 until 1200, October 22, and Sergeant Russell went straight to the SOG booth at 1300, October 22, to relieve the sergeant who had been filling in for him. This is to be his final stint, for the BLT will be gone from Beirut by mid-November. He is to be relieved at 0800, just two hours from now. Another milestone.

The only excitement on the afternoon of October 22 was a brief concert held by a country-western band provided by the MARG. Pizza baked aboard the ships was flown to the BLT and distributed, along with cold canned soda, to the audience. Sergeant Russell saw that each Marine standing post around the BLT building received his share of the treat.

That night, the BLT compound was hit by several bursts of direct small-arms fire. Russell was looking at the parking lot between posts 6 and 7 when he saw sparks from several bullets impacting on the macadam surface. Condition I, the highest state of alert, was sounded in the wee hours when several rockets landed a bit too close for comfort. Condition II remained in effect for the balance of the night, which was still and quiet.

At about 0500, a large yellow Mercedes truck entered the public parking lot just south of the BLT compound, circled once, and exited through the parking-lot entrance. The incident was observed by the sentry manning Post 6 but not reported because the truck did not stop.

It is now 0600.

LCpl John Berthiaume, a TOW gunner standing watch at Post 5, at the southwest corner of the BLT compound, calls in to ask permission to make a head call. Steve Russell sends his corporal of the guard to Post 5 to relieve Berthiaume, who stops in at the SOG shack to drop off his night-vision goggles, which he no longer needs.

Sergeant Russell notes that it is "a typical Beirut morning, the sunrise bright and beautiful."

Lance Corporal Berthiaume returns to Post 5 within a few minutes and calls Sergeant Russell to say that an early-morning jogger dressed in physical-training gear is tramping the lot between posts 6 and 7. This sort of activity is forbidden during conditions I and II, so Russell asks Berthiaume to tell the jogger to report to the SOG shack. The Marine shows up within the minute, and Sergeant Russell explains that he will have to stop jogging until the Condition II alert is relaxed. The two engage in some small talk, which peters out. Then the jogger remains, looking at Russell as though he cannot decide what to do next.

Sergeant Russell is sitting in the SOG shack, facing away from the lot. The shack is an eight-foot-by-three-foot plywood affair with a four-and-a-half-foot-high double-thickness sandbag wall on the south side, facing the parking lot. An array of squad radios, one for each of nine posts and one to the COC, is on either side of the sergeant of the guard's chair, which is set right up against the south wall.

It is coming up 0622.

There is a sudden noise. Steve Russell cannot quite figure out what he is hearing—"a sort of popping or crackling sound from the direction of the parking lot," from right in front of the BLT building. The sound is not loud and does not immediately cause Russell to turn and look. In a moment, however, he does turn because the sound has changed to something like a roaring diesel engine. He sees "a large, yellow Mercedes stake-bed truck bounding through the chain-link gate." Russell is not alarmed, but he is curious.

LCpl Eddie DiFranco is manning Post 7, just east of the gate leading from the parking lot to the BLT building. He sees a large yellow Mercedes truck heading right for the chain-link gate. The truck has circled once in the parking lot at high speed, just as the yellow Mercedes truck—the *same* yellow Mercedes truck?—did at 0500. It is the sort of truck—indeed, it might be one of the very trucks—that constantly transits the BIA compound to haul goods and equipment from the cargo terminal to Beirut and beyond. All the Marines at the BIA are used to seeing such vehicles. The only difference between this yellow Mercedes truck and all the others is that it has just crashed through the barbed-wire barrier separating the south public parking lot from the BLT headquarters compound.

Lance Corporal DiFranco is too stunned to act for several

seconds, but his mind's eye registers the swarthy bearded man at the wheel of the large truck. The man is dressed in a dark blue or green shirt. Finally, DiFranco shrugs his M-16 from his shoulder. The magazine is in place but the rifle must be locked and loaded. DiFranco pivots in the direction of the moving vehicle. It has already passed through the gate in the chain-link fence. DiFranco manages to get a round into the chamber, but he no longer has a clear shot. He lowers his rifle and heads for his bunker to place a call to Sergeant Russell. He realizes that the sergeant of the guard has probably already seen the truck, so he lowers the handset.

LCpl Henry Linkkila is the sentry at Post 6, which is right across from Post 7. He does not see the truck because his back is turned. When he does see it, he instinctively dives behind the corner of his bunker.

Lance Corporal Berthiaume, at Post 5, hears the commotion at the gate and turns in time to see the yellow truck pass the officers' and staff NCOs' mess tents. He pulls his M-16 from his shoulder, but the vehicle is past him before he can lock and load.

A Reconnaissance Platoon patrol leader who has just led his security patrol back to the BLT has stopped by a "water buffalo" —a large wheeled water tank—twenty-five meters across from the southeast corner of the BLT building. He is facing east when he hears a large vehicle engine accelerate at his back. The NCO believes the sound is coming from a speeding Marine vehicle, and he turns to see who it is. Perhaps he will make a report. He sees the yellow Mercedes truck as it accelerates from left to right across his field of vision. The event is so extraordinary that he simply turns to run for a nearby rain gutter.

Sergeant Russell is now on his feet, standing beside the guard shack and facing the intruding vehicle. The truck is heading straight for him—fast, at twenty-five or thirty miles per hour.

Russell does not think about his next act. He simply turns back toward the building's atrium lobby and runs. When he sees the jogger, he yells, "Get the fuck outa here!" Then he bolts across the lobby, heading for the back door, between the weight room and the S-4 shop. He has the presence of mind, and the time, to yell "HIT THE DECK!" two or three times. The whining sound of the truck engine is getting closer.

Russell exits the rear of the building and notices a Marine walking post at the motor pool. He yells, "Get down!" The Marine dives behind a two-foot-high concrete wall while Sergeant Russell cuts left at an angle into the open parking lot between the BLT building and the trash dump directly to the north. He looks back just as the big truck flattens the SOG shack. The moving debris of the shack looks to Russell "like a huge wave of water rushing into the lobby, filling every space." He legs another thirty feet, then turns for another look.

The truck is just coming to a stop in the center of the lobby. Russell sees absolutely no movement in the cab. There is extensive damage to the windshield and to the cab roof on the driver's side. He thinks the driver has been injured in the collision with the SOG shack. It is dead silent.

It is 0622 and eighteen seconds.

Still running, Russell looks directly at the truck. No more than two seconds have passed since he turned. He sees "a bright orange-yellow flash at the grill of the truck" and feels "a wave of intense heat and a powerful concussion."

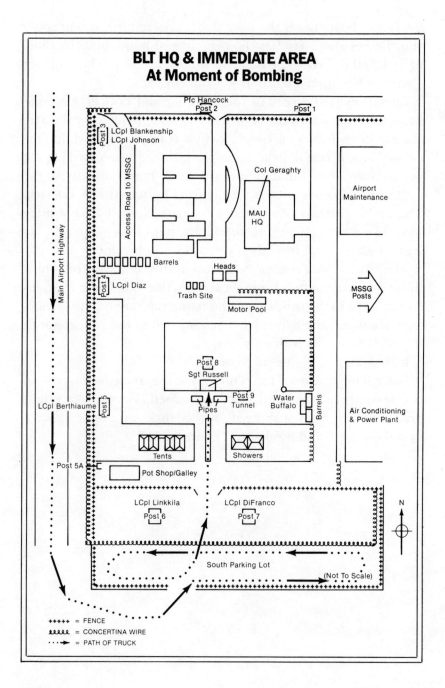

BLT HQ & IMMEDIATE AREA
At Moment of Bombing

Pfc Hancock
Post 2
Post 1

Post 3
LCpl Blankenship
LCpl Johnson

Access Road to MSSG

Col Geraghty

Airport
Maintenance

MAU
HQ

Barrels

Heads

Post 4
LCpl Diaz

Trash Site

Motor Pool

MSSG
Posts

Main Airport Highway

Post 8
Sgt Russell

Post 9
Tunnel

Water
Buffalo

Barrels

Air Conditioning
& Power Plant

LCpl Berthiaume

Post 5

Pipes

Post 5A

Tents

Showers

Pot Shop/Galley

LCpl Linkkila

Post 6

LCpl DiFranco

Post 7

N

South Parking Lot

(Not To Scale)

+++++ = FENCE
ꙮꙮꙮꙮ = CONCERTINA WIRE
····→ = PATH OF TRUCK

BLT HEADQUARTERS

BASEMENT

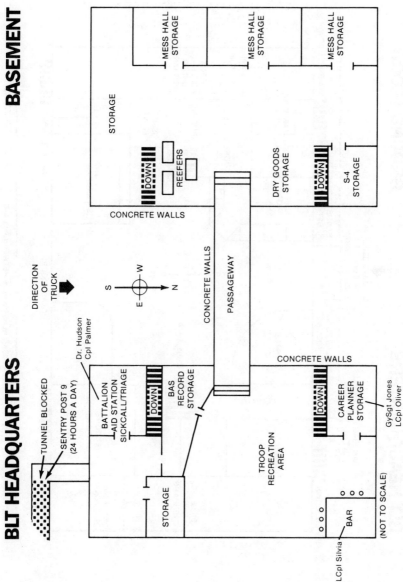

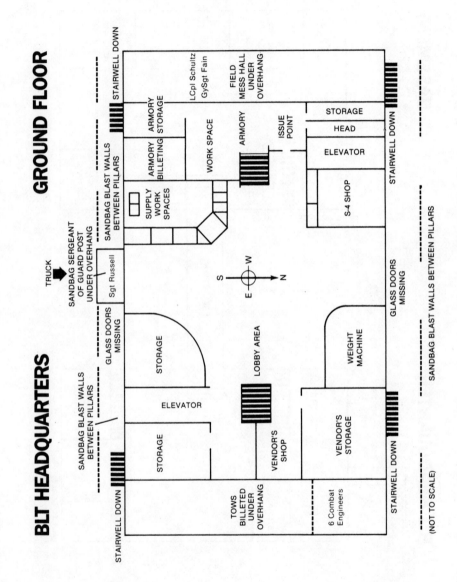

BLT HEADQUARTERS

1st DECK

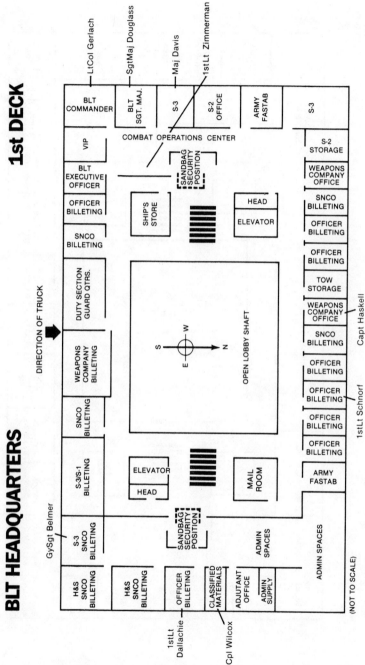

LtCol Gerlach
SgtMaj Douglass
Maj Davis
1stLt Zimmerman

BLT COMMANDER

BLT SGT. MAJ.

S-3

S-2 OFFICE

ARMY FASTAB

S-3

VIP

COMBAT OPERATIONS CENTER

S-2 STORAGE

BLT EXECUTIVE OFFICER

SANDBAG SECURITY POSITION

WEAPONS COMPANY OFFICE

OFFICER BILLETING

SHIP'S STORE

HEAD

SNCO BILLETING

ELEVATOR

OFFICER BILLETING

SNCO BILLETING

OFFICER BILLETING

DIRECTION OF TRUCK

DUTY SECTION GUARD QTRS.

TOW STORAGE

W

WEAPONS COMPANY OFFICE

Capt Haskell

WEAPONS COMPANY BILLETING

S
N
E

OPEN LOBBY SHAFT

SNCO BILLETING

SNCO BILLETING

OFFICER BILLETING

S-3/S-1 BILLETING

OFFICER BILLETING

1stLt Schnorf

OFFICER BILLETING

GySgt Belmer

S-3 SNCO BILLETING

ELEVATOR

MAIL ROOM

OFFICER BILLETING

HEAD

ARMY FASTAB

H&S SNCO BILLETING

H&S SNCO BILLETING

OFFICER BILLETING

SANDBAG SECURITY POSITION

ADMIN SPACES

CLASSIFIED MATERIALS

ADJUTANT OFFICE

ADMIN SUPPLY

ADMIN SPACES

1stLt Dallachie

Cpl Wilcox

(NOT TO SCALE)

BLT HEADQUARTERS

2d DECK

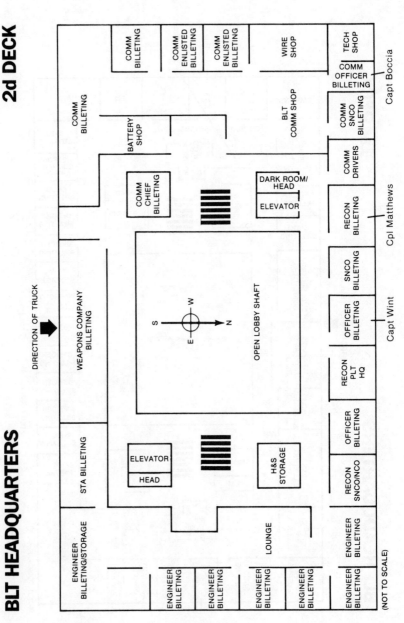

(NOT TO SCALE)

300

BLT HEADQUARTERS

3d DECK

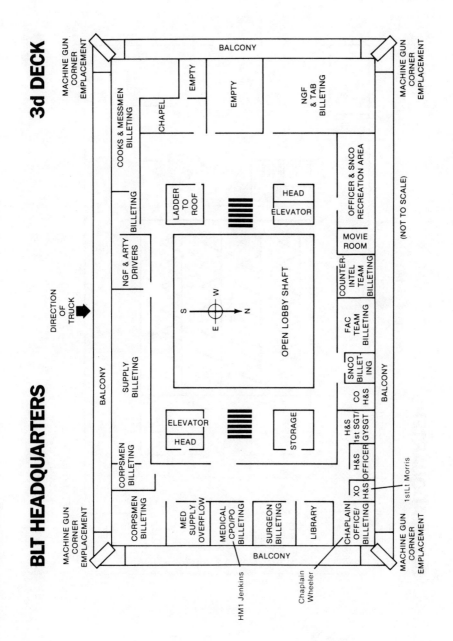

BLT HEADQUARTERS

ROOF

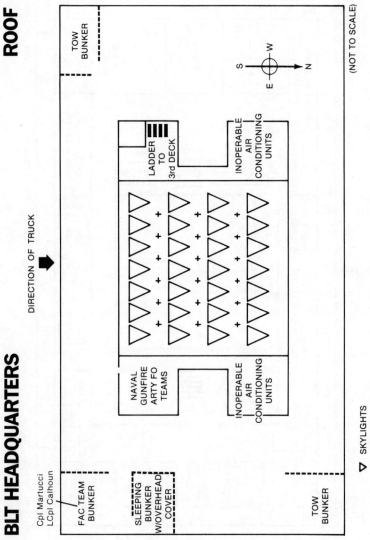

Cpl Martucci
LCpl Calhoun

FAC TEAM BUNKER

SLEEPING BUNKER W/OVERHEAD COVER

TOW BUNKER

TOW BUNKER

DIRECTION OF TRUCK

NAVAL GUNFIRE ARTY FO TEAMS

INOPERABLE AIR CONDITIONING UNITS

LADDER TO 3rd DECK

INOPERABLE AIR CONDITIONING UNITS

S
E — W
N

▽ SKYLIGHTS
+ + COMM ANTENNAS
■■■ SANDBAG
BLAST WALLS

(NOT TO SCALE)

24

The bomb in the bed of the big yellow Mercedes truck consisted of about 12,000 pounds of high explosives wrapped in canisters of flammable gases. It is said to have been the largest non-nuclear blast ever detonated on the face of the earth. Be that as it may, it was placed perfectly within the open atrium lobby of the concrete-and-steel Battalion Landing Team (BLT) head-quarters building. The force of the explosion initially lifted the entire four-story structure, shearing the bases of the concrete support columns, each measuring fifteen feet in circumference and reinforced by numerous one-and-three-quarter-inch steel rods. The airborne building then fell in upon itself. A massive shock wave and ball of flaming gas was hurled in all directions. The blast created an oblong crater measuring thirty-nine feet by twenty-nine feet, and eight feet eight inches in depth. This, after shattering the seven-inch-thick steel-reinforced-concrete basement floor.

First Lieutenant Bill Zimmerman, the combat operations center watch officer, was probably killed instantly as the ceiling and walls of the operations center fell in upon him and the other Marines in the room with total, crushing force. No one in that narrow compartment survived.

Cpl Denny Palmer, whose foot had been injured in a basketball game and who was occupying a rack next to a large pillar in the basement aid station, was knocked unconscious by the blast, which he did not even hear.

LCpl Scott Schultz, who had been sent to the rear from Bravo Company to stand mess duty as a reward for excellent performance in combat, was killed in the galley, which was located at ground level beneath an overhang on the west side of the building.

LCpl James LaRocque was about to leave his tent 150 meters from the building when the bomb was detonated. He received the full force of the concussion but was unhurt.

The front of Sgt Kim McKinney's tent fell in on him and nine other sergeants from the MAU Service and Support Group (MSSG) 24. Neither McKinney nor any of the others was hurt, but they were surprised and severely shaken by the magnitude of the blast. When McKinney realized that he was intact and unhurt, he hurtled from his sleeping bag, reflexively grabbed his flak jacket, and lifted the front of the fallen tent. A rising cloud of smoke, dust, and debris assailed his eyes.

SSgt Randy Gaddo had been stopped in midmotion by the sound of several small-arms rounds as he rose from the desk in the Joint Public Affairs Bureau staff NCOs' tent. He heard a dull, powerful thud that immediately reverberated off the hills to the east. Within seconds, he felt on his face a blast of heat that pulled loose folds of skin. The concussion hit him in the chest with sledgehammer force and threw him backward. The three other staff NCOs in the tent were awakened when they were hurled from their racks by that concussion. GySgt Herman Lange was slightly injured by broken glass. Gaddo and the others assumed, as did most people near the blast site, that their position had taken a direct mortar, rocket, or artillery hit.

LCpl Richard Bailey and Pfc Carl Hancock, the 81mm mortar-men on guard duty at Post 2, about 150 meters directly north of the BLT building, were certain that an artillery round had hit close by. Then Hancock saw smoke and dust rise over the nearby Lebanese Armed Forces liaison building, which partially blocked his view of the BLT. Hancock left the post to Lance Corporal Bailey and headed for the smoke.

First Lieutenant Leo Lachat, on Green Beach, heard the blast and saw a pillar of black smoke rise and spread from the knot of buildings within his view. He was not yet sure what had happened. Within seconds, the concussion, still powerful, rippled past him.

Cpl Joe Martucci and LCpl Bob Calhoun were only partway to their elbows, and still nestled in their sleeping bags, when they both saw the center of the BLT roof open up and issue a great gout of smoke and flame. Then the fissure sealed itself as the entire building slowly sagged beneath them.

Cpl David Wilcox had his .45-caliber automatic pistol in his hand and was heading for the door of his tiny room on the first deck of the building in response to gunfire from below when the door left its hinges and shot right at him.

LCpl Burnham Matthews, facing north out of a second-deck window, was hurled through the window and out into midair. He fell thirty feet to the ground and landed on his feet. He was not harmed until falling debris struck him on the head and shoulders. Nearly every other member of the Recon Platoon in Matthews's compartment was killed in the inferno.

Sgt Steve Russell, the only man to see the detonation itself, was caught in the spreading wave of concussion and hurled fifteen or twenty feet. He was mercifully unconscious by the time he came to rest.

The reconnaissance patrol leader was caught in midstride by

the blast as he ran from the water buffalo toward a nearby storm drain. He was lifted from his feet and slammed into the earth, injured but alive.

The sentries at posts 5, 6, and 7 were all shaken, but each was protected by an intervening barrier of one sort or another, and all survived without physical injury.

The Iranian behind the wheel of the big yellow Mercedes truck—and most of the truck itself—was vaporized.

On a hill about four kilometers from the center of the blast, an Iranian cameraman waited patiently until he heard the detonation. He released the shutter of his camera—which had been set up and focused at dawn—thirteen seconds after the driver of the big yellow Mercedes truck immolated himself.

Sgt Steve Russell came to in a deep cocoon of intense pain, especially in his legs. He repeated aloud, over and over again for many seconds, a simple litany, "Oh, my God, I can't believe it." It was strangely silent—a more profound silence than Steve Russell had ever experienced. Then there was the sound of incoming, though it could have been rounds cooking off in the battalion armory, which was inside the shattered building.

Then Steve Russell heard a voice: "Oh, God, help me." Another voice to his left said exactly the same thing. Sergeant Russell composed himself and instinctively moved to provide some assistance to the unseen men trapped within the rat's nest of concrete. But he could not move. The generalized pain that suffused his body reverberated through his twisted left leg. He looked to see what the matter was and saw that his left foot was twisted inward and pointing at the ground. He found blood on his left hand and saw that the skin and flesh had been blown open. He was wrapped in blood and dust, and his extremities felt eerily cold. The sharp tang of explosives was up his nose, and he thought that there was enough of it in the air to detonate. There was a gash on the left side of his head.

Everyone at or near Beirut International Airport (BIA) who heard the blast assumed that his position had taken a direct hit. This sensation was as profound for Marines and corpsmen on the beach or in fighting bunkers on the perimeter—kilometers from the BLT—as it was for men in the Marine Amphibious Unit and MSSG headquarters buildings—from 50 to 400 meters from the center of the explosion.

LCpl Dan Gaffney, a dump truck driver serving with the 1st Platoon, Charlie Company, 2d Combat Engineer Battalion, was asleep in a six-man sandbag hooch tucked under the overhang on the east side of the BLT building. He was awakened by the bomb and by debris falling on his head. He instinctively rolled over onto his stomach and covered his head with his arms.

LCpl Jeff O'Brien, a heavy-equipment operator, had gotten off guard duty an hour earlier and was not quite asleep in a rack near Gaffney's. He had heard the truck, assumed it was a Marine on a spree, and curled instinctively into a tight little ball as the heat and concussion of the blast raced over his body.

O'Brien yelled, "Is everyone all right?" Everyone responded with an affirmative except Lance Corporal Gaffney, who said, "I don't know." This got a chuckle from all hands because Gaffney had once been trapped in his sleeping bag during a rocket attack, unable to get free because of his mosquito net, his panic, and a mild case of alcohol intoxication.

O'Brien tried to get up to help Gaffney, but he was impeded by a pile of debris that had fallen upon his mosquito netting. LCpl Richard Macaluso pulled O'Brien clear. Cpl Neale Bolen then asked for help getting out of his rack, so O'Brien, Macaluso, and Gaffney—who had managed to free himself—went to his aid. Bolen was dazed and bleeding from a cut above one eye. He was the only man in the tent with visible injuries, though one other, LCpl Charles Melefsky, had a fractured arm.

The smell of cordite or gunpowder—some sort of tangy explosive—was in the air, burning nostrils and throats. The consensus was that the hooch had taken a direct hit, no doubt by an artillery round.

Corporal Bolen's shaky voice interrupted the speculation and self-congratulations: "What's this jeep doing here?"

Sure enough, a jeep had been blown into the hooch from the motor pool across the way. It was wadded up like a tin toy. The thing that had saved several of the engineers from being crushed was a new sandbag wall they had constructed earlier in the week to alleviate the boredom of a dry spell in their work load.

It was strangely quiet, and very still.

Only then did someone notice that the BLT building, against which the hooch had been built, was leveled. The profound silence was replaced by the cries of men who had been pulled from their sleep to find themselves trapped within the rubble. There were soft, gray, dust-covered lumps everywhere—bodies and parts of bodies, in the open, impaled on crazed steel rods, half-crushed beneath concrete slabs.

The rest of the combat engineers were in the building. Nearly all had been killed or suffered mortal injuries in the blast.

There is no telling why the six engineers were spared. Twenty-two members of the TOW antitank section—Sgt Steve Russell's unit—were asleep in two tents just forward of the engineer hooch. Nineteen were killed outright or died of their massive injuries before any help arrived. The wall and overhang both collapsed on the sleeping men, crushing every one of them.

LCpl Bill Blankenship, a strapping 81mm mortarman who would complete his third year in the Marine Corps this very day, and who had stood the 0400–0800 shift at Post 3 for about four weeks, could not at first choose a direction from which the sudden, engulfing blast emanated. He was simply bathed in the maelstrom of noise and dust as he ducked into the bunker. He instinctively dove, as did his partner, LCpl Harry Johnson. The earth shook, and the sound of stones hitting the ground could be clearly heard through the sandbag walls. Then there was a huge *CRUNCH,* and another.

Certain that something had hit the concrete fence right behind the bunker, Blankenship grabbed his radio handset and tried to talk to Sergeant Russell at the BLT building, but he knew in a moment that the line was dead, so he threw the handset down and told Johnson he could not get the guard shack. Johnson offered to try while Blankenship left the bunker for a cautious look around.

Small chunks of concrete were still falling, and the smoke and dust was so thick that Blankenship could barely see five feet. He simply could not tell from where the noise and smoke and debris were coming. Blankenship was momentarily unhinged by the disorientation. His first act on the road to recovery was to retrieve his camera and use the last two frames to record the smoky vista. Then he glanced southward, toward Post 4, which was manned by LCpl Steven Diaz, a burly Chicagoan who was slumped against his bunker, unmoving. This convinced Blankenship that Post 4 had been hit, so he jumped to the top of the concrete fence for a better view. He took his first look at the airport road, which was covered with trash and debris. A dust-covered lump beside the road caught his eye. It later proved to be the upper torso of a dismembered corpse.

"Hey, Diaz, are you okay? You all right?"

Diaz did not move, so Blankenship told Johnson to hold the fort while he ran to Post 4 to help. Johnson was still fiddling with the radio. "Hey, Blank, see if you can see the BLT."

Blankenship passed through the line of trees that normally obscured his view of the BLT building. A multitude of impressions struck at once: Maybe the BLT has been hit; no, it can't be; something big is going on; is this real; what's going on? There was still a great volume of smoke, but Bill Blankenship could clearly see the BIA control tower—a structure he had never before seen from Post 3 because it was on the far side of the BLT.

Johnson yelled from the bunker, "Blank, can you see the building?" The dust was rapidly clearing. Yes, Bill Blankenship could see the building: it was compressed into the height of a story and a half. Great chunks of concrete were strewn as far as his eyes could see. Twisted pillars of reinforced concrete and floors and ceilings and equipment and dust-shrouded lumps of every size and description lay in piles radiating hundreds of feet from the structure.

"Johnny, there ain't no BLT building."

"What?!" Johnson stepped from the bunker and stared slack-jawed at the scene of devastation.

Blankenship tore his gaze from the building and stared into Johnson's huge, disbelieving eyes. "I'll go down and see if Diaz is all right."

As Blankenship neared Post 4, Lance Corporal Diaz started coming to, shaking his head emphatically from side to side to clear a noise only he could hear. Blankenship knelt beside him, and Diaz looked up with a vacant expression on his round face. He rubbed his knee and moved to get up. He looked at Blankenship once more and seemed to come around. Steve Diaz stared at the building and asked, "What happened?"

Bill Blankenship moved to help Diaz into the bunker, but something he saw overhead stopped him in midmotion. The trees had been stripped of all their leaves and many had been lopped off at crazy angles by flying debris or the great concussion. This was just registering upon Lance Corporal Blankenship when he saw a sleeping-bag-shrouded Marine impaled upon a leaf-stripped branch just over his head.

LCpl Bob Calhoun, one of the two forward air control communicators on the roof, found an instant grasp on his situation. He was fully aware that the roof beneath his body had been bifurcated by a massive detonation, that the two halves and the building itself had undulated in the shock wave, and that pieces of concrete, fortunately not large, were hitting him. Cpl Joe Martucci, who was right beside Calhoun, was in a fog.

The two slid in their sleeping bags from the northeast to the southwest corners of the roof as the building tilted away beneath their recumbent forms. Calhoun felt the resounding jars as one deck after another collapsed in sequence, from bottom to top. Neither even tried to get to his feet, but just lay still, terrified, and rode out the storm of jarring sensations.

When the two sleeping bags shuddered to a halt, Calhoun lay still, asking himself if he was alive. He had his answer when he began moving parts of his body. He knew then that he had survived, but he also became aware that he was buried beneath sandbags and rubble. Calhoun lay still for about thirty seconds while Martucci tried to lift himself from beneath the rubble. Martucci was running on automatic, still unable to grasp the enormity of the situation. Calhoun was sure his corner of the roof had taken a direct hit from incoming artillery.

When Calhoun managed to claw his way out of the rubble, he stood to survey the damage. He was simply stunned to find himself so close to the ground—hardly more than twenty feet. The scene before his eyes was astounding. Mangled bodies lay in the open, on the ground, and in the rubble. Trees had been snapped off like matchsticks. There was rubble and debris everywhere, and columns and fountains of smoke and dust were rising into the otherwise clear sky. He was snapped out of a trance by Corporal Martucci's plaintive voice; he found his friend buried from the waist down, and quickly shifted the sandbags and rubble to free him. It was then that Bob Calhoun lost it, screaming irrationally at Martucci to shut up, though Martucci was certain he was silent. As Calhoun moved sandbags, he told his friend that he would not leave him.

Cpl David Wilcox was suspended in eternity, pistol in hand, when he was slammed to the deck as the door and inner wall of his compartment moved to meet him at light speed. The falling concrete formed a tiny foot-high haven and sealed Wilcox into it, fully conscious and dazed by the noise and the rush of events.

He was pinned by debris on his right side, and a piece of exposed steel rod had forced its way through his right upper arm. His right shoulder was dislocated, his right shoulder blade was chipped and cracked, and his right wrist was snapped. The impact of a pipe that had come to rest across Wilcox's lower back had traumatized his kidneys, shutting them down, and he had suffered several wounds and lacerations of the scalp. Wilcox knew from his emergency medical technician's training that he was not going to die of his wounds, that he was in surprisingly good shape despite the injuries about which he then knew. He was concerned about slipping into a shocky coma.

Wilcox could hear quite well, which is surprising, given his proximity to the blast, which had occurred one level down and right outside his room. He soon established voice contact with an engineer lance corporal who had been occupying a room on the next deck up and directly overhead. The combat engineer came to rest about five feet from Wilcox, on the far side of a huge concrete slab. Another slab was resting on the engineer's chest, pressuring a cage of cracked ribs. The other Marine's plight—he had difficulty breathing—took Wilcox's attention from his own painful injuries. The two spoke about commonplace things to pass the time.

First Lieutenant Chuck Dallachie and WO Paul Innocenzi were asleep in the compartment next to Cpl David Wilcox's, on the eastern side of the first deck. Innocenzi was crushed beneath falling debris and Dallachie awoke in the immediate aftermath of the blast, though he had heard no detonation.

His first sensation was of being enveloped in white smoke—really an incredible volume of fine gray dust that settled on everything and everyone in measurable thicknesses. Dallachie had trouble breathing because of the fine suspension, and when he moved his tongue around in his mouth he thought he had cotton mouth but could not recall drinking, let alone becoming drunk enough to have earned a case of the miseries. He coughed to clear his throat, and only then did he discover that he was wedged in his twisted metal bed, pinned across the chest by a huge slab of steel-reinforced concrete; one arm was pinned beneath his head, and he could not move it.

As Dallachie's amazing predicament began dawning on him, he was twisted still farther as the weight of the building shifted downward in search of a new equilibrium. His feet were forced back over his head, though his chest was still pinned. Another tremor turned him almost head-to-ground, and he was choking on real smoke, for there was a fire smoldering beneath the twisted heaps of rubble. Dallachie had not yet accepted the severity of his plight. His predicament was so bizarre that he could not quite allow himself to admit that he was really awake. He felt that his shirt was wet and knew he was bleeding, but he passed out before a thorough comprehension sank in.

Chaplain Danny Wheeler and his clerk, Cpl John Olson, had gone to sleep after the Condition I alert in their room on the northwest corner of the third deck. Olson was instantly crushed by the falling roof, but Wheeler was saved when the concrete pillars around him formed a lean-to almost at ground level.

Danny Wheeler, thirty-five years old, in the best shape he had been in since his days as an Army mail clerk in Vietnam, awoke confused and disoriented. He felt a cold breath of air on his legs, so he reached down to adjust his sleeping bag, which he could not find. He had an eerie feeling that something was amiss, but the numbness that had settled over his body prevented him from immediately discerning the source of his soul-deep foreboding.

Suddenly, Danny Wheeler gave in to panic. He tried to wake up from the dream, but he knew he was already awake. Then he screamed himself hoarse, pleading for help, though only ghosts then moved in that heap of rubble that had sheltered 350 living souls an instant, an eternity, in the immutable past.

When Wheeler had yelled to his heart's content, he pulled himself together, grasped his very essence, and got down to practical matters. He mentally checked the parts of his body. He could move his left hand, and did so, toward an open space on his left. He could feel his feet, but he could not move them. He felt that his steel cot was in a vertical position, and that he was bent into a very finite space at least a foot less than his standing height, almost into a right-listing sitting position. His right arm was jammed up behind his head and there was a continuous trickle of blood from near his left ear, where a steel bar crossed only millimeters away. His whole right side was slightly numb. His hearing was impaired, but a reflexive move to clean his ears with his free left hand loosened enough dust to restore his auditory senses. He felt no pain. There was a tiny shaft of light to the left, just enough to see with, and thus enough air, though breathing was a chore because of the position of his body and the many things that restrained him.

After taking his inventory, Wheeler concentrated his strength in his shoulders and attempted to lift the concrete pillar that had him pinned. He nearly burst his muscles in the attempt but did not move the obstruction at all. He loosened his muscles and tried to regain his strength. He knew he was trapped and that massive assistance would be required to free him, but Danny Wheeler thought he could fruitfully pass the time and better utilize the tiny space by dismantling his cot. He had nothing but his hands, and the will to survive.

GySgt Ron Jones, the battalion career planner, had decided to stay in the basement rather than climb back to the third deck following the nocturnal Condition I alert. As Jones had often done during the September War, he stretched out in the career-planner storage cubicle in a corner of the basement Enlisted Club, of which he was also the manager. LCpls John Oliver and Timothy Mitchell also bedded down in the cubicle.

Ron Jones awoke when he heard Lance Corporal Oliver call his name. He found himself beneath a pile of debris and rubble. He had been knocked unconscious by the blast and had no idea how long he had been comatose, but he knew that the first sounds he heard were gunfire going over or cooking off within the building. Jones was certain the building had been overrun by a ground attack. He responded to Lance Corporal Oliver's call and was rewarded by Oliver's immediate presence. The two moved debris from Jones's back and legs and then stood up in the absolute darkness to try to find a way to safety. Jones had a severe head injury, a shoulder injury, a hole in the bottom of his right foot, and multiple lacerations and contusions where he had been struck by falling concrete. He was dazed and disoriented.

Jones and Oliver found a thin shaft of sunlight and tried to squeeze through to the bomb crater, but they were stopped by the exposed steel bars that laced the shattered concrete blocks.

Lance Corporal Mitchell was separated from the career planners by the debris, so he burrowed out on his own.

Several feet away from Jones and Oliver, LCpl Jim Silvia, who had gone to sleep beside the Enlisted Club bar he had tended on Saturday night, was crushed to death by the falling concrete.

25

The deafening roar, the waves of heat and concussion, the destruction of sandbag and plywood walls, and the levitation of equipment and furniture of every description passed across Beirut International Airport (BIA) like a sudden summer thunderstorm, rousting everyone, everywhere, from sleep or solitude, forcing each to question the motive of the onslaught against his senses and sensibilities.

No one outside the Battalion Landing Team (BLT) building itself even began to suspect the enormity of the disaster. The first priority—for everyone—was to sort out the strong sensory jolts and, for nearly everyone, to seek some sort of protection from dangers real and anticipated. There was also the organizational problem of finding out what had occurred and reacting to it.

Capt Mike Hagemeyer, Marine Medium Helicopter Squadron (HMM) 162's embarkation officer, was occupying a tent beside the MAU Service and Support Group (MSSG) headquarters. He had been ashore since midweek, closing down Rock Base, the vulnerable helicopter maintenance area ashore. Hagemeyer had finished work at the base the afternoon before and had stayed ashore in anticipation of sorting the squadron's gear on Sunday and, perhaps, Monday. Hagemeyer's tentmates included five enlisted squadron supply specialists and Capt Mike McAuley, who was to be relieved Sunday morning from the rotating duty as operations duty officer, the squadron dispatcher ashore.

The detonation sounded to half-awake Mike Hagemeyer like the sort of storm thunder he had heard throughout his life in Texas, "a flat crack with a sizzle to it." He had no idea what it was, but he did not want to open his eyes; he was sure that he was not going to like what he would see if he did. He was jolted when Mike McAuley grabbed him and yelled, "Hag! Hag! Are you all right? Can you move?"

They ran from the tent into the cloud of red dust that hung heavy, unmoving, in the air. Like everyone else, Hagemeyer was certain that the adjacent MSSG headquarters building had taken a direct hit, probably by a rocket. A quick head count revealed that all the squadron personnel were present and intact. A gunnery sergeant ran through the area yelling, "Man your posts! Man your posts!" All the air-wingers, who had no role in defending the compound, headed for the MSSG basement.

CWO-4 George Allen, the MSSG-24 Maintenance Platoon commander, was awakened by what he thought were two gunshots fired from within the maintenance compound. He was instantly awake and fully alert when the bomb was detonated less than 100 meters away, on the far side of a small building. The blast sounded just like what Gunner Allen thought a nuclear explosion might sound like. His tent was blown down, and the double-width sandbag walls were sucked into the vacuum created by the passing rush of air. Large chunks of masonry fell within the compound, injuring several Marines, including Allen,

317

who ignored the bruise on his right forearm. He reached out to turn on a siren, but found that it had been destroyed. So he hollered in the direction of the sergeants' tent and ordered the NCOs to get themselves and all the troops down to the bunkers.

SSgt Mike Isajewicz, the MSSG-24 ground radio maintenance chief, was blown out of his rack, which was in the tent next to Gunner Allen's. He sat up and rolled forward just as a heap of boxes he was using for drawers collapsed onto his pillow. An instant later, two chunks of concrete fell upon the pile of boxes. The reverberations of the blast and the concussion waves would not quit, and chunks of concrete and gear from the BLT fell and fell and fell without letup. Believing that he had been near-missed by a mortar round, which usually arrived in trios, Isajewicz shouted a warning to Gunner Allen, "Careful! That was only one!" Allen yelled back that it was "definitely not a mortar round."

Isajewicz slowly pulled himself together, gathering essential bits of clothing and collecting his radio. He noted that both the main poles of his tent had been snapped by the blast. Glass from light bulbs was everywhere.

Gunner Allen shouted into the collapsed tent, "Ski, you all right in there?"

"I don't know, Gunner. Has all that shit stopped falling?"

Allen said it was safe to come out, so Isajewicz crawled out of the tent dragging his gear behind him. The entire compound was a shambles. Most of the troops were in the bunkers; only George Allen, Mike Isajewicz, and a few other NCOs were in the open, assessing the damage, trying to figure out what had happened. The BLT could not be seen through the clouds of dust.

Gunner Allen left to organize his platoon's heavy equipment, and Isajewicz headed for his combat observation post. When he got there, he radioed MSSG headquarters and exchanged questions with the people on duty there. None of them knew anything, so Isajewicz offered to call back as soon as the smoke cleared and he could see what had occurred. Meantime, he said, he was waiting for personnel counts from the MSSG platoons. The MSSG radioman asked for news as soon as possible because he had lost comm with the BLT.

Just as the MSSG Engineer Platoon reported that all hands were safe, the smoke cleared enough for Isajewicz to determine that there was no BLT. He called the command post: "The BLT is gone."

Capt William Boden, the MSSG operations officer, came up on the MSSG command net and said, "I understand the BLT was hit."

"Yes, sir," Isajewicz replied. "The BLT is hit. It's gone."

"What's the damage to the building?"

"Sir, it's gone. It's just not there anymore."

"The BLT was hit?"

"Yes, sir. The BLT was hit."

"Well, exactly where on the building is there damage?"

"Captain, listen to me. The whole damn building is gone. It's leveled right down to the ground."

There was a pause, then Boden came on again. "You're telling me the building is leveled all the way to the ground?"

"Yes, sir. It's down to the ground."

"The whole building? It's down?"

"Captain, listen to me. The whole damn building—all four floors—is on the ground. There is nothing on that building left sitting there. I can barely see the rubble. It's just a big pile of gravel. That's it."

"Okay, that's what I'm going to report." But Boden did not sound as though he really believed Isajewicz.

Col Tim Geraghty had been up and about since about 0530. He checked in at the MAU's combat operations center (COC), where nothing much was going on, then headed back to the room he shared with his exec, LtCol Harry Slacum. The MAU commander had just stretched out on his rack "when the windows and sandbags on the window ledge were blown into the room" and the doors opposite were blown into the hallway. Slacum was cut by some of the flying glass—which, fortunately, had been taped to reduce shattering—and Geraghty was shaken but unhurt.

The colonel grabbed his helmet and flak jacket and ran downstairs, straight to the COC, which was directly beneath his room. He was certain that it had taken a direct hit. Dust and loose items were everywhere, as was the powerful smell of explosives. Finding nothing seriously amiss in the COC, Geraghty ran outside to inspect the building, certain he would find that it had been hit. He found nothing and was totally puzzled, so he headed toward where the dust was thickest.

The next building he came upon, an administration building used to billet some United Nations troops, was surely the target. But Geraghty found that it was intact. The colonel was joined by his S-4, Maj Bob Melton, and both ran to the next structure, a Lebanese Armed Forces (LAF) liaison office. There they found the broken body of an LAF liaison officer, but the amount of damage to the building did not suggest a direct hit. The two puzzled officers turned toward the dissipating dust cloud. Melton gasped, "My God! The BLT building's gone!" They stood in shocked silence for a moment, feeling the impact of realization and emotions, then legged it back to MAU to organize the rescue and to assume command and control of the rifle companies and Charlie Battery.

LCpl Bob Calhoun climbed from the BLT roof through shattered debris, and, though he was barefoot, waded through bodies and parts of bodies in response to voices from within the mound of rubble. There was nothing he or any of the other walking survivors could do with their hands. After blubbering in frustration for a few minutes, Calhoun ran on his bare feet to MAU headquarters. He was utterly hysterical, and no one believed what he had to say. Calhoun emphasized his tale by collaring the MAU sergeant major and threatening to kill him if he did not drop everything and rush to the BLT. The older Marine shook free, so Calhoun grabbed another man and threatened him if he did not help. Things might have gone badly for Bob Calhoun, but a MAU communicator rushed in and confirmed the tale.

Maj Doug Redlich, commanding MSSG-24, was totally stunned by the sound and reverberating violence of the bomb detonation. The concussion instantaneously rearranged the innards of the MSSG building, about 250 meters from the BLT, by hurling sandbags and loose materials, including desks, and then sucking them back in the vacuum that rode in its wake. Several people in the MSSG headquarters were hurt, including HMC John Vaughn, who was beaned by the cinderblock he had placed above his rack to hold down his mosquito netting.

Major Redlich was one of the first men to the entryway of the MSSG building, where he was joined by Lt Gil Bigelow, the strapping senior MAU dentist, a twice-decorated former Air Force commando. SSgt Dennis Allston, of explosive ordnance disposal, emerged from a hole in the wall where the back pressure had sucked away the front of his room. Allston was barefoot, boondockers in hand, a "what-is-it-this-time" scowl of confusion on his face.

As the three tried to discern what had been hit, and how badly, Redlich heard someone yell something about the BLT. He saw the rising dust column and decided to head for it.

First Lieutenant Leo Lachat, the MSSG-24 landing support officer, had seen the detonation from Green Beach, had heard the roar, and had felt the concussion. He was kilometers away from the BLT, but he plainly saw "huge chunks of concrete hurtle from the black-and-gray mushroom cloud." He knew that a building or a fuel-storage facility had been hit, but it took a call to Capt William Boden, the MSSG-24 operations officer, to receive "tentative" word that the BLT had been hit.

After checking on his troops, Lieutenant Lachat eyeballed the airport compound. He saw trees that had previously been obscured, and deduced that at least the top of the BLT building had been razed. Captain Boden came up on the MSSG tac net and confirmed that the BLT had been leveled. Lachat ordered all the equipment he had on the beach to be marshaled and dispatched to the BLT, informed the Seabee and Beachmaster commanders of the bombing, passed control of Green Beach to the Beachmaster officer, hopped in his jeep, and headed for the BLT to find members of his platoon who were at the command compound and to help if he could.

LCpl Jesse Frazier, a Headquarters and Service Company communicator on loan to the 81mm Mortar Platoon, was on radio watch when he heard an explosion that seemed to be coming from behind the mortar pits. He turned to look but saw nothing, and so informed the platoon commander. Seeing nothing either, the lieutenant ordered Frazier to contact Battalion and ask them to try to locate the impact area from one of their upper-story windows. Frazier then saw the mushroom cloud but had no idea what it meant. He placed his call but discovered that the land line was out. He switched to his radio, but all he could hear was negative-modulation bursts, which indicated that the frequency was manned but that someone was merely keying his handset rather than speaking. Frazier peered from his bunker again. He should have been able to see the top two stories of the BLT, but they were not there. A quick check of the tac net brought forth numerous voices discussing the disappearance of the BLT building. Frazier passed The Word, but only one staff NCO took the trouble to check with his binos. He confirmed Frazier's news just as word arrived over the command net that the BLT building was down.

The news sent waves of deep foreboding through the Mortar

Platoon, for the unit had contributed a large contingent to guard the building. The Marine who was most shaken by the news was LCpl Timothy Whitfield, who had wheedled out of weekend guard duty; another Marine had been sent in his place.

GySgt Steve Mellinger, Charlie Company's Weapons Platoon sergeant, had been on COC watch at the hilltop company command/observation post and was just coming off the hill when he heard the blast. He instantly dove into the nearest bunker and landed right on top of 1stLt Jerry Walsh, the company exec. They spent several frantic seconds getting untangled and trading apologies, exclamations, and theories. Nothing else happened—an odd variation for an artillery barrage, which always struck in loose salvos. Walsh and Mellinger looked outside and saw the smoke billowing upward. Mellinger was certain it was a car bomb and that the target was the main airport terminal building, which was about midway between his position and the BLT. That was a pretty good guess, given the distortion of distance and the type of violence Mellinger had been experiencing for many weeks.

Next, the company command radioman told Gunny Mellinger that he had lost comm with Battalion. That was a common enough occurrence. Then 1st Platoon called in with news that they could not see the BLT. Mellinger told the platoon radioman that the smoke from the car bomb was probably obstructing the usual view of the top two stories.

Then things started falling into place. Lieutenant Walsh asked Mellinger if he thought the blast had occurred at or near the BLT. Mellinger said he wasn't sure, but that he ought to call the company commander, Capt Chris Cowdrey.

Cowdrey was awake. He had heard the blast and was wondering what it was, but he stayed in his bunker because that was the place to be when things were exploding outside. Gunny Mellinger's call was something of a relief. Cowdrey told him to keep trying to raise Battalion by radio, then left his bunker to sweep the BIA with his binos. He could see only dust. A quick sweep of the company positions put his mind at rest over the possibility that the company was under ground attack.

Gunny Mellinger called 1st Platoon, which repeated that it could not see the top of the BLT, though much of the smoke had cleared. The gunny then grabbed the 81mm forward observer's binos, the most powerful optical device on the hill, and swept the BIA compound. He saw familiar buildings and mentally checked them off relative to the BLT. He fixed the spot where the BLT should have been and reluctantly concluded that the building was down. Lieutenant Walsh confirmed the nonsighting, and the two went to Captain Cowdrey's hooch.

Cowdrey still refused to believe his or Mellinger's eyes, so the gunny suggested that they make a run to the BLT to see about the severed comm link.

The point was still being debated when the MAU COC came up on the net to say, definitely, that the BLT building had been taken out and that MAU had assumed tactical control of BLT 1/8.

Chris Cowdrey was the senior rifle-company commander. If the BLT was indeed down, then command of BLT 1/8 might have devolved onto his shoulders.

Gunny Mellinger left the Charlie Company CP by jeep at about 0630, eight minutes after the detonation. Captain Cowdrey ordered all nonessential personnel from the company command element and Weapons Platoon, and one corpsman from the company CP and each of the rifle platoons, to prepare to head for the BLT. He and his company gunny boarded a jeep and the troops and corpsmen piled into a truck. Lieutenant Walsh stayed behind to organize the company to resist a ground attack.

Capt Monte Hoover had been on the radio to the battalion COC only moments before the blast, trying to find out when Bravo Company's rations would be ready to pick up. He was returning to his tent when he saw, then heard, then felt, the detonation.

Two thoughts went through Hoover's mind: the BIA had been hit by a tactical nuke, and he had to capture the moment for posterity. He immediately yelled to GySgt Danny Evans to bring his camera. As Evans snapped a frame, a second, more distant, detonation sounded: the Iranians who had hit the American BLT also hit the French Multinational Force headquarters with a somewhat smaller bomb. Gunny Evans snapped a frame that would show both mushroom clouds.

Hoover had no idea what had been hit. He tried to raise the BLT on the radio, but the link had been severed. So had the land line. Still unable to comprehend what had occurred, Hoover assumed that the proximity of the blast to the BLT had knocked the comm links out. The company radio jeep was cranked up and Hoover flicked over to the airport control tower frequency. The U.S. Navy air traffic controllers manning the tower filled the ether with yells of "Get us out of here! The BLT's gone." A call to Charlie Battery provided unwanted confirmation.

Captain Hoover turned to Gunny Evans. "Go on down there and give me a call when you find out what's going on." Evans grabbed a Marine to ride shotgun and departed. Meantime, Bravo Company would stand to full alert to "repel boarders," or react to whatever else the bombers had in store for the battalion.

Capt Bob Funk, commanding Charlie Battery, was awakened when his cot was shifted by the concussion from one side of his bunker to the other. He naturally ran outside to the battery exec's pit, from which he saw the column of smoke and dust. His first assumption was that the Syrian army had fired some very heavy artillery, or even a FROG ground-to-ground missile. It was clear from Charlie Battery's hill that the BLT building had been the target. Attempts to reach the BLT by radio were fruitless, but Funk could hear other components of the rifle battalion talking frantically among themselves. No one on the tac net seemed to know what had happened. Battery officers and staff NCOs who joined Funk speculated among themselves for a few moments, then 1stSgt Kenneth Santo announced, "The whole fuckin' building is gone." Bob Funk was emotionally poleaxed by the realization that Santo was right. He ordered his exec, 1stLt Dave Kelley, to "drive down and see what happened."

The last MAU unit to receive firm news about the bombing was HMM-162, which was based between five and ten miles offshore, aboard helicopter carrier *Iwo Jima*.

The squadron had always been prepared to do its part in a medical emergency, and it swung into action soon after receiving news that there was trouble ashore. The two Cobra gunship helos were prepped for launch, and the crews of two ready CH-46 helos—one configured to carry up to fifteen litters—were ordered to flight quarters.

PART VIII

Rescue

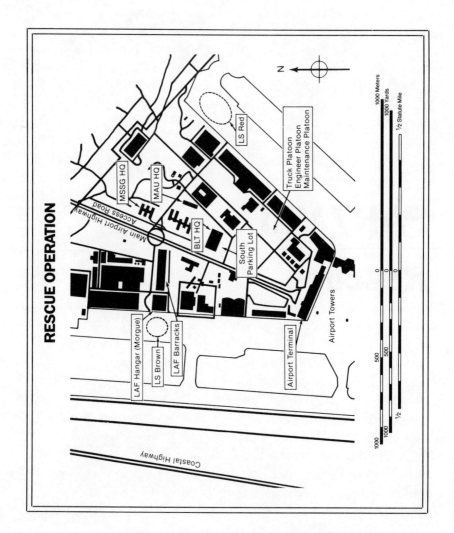

RESCUE OPERATION

LAF Hangar (Morgue)

LS Brown

LAF Barracks

MSSG HQ

MAU HQ

BLT HQ

Main Airport Highway

Access Road

South Parking Lot

LS Red

Truck Platoon
Engineer Platoon
Maintenance Platoon

Airport Terminal

Airport Towers

Coastal Highway

N

1000 Meters
1000 Yards
½ Statute Mile

500
500

0
0
0

1000
1000
½

26

The organized rescue effort was launched at about 0625, only three minutes after the detonation. It took that long—an eternity, really—for the people in authority and their stunned organizations to come to the realization that the Battalion Landing Team (BLT) headquarters was down and that scores of men were certainly injured or killed. It took many more minutes for the enormity of the tragedy to sink in.

Though Col Tim Geraghty had only a vague initial comprehension of the extent to which the BLT headquarters building had been devastated, his instincts told him that 24th Marine Amphibious Unit (MAU) had been badly wounded. It was a tough personal decision, but Geraghty decided to keep his MAU staff intact; it would have to run the surviving elements of BLT 1/8 as well as take up the responsibility for fire support coordination between the battalion and Charlie Battery, the flotilla of surface warships offshore, and the naval air wing working off the fleet carrier stationed over the horizon. The rescue and cleanup would have to be run by MAU Service and Support Group (MSSG) 24 and other people who could be spared from their duties.

The first people to provide aid for the trapped and injured men in the BLT building were survivors of the blast itself. The engineers who were in the hooch beside the east wall collected their wits within a minute or two of the detonation and rushed into the open. LCpl Dan Gaffney pulled a grievously injured Marine from the TOW-section tent, and two of his companions gently led a dazed and staggering Marine to an out-of-the-way corner. Cpl Galen Weber was the first to suggest that the engineers clear a path through the rubble to the nearest road. The dazed engineers began moving rubble.

Moments after Pfc Carl Hancock left Post 2 to learn what had been hit, he came upon a screaming, terrified Marine pinned beneath a heavy chunk of wood outside the Lebanese Armed Forces (LAF) liaison building. Hancock freed the injured man and called over one of the first corpsmen to arrive on the scene to care for him, then he headed toward the dust cloud. A passerby told Hancock the BLT building was down, but he did not believe it until he rounded a corner and saw for himself. He ran to the rubble and started searching for survivors among the loose hands, heads, legs, arms, and torsos that littered the rubble-strewn ground.

At the entryway to the MSSG headquarters building, Maj Doug Redlich, Dr. Gil Bigelow, and SSgt Dennis Allston, who had not yet finished lacing his boots, jumped into the nearest jeep and drove directly to the BLT building, which was the obvious focus of the radiating lines of dust and debris that covered the area. First Sergeant Kenneth Bell and GySgt Tim Sansbury were in a second jeep, right behind them.

On the way, they encountered several walking wounded, some escorted, some alone. Dr. Bigelow quickly checked each one and directed them to the MSSG headquarters for treatment. They found the first bodies and parts of bodies fifty or sixty meters from the shattered building.

Redlich and his companions and driver were the first "outsiders" on the scene. Dr. Bigelow took one look at the twisted heaps of outlying rubble, the ghastly dust-covered lumps of human flesh, the dazed individual survivors who had somehow freed themselves from the vortex of destruction, and legged it back in the direction of the MSSG building to find and organize help. Major Redlich sent Staff Sergeant Allston to the MSSG Engineer and Truck Platoon areas to rustle up some earth-moving equipment, trucks, and, most important, people to help with the digging and casualty evacuation. Allston was also to direct all the MSSG platoon commanders to meet with Major Redlich in front of the BLT.

When Bigelow and Allston left him alone, Major Redlich walked directly to the enormous rubble heap that had been the four-story BLT headquarters. He came upon Sgt Steve Russell, who was belly down on the ground. Redlich knelt beside Russell, who told him what he had seen in the moments before the blast. The severely shaken sergeant asked for help getting to his elbows so he could take a look at the building. Redlich complied and then called over a pair of MSSG corpsmen who had responded to the emergency on their own. As the major left, the corpsmen splinted Russell's shattered left leg from knee to ankle and placed a thick bandage about his head and another about his left hand. Two Marines arrived with a cot, upon which Russell was placed and carried to an impromptu casualty-collection point at Post 4.

Dr. Bigelow ran the 400 meters to the MSSG headquarters building in a thoroughly dazed state. When his colleague, Lt Jim Ware, saw him, the normally robust senior dentist looked frail, and his skin had the grayish hue of a man in shock. Ware asked, "What happened, Gil?" Bigelow gasped his alert: "Jim, the BLT has been hit. The aid station is gone. There's a lot of wounded people. Prepare for mass casualties."

Dr. Ware and the MSSG corpsmen were manning two aid stations on the theory that at least one would survive a direct hit upon the building. They assumed that they would be seeing upward of a dozen patients, which is about as "mass" as the Marine Corps had seen at one time, in one incident, in many years.

As soon as he had issued his alert, Dr. Bigelow grabbed his emergency medical kit, counted off four corpsmen, and charged back in the direction of the BLT to set up an on-site triage station.

LCpl Tony McVeigh, of the MSSG-24 Medical Platoon, collected several military policemen and other strays and moved vehicles from right in front of the MSSG headquarters building so that incoming trucks and jeeps could be off-loaded at the doorway. First Lieutenant Dave Gillespie, the MSSG-24 Truck Platoon commander, counted off drivers and assistant drivers for four trucks and ordered them to head to the BLT.

Within moments of Dr. Bigelow's departure from the MSSG building, Dr. Ware was confronted by his first patient, Cpl Burnham Matthews, who had been blown out of his room on the second deck of the BLT. Ware knew Matthews, but he had a hard time recognizing him, so thick was the layer of dust that coated him and the several other walking wounded who followed him into the MSSG building; there was no way to tell a black Marine from a white Marine; everyone was gray. Blood was absorbed by the cornstarchlike powder, which made wounds hard to locate. The first serious casualty was Sgt Pablo Arroyo, a reconnaissance NCO whose cheek and jaw had been torn open and shattered by flying debris. Fortunately, repairing facial injuries was Jim Ware's specialty, so he went right to work in the hope of reconstructing Arroyo's mouth and facial features. Other early arrivals were more stunned than severely injured, and the corpsmen inspected their wounds and provided first aid.

Another early arrival was LCpl Joe Martucci, who had been on the BLT roof. He had frantically tried to dig out buried men for awhile, but he had an awful headache from his ruptured eardrums, and his skin had been badly scraped, so he had allowed himself to be transported to the MSSG aid station.

Second Lieutenant Craig Hales, the MSSG-24 supply officer, was seated in the front of his bunker with 2dLt Mike Murphy, the MSSG-24 communicator, when he saw several of the walking wounded pass by. Hales was shocked to see injured men coming from the direction of the BLT because he just knew beyond a doubt that his own building had just taken a direct hit. Lieutenant Murphy thought the expressions on the faces of the walking wounded were strange, that perhaps they had seen something no man had ever seen before. Lieutenant Hales called out, "Hey! What's going on?" One of the wounded Marines called back that the BLT was down, but Hales could not believe that. He and Murphy left the bunker to guide the casualties into the MSSG headquarters building, but he had no conviction that this was not a dream. The scene inside the building shocked him into decisive action. He headed for his supply block and grabbed all the narcotics he had under his control, then distributed them among the corpsmen. Lieutenant Murphy was drawn into the rush to collect litters. When Capt Keith Arthur, the MSSG exec, ordered the litters to the BLT, Murphy went along.

SSgt Ronnie Walker, the MSSG-24 engineer NCO in charge, had just accounted for all his people when he saw one of the victims walking up the road from the BLT. The man was screaming, "Everyone's gone! Everyone's gone!" Walker saw that a large fold of skin over one of the Marine's eyes had been slit open and was hanging by a thread. He yelled for a corpsman and guided the injured man into the MSSG headquarters building. Like Lieutenant Hales, Walker simply reacted to the situation; he had no idea what was really going on. By the time he dropped the wounded Marine off at the aid station, the engineers had been ordered to get their equipment down to the BLT. Walker led the stampede.

Sgt Bob Muchler, of the MSSG-24 Maintenance Platoon, headed for the BLT building from the maintenance compound as soon as the dust cleared enough for him to see that the building was down. He had close friends in the battalion motor pool and wanted to see to their safety. He was just getting on his way when he crossed paths with a raving motor mechanic who was yelling that the BLT was down. The Marine's head, shoulders, and chest were drenched in blood, so Muchler and several others surrounded him and guided him to the Maintenance Platoon sick bay tent. They learned that the victim had been involved in the October 19 car bombing, and they had to shout directly into his ears in order to calm him down. SSgt Mike Isajewicz came away from the encounter with a deeper sense of gloom and doom than he had ever suffered.

Muchler headed for the BLT on foot while Isajewicz helped CWO-4 George Allen muster the troops and gear and get them on their way. The gunner was marvelous, coolly ordering specific details to collect fire extinguishers and jacks from vehicles in the area, telling a sergeant and his squad to load portable power units into the trucks and wreckers that would be going, sending individual maintenance personnel to collect the dozens of tools he instinctively understood would be needed at the blast site. Allen and the first elements of Maintenance Platoon were rolling by 0630.

While the first groups of rescuers headed for the BLT, Captain Arthur grabbed officers and NCOs as they emerged from the bunkers and ordered them to get help and begin setting up for the expected heavy influx of casualties. Arthur detailed several Marines to beef up the building's security against attack, then sent whomever he felt he could spare to help at the BLT. He immediately lost his sense of time.

The dozen-odd Marine Medium Helicopter Squadron (HMM) 162 personnel ashore had been in the MSSG basement shelter for about five minutes when an NCO announced that a car bomb had been detonated next to the BLT and that casualties would soon be arriving. The voice ordered all the duty drivers out of the shelter, and the squadron duty personnel and members of the Helicopter Support Team (HST) were ordered to Landing Site (LS) Brown to support medevacs. Capt Mike Hagemeyer and the squadron supply team he had ashore to close Rock Base were asked to help prepare the MSSG for "mass casualties." Everyone piled up the stairs. Hagemeyer and his people grabbed cots from the squadron tents and set them up in passageways on the first deck of the MSSG headquarters building.

HM3 Tom Young, an MSSG corpsman, was called out of his bunker right after Dr. Bigelow's departure. He went to work with HMC B.C. Miller, setting up treatment areas in the passageway, stocking each with battle dressings and medicines, plasma and intravenous solutions. No sooner done than Chief Miller's team began working on several early arrivals.

Conditions right outside the MSSG headquarters building immediately threatened to swamp the lifesaving effort. There was only a one-lane road leading through the narrow MSSG headquarters compound gate, and it seemed like everyone in Beirut was trying to enter or exit the compound. First Lieutenant Jim Martino, the MSSG supply operations officer, gravitated to the gate and was put in charge of traffic control by Captain Arthur. Martino went to work organizing the flow of vehicles. Everyone wanted to get in and out first. It was a total mess.

Maj Doug Redlich, 1stSgt Kenneth Bell, and GySgt Tim Sansbury were the first outsiders to remain on the scene, but they were joined almost immediately by alarmed Marines from all over the MAU compound as they made their way to the front of the building.

Second Lieutenant Mike Murphy, the MSSG communicator, broke through the treeline separating the BLT from the MSSG headquarters with the first litter bearers. The sight of the rubble rocked him back on his heels. He noted that "most of the people at the site who were on their feet were just standing around looking" at the smoldering ruin. Murphy could hear screaming from within the heap of concrete and steel, but no one could figure out how to get into the building to help the trapped men. It took that long for Murphy to realize that the rescuers would have to dig the survivors out.

Sgt Bob Muchler arrived at the southern parking lot with the first rush of rescuers and went into a state of shock. SSgt Ronnie Walker, the senior MSSG engineer on the scene, also froze when he first saw the rubble heap. MSgt George Jenkins, the MSSG maintenance chief, was not so much frozen by shock as by frustration. He arrived on foot from the maintenance compound with a shovel in his hand, but instantly realized that it was virtually useless.

Maj Doug Redlich found these and a slowly growing herd of other Marines when he rounded the corner of the rubble heap with First Sergeant Bell and Gunny Sansbury. He ordered the group to break down into twos and threes and begin looking for live bodies, to "quit gawking" at the destruction.

Sergeant Muchler was unable to move until someone jarred him from behind. He went to work rooting around in the rubble for living victims. Staff Sergeant Walker quickly detailed pairs of his men to circle the building and pull whomever they could from the rubble. Master Sergeant Jenkins dropped his shovel and waded into the debris to help collect the living.

Elements of the MSSG-24 Truck Platoon and Engineer Platoon were the first organized units on the scene. The first piece of heavy equipment to reach the scene was a 10,000-pound forklift driven by Pfc John Hlywiak, an MSSG engineer. As Hlywiak went to work clearing a path for incoming trucks and other rolling stock, Major Redlich grabbed a few Marines and told them to start moving bodies and body parts from the work area. These Marines were unable to even begin the grisly task until Redlich and First Sergeant Bell grabbed a stretcher and placed an assortment of arms and legs on it. This broke the spell, and the first group went frantically to work.

Col Tim Geraghty left the MAU combat operations center (COC) as soon as he felt it was in control of airport security and established a remote command post, incorporating only himself and the driver of his command radio jeep, at a spot from which he could see most of what was going on and past which most help from the outside had to flow. From this vantage point, the MAU commander worked to influence events without actually becoming mired in them. Someone needed to maintain a cool perspective, and that someone, for the moment, had to be Tim Geraghty—despite his personal impulse to dig into the rubble to save lives.

For his part, though he had no idea yet what had been detonated in the BLT, Geraghty was incredulous that so powerful an explosive device had been put together at all. He had seen more than enough death and destruction in his career, but he had never seen anything with the destructive power that had been unleashed upon the BLT. He grieved silently for the dead and for their families.

Geraghty grabbed every officer and NCO he could find as the rescue effort brought more and more Marines and corpsmen from the outside. These men were brought back to a calm demeanor by the colonel, then given specific tasks, which Geraghty ticked off from a growing list he maintained in his head.

Major Redlich was directing the forklift when he was approached by Colonel Geraghty, who wanted a rundown on the MSSG commander's initial assessment and plan. The two exchanged impressions on the enormity of the devastation, then Redlich rattled off details of what he was trying to accomplish. Geraghty nodded his assent and returned to his CP.

As Geraghty left, the MSSG Maintenance Platoon arrived, led by CWO-4 George Allen. SSgt Mike Isajewicz was nearly floored by the destruction, but he quickly recovered and joined the rush to collect bodies and parts of bodies that littered the area. Gunner Allen organized a carrying party and pulled the plywood walls from what had been the battalion officers' mess tent for use as stretchers to carry the bodies to the parking lot.

The first MSSG trucks to arrive on the scene were immediately filled with walking wounded and the first of the victims to be carried from the rubble by dazed fellow survivors.

LCpl Ken Spencer arrived with the first group of trucks. He helped load the walking wounded, then began poking through the rubble in search of additional casualties. The first man he found was pinned beneath a concrete slab. All available hands were called over, and they tried several times to lift the slab in unison before strength and willpower overcame gravity and inertia. The Marine was pulled from beneath the concrete, treated, and sent to the MSSG aid station on the next truck out.

Sgt Dean Randgaard, a Truck Platoon squad leader, went straight to the combat-engineer hooch to find friends with whom he had berthed on the float to Beirut and with whom he had palled around in succeeding months. He saw that the hooch was crushed, but was relieved that all his friends had escaped with only cuts and bruises and one broken arm.

Major Redlich soon found that there were almost too many vehicles converging on the blast site. He called aside 1stLt Dave Gillespie, his Truck Platoon commander, and directed him to reroute vehicles to the rear of the building, where there was an access road directly from the MSSG headquarters and inside the fence separating the main airport highway from the BLT compound. A casualty collection and triage site could thus be established at the rear of the building, at the terminus of the access road. After Redlich sent Lieutenant Gillespie on his way, he had First Sergeant Bell and Gunny Sansbury move among the casualty-collection teams to tell all hands where the injured were to be taken.

While the six stunned and shaky combat engineers cranked up

a dump truck and worked to clear a path outward from the rubble to the access road, Major Redlich put his MSSG engineers to work clearing huge chunks of concrete along the shortest line from the roadway to the rubble. One of the combat engineers, LCpl Dan Gaffney, backed his dump truck as close as he could to the rubble and soon hauled away a truckload of victims. However, until at least one serviceable path could be cleared, the many immobile victims of the holocaust could not be effectively moved. MSSG-24's only bulldozer was guided toward the building to help in a rescue, but was stopped before it mangled dust-camouflaged men awaiting help.

Staff Sergeant Isajewicz searched for wounded and trapped survivors, but he found only dead men. Each time he came upon a body, he detailed a pair of Marines to carry it to one of several collection points that had come into being. He counseled everyone who looked queasy: "Don't think about what you're doing; just do it" or "Don't stand around thinking; get to work." The emotional impact of the carnage was palpable.

The moans from within the rubble heap gave Isajewicz the impression that "the ground itself was crying."

The rescue effort was mounting in speed and power by 0635.

GySgt Ron Jones and LCpl John Oliver emerged from the basement Career Planning storage compartment into the bomb crater within fifteen minutes of the blast. Their first look around provided their first realization that the whole BLT was down. People nearby were screaming and yelling for help. Four people on the far side of the crater were at work digging someone out. The way out of the crater was barred by huge concrete slabs, too smooth and too steep for the dazed gunny. Lance Corporal Oliver guided Jones to a place where he could safely sit and then went to find help. He returned minutes later and led Jones up along a broken but negotiable path, at the top of which strong waiting hands guided him to a jeep. He was driven to the MSSG and treated in the open.

When Dr. Gil Bigelow returned to the BLT, he found only a few dozen Marines and a sprinkling of corpsmen at work, pulling dead and wounded Marines from the periphery of the rubble heap. He was immediately joined in an open area to the north of the building by First Sergeant Bell and Gunny Sansbury. The three of them were casting about near the end of the access road to the MSSG headquarters building in search of a clear spot to set up a triage station when they found a live Marine trapped between a wrecked jeep and a wall. Bigelow and Sansbury pulled him out, looked him over, and sent him on his way.

One of the first corpsmen to head for the BLT in Dr. Bigelow's wake was HM3 Steve Brown, an operating-room technician with three years Navy service and four years in the Army. Steve Brown had not had time to shrug into a cammie blouse but had thrown a flak jacket over his T-shirt, grabbed his Unit-1 aid kit, clapped on his helmet, and ran like the wind, which surprised him because he was still hung over from his twenty-eighth birthday party on Friday night. The impressions during his approach to the BLT were slow in coming, but typical at that early juncture. He noted that the trees surrounding the building were stripped, and he saw that there was a great deal of dust and debris in the air. In fact, he was just thinking that there might be "a lot" of casualties when he rounded the corner of the hedge and stopped in his tracks, totally awed by the scene of destruction. The screaming of trapped victims struck his soul.

As Dr. Bigelow sought to organize his corpsmen as they arrived, First Sergeant Bell and Gunny Sansbury organized the flow of men through the triage station, which by then had become a sort of forward command post. A temporary morgue was set up a few feet from the treatment area, and the casualties were sorted by the extent of their injuries, with the most severe being sent to the MSSG earliest. All of the walking wounded who were not still helping at and around the blast site had long since made their way to the aid station.

Gil Bigelow had been well and expensively trained by the Navy to evaluate and treat casualties of all types and to manage the continuing treatment by corpsmen. It was not his job, nor Dr. Jim Ware's, to perform intricate surgery. The MSSG aid station, and its impromptu satellites, were designed and equipped to provide emergency medical treatment, to stabilize patients, and to organize medical evacuations to the primary-care center, *Iwo Jima*, where a fully staffed, well-equipped medical-surgical team had been whiling away the months in sheer boredom.

HM3 Steve Brown and a Marine who joined him first chose an arm from among the limbs and torsos that projected from the rubble at their feet. Brown briefly prayed it was attached to something, then heaved. A live Marine emerged from the dusty gray background. The man's left thigh had been stripped from the bone, his right leg was hanging by a thread of sinew, his left bicep was torn away at the elbow, and Brown suspected the man had suffered some spinal damage. The victim was screaming in agony. Dr. Bigelow ran up and took control of the situation, issuing orders, caring for the man. As Bigelow worked over the first victim, Steve Brown saw that another Marine was impaled back to front—eviscerated—on the muffler guard of one of four twisted jeeps in the nearby motor pool. Brown moved down the line, reaching for an arm to search for a pulse, directing Marines to a body here or a body there that might retain a spark of life. He soon found himself working with LCdr Arnie Resnicoff, the 6th Fleet Jewish chaplain, who had come to the Beirut International Airport (BIA) to conduct a memorial service for Allen Soifert. The rabbi, who wore a camouflaged skullcap given to him by his Marine congregation before the memorial service, administered last rites to each victim in a singsong litany.

The first live Marine HM3 Steve Brown saw emerge from the building was a close friend, Cpl Dan Turner, of Headquarters and Service Company. Turner had been in the basement galley when the bomb detonated and had suffered only a leg injury. He limped past Brown, who was too busy and too stricken to follow through on his impulse to embrace his friend.

Brown ran out of bandages within five minutes, and he had no morphine to quell the pain of the men he found alive. One of those agonized men groped along Brown's thigh in the hope of finding a loaded .45 with which to stop the searing pain.

MSgt George Jenkins helped pull the living from the rubble for a short time before he headed across the airport highway on foot. He knew where the Lebanese Ministry of Transportation was storing a fifteen-ton P&H Omega crane.

Sgt Kim McKinney had been among the first to leave the MSSG maintenance compound, but his wrecker had been diverted out onto the main airport highway and he had become ensnared in traffic and debris—including the upper torso of a victim that had been blown out onto the four-lane highway. McKinney finally arrived at the BLT just as Top Jenkins rolled in with the fifteen-ton crane. He jumped to the ground and organized a detail to move corpses from the path of the crane and several civilian bulldozers that had also just arrived.

GySgt Danny Evans, who had been dispatched from Bravo Company within minutes of the blast, returned to the company CP with tears in his eyes, explaining to a disbelieving Capt Monte Hoover that the BLT building had been leveled and that there seemed to be no survivors. Hoover took a more positive view, detailing the few riflemen and corpsmen he could spare from his thinned-out ranks (he had about eighty of his Marines at the embassy) for work at the blast site.

First Lieutenant Dave Kelley, Charlie Battery's exec, was down to the BLT and back to the battery within five minutes of being sent, within fifteen minutes of the blast. He reported his findings—"There are arms and legs everywhere"—to Capt Bob Funk, who ordered 1stLt Mark Singleton to hit the road with his reaction force, thirty cannoneers mounted in three amtracs. Singleton had been on duty all night, but the call to arms galvanized his reserves; he was set for a fight. Captain Funk also ordered 1stLt Nick Nanna to MAU headquarters to act as artillery liaison officer until the fate of 1stLt Chuck Schnorf, the battery's representative at Battalion, could be ascertained. (Schnorf, who had spent Saturday evening at the battery, and who had turned down Mark Singleton's offer of a place to stay, died in his bed.)

The first security force at the BLT was organized at about 0645 when Colonel Geraghty ordered CWO-4 George Allen to outpost a line from the BLT parking lot to the MSSG engineer compound. Gunner Allen handed the assignment to Sgt José Febobigio, whose fourteen-man squad scavenged several M-60 machine guns from abandoned bunkers around the BLT building. By 0700 Febobigio was bolstered by the thirty-man battalion reaction force led by Lieutenant Singleton. Singleton had no idea where Sergeant Febobigio had posted his sentries, but he neatly complemented the MSSG security effort by deploying his amtracs and Marines at the edge of the airport parking lot, just to the south of the BLT, and out along the main airport road. Singleton's orders to his cannoneers were simple: first, he told them all to lock and load their weapons; then he told them, "If it isn't a rescue vehicle, and it doesn't stop for you, put a fucking round through it."

Amazing to most Marines working at the blast site were the odd small-arms rounds that zinged across the compound. Many of these were American rounds cooking off in the BLT armory, but a significant number were being fired by gunmen across the runway, in Hooterville. Neither Lieutenant Singleton nor Sergeant Febobigio did a thing to stalk the snipers. Their attention was riveted on incoming vehicles in the expectation that a follow-up bombing would be staged to take out people working in the rubble.

News reporters arriving at the MAU compound within fifteen minutes of the blast were held outside the gates from the main airport highway by sentries operating under the express orders of Capt Keith Arthur, the MSSG-24 exec. The newsmen became irate, then hostile, but Arthur would not relent. His attitude was that anyone who would not or could not materially help in the rescue was a liability. Like many of his colleagues in positions of authority, Arthur anticipated a second bombing once crowds of rescuers had been drawn to the site of the first.

Capt Chris Cowdrey and GySgt Steve Mellinger, of Charlie Company, expected to see the BLT in some state of disrepair, but the shock of the reality, when they got there, was profound, awesome. Dust was still in the air and bodies were still strewn all over the area. Both were sure the BLT had been hit by a missile.

LCpl Tim Hardy, a 60mm mortarman who had hopped aboard one of the Charlie Company trucks, joked with his comrades the whole way to the BLT. They all knew that the building was impregnable, so they thought the furor was much ado about nothing. The impact of the desolation was staggering. HM3 Mark Knight was reminded of a landfill site.

The smell of death—congealing blood and body fluids and wastes—was nauseatingly mixed with the sharp tang of explosives. The odors would become worse as the day heated up.

The Charlie Company commander restrained his work party and corpsmen when they arrived. He preferred to impose order upon the rescue effort rather than add to what appeared to him to be mass confusion. While Cowdrey checked in with Major Redlich, the company's gear was off-loaded by the northeast corner of the building, near the battalion motor pool. The Charlie Company corpsmen were detailed to find stretchers, cots, ponchos, and poncho liners and ordered to report back as soon as they had some. (This gear was provided by MSSG personnel.) The company drivers were sent to root through the wrecked vehicles at the motor pool to salvage shovels, crowbars, sledgehammers, jacks, jack stands, and fire extinguishers. (The motor pool had already been picked clean by MSSG personnel.) Bolt cutters and crowbars were commandeered from civilian ambulances. Hacksaws appeared from out of the ether, while a second Charlie Company work party brought down picks, shovels, axes, and other digging tools.

HM2 Julio Calder, Charlie Company's senior corpsman, found the situation initially chaotic. He was surprised to find no corpsmen on the scene (all the MSSG corpsmen were at the opposite corner of the building, obscured by the rubble) other than the three other Charlie Company docs and two from Bravo Company who arrived minutes later. Calder also realized at the outset that he had brought nowhere near enough medical supplies.

Gunny Mellinger organized a crew and swept the surface of the northeast quadrant to locate bodies and body parts that had not previously been collected. Then scouts were sent into the rubble to locate the living; each was to report back to Cowdrey's impromptu CP and select a crew large enough to dig out the victim he had found. Corpsmen would be sent, if needed, as soon as the victim had been freed. Cowdrey cautioned everyone leaving his area that he was to report back, with his equipment, at the conclusion of each rescue. Individual Marines were detailed to sit by trapped men who were awaiting rescue or, in several cases, who might never be freed alive.

GySgt Carlos Ramirez, the Charlie Company gunny, expressed a desire to secure the nearest stretch of road, so Captain Cowdrey authorized him to find the people he needed from among the strays who had by then gravitated to the CP and establish sentry posts. Ramirez's detail tied in with Lieutenant Singleton's cannoneers, who were already guarding the main airport road. Singleton ordered the Charlie Company troops to lock and load their weapons, and to shoot first and ask questions later if anyone gave them any trouble.

The rescue was considerably hampered by smoldering fires in the ground-deck armory and in the first-deck lithium-battery storage compartment. There was the nagging fear that TOWs and other heavy ordnance stored in the armory would erupt in a grand conflagration. The burning batteries, which were potentially explosive themselves, poured out a noxious gas that might have smothered several men confined in the rubble.

As organized as Cowdrey's group tried to remain, success hinged on individuals in sufficient possession of themselves to come back in once a job was completed and to bring their gear with them. When it was seen that the system could not be self-sustaining, Cowdrey sent out Marines to police up the tools left throughout the rubble heap. There were never enough tools.

HM3 Mark Knight's first patient was a dust-covered youngster pulled from the rubble by a pair of Lebanese Red Cross workers, who started cardiopulmonary resuscitation (CPR) as soon as the victim was in the open. Doc Knight checked for a pulse and applied an oral airway before assuming responsibility for the CPR. A civilian ambulance was brought up, and the victim was rushed away, probably to a Lebanese hospital.

It was surprising to most rescuers that a number of Marines who were thought to be dead were brought back to life by corpsmen who would not stop trying. Chris Cowdrey ran into one victim who had literally been scalped, had both arms and legs broken, and had no discernible wrist pulse. A civilian doctor knelt beside the cadaver and found a neck pulse, then went to work stabilizing him and arranging for his evacuation. Gunny Mellinger was also fooled by several men who seemed long dead.

On the other hand, HM2 Julio Calder found that many rescuers insisted that victims who had already smothered were alive.

One of the most paranoia-inducing thoughts to strike most rescuers was the idea that the rubble from one rescue might be placed atop another live victim. The worry was real: rubble excavated to free one live Marine was piled on top of two others, one of whom realized what was going on and became extremely belligerent, an attitude that probably helped save his life.

The task of prying reinforced concrete from some of the accessible living was solved by Master Sergeant Jenkins, who had holes punched through the concrete and wrecker chains strung through the holes. If possible, the wreckers lifted the concrete. If not, torches were brought in and the steel reinforcing rods, which were often exposed where concrete had shattered, were severed. While the tedious process of punching holes and torching steel was going on, rescuers spoke with the trapped victims, asking about their families, cars, girlfriends—anything but their injuries.

As Gunner Allen was picking his way through the rubble between rescues, he stopped to pick up a paperback book that caught his eye, an action novel entitled *Nobody Gets Out Alive*. Those words were to run through Allen's mind for days.

Top Jenkins initially moved the fifteen-ton crane he had commandeered from a Lebanese Ministry of Transportation storage shed to the west side of the building and attempted to lift the collapsed overhang that lay across the BLT mess hall. The effort failed, for there were many tons of rubble pinning the large slab Jenkins was trying to move. He soon drove the crane to the northeast corner of the building—from which most of the live ones seemed to be emerging. The crane managed to lift a huge piece of concrete and steel, allowing rescuers to snatch a live Marine who had been sealed in.

When HM3 Steve Brown wriggled into the mess hall after Top Jenkins left, he found GySgt Evan Fain alive and well, leaning up against a concrete slab nursing his broken arm. Fain had baked Brown's birthday cake two days earlier, so he nodded a friendly greeting before insisting that Brown and several other rescuers who followed him in look after the surviving cooks before spending their time on him.

Sgt Greg Gagner, a Maintenance Platoon squad leader, climbed to the pinnacle of the rubble heap and found two Lebanese paramedics working over a victim trapped in a vertical concrete-and-steel lean-to. Gagner did not have enough light available to see what was holding the man in, nor even who the man was. He could see the victim's head, which had acquired a horrible crack, through which Gagner was certain he could see brain matter. Though he felt the man would not survive, Gagner persisted in his efforts to free him. Another Marine arrived to help, and they tried to lift the man out with the help of the two Lebanese. He would not budge because he was tangled up in a twist of steel rod. Someone got a hacksaw, and everyone took turns slicing through the rod. At great length, the two wiry Lebanese climbed into the hole, but they were too small to lift the helpless man.

Greg Gagner was short and stocky, and powerfully built— ideal for lifting, but a little too wide to crawl far enough into the angled hole. He got partway in but was stopped over the trapped man's head. The Marine was conscious, so Gagner asked him who he was. He identified himself as 1stLt Neal Morris, the BLT 1/8 Headquarters and Service Company executive officer who had become famous when he was hit in the butt by shrapnel while in the officers' head during the first Druse artillery barrage in late July. Gagner asked Morris what he thought was holding him in. The lieutenant said that one of his arms was pinned beneath his body. The maintenance sergeant dug around a bit, but could not pry the limb free. Each time he tried, Morris screamed in agony.

Gagner offered this advice: "Buddy, you have a chance of getting out of there if you help yourself. You can make it home, but I can't do it for you. You're going to have to pick your shit up and do it on your own." Neal Morris pulled his arm free.

Gagner was on his back, braced against a concrete pillar, over Morris's head. He could not help Morris crawl out, but he could provide the means for the lieutenant to gain purchase. Morris made it far enough for Gagner to grab his hands. The burly squad leader heaved the big lieutenant up a few inches at a time and eventually had Morris on his chest. Another Marine removed his shirt and leaned into the cavity headfirst to place the shirt beneath Morris's bare feet, which were becoming painfully bruised by loose debris. Gagner cautioned Morris to rest on his chest until he felt he had the strength to continue. When Morris was set, Gagner lifted him up through the top of the cavity, where he was pulled into the clear by jubilant rescuers.

The lieutenant was carried from the rubble by the time a drained Greg Gagner lifted himself from the cavity. Gagner took a breather and then went in search of someone he could hear knocking on debris within the building. Unfortunately, he pulled only dead men from the rubble after he freed Neal Morris.

By 0640, the area around the building was swarming with scores of LAF soldiers from the adjacent barracks and countless Lebanese civilians, many of whom arrived in ambulances and medical-type vehicles while others poured through gaps in the fences around the BLT. Many were merely rubberneckers, and there were several potential looters in the crowd, but most of these good people went right to work in the rubble, exhibiting life-saving talents learned the hardest way over seven years of urban civil warfare. Only later did it dawn on any of the Marines and Navy men on the scene to question among themselves how so many outsiders had so quickly gotten The Word. They arrived from literally all over the war-ravaged city and its suburbs, and their numbers included Amal-sponsored medical teams (whose symbol was a red blood drop) from Khalde and Hooterville. The medical help provided by various Lebanese health and paramedical agencies was, in most cases, selfless.

SSgt Dennis Allston, who had been working with Explosive Ordnance Disposal in Beirut for over a year, was surprised to find several of his Lebanese colleagues on the scene within thirty minutes of the blast. When he thought about it later, Allston realized that the men he had seen—and to whose homes he had been during the halcyon days—all lived in Christian suburbs more than an hour's drive from the BIA.

Individual Lebanese civilian construction workers began gravitating to the blast site quite early in the effort. A few were merely gawkers, but most of them told Major Redlich and others in authority what they could do to help. The offers were quickly and gratefully accepted; the MAU had very little heavy equipment, and what it did have was clearly not enough to even begin a meaningful demolition of the rubble heap to get at the dead and injured who lay within. Thus heavy equipment owned and operated by the Oger-Liban Company, the prime airport construction contracting firm, was pulled off airport sites and moved to the BLT. While individuals and small crews went to work almost from the outset, it took a bit longer for Maj Bob Melton, the MAU S-4, to contact Oger-Liban's senior engineer. As soon as the key man arrived on the scene, he accompanied Major Melton and Major Redlich on a survey of the building, making recommendations and pointing out how the most work could be accomplished in the shortest time. Doug Redlich was so impressed with the Lebanese engineer's expertise that he left him to run his own show. Within an hour of the blast, Lebanese civilian construction workers had staged a huge bulldozer and a mobile forty-ton P&H crane at the building site, and numerous smaller vehicles of every description were in among the rubble, working with Marines and Lebanese medical workers. Meantime, Major Melton and his subordinates called all over Beirut in search of more vital equipment and skilled men to run it.

They found LtCol Larry Gerlach beside a fence near the southwest corner of the building, beneath what had been the window of his first-deck quarters. He was just about the only man in that quadrant of the building to be blown clear. Indeed, he was just about the only living being in that quadrant. He was unconscious, a total mess; no one expected him to survive. He was thrown into the back of a Lebanese ambulance—fortunately, under the gaze of Col Tim Geraghty—and driven off to the Italian MNF dispensary.

GySgt Alvin Belmer, the battalion training chief, was found, virtually in the open, unconscious and broken. Belmer, whom everyone called Hard Dick (after his own standard greeting, "Hey, how you doin', Hard Dick?"), was considered the most motivated staff NCO in the battalion. His reputation survived intact, for he had his .45-caliber pistol in his hand when he was pulled from the rubble. He was also driven off by Lebanese rescue workers to one of the civilian hospitals.

HM3 Tom Young set up a little station of his own in the vacant MSSG officers' club and treated a half-dozen badly injured victims by himself. In addition to their traumatic injuries, most of Young's patients were badly burned. Those who were conscious kept calling out, "What happened, Doc," but Tom Young was not sure he knew. Most of Young's patients had shredded skin adhering to their lower legs and feet, an odd condition he thought was caused by the force of the blast. Most had difficulty breathing, no doubt the result of inhaling huge volumes of dust. All of them were extremely restive, prone to thrashing around on their cots, loosening bandages and reopening barely controlled wounds. A delirious victim whose left arm had been nearly severed in the blast kept grabbing the blanket of the man next to him with his right hand. On the other side of the amputee, a senior NCO in a great deal of pain demanded morphine over and over. Young was utterly overwhelmed until joined by HN David Hall. Dr. Ware soon stopped in and doled out some morphine. Several of Young's patients had sustained head injuries, so they were denied morphine. The amputee died from shock and, perhaps, severe internal injuries.

First Lieutenant Leo Lachat arrived at LS Brown from Green Beach at about 0650. There he saw that members of the HST, which was part of his Shore Party Platoon, were all okay, awaiting the arrival of the first medevac helos, so he proceeded to the blast site to see Major Redlich. The air was "still gray and hazy, and the smell of explosives was still powerful." There were shards of clear Plexiglas all over the road. Concrete boulders were everywhere, and all adjacent buildings had been scarred by flying debris. Lachat was utterly unprepared for what he encountered as he rounded the corner of the Lebanese fire-fighting school.

Major Redlich was nowhere to be found in the growing crowd of workers, so Lachat left the jeep to find him. He saw his first victim then, a Marine who had been pancaked between the first and second decks. All that was visible was the victim's head and one dangling arm; the rest of the man had been crushed between huge concrete slabs. Lachat gravitated toward the north side of the building. There he found a huge cavern at ground level where the upper floors had not quite broken through to the lobby. Father George Pucciarelli, the MAU chaplain, asked Lachat to join him for a look into the cavern.

Huge blocks of steel-laced concrete angled in all directions and the huge support columns displayed great cracks. Metal reinforcing rods dangled from all the walls and the ceiling. Much of it was coiled and reminded Lachat of "tangled fishing line." About a dozen twisted corpses dangled from cracks in the overhead. Some were only legs, others were upper torsos. The padre advanced through otherworldly motes of gray cement dust dancing eerily in shafts of sunlight. He approached each of the dangling corpses, genuflected, and administered silent last rites. Body parts were lying helter-skelter amid military gear and personal possessions. Leo Lachat found a pool of fresh, red blood, the only sign of color in the gray vault. It dripped slowly from a body crushed in the rubble somewhere overhead.

27

Marine Medium Helicopter Squadron (HMM) 162 launched its two ready ships at about 0645. One was a medevac-configured CH-46 equipped to carry fifteen litter cases and the other was a CH-46 configured to carry up to twenty-five seated personnel or several deck-mounted stretchers. Each of the ready helos carried ground-support reinforcements and their equipment.

As additional aircrewmen and pilots reported in to Primary Flight, *Iwo Jima*'s aerial cortex, LtCol Jack Cress, the squadron operations officer, assigned them to additional airplanes, which he ordered to the beach in pairs. Once over land, the helos came under the control of Capt Mike McAuley, the squadron operations duty officer (ODO), who assigned them airspace, brought them into Landing Site (LS) Brown, saw to their loading, and launched them as he saw fit. While on the ground, the helos were serviced by the Helicopter Support Team (HST), a twelve-man ground unit belonging to MAU Service and Supply Group (MSSG) 24's Shore Party Platoon.

Capt Mike King, copilot of the first medevac helo, found the sky over Beirut typically hazy, much as it was every morning. But the haze over the blast site, which was really dust, prevented him from seeing the degree of destruction.

The first pair of birds made routine landings at LS Brown, their crews not yet certain what the furor was about. They could see frenetic activity on the ground near the landing site, but nearly all the airmen chalked that up to the way Marines operate.

Capt John Degelow, copilot of the first troop-configured bird, thought that casualties would already be at the LS, awaiting his arrival, but he was wrong. Though it took about thirty minutes from the moment of the blast to get the first helos to the beach, none of the injured had yet been brought up from the MSSG aid stations. One of the command pilots suggested that the helos move to LS Red, which was located beside the inner perimeter road and closer to the Battalion Landing Team (BLT) head-quarters; that, he averred, would save time. Captain McAuley, the ODO, told him to stay where he was but gave no reason.

The two helos sat for about twenty minutes. In that interim, two more birds, both configured for carrying troops, arrived. Captain McAuley had to call the ship to tell Lieutenant Colonel Cress to stop the flow; the LS was choked and the four birds were providing potential targets for follow-on attacks as they squatted at the edge of the landing site, their huge twin rotors slowly turning. All the pilots were keyed up, ready to fly at the first inkling of trouble. The pilots and aircrewmen were dismally uninformed about events ashore. The only word Captain Degelow had was that "the headquarters" had been bombed; he did not know which headquarters, nor did he have any idea how many casualties there might be.

Captain McAuley became extremely concerned over the amount of fuel the waiting helos were consuming. He could not decide whether to order them to shut down or run the risk that one or more would run out of fuel and clog his landing site. If many more minutes passed, he would launch the waiting birds and replace them with fresh aircraft from *Iwo Jima.*

In the meantime, as the birds sat on LS Brown, jeeps and trucks began arriving to deposit corpses in a Lebanese Air Force hangar beside the runway. Mike McAuley had no direct role in the staging of the bodies, but he was desperately concerned that no corpsmen were around to confirm that the expanding rows of litters and cots indeed contained dead men. He need not have worried; all the bodies had been pronounced dead before leaving the MSSG aid stations or the BLT triage stations.

When MSgt Tony DeMonti, the base clubs manager, saw that most of the MSSG senior staff had left for the BLT, he decided to stay at the MSSG headquarters. He initially helped set up cots but soon gravitated to one of the first of the litter cases, who had been treated and set aside. The young Marine had a severe head wound, so the docs wanted him to remain fully conscious. DeMonti tried talking football, but the kid showed no interest. Baseball? Nothing. His girlfriend? That got a response, but the kid was dopey from the blow to his head, and it was really hard to keep him focused. Finally, word arrived that helos were at LS Brown, so the kid was loaded aboard a truck. Things were getting slow at the MSSG, so DeMonti decided to accompany the first truckload of casualties to the LS.

While two young Marines worked to get the wounded safely and comfortably aboard the truck, Top DeMonti consoled the injured men, telling them that they were well on the road to recovery. Then he swung into the cab to direct the driver to the LS. As the large truck neared the airport highway, DeMonti suddenly became edgy over all the civilian traffic. He could see that armed Marines were deployed across the road, but he felt the kids in back had come too far to be denied their lives by another bomber. "Just go straight across the highway," DeMonti ordered, "don't stop for anything." DeMonti heard the squeal of brakes and the blare of horns, but the truck barreled on.

The Marine security guards along the roadway and at the main gate realized that DeMonti's was just the first of many evacuation vehicles on the way to LS Brown, so they moved to curtail and control the flow of traffic on the road.

The first casualty arrived at LS Brown in a jeep. Waiting bearers picked up the litter and rushed it to the medevac bird, but someone thought the victim should be checked over before going aboard.

Captain King looked back from the copilot's seat of the medevac bird and saw several silhouetted forms "fussing over a litter or a cot" that had been set down right on the clamshell ramp. King's first impression was that the bearers did not know how to place the victim aboard the helo, which is nothing compared to what he thought when the litter was carried back off the ramp. King assumed that an overefficient officer or NCO had decided to collect a full load of casualties before loading anyone. He had seen stranger things in the five years since he had graduated from the Naval Academy.

"Hey! What's going on? Let's get this guy on and get him out to the ship!"

The crew chief announced that the Marine had died. King was dazed for the rest of the time it took to load Top DeMonti's truckload of casualties, which arrived within a minute. Many of these men were burn victims who required immediate attention.

There were initially only enough casualties to load the first two birds, so, as soon as they left, Captain McAuley ordered Capt Ron Smith to take off empty and fly around the Mediterranean Amphibious Ready Group (MARG) to pick up body bags and litters, both of which were in desperately short supply. Fresh birds landed almost immediately.

When the main flow of casualties finally hit, LS Brown became the scene of incredible confusion. A dozen ambulances and other vehicles of every description rushed to the LS with dead, dying, dazed, and debilitated Americans. There were not enough litters at Beirut International Airport (BIA), so most of the severely injured arrived on cots, which were bulky and which severely restricted the number of injured who could be carried out on each helo. Each victim was loaded as quickly as possible, and the helos were sent off either as soon as they were filled or as soon as there was a lull; no one was kept waiting on the ground. There were plenty of helos, and flying time to *Iwo Jima* was, at most, five minutes. Captain McAuley thought everyone was going out alive, but someone aboard *Iwo Jima* soon complained that there were dead ones arriving, too.

Part of the problem was alleviated as soon as Captain Smith arrived from a circuit of the MARG. In addition to medical supplies and body bags, he brought in surgeons and corpsmen from two of the ships. One team set up at the LS and screened all casualties, with particular attention to victims brought in by agencies other than the MSSG. Smith took on his first load of four cots—all that would fit in his CH-46's cargo bay—and flew out to *Iwo Jima*. On the way back, he diverted to *New Jersey* to pick up yet another surgical team and more supplies. He left word aboard the battleship that litters were vitally needed.

LCpl Mike Wittenbrook, a member of the HST, tried to direct the huge influx of vehicular traffic around the LS, but he was severely hampered by the arrival of a score of newspeople, who insisted upon getting in among the evacuees to take photos and record interviews. Wittenbrook was incensed by the insensitivity of the rush for news, and he had words with those he considered farthest out of line.

Whenever there was a lull, Captain McAuley diverted some of the idle helos to the MARG to pick up needed supplies—particularly medical gear, body bags, and litters—and, eventually, the scores of Navy officers and sailors who demanded that they be allowed to help at the BLT.

Once the evacuation got going, there were at least eight CH-46s in the air or waiting on LS Brown at all times. Each pilot was responsible for selecting his routes to and from the ships while

Iwo Jima's air officer, a Navy commander, was responsible for carrier flight operations. Captain McAuley was responsible for traffic over the beach or at the LS. Aircrewmen and pilots took breathers while maintenance crews rotated aircraft in and out of service as required by their standard operating procedures. The greatest advantage HMM-162 had going for it was the readiness of its airplanes. At the moment the bomb was detonated, the squadron had no helos on repair or maintenance status. HMM-162 functioned flawlessly throughout the terror-filled morning.

Iwo Jima had been preparing to receive "mass casualties" from the moment word of the bombing arrived from the beach. As with every other organization directly involved in the rescue and treatment of the survivors, HMM-162 and the Navy medical-surgical team aboard the *Iwo* seriously underestimated the meaning of "mass casualties." Still, both did a creditable job of preparing for their arrival. The extra time afforded the ship-bound Marines and the helo carrier's crew was used to good advantage.

GySgt Warren Clopper, a wiry thirty-five-year-old West Virginian who had seen ground combat in Vietnam, became the spark plug because his duties as squadron career planner had left him with plenty of time on his hands. He had gravitated to the position of taking charge of the Marines from ground units who lived aboard *Iwo Jima*—fire-watch and security personnel and ill Marines who spent days or weeks recuperating aboard ship. When 24th MAU had started sustaining casualties in July, Clopper had made it his job to spend time with the injured men or to see that other squadron personnel were on hand to spread good cheer.

As soon as Gunny Clopper heard "Stand by to receive mass casualties" over the loudspeaker near his compartment, he jumped out of his rack and rushed to the hangar deck, ready to do whatever he could to make himself useful. When Clopper thought about all the military-type gear that would probably arrive with the ten or fifteen wounded he expected, he decided to take charge of collecting and tagging it. He headed for the troop berthing compartments to snatch the Charlie Company and Weapons Company personnel there, a total of about fifteen Marines.

The first two helos returned to *Iwo Jima* at about 0730. They both dropped lightly to the deck, opened their clamshell ramps, and became the immediate focus of furious activity as keyed-up corpsmen and litter bearers rushed aboard and pulled off all the victims within a minute. As soon as the victims were clear, re-fueling lines were run out and both helos were filled to brim-ming with aviation gasoline. Then they whirred off the flight deck, bound once again for the beach.

The first time the midships overhanging elevator was lowered to the hangar deck, Gunny Clopper counted two dead and a dozen wounded. As corpsmen and doctors moved to work on the critical cases right on the elevator, which had been stopped at waist-level, Clopper and his crew jumped in to collect per-sonal effects, which were placed in individual bags and tagged with as much identification as the circumstances allowed. All the gear was placed in a roped-off area Clopper thought would be ample. The arrival of more casualty-filled helos immediately resulted in the need for more space for personal effects and gear.

Capt Leon Huss, who was on standby flight status, naturally gravitated to the hangar deck, where he saw a blood-covered surgeon dressed in combat boots, white T-shirt, and khaki trou-sers working over the waist-level elevator, simultaneously caring for three victims. The doctor had one hand in one victim's abdominal cavity, was talking to another patient over his shoul-der, and palpating the abdomen of a third victim. The surgeon took time to put on rubber surgical gloves, cap, and gown only after the first rush had been expended.

As Gunny Clopper's equipment-recovery team worked on expanding its area of control, the corpsmen on the hangar deck became totally overwhelmed with new arrivals. Clopper soon noticed that victims who had been treated and stabilized were left alone, so he sent a few of his Marines over to see to their needs. In a short time, sailors from the ship's crew and squadron personnel who could take the time gravitated to the gunny, asking if they could help. Even off-duty ship's officers and Marine aviators placed themselves at the gunny's disposal. Clopper assigned each of the volunteers to an untended victim. In no time at all, the volunteers were going far beyond mere hand-holding; they checked pulses, monitored IVs, and called corpsmen over when they thought their patients needed help. Clopper was sensitive to the needs not only of the wounded but of the volunteers. If he saw someone looking queasy, he gave him another job to help get his mind off the blood and gore. And he stopped by as many of the tended victims as time allowed, to speak words of encouragement or answer their burning questions.

When Gunny Clopper remembered that Cpl Richard Truman was a trained emergency medical technician, he got him released from his regular duties. Truman climbed to the flight deck with his own medical gear and worked with the corpsmen, saving lives.

By 0900, the hangar deck was bulkhead to bulkhead with victims, some dead, some still alive.

28

Second Lieutenant Mike Murphy, MAU Service and Support Group (MSSG) 24 communicator, stepped into the lobby cavern for the second time that bloody morning at about 0800. He had been in the cavern within thirty minutes of the blast, looking for the living. On this, his second trip inside, he was chagrined to find Lebanese civilians, including women dressed in their Sunday finery, gawking at the dangling bodies. Murphy sent several enlisted Marines to find sleeping bags, with which he shrouded the bodies. To his amazement and fury, several of the civilians actually pulled the shrouds down to satisfy their curiosity about how dead Americans might have differed from dead Lebanese.

A pair of Red Cross girls laughed aloud when an injured Marine emerged from the rubble wearing only skimpy underpants.

Civilian rubberneckers gravitated toward the MSSG headquarters. During one brief break in the flow of wounded, Dr. Jim

Ware glanced out a window and saw them closing in on the building. He sent word to sentries to keep them back. A vacant car outside the building was also disposed of because someone thought it might house a bomb. On the other hand, Ware welcomed the arrival of a silent Lebanese doctor, who stayed only long enough to turn over needed medical supplies.

From the very start, individual Lebanese stole from the dead and even from the crowds of workers. LCpl Tom Robinson, an MSSG-24 supply clerk, saw one Lebanese man grab an untended M-16 and take off. About twenty Marines took off after him, and he meekly surrendered the weapon. Another was chased off when he was caught riffling through a stack of mail. Lebanese soldiers from the nearby barracks took the opportunity to scavenge combat boots and deuce gear, and an Amal paramedic temporarily improved his lifesaving abilities by lifting a Unit-1 first-aid bag from behind a corpsman. Another Amal paramedic grabbed a K-bar knife from behind a Marine who had stuck it in the ground when he dropped to his knees to check an injured Marine's wounds.

LCpl Tim Hardy, of Charlie Company, was commiserating with a disembodied voice that whispered out of the rubble when he glanced over in time to see a Lebanese soldier trying on combat boots. When the Lebanese found a pair that fit, he also grabbed a new belt. Then he started drooling over several loose photos he found, probably of a victim's wife or girlfriend. Hardy watched a Marine stalk over and coldcock the scavenger, then ran to help drag the attacker off the allied soldier.

First Lieutenant Mark Singleton, who was beyond fury, told his sentries to collar a thief and "knock him on his ass." Col Tim Geraghty happened on one of Singleton's people who was about to butt-stroke a looter with his M-16. Singleton was game to let the sentry do his thing, but the enlisted Marine was put off by the colonel's presence. Singleton forced the looter's hand open and retrieved a beat-up cigarette lighter. The two conversed in heated English for a moment, but the artillery lieutenant turned away when he realized the Lebanese had no idea why the Marines were infuriated over the scavenging.

By and large, however, most of the Lebanese soldiers and civilians on the scene were there to help, which they did.

The crowd of reporters that descended upon the blast site, beginning almost before the concrete blocks stopped falling, received mixed reviews. Most of the American newspeople were businesslike, even compassionate, in their coverage, though there were several who now and again displayed an appalling insensitivity. Marines reflexively closed ranks every time a body was recovered—specifically to deny news cameras a clear shot.

There was a graceless tendency on the part of many Marines to lump all newsmen together. However, the more discerning noticed that the American teams were graver and more respectful than foreign journalists, who clumped together, laughing, joking, and swigging from sodas cans, between exciting episodes. One of the American wire-service bureau chiefs toured the area, taking names of survivors and workers and their families' phone numbers. The information was passed to his New York headquarters, and each of those families received a cheering call. This practice spread in subsequent days.

Colonel Geraghty eventually gravitated from his remote command post, between MAU headquarters and the Battalion Landing Team (BLT) headquarters, to the rubble heap. Other men —the MAU executive and operations officers—were in control of the overall situation, and he felt it was a commander's responsibility to be seen, to impart to the troops a sense of continuity and the confirmation that someone at the top had their interests at heart. Years of ingrained habit brought forth standard questions like "How's it going?" and "Is everything okay?" The responses from grim-faced, grief-striken Marines were also pro forma: "Okay, sir" and "We're getting it done, sir." However, only a few Marines responded with the Marine Devildog grunt, "Oorah!" Somehow, the familiar litanies helped instill or preserve a sense of continuity, which is what everyone needed to heal so massive a fracture in their lives.

Everyone who saw the colonel noticed an incredible sadness reflected in his eyes—and how, despite the sadness, he maintained an expression of firmness, complete with clenched, outthrust jaw.

Cpl Denny Palmer, of Bravo Company, came to in the basement battalion aid station about an hour after he had been hit on the head by a large chunk of concrete. He awoke in pitch darkness, unable to draw a full breath because of dust and smoke that still hung suspended in the air. He had no idea what was going on, and it took long moments for him to recall where he was. There was no end of screaming, hollering, and moaning from beyond the concrete walls of the aid station, but none of the noise was in any way enlightening. It only increased Palmer's incredulity. Rounds cooking off in the armory sounded like incoming, and the throaty rumble of a large piece of heavy equipment profoundly added to Palmer's disorientation and concern.

Three live corpsmen, and about eighteen dead ones, shared the aid station with Palmer. The living corpsmen were in generally the same shape as the Marine, but they had been conscious longer. None of them had done anything to find a way out of the hole. The four living men hollered for a time, then one of the docs said, "We gotta get the fuck outa here."

Denny Palmer stood shakily and headed cautiously for the stairway, which he found without incident. He climbed about halfway up, then found the way barred by concrete boulders. The four thoroughly terrified men worked in relays, clawing through about ten feet of loosely packed rubble, using gravity to move the really big stuff. At length, Palmer's hand punched through a barrier. A passing rescuer saw it and called, "Hey!

Somebody's over here!" The four survivors were helped into the open.

SSgt Mike Isajewicz was stymied in his efforts to locate the source of a voice filtering through the rubble. He spent twenty minutes homing in, exchanging information, and bantering to provide some hope. Then the voice petered out.

The only living victim Isajewicz found in the rubble following the first rush of survivors collected in the wake of the bombing was GySgt Winston Oxendine, a personal friend. The gunny had heard the big yellow Mercedes truck bearing down on the building and was just stepping onto a balcony when the bomb was detonated. He was blown off the second deck and covered with falling debris. One of Oxendine's elbows was damaged, and he suffered numerous lacerations and contusions, but he would survive.

HM3 Tom Young and HN David Hall were relieved at the MSSG and sent to the BLT after the main flow of wounded left for Landing Site (LS) Brown. They wandered about the rubble for a time but could find no one to treat. Young finally saw what he thought was a dead body by the outdoor heads to the north of the building. He went ahead of Hall to see who it was. It was the torso of a man ripped apart in the blast. Sickened, Young warned Hall to stay away. He marked the spot and then climbed with Doc Hall to the top of the rubble heap, where they found Dr. Gil Bigelow. As Young and Hall were checking in with the dentist, a Marine came by to point out the location of a trapped survivor.

Dr. Bigelow and Doc Young found the Marine pinned up to his waist between two floors. The top slab overhung the bottom one, and there was a tiny open space beside the trapped man. Doc Young crawled into the dark cave with his Unit-1 aid kit to see if he could alleviate the man's intense pain. One look told him the Marine was nearly gone, that there was virtually no chance of extracting him before he slipped into a coma and died. A jackhammer was eventually brought up, but the job before it was a monster. Time was running out. Doc Young administered a dose of morphine and started an IV to stabilize him, but the man's blood pressure was low from shock and the IV would not take. Oxygen was administered until a torch was brought up for cutting the steel reinforcement rods. The victim's breathing was regular, and he responded to questions and conversational gambits aimed at keeping his mind off the pain. In time, the trapped man became delirious, then he slipped away and died. Doc Young was shaking so badly that he had to ask another corpsman to confirm the loss of a pulse.

When Maj Doug Redlich looked into Doc Young's face a few moments later, he ordered Young to sit down. Another passerby told him he looked terrible, as did another corpsman, who offered to sit with him.

The first American physician to reach the BLT was Lt Larry Wood, Marine Medium Helicopter Squadron 162 flight surgeon, who arrived from *Iwo Jima* with five corpsmen and a nurse at about 0730. This was the gentle six-and-a-half-footer's second experience at treating mass casualties; he had been at the BLT on August 29, when they brought in George Losey and the other wounded Marines from Alpha Company. But that had been in another life.

Dr. Wood did not even learn that the BLT was down until he saw the disfigured skyline as he was approaching the rubble heap in a jeep that had picked him up at LS Brown.

Wood ordered his medical team to establish a triage site in the parking lot on the south side of the building while he inspected the rubble to see if there were other medical teams at work and to try to get a handle on the number of casualties. He came upon Colonel Geraghty, who was standing silently in front of the building, just staring at the destruction. Wood asked the MAU commander if there was any chance of his communicating directly with the ship, but Geraghty said that all communications to the Mediterranean Amphibious Ready Group (MARG) would have to be routed through MAU headquarters.

Next, Wood got sidetracked for about twenty minutes rescuing a single Marine. The surgeon was, by then, a little angry with himself for having become immersed for so long in just one rescue, so he decided to remain at the triage station. He fell back on his training, intervening in treatment undertaken by his corpsmen only if asked or if he saw things going awry. His job was to manage and provide his advanced skills only as required.

Shortly after Dr. Wood settled in at his station, it dawned on him that Lebanese rescue workers were taking injured Americans directly from the rubble to their fleet of ambulances, completely bypassing his facility. He stopped the very next Lebanese litter team as it was loading a body and asked to meet with the Lebanese physician overseeing their operation. Dr. Wood held a brief powwow with his Lebanese colleague, insisting that all victims be turned over to American medics, that they would be taken to Lebanese facilities only if an American doctor or senior corpsman felt it was warranted. The Lebanese doctor agreed.

A short time later, Wood moved his station from the parking lot, which was filled with vehicles, to a quieter spot beside the BLT. Maj Bob Melton, the MAU S-4, arrived just as the squadron team was getting reestablished and offered to provide Wood with whatever supplies he felt he needed. The surgeon's first request was for a radio, which Melton immediately produced. Wood asked that patient-snatching Lebanese ambulances be restricted and that all victims, dead or alive, pass through his triage station. Melton sent word to the sentries in the parking lot to control the flow of medical traffic.

Dr. Gil Bigelow sensed around 0930 that most of the living had been freed from the rubble. Since all the casualties had been sent up to the MSSG aid stations, he decided to leave the primary care of additional victims to Dr. Wood, and he returned to the MSSG building to help Dr. Jim Ware.

LCpl Jesse Frazier, of the BLT 1/8 Communications Platoon, was trapped at the 81mm Mortar Platoon compound, unable to get permission to get to the BLT building. When MAU asked Mortar Platoon to donate some crypto gear to the reassembling comm net, Frazier asked to fulfill the request, but a staff NCO pulled rank and went himself. A short time later, MAU asked Mortar Platoon to donate a communicator to man a new link. Frazier emphatically volunteered, and he was finally sent.

The first body Frazier saw come out of the rubble was that of SgtMaj Frederick Douglass. He went to the area where Communications Platoon had been billeted but most of the bodies were so badly mangled that he could recognize only one of them, Capt Joe Boccia's. A communications staff NCO was found alive, pinned between the first and second decks, half in and half out of the building. He had been made delirious by large doses of morphine administered by compassionate corpsmen who knew very well that he had no chance of surviving until tons of rubble could be removed. Lance Corporal Frazier circled the rubble, looking into the dusty gray faces of men he knew, but recognizing only a few. He had no stomach for working with the dead, so, as soon as he gathered his wits, he went to work collecting weapons and stray communications gear, especially crypto devices.

The really chilling part of Frazier's experience was that he had been scheduled to call home from the BLT building on Saturday night. It was standard procedure that anyone placing a night call remain in the building until morning. By sheer good luck, Frazier had placed his call and stayed over Friday night.

Another communicator, LCpl Samuel Guice, arrived from the French Multinational Force headquarters, where he had been serving with the BLT liaison officer since Saturday morning. He had received news of the bombing from a Charlie Battery radioman at 0625, but it took him until about 0900 to get away. In the interim, Guice had followed developments on the radio in utter disbelief. He had heard requests for body bags, more body bags, and still more body bags. He crossed paths with Lance Corporal Frazier as he wandered about in shocked disbelief. Guice detailed himself to collect the hundreds of letters and photos that littered the bomb site. When he found a photo taken at a birthday party he had attended a few weeks earlier, he went to pieces and was unable to pull himself together. He tried to drown his sorrow in work but did himself in by absently picking up a stray leg. That was all he could bear. He wandered up to the MSSG headquarters to chill out with two fellow communicators, Cpl Joe Martucci and LCpl Bob Calhoun.

After several hours of working around the northeast quadrant of the BLT, HM2 Julio Calder, of Charlie Company, was detailed to man a post on the main road to stop Lebanese ambulances and reroute the bodies of victims to a holding area. He found the situation on the roadway utterly chaotic. The Lebanese were in such a rush to get away that they inadvertently desecrated several bodies. Doc Calder saw the rear doors of one ambulance pop open and the stretcher slide out. The stretcher's wheels caught on the rear bumper and the body was dragged through the parking lot until the ambulance could be flagged to a halt. The staff sergeant in charge of the security post had to be restrained as he lunged at the ambulance driver.

During one brief lull, Calder's eyes wandered to the rubble heap, where he saw two Lebanese rescue workers pulling mightily on a pair of legs that protruded from the crushed concrete. All the two got for their troubles was a body severed at the waist.

As the hours passed, it became less and less possible to free the living. HM3 Mark Knight and HN Steve Sibille, of Charlie Company, found a victim in a tiny cavity where the first deck had been. He was wedged upside down between the wall and the floor, and it looked as though he was pinned across the chest by a machine-gun tripod. The only way to get to him was to break through about eight inches of concrete and steel rods. While Marines did the heavy work, Knight and Sibille kept stopping by, relieving one another for brief periods, in order to comfort the victim, who was a bit confused. He said he was having difficulty breathing, but he refused all offers of oxygen. He also said that his legs hurt a lot and that he really craved water. Because the corpsmen could not assess the kid's injuries, and because he was upside down, they could not give him anything to drink. They took turns holding a constantly replenished wet gauze bandage to his lips so he could suck some of the moisture. LCpl Tim Hardy, a Charlie Company 60mm mortarman, spent two hours trying to dig the trapped Marine out of the rubble. During that time, the pinned youngster cried and pleaded with his rescuers to please get him out. They kept telling him that he would be okay, to hang in there. The injured man succumbed to his injuries only five minutes before his body was freed.

Another Marine was found leaning against the wall of a tiny lean-to deep in the rubble. He had applied a tourniquet to his bleeding leg but had bled to death before help arrived.

But it wasn't all bad news.

Cpl David Wilcox was about eight feet down in the rubble, fully conscious and in pain. It was pitch dark, and the clinging odor of smoke, combined with suspended dust, made breathing a chore. He heard people screaming for a time, then heard the shouts of rescuers and victims trying to locate one another. Wilcox kept up a running dialogue with a combat engineer who was a few feet higher and on the far side of a concrete-and-steel slab, pinned across the chest by another concrete slab. The engineer was extremely concerned about his breathing, which was impeded by the weight on his chest, so Wilcox tried to soothe him with innocuous conversation.

In time—hours—rescuers digging down from above got close enough to be distinctly heard. Wilcox shouted for help. SSgt Randy Gaddo heard him but could not locate him.

"Keep talking!"

Wilcox thought for a moment, then sang, at the top of his lungs, the only song to which he knew all the words: "From the Halls of Montezuma, to the shores of Tripoli . . ."

They found the engineer first, alive but pinned beneath his concrete slab. Neither the victim nor his rescuers knew that his cracked ribs were being held in place by the weight on his chest. When the slab was finally lifted, the trapped man's lungs expanded, driving the sharp ends of the ribs into the pink sacs. Both lungs deflated and the engineer smothered.

Staff Sergeant Gaddo strode across the slab on Wilcox's chest without any idea that his quarry was beneath his feet. Wilcox bleated, "Get off!" Gaddo asked Wilcox to keep making noise to guide him. Once the corporal's exact location had been ascertained, Gaddo and his ad hoc work crew dug down past the entrapping slab and burrowed back up at an angle to arrive beneath Wilcox and to one side. There was enough light for Wilcox to see for the first time where he was. He offered to crawl to the rescuers, but his first move ripped the flesh of his right arm, which was skewered by a steel reinforcing rod. He reached up with his left hand and told the man in the tunnel to grab it. Wilcox was pulled through the gap and placed on a cot. When the bearers nearly dropped the cot, Wilcox got to his feet and walked through the rubble with a pair of Marines supporting his arms and torso. He could see little, for he was badly nearsighted and his glasses were lost in the rubble. What he could see registered dimly.

"Oh, my God!"

Wilcox climbed aboard a jeep that already had a stretcher case strapped over the rear compartment and was driven to the MSSG aid station. Corpsmen pulled pieces of metal from Wilcox's body and bandaged his bleeding wounds. The corporal told them that his ribs were broken, but this was not the place to have them bound. He was taken to LS Brown and flown to *Iwo Jima* within an hour of being pulled from the rubble. Once aboard, he asked after his brother, Burton, a lance corporal serving with Charlie Battery. Burton was okay, but he had heard that David had been killed in the building.

After hours of working on shattered bodies, HM3 Steve Brown took a needed break by heading into the crater in the hope of unearthing the medical records that had been left in the battalion aid station. He had seen enough body parts to know the value of the records in establishing positive identification.

As Brown and another MSSG corpsman moved into the crater, a Marine captain stopped them and asked where they were headed. They told him, and he ordered them to stay clear of the place because it was considered a safety hazard. Brown tried to parry the issue by claiming that he wanted to search for dead corpsmen, but the officer was insistent. Brown asked for five minutes to see what there was to find. The captain relented.

Brown and the other corpsman spent twenty minutes in the aid station. In addition to grabbing several boxes of vital records, they brought the body of HM3 Joseph Milano into the daylight.

Five or six Marines, mostly staff NCOs, were trapped between the fallen floors and ceilings, partially in and partially out of the building. It was obvious by late morning that they could not survive long enough for the building to be peeled off their bodies. Work crews did everything they could to relieve the pressure, and many of the corpsmen made it a point to stop by to relieve one another from the agonizing vigils. Rabbi Arnie Resnicoff repeatedly stopped by to succor the trapped men. In time, however, each of these hopelessly trapped Marines went into shock. Each was given large doses of morphine—quietly and gently sent off into oblivion until, one after another, they all died.

Father George Pucciarelli found Chaplain Danny Wheeler's purple stole in the rubble and managed to convince a Charlie

Company rescue team that his Lutheran colleague was trapped directly beneath the vestment. It was mighty slim evidence, but it was also right above Danny Wheeler's crypt.

Wheeler had had his ups and downs in the three hours of solitude between the blast and Father Pucciarelli's chance discovery. A man of deep religious conviction, Wheeler nonetheless grieved for his soon-to-be-fatherless children. He had prepared for the eventuality of a violent death in Beirut, but the hours of enforced thought taught him that his preparations had been more practical than spiritual. He tried to close the gap, but was prevented from achieving spiritual peace by the nagging conviction that he would survive if he found the right combination of actions. He passed between moments of overpowering spiritual revelation and painful pleas for life.

"Who's there?"

Danny Wheeler was drawn back from the center of his soul. The calm words from above were Hope personified.

"Chaplain Wheeler."

"Are you going to make it?" It was Father Pucciarelli.

"I think I'll make it."

"Just hang on, buddy, we'll be right there."

There were more voices, then the sounds of digging. The rescuers had discovered that it was often simpler, and safer, to burrow down past entombed victims, then tunnel back up. Wheeler's voice was gone, so he guided the rescue team by beating upon a cardboard box within reach of his left arm. The burrowing was fraught with danger because loose chunks of concrete kept falling into the tunnel and hitting the workers.

At long last, hands reached into the crypt from the chaplain's left rear, and he called out.

They almost lost Danny Wheeler. A large piece of debris was pulled from the tunnel and the entire weight of the rubble settled on the minister's back, pinning his head within a vise of pressure too deep to sustain. Wheeler felt himself blacking out, and he panicked. He flailed with his hands but could do no good.

He was within millimeters of being rescued or crushed to death. He screamed at the diggers to try a fresh approach, to hurry. A voice—Father Pucciarelli again—told him he would be fine. Wheeler could not have been less inclined to believe that. He tensed every muscle in his body to hold back the six solid feet of rubble that was pressing in on him, hung on with every fiber of his being. He wanted to live. Period.

He thought of his wife. He thought of his sons. He thought of the taste of cold water. He thought of all the things he loved in life, of all the things he had never had an opportunity to experience. He prayed. He fought drowsiness. He fought a sleep he knew would be eternal. He nurtured the sparks of his anger, fanned them to a roaring conflagration of rage.

The burrowers burrowed on as fast as they could without getting Wheeler in deeper. He heard a voice say, "I can't get him." And he responded the way they had taught him an officer should respond, "Get him *now!*" Hands reached in and cut away portions of Wheeler's cot.

Then Chris Cowdrey's face appeared in Danny Wheeler's line of sight. "Hey, Chaplain! Can you move your legs?"

Both legs were pinned by rubble. He got his left leg free after much frantic pulling, but the right was trapped. A Marine they called Ski tried to dig the leg out, but falling debris made a hazard of the effort. He tried breaking the concrete with a sledgehammer, but even more concrete cascaded into the crypt.

"Pull me out!" Danny Wheeler had decided that the loss of a leg was acceptable.

Willing hands grabbed his body. He went out like a cork, free at last, intact.

He stood on his own two feet and luxuriously stretched his kinked muscles. Then he settled gratefully to the ground and asked for water. He drank deeply, stood up with Chris Cowdrey's help, took a few steps, and momentarily passed out. He awoke to the gentle ministrations of young Marines, who placed him on a stretcher and carried him to a waiting ambulance. A

Marine escort climbed in, and Wheeler was driven to the Italian aid station, where he was expertly and gently treated while a beautiful nurse held his hand.

Sgt Kim McKinney was called to the northwest corner of the building by Maj Doug Redlich to try to divine a solution to getting out two Marines, one alive and one dead, who were pinned by debris and steel reinforcing rods. There was so much junk clogging access to the lean-to that McKinney could not come up with an answer without actually getting to work. He was joined by several other Marines, including MSgt George Jenkins, who took charge of the cutting operation. When the steel rods had all been severed, a pair of corpsmen lowered an oxygen tank and breathing equipment to the live Marine in the hole, then Jenkins got to work cutting an access way through the concrete. It looked like it was going to be a race against time to bring the surviving Marine out alive.

While Jenkins and McKinney worked between the first and second decks, Sgts Greg Gagner and Dean Randgaard took it upon themselves to search for the BLT 1/8 armory and haul out live ammunition before smoldering blazes that were already cooking off small-arms rounds reached the areas where hand grenades, LAAWs, and TOWs were stowed. The armory was on the ground deck, on the west side of the lobby, and inboard of the BLT mess hall. Thus it was initially beneath four stories of rubble and several yards from the outer edge of the heap. It was also virtually beneath the spot where Top Jenkins was cutting concrete.

Sergeant Gagner found a way in, but was nearly brained when a slab of concrete cut from the overhead crashed at his feet. Top Jenkins looked into the hole his crew had made and grimly smiled at Gagner, who shrugged his shoulders and said, "I know."

Gagner and Randgaard wriggled into the armory and attached ropes to the cases of ammunition, then pulled the explosives out of the crypt and rushed them to a safe and secure place well away from the building.

In the meantime, the Marine who Top Jenkins and Sergeant McKinney were working to save slipped into a coma and died.

In fact, the last victim to be rescued alive was Chaplain Wheeler.

Most of the helo pilots who had started flying in the morning were taken off flight status in the hour after noon, when their airplanes were shut down for routine maintenance. Several wound up on the beach to help as needed while others crashed in their bunks, hopeful that a little rest would prepare them for more flying. It is doubtful that any of them slept. Capt Ron Smith didn't even try, though he was relieved after six grueling hours at the controls of his CH-46. He went to the squadron ready room and relieved a pilot who had been immersed in shipboard duties and who wanted to get airborne. Capt Mike McAuley, who had run LS Brown from the start, was relieved at noon but hung around until late afternoon. He was flown out to *Iwo Jima* and went straight to his stateroom, where he finally allowed his emotions to straighten themselves out.

Incoming small-arms fire began impacting at about 1300 near 1stLt Mark Singleton's reaction force amtracs, which were staged near the parking lot on the south side of the BLT. It appeared to be the work of just one sick soul. Understandably fearful that the shooting was a ploy to weaken the security detail by sucking sentries into a fruitless search, Singleton ordered everyone to get under cover. If Lebanese soldiers wanted to stalk the sniper, Singleton thought, it was okay with him. The gunfire went on for about forty-five minutes, then abruptly ceased. No one was hit. Singleton's reaction force was relieved later that afternoon and sent back to strengthen Charlie Battery's gun line.

News arrived at about 1400 from the northern perimeter that

sniping by Amal gunmen was picking up. No one had been found alive in the rubble for some time, so Capt Chris Cowdrey decided to return to his command. He left two corpsmen and sped north with everyone else he had brought to the blast sight.

The Italians sent fifty fresh combat engineers and their equipment at about 1400 hours. A section of grim-faced British Dragoon Guards worked until nightfall, and even the French, whose headquarters had been bombed and who had nearly fifty killed, sent a small group to help at the BLT. The most massive outside help arrived from the MARG, which sent so many sailors to the beach and LS Brown that Major Redlich had to get the flow turned off. Somber, furious sea-going Marines from *New Jersey*'s Marine Detachment arrived, ready to "kick ass and take names" or succor injured comrades, whatever was required. All were put to work searching for dead and, hopefully, trapped living men in the rubble.

29

Sergeant Steve Russell was given two doses of morphine aboard *Iwo Jima,* relief of the first magnitude. While he was still on the helo carrier's flight deck, he found three other members of the TOW section. All were in pretty bad shape, having been crushed by the east wall of the ground deck. Russell and the other three were the only survivors of the section.

GySgt Ron Jones's head injuries were bandaged and his arm was immobilized, then he was put off in a corner with several other walking wounded and checked from time to time.

First Lieutenant Chuck Dallachie briefly regained his senses aboard *Iwo Jima.* He had been out since a minute or two after the blast and did not yet know that the Battalion Landing Team (BLT) headquarters had been leveled or, for that matter, where he was. The first thing he noticed was a crazed thirst, so he asked for water. This was not possible, given his severe internal injuries, so a corpsman moistened some cotton balls and fed them into Dallachie's dust-rimmed mouth. A chaplain came by to administer late rites and a doctor knelt beside him for a few moments to describe the lieutenant's injuries: a collapsed lung, a damaged gall bladder, a lacerated spleen, a fractured skull, broken ribs, some liver damage, severe body gashes, a hole through one arm, and burned feet. The doctor then told Dallachie that his abdomen would have to be opened to learn the full extent of his internal injuries. As he was wheeled down long gray steel passageways, he kept pushing back a blood-soaked bandage that slipped over his eyes. Each time Dallachie received a dose of morphine, a corpsman wrote the time on his forehead. He was placed in an out-of-the-way corner when a new load of casualties arrived, apparently stable enough to await needed surgery until the new group had been triaged. He passed out again.

Dallachie's roommate, WO Paul Innocenzi, was also pulled alive from the rubble and rushed by Red Crescent workers to a hospital in the city. His head was shaved for cranial surgery, but he died before the operation began.

Cpl David Wilcox arrived aboard *Iwo Jima* before noon and was taken down to the hangar deck. He was examined by a Navy doctor, stabilized with an intravenous solution, given a tetanus shot, and set aside. He was in pain, but he was allergic to morphine, so he had to suffer.

The job of locating victims who had been whisked away to medical facilities throughout Beirut began almost the moment the MAU Service and Support Group (MSSG) aid station evacuated the last casualty late in the morning.

HM3 Ken Boyer was ready to unwind when the last of the wounded was taken from his MSSG aid station. He had been on Saturday-night duty until about 0230 and had counted on sleeping through the morning. Of course, he had been up since 0622. Boyer was just sipping his first drink of water of the day when he was ordered to the Italian Multinational Force (MNF) dispensary to locate injured Americans who had been taken there in the press of events immediately after the bombing.

Boyer found six injured and three dead Marines at the Italian medical facility. He collected all the vital information he could and filled out medical evacuation tags, which he later gave to Dr. Jim Ware. Boyer drove back to the Italian camp at about 1300 to deliver body bags and arrange for the evacuation of the dead and the injured who could be moved.

While Boyer was looking for casualties at the Italian camp, 1stLt Miles Burdine, the Bravo Company exec and commander of the embassy guard detachment, was providing Marines to escort several lost Italian ambulances to the American University Hospital. When Burdine went to the hospital to see what he could do to help, he was first taken to the morgue to identify several American corpses. They were all unrecognizable. He was next taken to an emergency treatment area and asked to identify the living. When Burdine looked into the battered face of GySgt Alvin Belmer, the BLT's extremely popular and gregarious training chief, he did not recognize him, and Belmer was unable to speak. Burdine was devastated. He toured other areas of the hospital and, fortunately, was able to speak to men who could identify themselves.

One of the most grievously injured was LCpl Terry Valore, a combat engineer who had sustained severe burns over most of his body. When Miles Burdine found him, Valore was the color of burned beef and covered in grease. Burdine could see that Valore was in extreme pain, but the youngster only wanted to know about his comrades. Minutes of conversation passed before the lieutenant brought up the matter of Valore's own condition, and only then did the burn victim show any concern for himself.

Burdine was leaving the ward when Valore called out, "Sir!"

The lieutenant turned.

"Semper fidelis, sir."

Burdine fought to contain the tears, but they rolled down his cheeks. It took him an eternity to regain enough of his composure to croak, "Semper fidelis, Lance Corporal Valore."

As soon as he could, Miles Burdine established a post at the hospital, using members of his embassy guard detachment headquarters team to both guard and succor the injured.

At about 1430, HM3 Ken Boyer and Capt Barry Ford, a MAU staffer, began a tour of Lebanese civilian hospitals to which American victims were believed to have been taken. Thanks to Lieutenant Burdine's report, they found patients being treated at the American University Hospital and another facility, and they learned that yet more Americans had been taken to several other treatment centers.

Though Dr. Larry Wood's hyperactive imagination warned him that he would be shot dead if he stepped beyond the security lines around the BLT, the flight surgeon also conducted a tour of Lebanese medical facilities to learn if any of the bombing victims needed to be moved to the American University Hospital, where care was superb, or could be moved to *Iwo Jima* or even prepared for evacuation to American military hospitals outside Lebanon. Dr. Wood happened to cross paths with Captain Ford and Doc Boyer, and they all compared notes, which provided the basis for locating nearly twenty Americans who had been whisked from the BLT before they could be treated or tracked. Several others were not found that afternoon, but they were being treated by Lebanese agencies.

One of the missing was LtCol Larry Gerlach, who had initially been taken to the Italian dispensary, unconscious and suffering compound fractures of his left arm and right leg and numerous facial fractures. He was transferred before the search parties were sent out to Sahel General Hospital, which was, of all things, a Shiite Moslem facility.

One of the first outside agencies to offer help to the victims of the bombing was the government of Israel, which announced within twenty minutes of the blast that it was prepared to scramble numerous medevac helicopters directly from military hospitals possessing mass casualty burn and trauma centers. Though the Israeli facilities were among the best in the world, and only a twenty-minute flight from Beirut, the U.S. government spurned the offer. Self-serving explanations later beclouded the essentially political nature of the decision. And, though administration spokesmen later averred that no American serviceman died as a result of the decision, there were deaths among the survivors held aboard *Iwo Jima* or at Beirut International Airport (BIA) for periods far in excess of the time it would have taken to get victims to the highly skilled Israeli surgical teams.

The four TOW-section survivors were split up in the afternoon. Sgt Steve Russell and two of the others, LCpl Michael Toma and LCpl Guillermo Sanpedro, were flown back to Landing Site (LS) Brown around noon and almost immediately shipped to Cyprus aboard a white-painted Royal Air Force C-130 transport, the first medevac flight to leave the BIA. The fourth TOW gunner, LCpl Jeff Nashton, was barely alive; he was slated to fly direct to one of the U.S. military hospitals in Germany. Lance Corporal Sanpedro died in Cyprus.

Steve Russell's injuries were treated at the superb, though spartan, British military hospital at Akrotiri, Cyprus. The blast that had hurled him at least fifteen feet from the rear of the BLT building had left him with a broken left femur, a fractured left ankle, a cracked pelvis, and a fracture in his left hand. In addition, his left leg was split open from knee to ankle, and a huge gash that opened his left hand required thirty-five sutures. A large chunk of flesh had been gouged from his right thigh, and there was a hole through his right shin. He had several head lacerations, and the rest of his body had sustained numerous cuts and bruises.

GySgt Ron Jones and Cpl David Wilcox were also flown to Cyprus aboard the British C-130. Twenty-one survivors in all made the flight.

Chaplain Danny Wheeler was evacuated from the Italian aid station to *Iwo Jima* in midafternoon. He was inspected and carted off to the hospital ward, where he was painfully catheter-ized. Danny Wheeler did not want to be alone. He had been in utter solitude for over four hours that Sunday, and he never wanted to be alone again. He greedily talked with the young sailor who had been detailed to keep him company until he was flown to LS Brown at about 1800 hours. He was met there by Father George Pucciarelli and Rabbi Arnie Resnicoff. The three men of God exchanged blessings and good cheer, and then Danny Wheeler was loaded with eleven other survivors aboard a Navy C-9 hospital plane for a flight to the Navy hospital at Naples. He carried away nothing but his dog tags. He had no possessions, not even a stitch of clothing. But Danny Wheeler had his life and his future.

First Lieutenant Chuck Dallachie came around again aboard one of the Air Force C-9 Nightingales bound for Germany. Cool, efficient hands were shaving his chest, abdomen, and groin. Then he went out again. Dallachie was kept unconscious by his physicians between Sunday evening and Wednesday. He had been blown up at 0622 on Sunday, and his damaged spleen and gall bladder were removed in Germany sometime that same night. His injuries could easily have been lethal, but Dallachie was a strapping young man in peak physical condition. No doubt, his strong constitution saved him. When the circum-stances of his injuries and presence in Germany were revealed, Chuck Dallachie stared at his doctor in utter disbelief. He had not had a clue, would not remember until days later the mo-ments of sheer panic he had experienced when he came to in the rubble, nor his time aboard *Iwo Jima,* nor being prepped for surgery aboard the Air Force Nightingale. He even learned, much later, that he had carried on a lucid conversation with his rescuers at the blast site, but he was unable to conjure up even the dimmest recollection of the incident. When Dallachie finally absorbed the few facts at his disposal, and as he read the lists of dead and wounded comrades, he could think of no reason under the sun for his having survived. Not one.

LCpl Dale Garner, of the BLT 1/8 Dragon Platoon, came to in a Lebanese hospital early Monday morning. He had no idea what he was doing between clean sheets in a scrubbed white room. The last thing he could recall was going to sleep after the country-western show on Saturday evening. He had been in the front of the building, on the second deck, when the bomb was detonated, and was the only man in his room to survive. He had already been through one operation on his ear, a chest tube was connected to a collapsed lung, a blood clot had been removed from his head, an ankle was broken, and the heel of one foot had been deeply gashed. His body was covered with abrasions and contusions. Garner was alone for awhile, but Cpl Terry Hudson, one of the battalion armorers, was later brought unconscious from surgery. The treatment was excellent. A teenaged male nurse spent all his time with Garner, who did not believe that the BLT had been bombed and that he was one of a very few survivors. Garner was eventually flown to Frankfurt, Germany. Corporal Hudson succumbed to his injuries.

HM1 Larry Jenkins, of BLT 1/8's medical section, came to at the Air Force hospital in Wiesbaden on Thursday morning. Like Lance Corporal Garner, his last memory was of turning in after the country-western show on Saturday evening. Unlike all the other corpsmen, Jenkins was found in his rack in the remains of his third-deck room, on the east side of the building. He had been pinned by concrete beams across the chest and knees, and was pulled unconscious from the rubble by two MSSG-24 corpsmen. He had no recollection of responding to the Condition I alert, nor of climbing back to the third deck to continue his night's sleep, though he must have done both. He was the senior survivor from the battalion aid station, one of only five or six battalion corpsmen to survive at all. One of them, HM3 Pedro Alvarado, was in the next bed. It fell to him to tell Jenkins what had occurred and why he was in Germany.

Lieutenant Colonel Gerlach remained in a coma for three

days at the Shiite Sahel General Hospital. He was frankly expected to succumb to his massive injuries. He was visited at the hospital by Robin Wright, an American journalist, and carried on a lucid conversation with her, but could recall no details of their talk a year after the event. He was flown to West Germany a week after the bombing. Highly specialized X rays revealed that the battalion commander's neck had been broken and that his spinal cord had been damaged. Sixteen years earlier, Larry Gerlach had been shot several times in the abdomen in Vietnam and had required a year of intense physical therapy to return to duty. Gerlach could not resign himself to living the life of a quadriplegic; he vowed to leave the Marine Corps the same way he had entered it—walking.

GySgt Alvin Belmer, the BLT training chief, was operated on at the American University Hospital several days after the bombing. He had been semiconscious since the bombing and had not responded to any of the conversational gambits offered by Lieutenant Burdine or members of the embassy guard detachment. Burdine reluctantly agreed to allow the surgery only after doctors assured him that it would provide Gunny Belmer with his only chance for survival. Belmer succumbed to his injuries.

It took the troops at the American University Hospital days to identify LCpl Larry Simpson of Headquarters and Service Company. Simpson was conscious and could move part of his body, but he could not speak. After several days of sitting with Simpson, LCpl Guy Fortier, a Bravo Company machine gunner, figured out that the victim's hearing was unimpaired, so he held Simpson's hand and asked the mute man to squeeze in response to questions. Simpson was able to spell out his name and provide his social security number and the phone number of his next of kin, who were called direct from the hospital with the news that he was alive.

As long as there were Marines being treated at the American University Hospital, members of Lieutenant Burdine's embassy guard detachment and the regular Marine security guard at the embassy, spent all their off-duty hours with their comrades, holding hands or supplementing the beleaguered nursing staff.

The best determinations indicate that a total of 128 American servicemen were treated in the wake of the bombing. Of these, eighty-three were initially treated at the MSSG-24 aid stations, eighteen were initially treated at LS Brown or aboard *Iwo Jima*, and twenty-seven were initially treated at the Italian MNF dispensary or Lebanese hospitals. Twenty-nine of the eighty-three treated by the MSSG were returned to duty on October 23, and seven others turned themselves in and were treated over the next several days. Eight of the Americans treated in local hospitals died of their injuries, including all three Marines who were taken to the Ghaza Hospital, in the Sabra refugee camp. By a week after the bombing, only five of the eighty-three patients initially treated by the MSSG had succumbed to their injuries—a survival rate of 94 percent.

The impact of the tragedy upon the living was both awesome and touching. The rescue workers were, by and large, young men totally caught up in the macho spirit of the Marine Corps. The tenderness with which they treated the survivors and the dead was often remarked upon by observers.

GySgt Steve Mellinger, of Charlie Company, had enlisted in the Marine Corps at age seventeen and had become a gunny by age twenty-six. He was a former drill instructor and recruiter, a totally squared-away young man with a bright future in the Corps. Late that Sunday evening, Steve Mellinger found a quiet place to himself and cried his heart out as he thought of the things he had seen that day, as he reflected on the cold, dead faces of men he had known and about whom he profoundly cared, as he thought of their widows and orphans. Steve Mellinger preferred to express his grief in solitude, but he would not have been embarrassed if he had broken down in front of the troops who looked to him for leadership and guidance. They were all crying, too.

Following Chaplain Wheeler's rescue, at about noon, rescuers continued to find living victims trapped within the rubble. None of these was recovered alive, however, so, at some indeterminate moment, the "rescue and recovery" effort became purely a "recovery" effort, and that was divided into four distinct parts: recovery of the dead from the rubble; positive identification of the bodies and body parts; preparation of the bodies and body parts for repatriation to the United States; and collection, identification, and return of personal effects.

Each phase of the recovery and identification was handled by scores of volunteers, but each also became the compulsion of a small band of stalwarts who pretty much ignored their other duties to remain on the job, working with the dead or their possessions. Each group maintained a core of dedicated individuals who ultimately had to be pried from their work.

The recovery of bodies from the rubble took a full week, though the bulk of the work was completed on Wednesday. The job entailed the dismantling of the rubble heap from top to bottom. MSSG-24 maintained full control of the job, and many members of the 380-man unit contributed blood, sweat, and tears to the task. Four squad leaders, however, constituted the vital core of the effort. They were Sgts Kim McKinney, Greg Gagner, and José Febobigio of the Maintenance Platoon and Sgt Dean Randgaard of the Truck Platoon. The four stuck together, building a group ethos that withstood the onslaught of impatient Lebanese workers and the insensitivity of news teams and VIPs, who rushed to Beirut in the immediate wake of the bombing. The four were utterly compulsive in their work, unable to rest or stop for more than a few bites of food and a few sips of water pressed on them by concerned comrades and superiors. By Monday morning, nearly everyone on the site was deferring to the four sergeants on matters concerning the recovery of the dead.

The horror stories are legion: the time on Tuesday that one of the sergeants spent hours freeing a body from a tight corner, only to discover that it was warm, no doubt having expired only moments before he reached it; the time several of the sergeants were told in the midst of a recovery to shut down a hard-to-start light earth mover because the noise disturbed Vice President George Bush, who was touring the bomb site in place of the Commander in Chief; the time an impatient Lebanese bulldozer operator scraped arms and legs off three or four corpses as he tidied up a corner of the rubble heap; the numerous times they had to threaten newspeople to stop photographing the faces of the dead and their dismembered corpses; the numerous in-stances when one or another would nearly "lose it" until pulled back from the brink by one of the others; the time when one of the four found one body and two heads in the same crypt but could not begin to determine which head went with the corpse, nor where the second body might be; the incessant low moans and cries for help emanating from "somewhere" in the rubble; the knowing that the chance of pulling living men out dwindled with each passing minute; the realization, at the end, that all they had been able to do since noon Sunday was preserve the dignity of the dead.

MSSG-24 bore the lion's share of the recovery, but hundreds of sailors from all the U.S. Navy ships in the area made heroic contributions, as did engineers and volunteer infantrymen from the Italian, British, and French MNF contingents. Chief among these, as compulsive in his way as the four sergeants, was an Italian engineer, Lt Mario Rosetti, upon whom the putrefaction became a garland of honor and brotherhood.

Two temporary morgues were established at the outset of the rescue operation, one adjacent to the blast site, the other within the MSSG headquarters. As long as there were wounded, little effort was expended on the dead. As the lines of bodies length-ened, as "assorted parts" were collected in gruesome heaps, Maj Doug Redlich had to think about beginning the process of iden-tifying . . . how many? A hundred? More?

It was evident by 0700 that hundreds of bodies were going to be pulled from the rubble, so Redlich ordered the establishment of a central morgue in a Lebanese Air Force hangar adjacent to LS Brown. It appears that the morgue was opened by a MAU staffer. He was joined early by Lt Charles Morrison, a Navy chaplain who arrived on the beach aboard the first helo from *El Paso.* By 0750, 1stLt Leo Lachat, the MSSG Shore Party Platoon commander, had gravitated to it and taken temporary charge. Lachat found it a going concern, with over sixty corpses in residence, all awaiting body bags, which were in desperately short supply.

Cpl Neale Bolen glanced into the hangar at about 0830, as he waited beside LS Brown for a helo bound for *Iwo Jima.* He saw rows of stretchers with men on them, so he grabbed a passerby. "Why are we going first when these guys on the litters are waiting to go?" No answer was given, so Bolen became insistent.

"Hey," the Marine replied, "those guys are dead."

Bolen was rocked back on his heels. "No!" There were rows of bodies as far back into the hangar as he could see.

The gruesome task of staging bodies and parts of bodies, wrapping them in plastic, placing them in body bags, and plac-ing the body bags in aluminum "transfer cases" fell to a core group of dedicated officers and enlisted Marines and rotating crews from virtually every American unit at or near the BIA.

Capt Mike Hagemeyer, the Marine Medium Helicopter Squadron (HMM) 162 embarkation officer, got into the work of ministering to the dead by accident. When work at the MSSG sick bay began petering out late Sunday morning, the twenty-eight-year-old Texan asked permission to take his squadron supply team to LS Brown to help with flight operations. In-formed that the LS was being used as the main mortuary,

Hagemeyer agreed to take care of things there. After helping get the LS up to smooth operating status, Hagemeyer joined Leo Lachat and the volunteers who were laying the dead in the main hangar bay and clearing side rooms to receive additional fatalities.

MSgt Obie Gandy, who had been in charge of Rock Base until Saturday, flew in from *Iwo Jima* with nine other squadron volunteers early Sunday morning. Gandy had left the beach on Saturday, on the last flight out, after turning down an invitation to spend the night with the BLT's senior NCOs, all of whom were killed outright in the bombing. During Obie Gandy's time at the Lebanese Air Force hangar, he found nearly all of his comrades.

There were well over seventy bodies staged at the LAF maintenance hangar beside LS Brown by 1100, Sunday. The heavy flow was really just beginning, for *Iwo Jima* sent back the first of the victims who had succumbed on the way to or aboard the carrier, and impromptu morgues at the MSSG headquarters and around the BLT were cleared as transportation previously reserved for the wounded became available.

The body handlers faced an initial shortage of all types of materials required to care for the dead. No one could have anticipated the magnitude of the tragedy, so there were not nearly enough body bags or aluminum transfer cases in or near Lebanon for the job at hand. What there was was spread through the Mediterranean Amphibious Ready Group and the loads of supplies the MAU had been preparing to backload. Dozens of sailors and Marines did little more than dig out the meager supply of plastic bags and aluminum caskets and see to their shipment to the MSSG aid stations and the Lebanese Air Force hangar. It was not until Sunday evening that an Air Force C-9 arrived with a pallet of body bags.

First Lieutenant Leo Lachat thought that "packing the bodies and parts of bodies in the bags did nothing to hide the destruction. We were still left with row after row of green bags awaiting transfer cases."

The last large load of injured was slated to go out aboard an Air Force C-141 medevac aircraft that landed at the BIA late Sunday. Injured Americans arrived from hospitals throughout Beirut and from *Iwo Jima.* Since there was still ample room aboard the airplane, MSgt Obie Gandy asked the crew to take out as many bodies as he could fit aboard. The request was refused because of regulations forbidding wounded and dead to be mixed unless the dead were in metal transfer cases. None of the dead had yet been placed in the cases, but rather persuasive arguments were brought to bear. At length, the airplane commander swallowed and told Top Gandy, "Okay, I'll take as many as I can." All the wounded were placed in the forward end of the C-141, a canvas curtain was strung, and the body bags were placed in litters. Thus the first fifty American dead left Beirut at about 0430, Monday, for a forensic center that was being set up for them in Germany. Ultimately, every corpse would be assembled, positively identified, and embalmed in that center.

The very next airplane, another Air Force C-141, brought 144 transfer cases, packed sixteen to a pallet. There were no wounded, so the C-141 left empty. The pallets were immediately broken down and all the filled body bags on hand were placed in the aluminum transfer cases. The Helicopter Support Team stacked the cases four wide and four high on aluminum aircraft pallets, then netted and strapped each pallet-load for security and stability in flight.

The 144 transfer cases were loaded aboard a C-141—which had brought in seventy empty transfer cases—at about 1300, Monday. GySgt Warren Clopper, who had just arrived at LS Brown from *Iwo Jima,* stopped to watch the loading. He unconsciously counted the transfer cases and found himself repeating over and over in his head, "Bodies by the gross."

Late Monday night, on a rain-swept runway in Germany, Gen PX Kelley, Commandant of the Marine Corps, left his airplane on arrival from Washington to drive to the nearest American military hospital to visit injured Marines and corpsmen. As Kelley stepped to the runway, he saw another newly landed plane and was drawn to the lights burning brightly within. Aides saw him stop cold at the ramp in the rear of the plane. There, bathed in the lights, were 144 gleaming aluminum transfer cases, each bearing the body of an American serviceman.

Those body handlers who could see it were impressed by the arrival on Tuesday of French President François Mitterand, who stopped in at the Lebanese Air Force hangar after visiting the French MNF headquarters, where nearly fifty of his countrymen had been killed. The French president's entourage, which included numerous security troops and the spiffiest honor guard most Marines had ever seen, was as unobtrusive as possible. President Mitterand drew away from the crowd and strode through the work area, stopping here and there to utter silent prayers or bow his head in grieved silence. The Vice President of the United States, George Bush, arrived after Mitterand left and after he had toured the blast site. He made a quick pass through the hangar and led a long period of silent prayer amid the popping of camera flashes and the glare of movie lights. A short time later, Marines working with the bodies saw General Kelley fight back tears as he toured the hangar.

The activity among the "permanent cadre" at the Lebanese Air Force hangar was so consuming that Capt Mike Hagemeyer and most of the squadron personnel took no time to shave or shower and only minimal time to eat. Top Gandy kept his motor running on thick, strong Turkish coffee provided by the hordes of Lebanese civilians who arrived to pay their respects.

There was a long lull in the work on Tuesday morning, so Mike Hagemeyer asked Father George Pucciarelli to come to the LAF hangar to bless a body bag filled with assorted arms and legs. The entire body-handling operation shut down while the priest chanted his blessing and sprinkled holy water on the green vinyl case. Then every man in the hangar "cried his eyes out."

Finally, on Wednesday, LtCol Jack Cress, the squadron operations officer, ordered Mike Hagemeyer and his team to clear out.

First Lieutenant Leo Lachat remained on duty at the hangar until the last transfer cases were loaded aboard a pair of C-141s on the morning of October 30.

Every member of the MAU who wanted to call home was able to do so within a week of the bombing. There were also incoming calls, which the recipients used to spread the word that they and their comrades were alive and well. First Lieutenant Miles Burdine was called at the embassy early Sunday morning by a college friend who had not yet heard about the bombing. That saved the Burdine family unneeded anxiety. And MSgt Tony DeMonti received a call at MSSG headquarters from his wife, Linda, on Sunday evening. While they spoke of family matters, Marines ran through the building collecting names and phone numbers of next of kin. DeMonti rattled off the names of about forty MSSG personnel and asked his wife to call each of their families with good news. Linda DeMonti got so wrapped up in making mercy calls that she forgot to call her in-laws until she was halfway through the list.

In addition to a few outgoing calls, Lieutenant Burdine took numerous incoming calls at the embassy from families of MAU personnel. He told each of them what he could, which was not much. In one case, a father who had called on one day called back the very next day, only minutes after a casualty assistance officer had told him that his son was dead. The man just wanted to talk to a Marine, and Miles Burdine obliged him.

Many of the next of kin of the dead paid a heavy price in time. Many, many bodies were mangled beyond recognition and could not be immediately identified. Even when a victim could be identified by close friends, he had to be processed and re-processed until there was absolutely no doubt who he was. That took time, and families had to wait. Mistakes were made. In several cases, families were informed that their Marine was alive, then contacted again with news of a death. The opposite happened; one mother had just finished hearing of her son's death when the youngster called to say he had not been hurt. Cpl David Wilcox's mother heard that David was being treated in a hospital in Germany before her other son, Burton, called from Beirut to say that he was okay. In the meantime, Burton had been listed as missing in action. The Giblin family also had two sons in Beirut. Donald, a corporal with Alpha Company, was unhurt, but Tim, a corporal in Headquarters and Service Company, was killed. Donald was sent home to Rhode Island with his brother's remains.

For two solid weeks after the bombing, forensic teams in Germany worked to establish positive identification. They were assisted in large part by a team of dedicated MSSG-24 personnel led by 1stLt Dennis Emperley and MSgt Tony DeMonti. These men spent many emotion-filled days sorting and cataloging the bundles of personal effects salvaged from the building. Since all unit records were lost, the cataloging effort was used to establish a base list of men who might have been in the BLT at the time of the bombing. In a few instances, personal effects found in proximity to an otherwise unidentifiable body were the only clues available for establishing even a tentative identity. (Top DeMonti gazed at enough photos of orphaned children and new widows to last an eternity. He even found an unrecorded wedding certificate dated two days before 24th MAU left the States.)

In the end, 1stLt Greg Balzer, the only BLT staff officer to survive unscathed, and Cpl Joe Martucci and LCpl Bob Calhoun, the forward air control communicators who had been on the BLT roof at the moment of detonation, were flown to Germany in the hope they could identify the last half-dozen bodies. It turned out that they could identify only one, the nearly vaporized thorax and jawbone of an elderly Lebanese man who had habitually slept in the tiny snack concession booth he operated on the ground deck of the BLT building.

The remaining American bodies were identified by extremely sophisticated tissue-identification techniques.

The dispatch of casualty-assistance teams, usually comprising a chaplain and a Marine officer or staff NCO, has long been the tried and true method for informing families that their sons are wounded, dead, or missing and for dealing with immediate grief. No one can be trained well enough to handle every situation or need when the news is given out, but most survivors agree that a personal visit by men in uniform is better than a telegram or phone call.

The most horrid part of the process was the morbid exploitation of Marine and Navy families, mostly by local news media. News crews with lights on and cameras and tape recorders rolling doggedly searched for stories depicting the vigils and moments of truth and relief of MAU families throughout the nation. At Camp Lejeune, North Carolina, where the greatest concentration of wives and families resided, the base command finally placed living quarters off limits to the press. Neighbors and friends of MAU families in surrounding towns banded together to keep the camera teams out of their neighborhoods.

The rest was all politics and finger pointing.

PART IX

Parting Shots

30

Camp Lejeune, North Carolina, home of 2d Marine Division.

The call came at about 0530. LtCol Ed Kelley, the new commander of Battalion Landing Team (BLT) 2/6, was at home, asleep. He answered the phone and was told by his officer of the day that there was "a problem" in Beirut and that the division operations officer was going to call with more information.

This was no mere gossip. BLT 2/6 was the Division Air Alert Battalion. It had been held in readiness for months to mount out on short notice to virtually anywhere in the world. No air alert battalion had ever before flown to a real crisis, but Ed Kelley was ready to go, having spent months fine-tuning his BLT's readiness procedures. Ironically, 2/6 was to be relieved of the air-alert duty in only three days.

Kelley ordered the lieutenant to begin recalling the battalion —everyone who was at home, and everyone who was away from home. As soon as he got up, he turned on his television and watched, incredulous, the early reports reaching the American home audience. He dressed and headed for his office to begin final preparations. Company commanders and members of the battalion staff had already arrived, so he put them to work while he headed up to Division for his first briefing. The first message from 24th Marine Amphibious Unit (MAU) indicated that Col Tim Geraghty needed a complete battalion headquarters, with attachments, most of a weapons company, and a rifle company. This was Ed Kelley's first inkling that the battalion staff in Beirut had been destroyed.

Lt Ray Michener, the battalion chaplain, a veteran of the spring deployment in The Root, received his call at about 0700. It was the assistant division chaplain with orders to prepare to undertake casualty assistance calls. Michener had not yet received a call from Battalion, so he had no idea what the senior chaplain was talking about. He immediately turned on the television and watched a few moments of incoming news until the phone rang again. It was Danny Wheeler's wife, who wanted to know if her husband could have been hurt. Ray Michener had no idea, but he tried to reassure her. Minutes later, Michener saw a film of the building and was horrified. He left his house for the BLT command post, certain that Danny Wheeler had died.

Though fewer than half the officers who had been to Beirut with BLT 2/6 remained in the unit, Lieutenant Colonel Kelley was able to piece together a virtually precise picture of what needed to be replaced. The bulk of the list was written by Maj G.K. Cunningham, a former rifle-company commander, now the battalion S-3. Division blessed the list as soon as it was submitted, and the platoons and sections needed to fill out a battalion landing team headquarters were turned over to Ed Kelley.

While Lieutenant Colonel Kelly and Major Cunningham were putting together the pieces, other BLT officers, with a big hand from Division, were redrawing the load plans. It had always been

anticipated that the Air Alert Battalion would first send a reinforced rifle company, then follow with more combat components and, finally, the BLT headquarters. BLT 2/6 was going
out backward, headquarters first, then at least one rifle company. Since Colonel Geraghty's request and Division's orders
stipulated that the *entire* headquarters was needed, the rump of
the battalion would have to fend for itself.

The Word about departure times shifted as the hours passed.
Division seemed to want to get Kelley on the road by 1600
hours; he led Headquarters and Service and Echo companies
out of the battalion parking lot at 1400. The convoy drove the
fifty miles to the Marine Corps Air Station at Cherry Point,
North Carolina, where the Alpha command element immediately loaded itself aboard four C-141 transports, command jeeps
and all.

No information of any sort reached Ed Kelley on the long first
leg of the flight, which took him to Frankfurt, Germany. Once
on the ground, while the airplanes were being refueled, Kelley
learned that Echo Company had been held up at Cherry Point,
but he did not learn why. (There was no real reason; the company was just held up, which caused all the troops to think that
they had been had by a phony weekend alert only three days
before their scheduled stand-down.) Kelley and his key staffers
tracked down several intelligence officers from the Military Air-
lift Command and received a sketchy update on the Beirut situation. Someone found a photograph of the shattered BLT building in the morning's issue of *Stars and Stripes.* No one could say
for certain if Beirut International Airport (BIA) was secure, or
if the landing there would be routine or "hot." Then it was off
again.

The C-141s began their final approach to the BIA at about
1800, October 24, less than thirty-six hours after the bombing,
excellent time given the distances involved and the very little
useful information the battalion headquarters had received.

Ed Kelley and his sergeant major were able to watch the

approach through windows in the rear of the cargo deck. They could easily spot tracer flying across the Shouf and throughout Khalde and other areas near the BIA. The pent-up excitement, the noise of the jet engines backing, and the pitted condition of the runway all combined to convince everyone in the first four C-141s that they were landing under fire.

The huge rear cargo ramp dropped and the command radio jeeps drove out onto the runway, where they were met by Col Tim Geraghty and the brand-new U.S. ambassador to Lebanon, Reginald Bartholomew. Ed Kelley knew Tim Geraghty from numerous encounters at Camp Lejeune. He found the MAU commander's demeanor essentially unimpaired by the traumatic events of the preceding day and a half.

Colonel Geraghty drove Lieutenant Colonel Kelley and Major Cunningham past the blast site and a neighboring building that was to serve as the temporary battalion headquarters and wound up at MAU headquarters, where the three discussed conditions at the BIA. As soon as the briefing was concluded, the new staff went to work collecting the strings, meeting with MAU and MAU Service and Support Group (MSSG) staffers and surviving BLT 1/8 headquarters people. A new battalion combat operations center was installed in the protected basement of the temporary BLT headquarters building even while work details were clearing junk from the compartment. The Bravo command element arrived early in the morning, and the new arrivals joined in the rush to reconstitute the BLT headquarters. It was only midmorning when Ed Kelley went up to MAU and told Colonel Geraghty, "I'm ready." He was named BLT 1/8's new commander.

Ed Kelley met with Capts Paul Roy, Monte Hoover, Chris Cowdrey, and Bob Funk, among others, at the first opportunity on October 25. The new staff had brought the BLT 2/6 colors, but they were never unsheathed. Ed Kelley announced to his ground unit commanders that Headquarters and Service Company 2/6 had simply been redesignated Headquarters and Service Company 1/8. This was a crucial decision, made on behalf of the shocked and grieved survivors, who had clung to little more than unit identity in the wake of the tragedy that had taken nearly one-fourth of their comrades.

The new staffers took immediate control and set out to win the confidence of the remainder of the battalion. The new battalion adjutant was 1stLt Bill Leftwich, who had been one of the first officers to arrive at the bombed American embassy in April and the first embassy guard-detachment commander. Leftwich went right to work piecing together battalion rosters, identifying by one means or another who had been lost and who was left. It also fell to him to oversee the collection of personal effects pulled from the rubble, though the actual work was handled by MSSG-24. Leftwich became so engrossed in his work that he nearly failed to notice visits by both Vice President Bush and the Commandant of the Marine Corps.

The new battalion S-2 spent sleepless days and nights piecing together events of the past weeks and patching them to the constant accumulation of new materials. Maj G.K. Cunningham, the new S-3, had to mesh what he had learned as a company commander with the new tactical situation, and he had to impose his methods upon the combat unit commanders and learn their personal strengths and weaknesses. The new battalion S-4 had to inventory everything BLT 1/8 owned and replace everything that was missing, a monumental job. His staff logistician was given the task of reestablishing the battalion galley and serving hot meals.

Chaplain Ray Michener also went right to work. He first checked in with Father George Pucciarelli beside the BLT building, where the priest was administering last rites to each body as it was freed from the rubble. Rabbi Arnie Resnicoff and Chaplain Charles Morrison were also on hand, ministering to the victims, so Michener assigned himself to overseeing the spiritual needs of the combat troops. He spent long hours daily touring the line companies, walking and talking with Marines and sailors of all faiths who had things they wanted to get off their chests or straight in their minds. Neither Ray Michener nor the troops knew it yet, but the serious emotional problems they thought they had evaded would begin in a few weeks, during the idle float home. For the time being, everyone was too busy to let down.

There was no escaping the reality. BLT 1/8 had had a great hole torn out from where its heart and brain had resided, and the graft would take time to merge with the body. Since there really was no time, and because Marines are, first and foremost, disciplined and obedient, Ed Kelley's word became law from the moment he assumed command of the BLT. The few men privileged to command Marine rifle battalions are so highly rated by Marines of all ranks and stations that Kelley was accepted, though not yet rated, with neither qualm nor question.

The new BLT commander looked at the tactical layout and went to work bringing things up to snuff in the face of new realities. He learned that Charlie Battery was occupying a frontline position on the northwest edge of the BIA because, in the early days, the batteries had filled in as BLT 2/8's and BLT 3/8's fourth rifle companies (which had been slashed a few years before because of manpower shortages). No one had bothered shifting the batteries to safer, more secure locations after Col Tom Stokes had brought the howitzers ashore. The need to keep Charlie Battery in frontline positions was obviated when Echo Company 2/6 arrived, so the battery was moved to a new site down the beach. Charlie Company was relieved by Echo and moved up into the old battery location. Kelley also learned that the Lebanese University had first been manned to provide an American buffer between the Israelis and the then-helpless Shiites in Hooterville. Now the Israelis were gone and the Shiites were hostile. The risk was no longer warranted. Kelley received permission to close the company outpost at the Lebanese University and withdraw Alpha Company.

One of the new arrivals who had not been requested by the new BLT staff was Capt Joe Peagler, the new commander of Charlie Company, 2d Combat Engineer Battalion. Peagler's 1st Platoon, which he had never seen, had been destroyed in the bombing. He had pulled a few strings and won a place on one of the C-141s that carried Headquarters and Service Company 2/6 to the BIA, but no one had taken the time to tell Lieutenant Colonel Kelley; there had been no time.

On arrival at the BIA, Joe Peagler had to make himself and his presence known to Lieutenant Colonel Kelley and find useful work for himself. He had it in mind to build formidable defenses and bunkers, but Ed Kelley was initially more interested in securing the BLT, MSSG, and MAU compounds, so he turned local security over to Peagler until he had the time to discuss fortifications. Peagler was disappointed at being shunted aside, but he attacked his new job with alacrity. In time, when a platoon of Golf Company 2/6 arrived to assume the task of securing the command compound, Joe Peagler assayed his slim resources and submitted a detailed plan for fortifying the MAU positions at the BIA. There were still objections from the Department of State, but the military hierarchy authorized the fortification of the BIA—though no additional engineers were committed, nor were any materials forthcoming.

Initially, Captain Peagler had to settle for ringing the BLT, MSSG, and MAU compounds with huge earthen berms (which were constantly washed away by winter rains) and constructing several steel gates across roads within the compound. Later, Peagler designed movable concrete barriers, which were built by the Oger-Liban Company. He also designed and built near the beach a secure command bunker for the BLT, and installed quickie personnel bunkers around buried commercial cargo containers purloined from the moribund Port of Beirut. (Most of the containers had Soviet-bloc markings; their theft made the Marines feel good, though documenting it created a flurry of paperwork for the State Department.)

For all the concern shown by new staffers to the feelings of BLT 1/8 Marines, there were several clods among the new arrivals who insisted upon exhibiting attitudes of superiority.

HM3 Steve Brown was on duty at the MSSG-24 sick bay when a newly arrived lance corporal had to have a split lip sutured. When the job was done, Brown learned that the laceration had been acquired only after the Marine had announced to old hands that "2/6 came to save your asses because you people fucked up." Brown wished he had known this before he sutured the lip—when there had been an opportunity to sew the man's mouth shut. Other, similar, incidents provoked similar altercations.

If there was one positive thought to which all the survivors of 24th MAU had clung, it was the knowledge that a new 22d MAU would arrive in early November, that 24th MAU was going home. That comfort was stripped away when news arrived, almost on the heels of the bombing, that 22d MAU had been diverted to Grenada and that the relief had been indefinitely postponed.

The Marines of BLT 1/8 had two thoughts about Grenada. First, many were convinced that the operation had been planned specifically to delay their departure from Beirut. Second, and stronger, was the sheer envy every Marine in Beirut felt for his counterpart on Grenada. The most wearing aspect of the September War had been the need to sit and take more than they could dole out, to defend the BIA when every man wanted to attack Hooterville, Khalde, and the Shouf. There was never a clearer example, they agreed, of adding insult to injury—for Grenada, a walk-through as it turned out, was considered legitimate combat, while the "presence" war in The Root was not.

For all the ministrations of the new battalion staff, BLT 1/8 had to heal its own wounds.

Second Lieutenant Dave Hough, for one, went out of his way to get his troops out of their funk. He had taken to reading a series of adventure books about a character named Mack Bolan, a fictional superman fighting "Commie" evil. In a move calculated to raise the moral of his troops, Hough soon took on the persona of the fictional hero, even encouraging the troops to call him "Mack Bolan" behind his back. Hough stalked the southern BIA lines with neither helmet nor flak jacket, and responded jokingly to his concerned but understanding superiors' instructions to don the proper attire with the standard plaint that "Mack Bolan wouldn't wear those things." In one memorable incident, the usually squared-away lieutenant emerged from his tent in disgraceful condition: T-shirt partway in and partway out of his trousers, trouser legs unbloused, and shoelaces untied. He also had a pistol in one hand and a K-bar knife in the other. As his incredulous troops looked on, Hough jumped to the top of an exposed berm and yelled across the way to a covey of active snipers in Khalde, "Hey, Muhammed, your father's a Christian!" It was a crude joke, but also a display of effective, affectionate leadership. It got the troops' minds off their problems.

The finest example of self-help came one night during the first week of November, when three Charlie Company machine gunners took unauthorized leave to remove a Shiite battle flag from an Amal command bunker.

Fighting around Beirut ebbed and flared during the last week of October as warring Lebanese factions neared completion of negotiations aimed at convening a national reconciliation conference. Marines on the line bore the brunt of much of the

407

fighting and were even directly threatened in bellicose broadcasts from Damascus, which was jockeying for position behind the Shiite and Druse factions. The most ironic of all developments in Arab-versus-Arab fighting in Lebanon was the bifurcation of the Palestine Liberation Organization (PLO). Syrian-backed PLO fighters opened a side war in Tripoli aimed at unseating Yasir Arafat as chairman of the terrorist organization. Hundreds of fighters—including, no doubt, many who had been saved from the Israelis by American intervention a year earlier—and more hundreds of Lebanese civilians were fated to die in the intramural bloodbaths.

All the Marines wanted to "get some." Whenever possible, young Americans—and some older ones—dispensed with the Rules of Engagement. Many militia fighters died that last week of October 1983, convinced to the end that Americans would not fight back.

31

Capt Paul Roy's Alpha Company was scheduled to pull out of its positions at the Lebanese University on the evening of November 7, 1983, about a week ahead of the scheduled relief of 24th Marine Amphibious Unit (MAU) by the victors of Grenada, 22d MAU. LtCol Ed Kelley had won his argument that the university outpost was superfluous and that Roy's company could better serve as a needed reserve while aboard its transport.

In the morning, Paul Roy left the university with a convoy—three jeeps and two trucks—and drove by a circuitous route to the new Battalion Landing Team (BLT) headquarters to get the latest intell and plan the withdrawal of his company from Green Beach. Roy started back to his company at 1400 via West Beirut, East Beirut, and Baabda, a long way out of the way but a proven safe route.

Roy still had four miles to go and had just picked up communications with the company combat operations center (COC) when LCpl Shawn Gallagher, manning the stanchion-mounted M-60 in the rear jeep, heard a round *crack* over the vehicle.

"What the fuck?"

Another round passed beside Gallagher's ear, then a whole burst. The driver floored it.

It was business as usual for the Surveillance and Target Acquisition (STA) Platoon snipers manning the rooftop bunker.

There had been minor skirmishes over the preceding two weeks, but this day looked like it was going to end with a real bang. For reasons none but the cynics could fathom, it seemed that the militias were preparing a going-away party for Alpha Company. Well over 100 militia fighters had been counted as they moved into position during the afternoon. Marines on the roof, in the Moat, and at outposts around the library had watched the militias install new heavy-machine-gun bunkers through the day.

Cpl Lee Norton was keeping an eye on things when he saw several militiamen man a newly installed .50-caliber machine gun. "Looks like trouble," he warned. "When I say duck, duck."

Norton saw a puff of smoke. "Duck!"

Militia fighters all around the library opened fire. The snipers reported in to the COC. The Alpha Company exec, 1stLt Ron Baczkowski, who was in the Moat, had the snipers and Alpha Company riflemen go to work on the perpetrators.

The convoy was closing on the university when Captain Roy was cautioned that the bulk of the company was receiving light fire from militia positions to the south, east, and northeast. He ordered the vehicles to speed up and soon reached the entryway to the company position, about a quarter mile west of the library. That was as far as Roy could get because of heavy fire sweeping the open areas between himself and the company.

As soon as the tail jeep rolled to a stop, Lance Corporal

Gallagher grabbed his M-60 and hit the dirt looking for targets. The others deployed to the front and flanks.

Captain Roy maintained communications with the company COC via his convoy's squad radio. He offered what suggestions he could, but the fight would have to be run by Lieutenant Baczkowski, who was in the Moat, with an assist from 1stLt Pete Ferraro, at the COC.

Despite the outside threat, Alpha Company maintained its normal deployment: Ferraro's 3d Platoon was manning five isolated squad and fire-team outposts spread all around the library building; 1stLt Andy May's 1st Platoon was in the Moat; 1stLt Brent Smith's 2d Platoon, the company reaction force, was in the stacks, off duty, resting, alert to reinforce as required.

First Platoon kept its cool. As the militia positions doing the firing were positively identified, Marines in the Moat countered with precise bursts, neither allowing the militia fighters to gain the upper hand nor raising the ante. All the troops wanted to leave in one piece. Many felt that they should use this last opportunity to get even, but others were willing to let bygones be bygones if the spreading fight quickly abated.

As Captain Roy saw the fight spreading, he ran to the nearby Lebanese Armed Forces (LAF) position and requested support in the form of tanks, jeep-mounted 106mm recoilless rifles, and .50-caliber machine guns mounted on armored personnel carriers. The LAF commander gladly complied. Roy pointed out friendly positions and indicated which specific targets he needed taken out by the LAF weapons.

The first two LAF tanks rolled out behind Lance Corporal Gallagher, who had moved to the center of the roadway and deployed his M-60 to cover the convoy's rear. Gallagher had been wounded less than a month before, on the night Mike Ohler was killed, and he was petrified of being hit again. He was so intent upon guarding the convoy's rear that he heard and saw nothing until the LAF tank gunners fired.

411

"BOOM! BOOM!"

"Hah!" Gallagher was lifted right off the ground when his body went rigid with fright.

While Alpha Company's 60mm mortars fired illume, the Lebanese placed heavy fire from the south and east against Amal positions to the northeast. When fire from the east threatened Roy's isolated convoy, a call to the LAF commander produced a mobile strike force, which fired with telling effect.

The five outposts were all extremely close to the Moslem fighting positions, which allowed Marines to pop off M-16 and M-203 rounds at extremely short ranges with telling accuracy. Because the outposts were between the main body of the company and the opposing lines, the troops in the Moat had to adhere strictly to carefully maintained fire zones in order to avoid hitting friendly troops. It took a little hitting power away from the main body, but the success of the system pointed up Alpha Company's superb fire discipline. However, the LAF units supporting Alpha Company recognized no such safety zones, which caused no end of concern for the Marine troop leaders and no end of consternation among the troops manning the outposts.

The three-man 3d Platoon fire team manning Post 2, located beneath a railroad trestle in the southeast quadrant of the company sector, had been out since noon, monitoring Moslem activity and answering frequent requests for activity reports.

As soon as the firing began, LCpl Dan Kovach sent his M-203 gunner, Pfc Terry Wells, to man a position on the railroad embankment while he and LCpl Gregory Wah manned positions beneath the trestle. LAF soldiers occupying an adjacent position also prepared to return fire with their machine gun, rifles, and rocket-propelled grenades (RPGs).

Kovach's main concern was an Amal checkpoint the Marines had tagged Target 7, an apt enough description in Marine eyes. The Amal position comprised a horseshoe-shaped bunker mounting a pair of .50-caliber machine guns. Amal warriors manning the bunker and outlying positions fired numerous RPGs at Post 2 and over it at the library building.

Lance Corporals Wah and Kovach spent most of the first hour hunkered down behind the chest-high sandbag wall of their bunker beneath the railroad trestle. They popped up to return fire whenever there was a lull, but that was rare. Wah was kneeling to talk on the radio, which was protected by a steel grate pilfered from a storm sewer, when sheets of 7.62mm rounds fired from a building about 100 meters away struck the grate. One round ricocheted into Wah's knee and he collapsed to the ground, writhing in agony. Kovach treated the wound with a pressure bandage, gave Wah the radio, and covered him with sandbags to protect him from ricochets.

As the hours passed, the bunker was hit by RPGs and so many 7.62mm and .50-caliber rounds that the sandbag wall drooped from chest-level to somewhere below Kovach's knees.

Private First Class Wells responded with a total of eighteen M-203 high-explosive (HE) rounds, all of which were observed to be on target. He also fired several LAAWs, which were also on target. But the Amal fire was massive. Target 6, a checkpoint located about 200 meters straight down the railroad tracks, poured heavy machine-gun fire right into the Marine bunker. Wells stood tall between streams of incoming to locate the source of the fire, then silenced Target 6 with three LAAWs.

Target 7 immediately started up again, but all the M-203 HE was gone. Lance Corporal Kovach called the COC and said that he would be forced to abandon Post 2 if he did not get some help right away. It took only a few moments to hit Target 7 with a salvo of 60mm HE followed by illume and Willy-Peter (white phosphorus).

Target 7 burned to a cinder, but bunkers from which the Marines had never before heard took up the slack. Kovach and Wah plotted the targets they could see, but not nearly all of them.

Since Captain Roy was still kept from the library by the intense incoming, the brunt of controlling the fight fell upon Lieutenant Baczkowski, who was in direct touch with Captain Roy, via a squad radio. The COC watch officer, Lieutenant Ferraro, who had a more powerful radio at his disposal, acted as an interface between higher authority and the fighting units. As soon as the heavy fighting erupted, Lieutenant Smith, whose 2d Platoon was standing down, arrived to help with the heavy message traffic. Battalion wanted to know exactly what was going on as it was happening, so Ferraro had to keep up a running commentary. He and Smith also had to impose on their fellow officers and their subordinates to provide fresh information. Since everyone involved in the fight was busy, the COC's constant interruptions brought forth some fairly emotional comments. Neither Ferraro nor Smith took offense; they had been on the receiving end on countless nights since late August. There was also a great deal of pressure from above, because the only way Captain Roy could communicate with Battalion, and vice versa, was through the COC.

Ferraro received an unprecedented offer from Battalion. LtCol Ed Kelley asked if Alpha Company wanted 81mm mortar support. The 81s had been requested by all the companies as a matter of form since late August, but had been infrequently fired; even then, they put out little more than illume. Ferraro passed the word to Captain Roy, who said he did not want the support until he knew that Alpha Company could not rid itself of targets with the weapons it had on hand.

Ferraro told Kelley, "Be advised that our actual says 'No.' We'll use our own 60s."

"Let me speak to your actual."

"Be advised he's not here."

"Well, how can he say you can't use them if he's not there?"

None of the Alpha Company officers was about to go along with firing the 81s if Captain Roy did not want to use them.

Kelley could see the fight, but he was several miles away. He was deeply concerned, but he well knew that there was no way he could run the fight in detail. Still, he could not quite understand that Roy was interested in pinpoint accuracy from explosives with small bursting radii—60mm mortar and 40mm M-203 rounds. Roy told the COC that he felt any slipups could result in friendly casualties at the five tiny posts nearest the Moslem bunkers. At that point 1stLt Brent Smith volunteered to climb to the rooftop bunker to adjust the proffered 81mm fire, but Captain Roy came up on the company tac net: "Stay right where you are!"

Still, Roy was not about to close the door. He requested that the 81mm mortars be laid on selected targets and held "on call." Kelley complied with the request. The company's 81 forward observer plotted potential targets and the 81mm gun line was manned and ready to put out rounds. The issue did not die during the ensuing hours; Battalion kept coming back with appeals that Alpha use the 81s and Alpha kept refusing. Kelley finally gave it up, telling Roy to do what he thought needed doing. This certainly suited Roy, who was repeatedly assured by his company officers and his own observations that Alpha Company was maintaining fire superiority over the militia bunkers and, more importantly, that the five outposts close to the Moslem positions were in no immediate danger of being overwhelmed.

Following the rebuff of his offer to spot for the mortars, 1stLt Brent Smith decided to move up to the Moat to help Lieutenants May and Baczkowski run the fight. He got as far as the outside exit, but was stopped by the sheer volume of bullets caroming through the concrete ditch. RPGs were flying every which way, detonating beside the Moat and against the LAF-occupied building next door. Smith headed back to the COC.

As the fight wound on into the evening, Battalion came up on the net with news relayed from MAU. It appeared that Alpha Company had become embroiled in a fight between Druse and

Amal factions, which had agreed between themselves to begin a truce at 1730. If Alpha Company stopped firing on time, the aggressor forces would likewise stop firing. Captain Roy ordered the company to comply. The outgoing fire was switched off on time, but the incoming did not abate one iota. Roy was patient, but only until it seemed that the opposing forces were about to gain fire superiority. He ordered the company to pull out the plug.

Another hour passed, then Battalion claimed that the Druse and Amal militia commanders were meeting to work out another truce. Roy was to cease firing at 2000, at which point the Moslem factions would also shut it off.

It was coming up to the appointed hour when most of the incoming stopped. There was still sporadic fire from all major Moslem fighting positions, but not much.

First Lieutenant Smith's 2d Platoon, which was about due to "get some," thundered into the Moat to relieve First Lieutenant May's 1st Platoon, which was about due for a respite. No one had any doubt but that Alpha Company had weathered its most intense fight of the deployment. And the night was still young. Rain started falling as soon as 2d Platoon moved into the open. The cold, wet torrents quickly translated to cold, knee-deep water throughout the Moat.

As soon as the lull seemed to take, Captain Roy checked in with Battalion and was ordered to withdraw the company as scheduled. Sufficient trucks from the MSSG-24 Truck Platoon were ready to rush to the library compound to collect all the troops and all the company's equipment. Roy was not the sort of man to disobey an order, but he was not shy about airing his views about an order he considered, at best, imprudent. He was faced with withdrawing troops from the company line to prepare for the move and, once that was done, exposing the company and the truckers to the whims and mercies of militia commanders he thought were barely rational beings. Battalion told him to withdraw.

Alpha Company began staging its gear by 2200, many hours late. Collecting ammunition and other supplies that had to be kept from Moslem hands was grueling, and made more so because most of the troops had to remain in fighting positions while diminished details hauled out gear that had been accumulating in the building for a year. One of the truly frustrating glitches involved getting the company's portable shower unit from the deepest part of the underground library stacks to the surface. It was a mean task that would not go right. Many of the troops were in favor of just blowing the unit to pieces, but Captain Roy was not one of them. As long as the trucks had not yet arrived, Roy was content to work on the shower unit. If the unit was not out by the time the trucks showed up, he would play it by ear.

First Lieutenant Dave Gillespie's MSSG Truck Platoon arrived on schedule. Unfortunately, two of the trucks had flat tires and a third had a cracked oil pan. Gillespie had foreseen the possibility of breakdowns, so he had brought along an extra truck and a wrecker. The flats could be fixed, but the cracked oil pan could not. That took out the spare truck and the wrecker before Alpha Company even got moving, and the repair job delayed the departure by a considerable margin.

The steady downpour did not help the loading, but it no doubt affected the will of the militias to fight and masked the Marine departure and the LAF takeover of the library building.

The outposts were pulled in beginning at 0100, when Lance Corporal Wah, the company's only casualty, was yanked from Post 2. The post itself was abandoned at 0120.

The Alpha Company convoy hit the road after 0300.

Night discipline required that truck lights be doused. The rain, the dark, the winding streets, and the circuitous route were especially wearing on the drivers. It was not until Captain Roy stopped at the first prearranged checkpoint that he discovered that the tail of the column had gone astray or dropped behind. The company commander was not overly perturbed because Lieutenant Baczkowski, who had been over the route many times, was riding drag. Both sections had ample combat power, so Roy decided to keep going. What Roy did not know was that the tail half of the column had become fragmented into several smaller groupings of trucks and jeeps. One section under GySgt Lewis Butler was stopped in a built-up area by troops manning an LAF checkpoint. The Marines were all locked and loaded, ready to do harm, and the streets were soon filled with curious residents. The Marines just sat for forty minutes, then proceeded without incident. Lieutenant Smith's section of two trucks and a jeep ran the entire route without encountering any other Marine-laden vehicles.

As soon as Paul Roy's element nosed into a French-controlled area of Christian East Beirut, the second truck blew a tire on loose debris. The column was ordered to a halt and all hands deployed in alleyways and streets ringing the stalled vehicle. The minute the new tire was secured, Ron Baczkowski rolled up with the largest of the missing sections of the convoy.

All of Alpha Company reached the new BLT command bunker by 0500, an hour late. Captain Roy's jeep passed Lieutenant Colonel Kelley's jeep, which was just leaving to meet the convoy. Roy ordered his driver to stop, then he jumped to the roadway and ran to meet the battalion commander. He expected to get chewed out over the 81mm mortar flap. Ed Kelley was standing tall, waiting with a bright smile on his face. He threw his arm across Roy's shoulders and said, "Well done!" Alpha Company had weathered its last awful night in The Root with but one Marine wounded. Roy started to state his case about the mortars, but Kelley cut him off: "No problem. I know you guys had control."

Alpha Company's ammunition-expenditure count for the

night listed over 100 rounds of 60mm HE, Willy-Peter, and illume; well over 2,000 .50-caliber machine-gun rounds; 35 LAAWs; many thousands of 5.56mm M-16 rounds; many thousands of 7.62mm M-60 machine-gun rounds; and nearly 100 rounds of M-203 HE and illume.

As soon as Alpha Company reached Green Beach, orders came down for all hands to turn in their ordnance. The company waited on the beach for about thirty minutes, then was carried to *Harlan County,* where everyone started to unwind. Immediately, the company officers ran an inspection to see that all ammunition had been turned in on the beach. Naturally, few of their combat veterans were found to be without the means to defend themselves. And, naturally, the officers could have repeatedly shaken down the troops without coming close to getting all the contraband.

"I can't describe the feeling of getting aboard that safe ship," 1stLt Brent Smith said. "I knew I had done something that no one could ever take away. I was really proud, and my Marines were proud."

Smith headed straight for his rack and immediately dropped into the soundest sleep he had experienced since May.

Epilogue

Col Tim Geraghty's 24th Marine Amphibious Unit (MAU) was relieved by 22d MAU on November 18, 1983. By that time, Beirut International Airport (BIA) was a prairie-dog town covered with Capt Joe Peagler's budget bunkers. In subsequent weeks, 22d MAU went underground to the point that combat-post reliefs often walked erect through covered bombproof trenches. By that time, also, the United States and Syria were embroiled in a mutually undeclared war neither side attempted to hide from public view.

The direct Syrian-American confrontations began on November 11, when Syrian SAM-5 surface-to-air missiles were launched against four U.S. Navy fighter-bombers conducting reconnaissance missions over the Shouf. Navy warplanes continued to fly their missions over succeeding days, and the Syrians continued to fire their SAMs without effect.

The Israeli Air Force blew away an Iranian training camp in Baalbek following the bombing of the Israel Defense Force regional headquarters in southern Lebanon. French warplanes struck another Iranian camp a few days later in retaliation for the bombing of their Multinational Force (MNF) headquarters on October 23. The United States carried out no known direct reprisals for the battalion headquarters bombing.

Truces came and truces went. A major American air strike on December 4 against Syrian positions in the Shouf resulted in the loss of two American fighter-bombers, the death of one pilot, Lt Mark Lange, and the capture of Lt Robert Goodman. On the same day, Druse gunners scored a direct hit on Combat Post 76, killing eight Marines and wounding two. Numerous Syrians and Lebanese were killed when the battleship *New Jersey* retaliated by firing her 14-inch naval rifles into the Shouf. Arab extremists, including the regime of Hafez al-Assad, publicly threatened to sink the battleship through terrorist action. Shellings and bombings by American warships and aircraft continued into the new year.

Twenty-fourth MAU arrived at Morehead City, North Carolina, on December 7, and was met by hundreds of cheering relatives and friends. The forty-mile route to Camp Lejeune was lined with cheering onlookers. This was possibly the first time since the end of World War II that approving citizens cheered in public a large group of returning American combat veterans.

Yasir Arafat was driven from the Palestine Liberation Organization (PLO) base at Tripoli by PLO contingents controlled and supported by Syria.

On December 15, President Reagan began dropping hints that his administration was ready to withdraw Marines from Lebanon. He made it seem like a new idea. On December 21, the President said, firmly, that the Marines would remain in Beirut unless "the Lebanese government no longer wants them there." Next day, only fifteen months after Battalion Landing Team (BLT) 2/8 had occupied the BIA, Reagan administration spokesmen said that they would soon "clarify" the role of the Marines in Lebanon. On December 30, the Lebanese ambassador to the United States followed the White House's lead by saying that the government of Lebanon wished it had never invited Marines into Lebanon. He then stated that his government probably would have fallen without the Marine presence.

Italy halved the size of its MNF contingent on January 1, 1984, and the Reagan administration announced on January 5 that "early troop withdrawals" were a distinct possibility.

On January 8, Cpl Joseph Gargano was killed by a rocket-propelled grenade as he participated in a troop rotation near the British embassy.

On January 12, after months of work, U.S. Senator Charles Percy announced that he had prevailed upon military authorities to reclassify American service fatalities in Beirut as "combat-related" rather than "nonbattle" and "accidental."

On January 31, LCpl George Dramis, aged nineteen, was shot to death during the course of day-long battles with Amal fighters around Hooterville. Two other Marines were wounded and evacuated in serious condition to Germany.

On February 8, President Reagan announced that 22d MAU would be withdrawn to its ships, which would continue to ply the waters off Beirut.

The decision to pull Marines out of the BIA chiefly resulted from strong congressional disapproval, the inability of the Reagan administration to articulate a cogent or consistent policy, and the growing incredulity of the American electorate at the start of an election year. A contributing factor was the self-destruction of the Lebanese Armed Forces (LAF), which, by February 8, was down to about 40 percent of its authorized strength, the balance of its soldiers having gone home or deserted to the Moslem militias. Most LAF units that had not simply melted away opted to remain in their barracks while the militias moved to secure all of West Beirut and the Moslem suburbs.

Also on February 8, the 115-man British MNF contingent was

completely withdrawn, and the Italian government announced plans for a "gradual" withdrawal of the remainder of its MNF contingent. Finally, on that same day, LCpl Rodolfo Hernandez died in Germany of wounds he sustained on January 31.

On February 9, Secretary of Defense Caspar Weinberger ordered that mild "nonpunitive letters of instruction" be issued to Col Tim Geraghty and LtCol Larry Gerlach. Geraghty's letter was eventually delivered by MGen Al Gray, and Gerlach's was delivered to his bedside at a Boston Veterans Administration hospital. When the letter arrived, Larry Gerlach was virtually a quadriplegic whose ears were still ringing from the blast and whose vision was unfocused because the bones stabilizing one of his eyes had not yet healed in place. Most 24th MAU veterans took the reprimand of their leaders as a personal insult.

On the day of Weinberger's announcement, Maj Albert Butler accidentally shot himself in the chest while cleaning his pistol in a BIA bunker. He died before help arrived.

Heavy fighting in Beirut killed scores of Lebanese. Scores of American and European nationals were evacuated to American ships under Marine escort throughout the balance of the week.

On February 15, Druse ground units swept down from the Shouf and cut through the LAF to occupy combat posts on the beach just south of the BIA. American warships continued to support the moribund LAF—or just get even—by pounding forces dubbed "antigovernment."

On February 17, President Amin Gemayal did the one thing Syria had wanted him to do from the start; he revoked the peace accord with Israel he had signed on May 17, 1983, at the insistence of the United States. This was the price he paid to remain president of his fragmented, tortured nation. If there were to be a peace in Lebanon, it would be a Syrian peace.

The last 1,200 Italian MNF troops turned over checkpoints to Shiite militiamen and completed their "gradual" withdrawal in one day, February 20. On the same day, the Israeli air force launched significant strikes against targets all along the Beirut-

Damascus highway. And, finally, a large portion of 22d MAU withdrew from the BIA via Green Beach.

President Reagan told reporters on February 22 that the American presence in Beirut had, from the start, been an effort to "prevent a war between Syria and Israel"—the first time that sentiment was ever revealed in that context, but not the last. This logically tortured newspeak statement was to become the official, retroactive administration rationale for the entire Lebanon adventure. (It was repeated, word for word, by Robert McFarlane on the "McNeil-Lehrer News Hour" as late as mid-September 1984, when McFarlane was asked to explain to American voters the reasons for the U.S. involvement in Lebanon.)

The last Marine of 22d MAU left Green Beach at 1237 hours, Monday, February 27, 1984. A 100-man security detachment from the MAU remained at the American embassy to supplement the Marine security guard. Amal gunmen moved cautiously into the underground bunker complex abandoned by the Marines, certain the Americans had booby-trapped the area. Once the final Marine amtrac was clear of the beach, American warships, including *New Jersey,* fired on targets in the Shouf.

The last 22d MAU Marines left the embassy in late August 1984. Less than a month later, on September 20, 1984, Moslem terrorists drove an explosives-laden truck into the new American embassy annex in Yardze and killed eight, including two American servicemen. The U.S. ambassador to Lebanon, Reginald Bartholomew, was injured in the blast along with the British ambassador and several other people. It appears the bomb was detonated after both drivers of the bomb-laden vehicle had been shot to death. The new Mediterranean Amphibious Ready Group—which happened to include BLT 1/8 and MSSG-24, back for an "uneventful" float—was dispatched to Lebanese waters.

On October 23, 1984, Ronald Reagan did *not* attend any of

the numerous memorial or commemorative ceremonies honoring the nearly 300 American servicemen who died in Beirut.

There is no consensus among the 200 participants who contributed their recollections to this book concerning what the adventure in Lebanon was about or for.

When they were asked, "How do you feel about it?" most of the members of 24th MAU who submitted to interviews for this book said, like 1stLt Brent Smith, "I am proud of what I did." But when they were then asked, "What, exactly, are you proud of?" they said again what Brent Smith said, that they are proud of having weathered combat. Their pride is a personal pride.

But when they were asked, "What did we accomplish?" about half answered, "We bought the Lebanese people more time." The responses of the other half amounted to "Nothing."

As time passes, "Nothing" looks more and more like the correct assessment.

Appendix I

Rules of Engagement

1. When on post, mobile or foot patrol, keep loaded magazine in weapon, bolt closed, weapon on safe, no round in the chamber.

2. Do not chamber a round unless told to do so by a commissioned officer unless you must act in immediate self-defense where deadly force is authorized.

3. Keep ammo for crew-served weapons readily available, but not loaded. Weapon is on safe.

4. Call local forces [LAF] to assist in self-defense effort. Notify headquarters.

5. Use only minimum degree of force to accomplish any mission.

6. Stop the use of force when it is no longer needed to accomplish the mission.

7. If you receive effective hostile fire, direct your fire at the source. If possible, use friendly snipers.

8. Respect civilian property; do not attack it unless absolutely necessary to protect friendly forces.

9. Protect innocent civilians from harm.

10. Respect and protect recognized medical agencies such as Red Cross, Red Crescent, etc.

Appendix II

U.S. Servicemen Killed in Lebanon
September 1982–February 1984*

September 29, 1982

Cpl David Reagan

August 29, 1983

2ndLt George D. Losey
SSgt Alexander M. Ortega

September 6, 1983

LCpl Randy Clark
Cpl Pedro Valle

October 15, 1983

SSgt Allen H. Soifert

October 16, 1983

Capt Michael J. Ohler

*October 23, 1983***

Cpl Terry W. Abbott

LCpl Clemon Alexander
Pfc John R. Allman
Cpl Moses Arnold, Jr.
Pfc Charles K. Bailey
LCpl Nicholas Baker
LCpl Johansen Banks
LCpl Richard E. Barrett
HM1 Ronny K. Bates, USN
1stSgt David L. Battle
LCpl James R. Baynard
HN Jesse W. Beamon, USN
GySgt Alvin Belmer
LCpl Stephen B. Bland
Cpl Richard L. Blankenship
Pfc John W. Blocker
Capt Joseph J. Boccia, Jr.
Sgt Leon W. Bohannon
SSgt John R. Bohnet, Jr.

* All those listed are USMC unless otherwise noted.
** Two of the Marines killed this day are not listed in deference to the wishes of their families.

Sgt John J. Bonk, Jr.
LCpl Jeffrey J. Boulous
Cpl David R. Bousum
1stLt John N. Boyett
Cpl Anthony K. Brown
LCpl David W. Brown
LCpl Bobby B. Buchanan, Jr.
Cpl John B. Buckmaster
Pfc William F. Burley
HN Jimmy R. Cain, USN
Cpl Paul L. Callahan
Sgt Mecot E. Camara
Pfc Bradley J. Campus
LCpl Johnnie D. Ceasar
Pfc Marc L. Cole
SP4 Marcus E. Coleman, USA
Pfc Juan M. Comas
Sgt Robert A. Conley
Cpl Charles D. Cook
Cpl Curtis J. Cooper
LCpl Johnny L. Copeland
Cpl Bert D. Corcoran
LCpl David L. Cosner
Sgt Kevin P. Coulman
LCpl Brett A. Croft
LCpl Rick R. Crudale
LCpl Kevin P. Custard
LCpl Russell E. Cyzick
Maj Andrew L. Davis
Pfc Sidney J. Decker
Pfc Michael J. Devlin
LCpl Thomas A. DiBenedetto
Pvt Nathaniel G. Dorsey
SgtMaj Frederick B. Douglass
Cpl Timothy J. Dunnigan
HN Bryan L. Earle, USN
MSgt Roy L. Edwards
HM3 William D. Elliott, Jr., USN
LCpl Jesse J. Ellison
LCpl Danny R. Estes

LCpl Sean F. Estler
HM3 James E. Faulk, USN
LCpl Richard A. Fluegel
Cpl Steven M. Forrester
HM3 William B. Foster, USN
LCpl Michael D. Fulcher
LCpl Benjamin E. Fuller
LCpl Michael S. Fulton
Cpl William R. Gaines, Jr.
Cpl Sean R. Gallagher
LCpl David B. Gander
LCpl George Gangur
SSgt Leland E. Gann
LCpl Randall J. Garcia
SSgt Ronald J. Garcia
LCpl David D. Gay
SSgt Harold D. Ghumm
LCpl Warner Gibbs
Cpl Timothy R. Giblin
ETC Michael W. Gorchinski, USN
LCpl Richard J. Gordon
LCpl Harold F. Gratton
Sgt Robert B. Greaser
LCpl Davin M. Green
LCpl Thomas A. Hairston
Sgt Freddie Haltiwanger, Jr.
LCpl Virgil D. Hamilton
Sgt Gilbert Hanton
LCpl William Hart
Capt Michael S. Haskell
Pfc Michael A. Hastings
Capt Paul A. Hein
LCpl Douglas E. Held
Pfc Mark A. Helms
LCpl Ferrandy D. Henderson
GySgt Matilde Hernandez, Jr.
Cpl Stanley G. Hester
SSgt Donald W. Hildreth
SSgt Richard H. Holberton
HM3 Robert S. Holland, USN

LCpl Bruce A. Hollingshead
LCpl Melvin D. Holmes
Cpl Bruce L. Howard
Lt(jg) John R. Hudson, USN
Cpl Terry L. Hudson
LCpl Lyndon J. Hue
2ndLt Maurice E. Hukill
LCpl Edward S. Iacovino, Jr.
Pfc John J. Ingalls
WO-1 Paul G. Innocenzi III
LCpl James J. Jakowski
LCpl Jeffrey W. James
Pfc Nathaniel W. Jenkins
HM2 Michael H. Johnson, USN
Cpl Edward A. Johnston
LCpl Steven Jones
Pfc Thomas A. Julian
HM2 Marion E. Kees, USN
Sgt Thomas C. Keown
GySgt Edward E. Kimm
Pfc Walter V. Kingsley
Sgt Daniel S. Kluck, USA
LCpl James C. Knipple
LCpl Freas H. Kreischer III
LCpl Keith J. Laise
LCpl Thomas G. Lamb
LCpl James J. Langon IV
Sgt Michael S. Lariviere
Cpl Steven B. Lariviere
MSgt Richard L. Lemnah
Cpl David A. Lewis
Sgt Val S. Lewis
LCpl Paul D. Lyon, Jr.
Maj John W. Macroglou
Cpl Samuel Maitland
SSgt Charlie R. Martin
Cpl David S. Massa
Pvt Joseph J. Mattacchione
LCpl John McCall
Cpl James E. McDonough

Pfc Timothy R. McMahon
LCpl Timothy D. McNeely
HM2 George N. McVicker II, USN
LCpl Louis Melendez
Sgt Michael D. Mercer
LCpl Ronald W. Meurer
HN Joseph P. Milano, USN
Cpl Joseph P. Moore
LCpl Richard A. Morrow
LCpl John F. Muffler
Pfc Alex Munoz
Cpl Harry D. Myers
1stLt David J. Nairn
LCpl Luis A. Nava
Cpl John A. Olson
LCpl Robert P. Olson
CWO-3 Richard Ortiz, USA
LCpl Jeffrey B. Owen
Cpl Joseph A. Owens
Cpl Ray Page
LCpl Ulysses G. Parker
LCpl Mark W. Payne
GySgt John L. Pearson
Pfc Thomas S. Perron
Sgt John A. Phillips, Jr.
HMC George W. Piercy, USN
1stLt Clyde W. Plymel
Sgt William H. Pollard
Sgt Rafael Pomalestorres
Cpl Victor M. Prevatt
Pfc James G. Price
SSgt Patrick K. Prindeville
LCpl Eric A. Pulliam
HM3 Diomedes S. Quirante, USN
LCpl David M. Randolph
GySgt Charles R. Ray
Pfc R.A. Relvas
LCpl Terrence L. Rich
LCpl Warren Richardson
Cpl Paul P. Rivers

Sgt Juan C. Rodriguez
LCpl Louis J. Rotondo
LCpl Guillermo Sanpedro, Jr.
LCpl Michael C. Sauls
1stLt Charles J. Schnorf
LCpl Scott L. Schultz
Capt Peter J. Scialabba
Cpl Gary R. Scott
Cpl Ronald L. Shallo
LCpl Thomas A. Shipp
LCpl Jerryl D. Shropshire
LCpl James F. Silvia
LCpl Stanley J. Sliwinski
LCpl Kirk H. Smith
SSgt Thomas C. Smith
Capt Vincent L. Smith
LCpl Edward Soares
1stLt William S. Sommerhof
LCpl Michael C. Spaulding
LCpl John W. Spearing
LCpl Stephen E. Spencer
LCpl Bill J. Stelpflug
Pfc Horace R. Stephens
Pfc Craig S. Stockton
LCpl Jeffrey G. Stokes
Cpl Thomas D. Stowe
LCpl Eric D. Sturghill
Cpl Devon L. Sundar
Lt James F. Surch, Jr., USN
Pfc Dennis A. Thompson
SSgt Thomas P. Thorstad
Pfc Stephen D. Tingley
LCpl John J. Tishmack
Cpl Henry Townsend, Jr.
Pfc Lex D. Trahan
Pfc Donald H. Vallone, Jr.
LCpl Eric R. Walker
Cpl Leonard W. Walker
Cpl Eric G. Washington
Cpl Obrian Weekes

1stSgt Tandy W. Wells
LCpl Steven B. Wentworth
Sgt Allen D. Wesley
GySgt Lloyd D. West
SSgt John R. Weyl
Cpl Burton D. Wherland
LCpl Dwayne W. Wigglesworth
LCpl Rodney J. Williams
GySgt Scipio Williams
LCpl Johnny A. Williamson
Capt Walter Wint, Jr.
Capt William W. Winter
Cpl John E. Wolfe
1stLt Donald E. Woollett
HN David E. Worley, USN
LCpl Craig L. Wyche
SFC James G. Yarber, USA
Cpl Jeffrey D. Young
1stLt William A. Zimmerman

December 4, 1983

Cpl Shannon D. Biddle
LCpl Sam Cherman
Sgt Manuel A. Cox
Cpl David L. Daugherty
LCpl Thomas A. Evans
LCpl Jeffrey T. Hattaway
LCpl Todd A. Kraft
Lt Mark A. Lange, USN
LCpl Marvin H. Perkins

January 8, 1984

Cpl Joseph Gargano

January 31, 1984

LCpl George Dramis
LCpl Rodolfo Hernandez

February 9, 1984

Maj Albert Butler

Selected Bibliography

The narrative is based solely upon information gleaned from the interviews described in the Introduction, numerous unbylined news articles, and the following bylined feature articles:

Dye, Capt Dale A., "Keeping the Peace In Lebanon," *Marine Corps Gazette*, August 1983.

Editors, "The Marines in Lebanon: An Interview With P. X. Kelley," *The Washington Post*, November 6, 1983.

Friedman, Thomas L., "America's Failure In Lebanon," *The New York Times Magazine*, April 8, 1984.

Gaddo, SSgt Randy, "The Price They Paid . . . ," *Leatherneck*, January 1984.

———, "Beirut Bombing," *Leatherneck*, February 1984.

Jordan, Maj Robert T., "They Came in Peace," *Marine Corps Gazette*, July 1984.

Mead, BGen James M., "The Lebanon Experience," *Marine Corps Gazette*, February 1983.

———, "Lebanon Revisited," *Marine Corps Gazette*, September 1983.

Sloyan, Patrick J., "Lebanon: Anatomy of A Foreign Policy Failure," *Newsday*, April 8, 1984.

———, "The Warnings Reagan Ignored," *The Nation*, October 27, 1984.

Taubman, Philip, and Joel Brinkley, "The Marine Tragedy: An Inquiry into Causes and Responsibility," *The New York Times*, December 11, 1983.

U.S. Government, "Report of the DOD Commission On Beirut International Airport Terrorist Act,October, 1983"(the sanitized *public* version of the Long Commission Report of December 20, 1983).

Index